£14·00

D0906622

Critic as Scientist

The modernist poetics of Ezra Pound

Critic as Scientist

The modernist poetics of Ezra Pound

Ian F. A. Bell

Methuen
London and New York

First published in 1981 by
Methuen & Co. Ltd
11 New Fetter Lane,
London EC4P 4EE

Published in the USA by
Methuen & Co.
in association with Methuen, Inc.
733 Third Avenue, New York,
NY 10017

Photoset in Great Britain by
Rowland Phototypesetting Ltd
Bury St Edmunds, Suffolk
and printed in Great Britain at the
University Press, Cambridge

British Library Cataloguing in Publication Data

Bell, Ian F A
    Critic as scientist.
    1. Pound, Ezra – Criticism and interpretation
    I. Title
     811'.52   PS3531.082Z/   80-41826
    ISBN 0-416-31350-7

For Lionel Kelly

Contents

Acknowledgements

This book's lengthy gestation began in the University of Reading, and it attempts to incorporate the example of the late D. J. Gordon. Its imprint of his ways of reading can only be a pale testimony to a remarkable mind. Lionel Kelly, with generosity and understanding, continued the lesson and has been integral to the entire exercise. John Goode and David Howard have presented instigatory models. Martin Kayman renewed my interest at an important time through his friendship and his own excellent work on Pound and science. Arnold Goldman commented sturdily on several chapters. Richard Godden enlivened my thinking. My students and colleagues in the Department of American Studies at the University of Keele provided an admirable context for composition. Linden Stafford, on behalf of Methuen, dissolved many obscurities. Dorothy Watson and Karen Harrison produced a typescript with humour and efficiency. Lizzie Tagart has sustained me throughout.

Introduction

> I hadn't in 1910 made a language, I don't mean a
> language to use, but even a language to think in.

'The proper METHOD for studying poetry and good letters', proclaimed Pound in 1934, 'is the method of contemporary biologists'.[1] This ambition, written 'in an age of science and of
abundance', had been true of the entire critical burden of his
London years between 1910 and 1920. The purpose of the present
exercise is to explicate this ambition: to demonstrate the relationship between Pound's use of scientific analogy and the more
familiar areas of his critical concerns, and to argue that his efforts
to create a poetics informed by the disciplines of science were the
characteristic gestures of his modernity. It was a science-based
terminology that gave Pound's literary criticism its characteristic
tone, a tone that in turn owed its allegiance to particular American
manners of literary debate.

Pound's critical vocabulary was a deliberately public gesture
during a specific period in literary history: it was a distinct verbal
exercise, a means of announcing his modernity in response to the
current conditions of the artist and of offering a programme to
sharpen up careless and inadequate discussions of letters. Pound
was impelled towards this vocabulary by the ruptures everywhere
apparent in matters of cultural responsibility, in the artist's increasingly awkward relationship to his audience and to his function
within the wider issues of his society. His search for a means
of healing these ruptures found its most significant resource in
analogies from science. It was here that Pound also sought answers
for his more immediate problems as a writer, which he first announced in 1910 as a need for 'a literary scholarship which will

weigh Theocritus and Mr Yeats with one balance'. This reflects his permanent belief that 'All ages are contemporaneous' – a historicism in which 'the real time is independent of the apparent' and where 'many dead men are our grandchildren's contemporaries, while many of our contemporaries have been already gathered into Abraham's bosom, or some more fitting receptacle.'[2] And Pound's historicism was fundamentally a matter of terminology: 'The history of literary criticism is largely the history of a vain struggle to find a terminology which will define something.'[3]

My discussion is confined to Pound's London years because this was the period during which his major battles were conducted,[4] battles, essentially, to cultivate an appropriate vocabulary for the modernist enterprise. Pound wrote retrospectively in 1929: 'I hadn't in 1910 made a language, I don't mean a language to use, but even a language to think in.'[5] The problem of vocabulary was in many ways a result of the radical shifts in perspective experienced by the turn of the century, most succinctly summarized in Arthur Symons's description of the demands implicit in the reaction against mechanistic materialism by symbolist literature, 'a literature in which the visible world is no longer a reality and the unseen world no longer a dream'.[6] The epistemological gap inherent in such a viewpoint was a problem that Pound sought to resolve through the discourses of science, through the new materialism they offered as a means of access to the interstitiality of the corporeal and the non-corporeal that was the habitation of the modernist writer.

The relationship between Pound's critical writings and science has not gone unnoticed in the commentaries, principally in the work of Noel Stock,[7] Max Nänny[8] and Hugh Kenner,[9] but, in the nature of my proposals, these are all felt to be, in varying degrees, unsatisfactory, mainly because they engage themselves with so little of the science that was actually available to Pound's campaign. Their reluctance is not in fact surprising: with the late exception of the Swiss-born naturalist, Louis Agassiz, there is little direct evidence of Pound's reading in the sciences. Such an absence is clearly problematical for a certain kind of critical commentary: I should make it clear that the present work is not concerned with 'sources' as such but with bodies of material that would unavoidably have informed Pound's thought, that were available to him in a variety of accessible ways and that cannot be ignored in any explication of the complicated series of analogies through which he chose to articulate the modernity of his poetics. His linguistic strategies are ultimately meaningless without a cognizance of the levels of discourse to which they properly belong.

There is thus an order of mystery attaching itself to my own procedure, close, perhaps, to that mystery I shall show was inherited by Pound himself from transcendentalist epistemologies. This mystery of origin became for Pound in one sense a means of sloughing off the cumbersome burdens of encyclopedic data in favour of retaining their pattern, their organic synthesis; in this sense we can clearly determine his totalitarian impulse (in its parallel contexts of anthropology and politics). In a practical sense, as a means of getting about, this mystery is inevitable as part of the assumptions we have to make in accounting for a writer's relationship to his culture, a relationship that rarely manifests itself in the flattened shapes of notated sources. In any case, as Pound himself observed in an essay in 1911, 'the best of knowledge is "in the air" ',[10] and in a letter of the same year he wryly remarked: 'Out of the 25 people who are variously supposed to have formed my mind, (acc. critics diversi), I have counted about 9 poets unknown to me, 7 whom I had only read casually':

> I think that the 'influences' in a man's work which matter are usually pretty well concealed. They are the forces that strike at the thought tone and into the meaning . . . strike the entrails not the complexion, or strike the complexion thru' the entrails and not as cosmetic.[11]

Here is a solid piece of advice to his subsequent commentators.

Since the present work seeks not only to locate the scientific provenance of Pound's major items of vocabulary but also to establish the *forma mentis* of his modernity, it concentrates on those aspects of Pound's poetics that are familiar: his analogies from geometry and electromagnetism, his campaign for the seriousness of the artist, his conceptions of the 'vortex' and of 'tradition'. It hopes not only to offer new readings, but to extend the contexts in which discussions of his poetics have tended to reside, by refocusing the issues of science that Pound's modernism incorporates and by suggesting the transcendentalist ideology to which, in Pound's use, they belong. The state of current critical accounts of Pound requires a shift in the perspectives through which he is usually seen; these have too often been confined by the figures and debates that Pound himself announced, by the unquestioning appropriation of Pound's own vocabulary, with the inevitable result of cutting Pound off from the wider motives and issues of literary culture.

1 Poet as geometer

The live man in a modern city feels this sort of thing or
perceives it as the savage perceives in the forest.

(Olson)

Prose under pressure

Stephen Dedalus found his mind 'fascinated and jaded' by the
'spectrelike symbols of force and velocity' he transcribed during a
lecture on applied physics, formulae that manifested themselves in
the professor's somnolent exposition of F. W. Martino's platinoid.
Stephen's education in naming things, in determining the meanings
and effects of words, led him later to a famous speculation on the
radiance of the scholastic *quidditas*, where the spiritual state of its
harmony and luminosity required the explication not so much of
Shelley's Neoplatonism as of the physiology suggested by a different branch of applied physics, Galvani's electrical interventions
in the cardiac system of the frog. This 'enchantment of the heart',
during the nebulous period of the day, and, indeed, of language
itself, demonstrated how 'the word was made flesh'. Yet Stephen's
villanelle, the fleshment of his theoretical 'enchantment', had to
negotiate the impediments of everyday living, the remnants of the
previous night's supper, the search for pencil and one remaining
cigarette, before its 'small neat letters' could appear on a 'rough
cardboard surface'.[1] It was not easy to talk of 'Art' in the modern
world; things spiritual, even with the sanction of scientific metaphor, had still to enjoy a somewhat awkward relationship with
things material. Henry Adams used such metaphor to describe the
difficult entry into modernity and emphasized the special reality of
the 'manikin' on which the process of education was draped:

The young man himself, the subject of education, is a certain form of energy; the object to be gained is economy of his force; the training is partly the clearing away of obstacles, partly the direct application of effort. Once acquired, the tools and models may be thrown away. The manikin, therefore, has the same value as any other geometrical figure of three or more dimensions, which is used for the study of relation. For that purpose it cannot be spared; it is the only measure of motion, of proportion, of human condition; it must have the air of reality; must be taken for real; must be treated as though it had life.[2]

Overwhelmingly, this entry was to involve not simply transition but translation, a quest for appropriate vocabularies, for a complicated series of alternative terminologies: the major crisis for the artist during the early years of the twentieth century was to be a crisis of discourse. For Pound in particular it was a crisis exacerbated by his nationality, which partly involved, as Wyndham Lewis noted, the awkward problem of combining an indigenous 'toughness' and practicality with the delicacy of the butterfly with which James McNeill Whistler habitually signed his paintings.[3] Pound valued the 'pagan' energy that suggested possibilities for an American *risorgimento* in 1912 but, to adopt his own terms from 'The Condolence' of the following year, he identified the impossibility of his 'fantastikon' within a milieu topographically conditioned against the gathering of 'delicate thoughts':

One knows that they [Americans] are the dominant people and that they are against all delicate things. They will never imagine beautiful plaisaunces. They will never 'sit on a midden and dream stars'. . . . This new metropolitan has his desire sated before it is aroused. Electricity has for him made the seeing of visions superfluous. There is the sham fairyland at Coney Island, and however sordid it is when one is in it, it is marvellous against the night as one approaches or leaves it.

Pound needed to view Coney Island from a distance, just as he was observing America itself from the distance of five years in Europe. He found it difficult during the early years of exile to narrow that distance, to decide what America and its failure of imaginative tractability had to do with 'lyric measures and the nature of "quantity"'.[4] Pound realized that the problem was one of translation; in 1907 he wrote of his prose-poem 'Malrin' that 'To give concrete for a symbol, to explain a parable, is for me always a limiting, a restricting.'[5] It was, however, a two-edged problem, since the delicacy of 'beautiful plaisaunces' required, as Donald Davie has put it, 'the accents of the present century'; exile always carries a double function of alienation: delicacy not only needed to be maintained against a philistine audience but had also to seek expression through a vigorous and precise discourse during what Pound felt to be an era of overwritten preciosity. As the pressures of modernity and of being modern increased after 1910, so too did those of diction: compare, for example, the very beautiful description of New York at night in 1912 ('Squares after squares of flame, set and cut into the ether . . . we have pulled down the stars to our will'), where the present city is seen as a proper expression of the ancient τὸ καλόν, with a poem of an ostentatiously truncated title, 'NY', on the same subject in the same year which crudely stylizes the tensions of diction between 'My city, my beloved, my white! Ah slender' and 'here are a million people surly with traffic'.[6] Whereas the prose, a marvellous exercise of visual perception, strenuously enacts the crisis of diction, the poem offers merely a banal shadow of that crisis; to put it another way, we are presented with differing modes of sincerity. One of Pound's most pervasive claims for sincerity was given in this same year as 'our American keynote' and defined as 'a certain generosity; a certain carelessness, or looseness, if you will; a hatred of the sordid, an ability to forget the part for the sake of the whole, a desire for largeness, a willingness to stand exposed'. This was essentially a testament to his two American predecessors who were most responsible for Pound's aesthetics during his London years, Whitman and Whistler; the phrase to be remembered is the 'willingness to stand exposed' which provides the clue to Pound's admiration for Whistler, in particular, who exhibited the process of education, the openness and the struggle:

> Here in brief is the work of a man, born American, with all our forces of confusion within him, who has contrived to keep order in his work, who has attained the highest mastery, and this not by a natural facility, but by constant labour and searching. . . . The man's life struggle was set before one. He had tried all means, he had spared himself nothing, he had struggled in one

direction until he had either achieved or found it inadequate for his expression.[7]

In a little-recognized essay of 1949, Marshall McLuhan has suggested an important resource for Pound's American diction. He distinguishes between the 'Senecal or Jonsonian vigour and precision' of Pound's style and the 'urbane sinuosities' characterizing that of Eliot, locating the roots of Pound's speech in 'the radical individualism of generations of sea-board Yankees . . . the intensity, the shrewdness, and the passion for technical precision'. McLuhan contrasts Pound's 'sharp and alert sentences', their 'evangelical' spirit instigating judgements that are 'vehement and explicit', with the 'gentle rhythms' of Eliot's paragraphs that produce a 'balm for minds which find only distress in the violence of intellectual penetration', that cause 'little perturbation in foolish ears'.[8] To borrow Berryman's phrase, it is the 'crumpled syntax' in Pound that occasions trust. Pound learned from Whitman the importance of a provisory, unfinished quality for writing, and it is this quality that marks the crucial difference from Eliot's 'urbane sinuosities'. This difference asks that we participate in Pound's writing in a manner wholly distinct from that in which we enter the world of Eliot; it distinguishes between Pound's expression and Eliot's manipulation, between the mobility of the reader–text relationship and the autonomy of that relationship, between a potential for flexibility and undisguised enclosure.

McLuhan offers a specific intellectual source for the manner of Pound's prose:

> the America which Mr Pound left about 1908 gave him a great deal which he translated into literary perception and activity. It was the technological America . . . the most authentic expression was widely sought and found in the contemplation of mechanical tools and devices, when intellectual energies were bent to discover by precise analysis of vital motion the means of bringing organic processes within the compass of technical means.[9]

It was this 'technological America' that Pound remembered during his vorticist battles, which necessitated a reliance on metaphors and analogies from the practical disciplines of the physical sciences that were explicit in the America suggested by McLuhan. Such metaphors defined above all Pound's insistence on the artist as a 'constructive individual', as the creative centre of a new *risorgimento*. Vorticism for Pound announced specific possibilities for the *risorgimento* in that it provided a 'programme', and Pound sought to express his view of such a programme through a model from technology:

> We believe that the Renaissance was in part the result of a programme. . . . The use and limitation of force need not bring about mental confusion. An engine is not a confusion merely because it uses the force of steam, and the physical principles of the lever and piston.[10]

The final sentence suggests not only a precise image for an aesthetic idea; crucially, it also implies that modernist critical activity must be programmatic as a public gesture. Hence we have Pound's pithy openness as opposed to what he later called Eliot's 'increasingly guarded abstract statement',[11] and we have Pound as the successor to the 'Yankee' temperament of James McNeill Whistler.

Whistler was, of course, emblematic for Pound as a defender of the avant-garde.[12] Whistler conducted his defence primarily by the Poundian means of a contempt for authority and a castigation of 'taste', the perennial rallying cry of the amateur. Time and again in Whistler we hear the voice that is to become so familiar in Pound; as Pound's demands in 'The Serious Artist' of 1913, for example, were supported by reference to the prerogatives of science and practical craftsmanship (the falsification of 'inaccurate art' being regarded as reprehensible as the falsification of a scientific report), so too were those of Whistler:

> An inroad into the laboratory would be looked upon as an intrusion; but before the triumphs of Art, the expounder is at his ease. . . . The people are to be educated upon the broad basis of 'Taste', forsooth, and it matters but little what 'gentleman and scholar' undertake the task. . . . The Observatory at Greenwich under the direction of an Apothecary! The College of Physicians with Tennyson as President! and we know that madness is about. But a school of art with an accomplished *littérateur* [Ruskin] at its head disturbs no-one![13]

For both Whistler and Pound, analogies from science and technology emphasized the professional and practical qualities they saw as essential for the critic; Whistler argued for the comparability of the 'unscientific' with the judgement of 'the hand that holds neither brush nor chisel', while Pound, in 1917, complained that the surgically antiseptic instruments of 'clear and clearer realism' were subjected to the censorship of 'the most debased and ignorant classes'.[14]

Pound began to preach Whistler as early as 1907,[15] but it was during the crucial years of 1912–16 that he fully elaborated Whistler's importance for modernism. The text that Pound usually cited to illustrate the contemporary relevance of Whistler was the famous lecture of 1885, 'The Ten O'Clock'. Primarily a defence of the artist's freedom against the intrusions of the professionally ill-equipped, the lecture exhibited little specific scientific analogy, but that analogy was clearly instrumental in its debate. Joseph Pennell, Whistler's friend and biographer, paraphrased the main line of its argument to emphasize the implicit reference to science as a means of underlining the special seriousness of the artist's work:

> Art is a science – the science by which the artist picks and chooses and groups the elements contained in Nature . . . art is a science not because painters maintain that it is concerned with the laws of light or chemistry of colours or scientific problems, but because it is exact in its methods and in its results. The artist can leave no more to chance than the chemist or the botanist or the biologist. . . . Because art is a science the critic who is not an artist speaks without authority.[16]

Whistler's advocacy of art as a science in the sense of a specialized craft, which incorporated the ethical dictum that immoral art was equated with untruthful art, and as a serious practical activity – with his accompanying derision of the critic who failed to participate in the first and to recognize the second – established a preoccupation that Pound continually displayed. Pound's poetic tribute of 1912, 'To Whistler, American',[17] registered admiration for an American who offered no compromise to the art world of Europe and who was willing not only to experiment but to exhibit the struggles of experiment. Pound placed himself in the Whistlerian tradition of those who bore 'the brunt of our America' and who (in the most significant of the poem's lines) tried to 'wrench her impulse into art'. The poem suggests Whistler not only as a model for behaviour but also, for the American artist in exile, as a model for reassurance.

Whistler stood at the centre of Pound's vorticist campaigns; a discrimination of 1910 – that 'there are works of art which are beautiful objects and works of art which are keys or passwords admitting one to a deeper knowledge, to a finer perception of beauty'[18] – placed Whistler in the latter category and clearly predicted the way in which the unfinished (in the non-enclosed sense) and the provisory elements in Whistler's work would, by 1915, make possible for Pound the 'new perception of form' instigated by vorticist paintings.[19] In particular, Whistler's importance for vorticism may be located in the unattributed axiom with which Pound opened his 1914 essay on Edward Wadsworth: 'It is no more ridiculous that one should receive or convey an emotion by an arrangement of planes, or by an arrangement of lines and colours than that one should convey or receive such an emotion by an arrangement of musical notes.' The principle of non-representational 'arrangements' was, for Pound by now, 'self-evident to all save the more retarded types of mentality'.[20] Pound's 'Vorticism' essay of January 1915 contained no specific mention of Whistler, by now too thoroughly assimilated to enter into the propaganda by name, but the essay radiated his presence. Within this thoroughly Whistlerian exercise, Pound turned to analogies from science to illustrate his dogma; using the diagnostic vocabulary from medicine that he usually reserved for his discussion of the situation of the novel, particularly for the place of Joyce, he referred to vorticist paintings as 'our antiseptic works', and, more importantly, he glossed the notion of 'arrangements' as an 'organization of forms' with a famous metaphor from electromagnetism:

> An organization of forms expresses a confluence of forces. . . . For example: if you clasp a strong magnet beneath a plateful of iron filings, the energies of the magnet will proceed to organize form. . . . The design in the magnetized iron filings expresses a confluence of energy.

By contrast with the energies of vorticist art, Pound chose figures from biology to describe the 'automatic paintings' of Florence Seth, defining those paintings as 'organic' and arguing that they were products of the mind 'in a state of lassitude or passivity', a reversion to 'the pattern-making faculty which lies in the flower-seed or in the grain or in the animal cell'.[21] Here, Pound was suggesting an impoverished version of the 'germinal' consciousness that he distinguished from the 'phantastikon' of the Greek world in his 1912 essay on 'Psychology and Troubadours'; there, he compared this 'germinal' consciousness with the sexual mysticism of Provence, figured in another metaphor from electromagnetism, the telegraph.[22] The difference in metaphor predicated a hierarchy of values pertaining to the modes of 'energy expressing [themselves] in pattern' and to the organizers of those modes; the vorticist, expressing a 'complex consciousness', topped the table: 'He is not like the iron filings, expressing electrical magnetism; nor like the automatist, expressing a state of cell-memory, a vegetable or visceral energy.'[23]

Poundian vorticism, focused by Whistlerian 'arrangements', chose to express the energy of those 'arrangements' through metaphors from science. This was the necessary conjunction of elements already 'in the air'; we are dealing not with the lines of relation between source and agent but with the shifts and syntheses of Pound's intellectual furniture. As Whistler became fused with vorticist London, so Pound thought of paintings and pieces of sculpture as ordered by the pattern and design potential of electromagnetism and, predominantly, of geometry and analytical mathematics. His 'Vorticism' of September 1914 began with the paragraph on 'arrangements' that had opened his assessment of Wadsworth a month previously, and, unlike the 'Vorticism' of January 1915, the essay abounded with Whistler's name. Here we find the major conjunction of Whistler and science; the climax of the essay was Pound's definition of vorticism as an 'intensive art' through the 'four different intensities of mathematical expression . . . the arithmetical, the algebraic, the geometrical, and that of analytical geometry'. The first two expressions dealt merely with facts and with their relationship to each other; the important movement was from the third expression, that of Euclid's 'plane or descriptive geometry', to the fourth expression, that of Descartes's 'analytical geometry' in which 'one is able *actually to create*'. The equations of the fourth expression (Pound gave the example of the equation for the circle) were those of universal truths, ruling over 'form and recurrence'. Pound's reconstruction of Whistler's 'arrangements' through the vocabulary of geometry was an attempt to bring them into the public sphere, to demonstrate that the vorticist movement 'is not a movement of mystification'.[24]

It was particularly appropriate that Pound chose Cartesian geometry to define the intensity and dynamism of vorticist painting in 1914. The previous year had witnessed the reprint of Sir Oliver

Lodge's *Pioneers of Science*, a popular textbook first published in 1893, which, as its title implied, consisted of a series of lectures designed to survey the major events in the history of science. Lecture VI bore the title 'Descartes and His Theory of Vortices' and insisted on the doctrine of vortices and the system of analytical geometry as the two theoretical achievements that gave Descartes his place as 'the man of first magnitude filling up the gap in scientific history between the death of Galileo and the maturity of Newton', as, in other words, the instigator of modern science. Lodge's account of the doctrine of vortices was directly preceded by his account of Cartesian geometry. From the organizing principle of this geometry – that it was 'the specification of the position of a point in a plane by two numbers' – Lodge demonstrated how this principle permitted, in the terminology of Pound's essay, the movement from 'numbers' to 'form'. The curves and surfaces defined by the equations of such geometry could, then, according to how many variables the equations involved, be seen to function in a corresponding number of dimensions. It was this new freedom that marked the advance, as Pound saw it, on the Euclidean system; Lodge noted:

> Thus algebra is wedded to geometry, and the investigation of geometric relations by means of algebraic equations is called analytical geometry, as opposed to the old Euclidean or synthetic mode of treating the subject by reasoning consciously directed to the subject by help of figures.[25]

Lodge's account helps considerably to clarify Pound's argument; his view of the reliance of Euclidean geometry on 'figures' showed analytics, by comparison, to be truly abstract, independent of the material world: thus Pound admired the equation for the circle because it was 'universal, existing in perfection, in freedom from space and time'.[26] Lodge offered Cartesian geometry not only as an easier and more accurate procedure but also as a means of overcoming the limitations of procedures dependent upon phenomenal models:

> Thus geometry can not only be reasoned about in a more mechanical and therefore much easier manner, but it can be extended into regions of which we have and can have no direct conception,

because we are deficient in sense organs for accumulating any kind of experience in connexion with such ideas.[27]

The purity of abstraction resulting from a programme of aesthetics organized within such an epistemology solidified absolutely the Whistlerian notion of 'arrangements' as (in Pound's phrase) 'equations of eternity', as the major denial of representationalism: so Pound misquoted Whistler's 'Trotty Veck' as 'Trotty Veg' in counter to 'an arrangement in colour' as a reminder of what he saw as the vegetable-like passivity of Florence Seth's paintings or those of the impressionist school (castigated famously as 'any decayed cabbage cast upon any pink satin sofa' or the 'imitating of light on a haystack').[28]

The double argument of vorticism relied not only on 'arrangements' but on the idea that such 'arrangements' were expressive of what Pound called 'the primary pigment' and 'the primary form' throughout his defences of the movement. The emphasis here was on that which was 'primary' in the emotion conveyed through the work of painting or sculpture. This quality of primacy is particularly relevant if we return to Lodge's lecture and find his discussion of the Cartesian doctrine of vortices, directly following his account of analytical geometry. Quite simply, this doctrine was used to describe primary universal motion:

> He regarded space as a plenum full of an all-pervading fluid. Certain portions of this fluid were in a state of whirling motion, as in a whirlpool or eddy of water; and each planet had its own eddy, in which it was whirled round and round, as a straw is caught and whirled in a common whirlpool. This idea he works out and elaborates very fully, applying it to the system of the world, and to the explanation of all the motions of the planets.

Descartes's doctrine thus had the satisfyingly universal and eternal qualities that Pound had admired in the equations of his geometry, and Lodge, aware of contemporary scepticism towards the doctrine, proposed that its true value lay in its application to the nebulous stage of the universe, its very beginnings 'when the whole thing was one great whirl, ready to split or shrink off planetary rings at their appropriate distances'. Contemporary science, suggested Lodge, found use for the doctrine on the microcosmic scale to offer a different mode of primacy, that of the properties of matter themselves:

the now imagined vortices are not the large whirls of planetary size, they are rather infinitesimal whirls of less than atomic dimensions; still a whirling fluid is believed in to this day, and many are seeking to deduce all the properties of matter (rigidity, elasticity, cohesion, gravitation, and the rest) from it.[29]

Descartes's mathematical investigation of nature thus provided an entirely apposite system of analogy for Pound's reconstruction of Whistler; both shared Pound's ambitions for 'equations' of eternity and primacy; and Pound's 'community' of vorticist activity included Whistler and the equation for the circle as well as Gaudier-Brzeska, Lewis and ancient fragments:

> we are indissolubly united against all non-artists and half-artists by our sense of this fundamental community, this unending adventure towards 'arrangement', this search for the equations of eternity. A search which may end in results as diverse as the portrait of Miss Alexander, at her rather disagreeable age of thirteen or thereabouts, or a formula like
>
> $$(x-a)^2 + (y-b)^2 = r^2,$$
>
> or Brzeska's last figure of a woman, or Lewis's 'Timon' or even a handful of sapphics.

Terms such as 'equations of eternity' are potentially deceptive; it is important to remember that emphasis should be placed on the first half of the phrase, since Pound's interest lay not in any notion of the *complete* art-object; he noted: 'Perhaps the finest thing said of Whistler is to be found in an essay by Symons: "And in none of these things does he try to follow a fine model or try to avoid following a model."' This was what he meant by Whistler's 'keys', entries into otherness that did not rely on mimesis, the entries provided also in the abstractions of an Epstein statue or a geometrical equation, essentially '*expérimenté*', which suggested 'new chords, new keys in design' to energize perception by their provisory function.[30]

Whistler's place in Pound's vorticist tracts instigated a public language for criticism that relied on the discourse of mathematics; Whistler's battles, not only with Ruskin but with art criticism in general, were, at root, battles over terminology with an audience as mystified by 'harmony' and 'arrangement' as they were to be by 'vortex'. For Pound, the discourse from geometry came to belong naturally to a discussion of painting and sculpture based on Whistler's principle of 'arrangements', a term that, announcing its field of reference in both music and mathematics, insisted on its function as 'key' and as instigation. Pound's Preface to the catalogue of the Gaudier-Brzeska Exhibition in 1918 contained a marvellous account of *The Dancer*:

> We have the triangle and the circle asserted, *labled* almost, upon the face and right breast. Into these so-called 'abstractions' life flows, the circle moves and elongates into the oval, it increases and takes volume in the sphere or hemisphere of the breast. The triangle moves towards organism it becomes a spherical triangle. . . . These two developed motifs works as themes in a fugue. We have the whole series of spherical triangles, as in the arm over the head, all combining and culminating in the great sweep of the back of the shoulders. . . . The 'abstract' or mathematical bareness of the triangle and circle are fully incarnate, made flesh, full of vitality and of energy.[31]

Here we see the suggesting of new shapes, the spaced energy of points that define a periphery.

Against explanation

The attitude that Whistler protested against continually was summarized by a critic's comments on an exhibition of his etchings: 'They rather resemble vague first intuitions, or memoranda for future use, than designs completely carried out.' The argument here for the 'completeness' of 'representation' was to Whistler one reason for 'ceasing to exist'; it implied not only a limiting mimesis, a misunderstanding of the artist's function to be provisional, to supply 'keys', but also a dangerous proximity to commercial enterprise:

> There is a cunning condition of mind that *requires to know*. On the Stock Exchange this insures safe investment. In the painting trade this would induce certain picture-makers to cross the river at noon, in a boat, before negotiating a Nocturne, in order to make sure of detail on the bank, that honestly the purchaser

might exact, and out of which he might have been tricked by the Night![32]

Pound, worried by the commercialism of the American magazine system in 1912, sought his simile in the world of technological production rather than in the share market:

> As the factory owner wants one man to make screws and one man to make wheels and each man in his employ to do some one mechanical thing that he can do almost without the expenditure of thought, so the magazine producer wants one man to provide one element, let us say one sort of story and another articles on Italian cities and above all, nothing personal.

Confronted by these immediate oppositions, Pound was forced into a famous analogy from the scientist's function that approximated closely to Whistler's complaint:

> The serious artist does not play up to the law of supply and demand. He is like the chemist experimenting, forty results are useless, his time is spent without payment, the forty-first or the four hundredth and first combination of elements produces the marvel, for posterity as likely as not. The tradesman must either cease from experiment, from discovery and confine himself to producing that for which there is a demand, or else he must sell his botches, and either of these courses is as fatal to the artist as it would be to the man of science.

The analogy was completed by a demand for the artist's freedom: 'The artist paints the thing as he sees it. . . . He must be as free as the mathematician.' In the vocabulary of pure technology that anticipated the major resource of the *ABC of Reading* some twenty years later, Pound, thinking of Henry James, distinguished between the novelist and the poet, drawing explicit attention to the strategy of his own rhetoric:

> it is the novelist's business to set down exactly manners and appearances: he must render the show, he must, if the metaphor be permitted, describe precisely the nature of the engine, the position and relation of its wheels . . . the poet is a sort of steam-gauge, voltameter and set of pipes for thermometric and barometric divination.[33]

Whistler's 'keys', ciphers of the provisory, became what Pound called 'points of departure' as he moved his attention from the art-object to the art-idea; a few sentences prior to his fullest appreciation of Whistler, in chapter 13 of *Gaudier-Brzeska: A Memoir*, Pound wrote:

> an artistic principle, even a 'formula' is not a circumscription. These 'dogmas' are not limits, not signs saying 'thus far and no further', but points of departure, and lines along which the thought or the work may advance.

This statement was important for the freedom and flexibility that promised an open function for art, its resistance to enclosure ('All poetic language is the language of exploration'). Pound took issue with criticism of Gaudier's later work as 'experimental', a term that, together with 'exploration' as evidence of a struggle for the 'right curve', was always antithetical to 'finish' and 'completion':

> Wolmark considers the later work 'experimental'; and says that Gaudier regarded it as a 'phase' not an end. I am not sure that there is any great work which is not 'experimental'. Some experiments land on 'discovery', but they are none the less 'experiments'.

It was the literally unfinished nature of Gaudier's bust of himself that Pound admired:

> The bust of me was most striking, perhaps, two weeks before it was finished. I do not mean to say that it was better, it was perhaps a *kinesis*, whereas it is now a *stasis*; but before the back was cut out, and before the middle lock was cut down, there was in the marble a titanic energy, it was like a great stubby catapult, the two masses bent for a blow.

The unfinished bust offered lines of potential, suggestions for new energies of design; when quoting Whistler's maxim that the artist ought 'in arrangement of colours to treat a flower *as his key, not as his model*', Pound emphasized the latter half and noted: 'The last italicized words are to me the most important.' In explaining his emphasis, he pointed to the resemblance between the activity of the artist and that of the mathematician:

The pine-tree in mist upon the far hill looks like a fragment of Japanese armour.

The beauty of this pine-tree in the mist is not caused by its resemblance to the plates of the armour.

The armour, if it be beautiful at all, is not beautiful *because* of its resemblance to the pine in the mist.

In either case the beauty, in so far as it is beauty of form, is the result of 'planes in relation'.

The tree and the armour are beautiful because their diverse planes overlie in a certain manner.

There is the sculptor's or the painter's *key*. . . . This is the common ground of the arts, this combat of arrangement or 'harmony'. The musician, the writer, the sculptor, the higher mathematician have here their common sanctuary.[34]

The provisory function of the Whistlerian 'key' was what Pound meant in 1938 by the 'wisdom' of Whistler's 1912 exhibition: 'Neither monopolizing the truth nor exhausting it'. Or, as he noted a few lines later within a framework more akin to Whitman, 'ultimately a greater trust in rough speech than in eloquence'.[35] As Whistler theorized about the provisory, instigative practice of art, Whitman used that function as his most characteristic strategy; one commentator has argued:

Almost from their first appearance, Whitman's poems were labelled 'materials of poetry', excellent in themselves perhaps, but not put together as poems. . . . Emerson expected Whitman to write the songs of the nation and found him writing only the inventories.[36]

Pound acknowledged the open-ended nature of Whitman's work in 1915:

he never pretended to have reached the goal. He knew himself and proclaimed himself 'a start in the right direction'. He never said, 'American poetry is to stay where I left it'; he said it was to go on from where he started it.[37]

For Pound, it was work in which Whitman's followers had necessarily to participate: 'I honour him for he prophesied me.'[38] The term 'inventories' is a good one to describe Whitman's poetry because it suggests the activity of those lengthy catalogues that constitute its major programme. Whitman's catalogues relied on the traditional epistemological principle that to 'name' was to 'create'; his sense of the relationship between words and their objects was nowhere better expressed than in 'Mannahatta', the poem that celebrates the indigenous name for Manhattan and begins by offering that name for the city itself:

> I was asking for something specific and perfect for my city,
> Whereupon lo! upsprang the aboriginal name.
>
> Now I see what there is in a name, a word, liquid, sane, unruly, musical, self-sufficient,
> I see that the word of my city is that word from of old,
> Because I see that word nested in nests of water-bays, superb,
> Rich, hemm'd thick all around with sailships and steamships, an island sixteen miles long, solid-founded . . .

The items of the city then constitute the remainder of the poem; the naming of the city's objects announces, essentially, the going of words into action. Whitman wrote another poem of the same title in which the chant of the first poem is replaced by pure lexicography; I quote it entire:

> My city's fit and noble name resumed,
> Choice aboriginal name, with marvellous beauty, meaning,
> *A rocky founded island – shores where ever gayly dash the coming, going, hurrying sea waves.*

Whitman's 'inventories' were part of a larger campaign to paint America at the beginning of what he saw as a new phase in history. Thus their open-endedness was not only a function of the necessary partiality of catalogues as rubrics of knowledge but was also expressive of experiment, of how words were to be related to objects. Whitman speculated famously in the 'Song of Myself', where his typography dramatizes exactly the problematic involved:

> My words are words of a questioning, and to indicate reality;
> This printed and bound book . . . but the printer and the printing-office boy?
> The marriage estate and settlement . . . but the body and mind of the bridegroom? also those of the bride?
> The panorama of the sea . . . but the sea itself?[39]

Such speculation assumed, of course, the burden of every nineteenth-century American writer, the burden not only of providing America with what Van Wyck Brooks called a 'usable past', but of providing a vocabulary to convey the novelty of American experience and American literary behaviour. Whitman faced up to the problems of that burden more thoroughly and more energetically than anyone else.[40] It entailed, essentially, an acknowledgement of poetry's provisory activity. He wrote in an essay of 1855, 'An English and an American Poet', about the duties of the 'new poet':

> He never presents for perusal a poem ready-made on the old models, and ending when you come to the end of it; but every sentence and every passage tells of an interior not always seen, and exudes an impalpable something which sticks to him that reads, and pervades and provokes him to tread the half-invisible road where the poet, like an apparition, is striding fearlessly before.[41]

Whitman was for Pound the 'reflex' of his time (counterbalancing the model of the 'artist' that he sought in Whistler), who 'established the national timbre', who provided 'reassurance' during the difficulties of exile,[42] and whose rhythms Pound found himself almost unconsciously using 'when I write of certain things'.[43] And, on occasion, Whitman's strictures on the writing of poetry anticipated specific axioms in the Poundian canon; those central axioms of simplicity and the avoidance of ornament, which sustained Pound's propaganda for the 'sincerity' of 'The Serious Artist', structured the basic argument of Whitman's 1855 Preface to the *Leaves of Grass*:

> The art of art, the glory of expression and the sunshine of the light of letters is simplicity. Nothing is better than simplicity . . . nothing can make up for excess or for the lack of definiteness. . . . I will not have in my writing any elegance or effect or originality to hang in the way between me and the rest like curtains. I will have nothing in the way. . . . What I tell I tell for precisely what it is.[44]

As Pound was to specify his modernist clarion-calls by analogies to science and technology, Whitman, too, persistently evinced his faith in machinery, technology's instruments of construction. Newton

Arvin put the case for Whitman when he noted that 'he saw in the machine not only a delight to the eye of the craftsman but an intrinsically constructive agent in the civilizing of mankind, the freeing of it from the primitive bonds of distance and inflexibility and weight.' Whitman's poetry, like Pound's critical prose, was thus resplendent with the objects of technology, 'unprecedentedly full of steam printing-presses, telegraph-wires, sewing-machines, forge-furnaces, steam-whistles, and even drain-pipes and gas-ometers'. Whitman's response to such material provided the foundations of his modernity: 'He was the poet for whom a locomotive was to be . . . a "fierce-throated beauty", a "type of the modern".'[45] In both Pound and Whitman (as with Whistler) we find a community of values underwritten by a shared vocabulary of practical science. Whitman's modernity lay not only in the con-temporaneity of his choice of material (an essential lesson that Pound learned more immediately from Ford), which articulated his own place in history, but in a temperament that was capable of responding to that contemporaneity in the first place, to the demands that practical science imposed upon modes of apprehend-ing the world. As an early commentator, himself of scientific persuasion, has claimed: 'He was among the first to perceive the grandeur of the scientific truths which are to give impulse to a new and loftier imagination.'[46] We need to remember, of course, that in the case of Whitman we are dealing with a use of science that expressed itself primarily in the body of his poetry, while with Pound we have a usage that is directed almost wholly towards the discourse of his propaganda, but there are moments in Whitman that clearly 'prophesy' that propaganda. In the section of the 'Song of Myself' where Whitman proclaimed 'Hurrah for positive science!', the figure of the scientist was acknowledged as the 'lexicographer' of the world, a view he elaborated during his 1855 Preface to the *Leaves of Grass* in a passage that, as Joseph Beaver, the best guide to the subject, has argued, contained 'the core of almost everything Whitman was to say of poetry and science':[47]

Exact science and its practical movements are no checks on the greatest poet but always his encouragement and support . . . the anatomist chemist astronomer geologist phrenologist spiritualist mathematician historian and lexicographer are not poets, but they are the lawgivers of poets and their construction underlies the structure of every perfect poem.[48]

Whitman's choice of the term 'lawgivers' indicates that he had more in mind than the greater accuracy of description that science made available for literature. It suggests the freedom that for Pound was conferred by the operations of Cartesian geometry in 1912, by the equation for the circle, for example, which led to 'the contemplation of the circle absolute, its law; the circle free in all space, unbounded, loosed from the accidents of time and place'. Pound's metaphor was an explication of the proposition that the 'main purpose' of all the arts was one of 'liberation':

Borrowing a terminology from Spinoza, we might say: The function of an art, is to free the intellect from the tyranny of the affects . . . to strengthen the perceptive faculties and free them from encumbrance, such encumbrances, for instance, as set moods, set ideas, conventions; from the results of experience which is common but unnecessary, experience induced by the stupidity of the experiencer and not by inevitable laws of nature.

Such 'liberation' was especially important for a poet committed to the practical world of objects, since that commitment inevitably incorporated a potential for imprisonment by those objects. It was by example that Pound illustrated particular modes of 'liberation':

Thus Greek sculpture freed men's minds from the habit of considering the human body merely with regard to its imperfections. The Japanese grotesque frees the mind from the conception of things merely as they *have been* seen. With the art of Beardsley we enter the realm of pure intellect; the beauty of the work is wholly independent of the appearance of the things portrayed. With Rembrandt we are brought to consider the exact nature of things seen, to consider the individual face, not the conventional or type face which we may have learned to expect on canvas.[49]

Pound's insistence on 'liberation' as the 'main purpose' of art marked the most important consequence of his simultaneous demand for art's provisory function. That he chose to explain both by mathematics was a product of radical changes in the epistemology of scientific language at the turn of the century. Although the commonplace debate between mechanistic and vitalistic accounts of the world continued to be argued (mainly by philosophers), it was required to shift its ground considerably. The scientist recognized, primarily as a result of advances in wave theory, field theory and the postulates of relativity and of quantum mechanics, that nature could no longer be seen as constituted by the enduring objects of traditional physics.[50] In 1914 Bertrand Russell wrote of the intellectual climate that science had created, stressing the provisory function which then circumscribed scientific investigation:

> Another reason which makes a philosophy of science especially useful at the present time is the revolutionary progress, the sweeping away of what had seemed fixed landmarks, which has so far characterized this century, especially in physics. The conception of the 'working hypothesis', provisional, approximate, and merely useful, has more and more pushed aside the comfortable eighteenth century conception of 'laws of nature'.[51]

Henry Adams, faced with the world of twentieth-century physics, understood, in a pessimistic and extremist frame of mind, that the scientific historian's concern was not so much with factual truth or factual knowledge but with 'measurement':

> The historian never stopped repeating to himself that he knew nothing about it; that he was a mere instrument of measure, a barometer, pedometer, radiometer; and that his whole share in the matter was restricted to the measurement of thought-motion as marked by the accepted thinkers. He took their facts for granted.[52]

Bergson and Whitehead argued the most famous and most popular case for nature to be seen as constituted not by enduring objects but by continuous flux. They proposed to substitute relations for qualities as the constitutive characteristics of phenomena, in order to move away from the view that had hitherto demanded the fixity of those qualities. Theirs was the most obvious response to the prohibitive determinism of Victorian science, using biology as the archetype, and they exemplified an attitude that was concerned with the specific content of the picture advanced by the scientist. There was also, however, a significant parallel line of response that concerned itself more with the idea of scientific method as a kind of metalanguage, of science not as an *explanation* of phenomena but as a *description*. This line of thought was associated mainly with the reductionist school of physicists who were deeply influential in areas of scientific theory throughout the period 1880–1930. A German physicist, Ernst Mach, provided the main voice, but the school's position was most widely announced in England in a book by one of Mach's disciples, Karl Pearson, *The Grammar of Science* (1892). In one sense it is easy to see why the book occasioned doubts for Henry Adams and a quarrel between the schoolboy T. E. Hulme and his headmaster,[53] since the method it advocated depended upon analysis conducted entirely in terms of organic chemistry and physics. This method seemed to move perilously close to a life-denying mechanistic conception of the world, particularly worrying for the biologist; a manual of physiology noted in 1913:

> all the methods available for the study of vital processes are physical or chemical, so that, even if there were a form of energy peculiar to living things, we could take no account of it, except when converted into known forms of chemical or physical energy of equivalent amount.[54]

Hence, of course, the title 'reductionist'. But to understand the school's principles in this way was to miss the most important point, because a *description* of phenomena in physico-chemical language by no means entails a physico-chemical *explanation* belonging to a mechanistic framework. Indeed, the reductionist philosophy of scientific language was designed precisely to avoid such a conclusion; to 'describe', to operate within a metalinguistic system, was to enter into a very different relation to the objects of investigation: it was to admit the partiality of method, to deny the authoritarian imposition of 'explanation'. Once again we are engaged in the function of the provisory against the falsehood of 'completeness' and 'representation' (the alternative cognitive modes of 'explanation'). Pearson's claim for the mechanical method was wonderfully simple:

> Step by step men of science are coming to recognize that mechanism is not at the bottom of phenomena, but is only the conceptual shorthand by aid of which they can briefly describe and resume phenomena. . . . All science is description and not explanation.

Science as a means to cognition was thus not intended to penetrate nature but rather to organize in an economical manner those aspects of phenomena that observation presented: 'it asserts no perceptual reality for its own shorthand'.[55] It was understood not as a guide to a full reality but as a lexical instrument for organizing our sensations with respect to external phenomena. This was the major revolution in the theoretical bases of scientific language during the formative period of Pound's literary criticism; Henri Poincaré's *La Valeur de la science* (1905) was organized almost entirely according to the view that the various theories postulated by science were to be understood as different languages for describing the facts, and in 1923 A. D. Ritchie's textbook on scientific method claimed that questions about purpose played only a small role in scientific investigation, with the strong implication that it was misguided to see science as providing explanation.[56] It is within this linguistic revolution that we find the strongest case for science's rejection of its own version of 'representation', for the establishing of an alternative and economical lexical system, which, in admitting the restrictions of its procedure, resisted the myth of a totalizing 'explanation'. For Poincaré and Pearson, science was essentially creative in precisely this sense, an imaginative language in its own right: 'it is not a mere catalogue of facts, but is the conceptual model by which we briefly resume our experience of those facts.'[57] Conceptual models do, of course, require some measure of correspondence to the operations of reality; the major denial of the deterministic aspects of the 'mechanical' method newly redefined by Mach and Pearson was the result of Planck's work on the quantum theory from 1900 onwards. Sir Arthur Eddington, in his Gifford Lectures of 1927, saw Planck's work as a radical dislocation of causal orthodoxy: 'It is a consequence of the advent of the quantum theory *that physics is no longer pledged to a scheme of deterministic law.*' This freedom from causal determinism resulted in a crucial difference in the ways in which the scientist utilized his tools and in the kinds of question that he asked about the phenomena under observation:

Considering an atom alone in the world in State 3, the classical theory would have asked, and hoped to answer, the question, What will it do next? The quantum theory substitutes the question, Which will it do next? Because it admits only two lower states for the atom to go. Further, it makes no attempt to find a definite answer, but contents itself with calculating the respective odds on the jumps to State 1 and State 2. The quantum physicist

does not fill the atom with gadgets for directing its future behaviour, as the classical physicist would have done; he fills it with
gadgets determining the odds on its future behaviour. He studies
the art of the bookmaker not of the trainer.[58]

Thus the new physics joined with analytical geometry to inform the
energies and the provisory function of the Poundian art-object and
to ensure the essential 'liberation' which that object instigated in its
relationship with the world by denying the illusory mimesis of
'representation' and 'explanation'.

The art of the practical: a conservation of energy

In 1910 Hudson Maxim, one of those curious American *littérateurs*
who attempted to synthesize a scientific base for the procedures of
literary criticism during the early twentieth century, published *The
Science of Poetry and the Philosophy of Language*. Pound reviewed
the book in the year of its publication and made an unacknowledged use of it in his important essay of 1912, 'The Wisdom of
Poetry'. He was ambivalent about the ultimate value of Maxim's
treatise and oddly reticent about its application to his own consequent theorizing; indeed, there was much in Maxim that was
simply foolish, but there was also a great deal that undeniably
anticipated the foundations of Pound's modernist critical programme, material that, inexplicably, Pound seemed reluctant to
cite. The reasons for this reluctance are hidden, but there is no
question that the tenor and the axioms of Pound's London period
owed far more than he was willing to admit to Maxim's work; it is
there that we find the most intensive application of Karl Pearson's
propositions about the epistemology of scientific language to the
vocabulary of the literary critic. Maxim established principles that
Pound was to advocate insistently for the next twenty years. He
stated the case for himself, and, by extension, for Pound, at the
beginning of his Introduction:

> The main object of this book is to provide a practical method for
> literary criticism and analysis, and a standard of uniform judge-
> ment for determining the relative merits of literary productions,
> and further, to supply a more practical and efficient means than
> we have had heretofore for the standardization of poetry, whereby

any poem may be assayed and the amount of its poetic gold determined and separated from the slag and dross.[59]

Here was exactly the framework of Pound's own ambitions for criticism: a 'practical' method, a 'standard of uniform judgement', an 'efficient' means of aesthetic discourse, all subsumed within his proclamation for *The Spirit of Romance*: 'What we need is a literary scholarship, which will weigh Theocritus and Mr Yeats with one balance', a scholarship on the principle of 'standardization', which would thereby illustrate the contemporaneity of all ages.[60] The contemporaneity consequent upon a uniform standard accounted for the fascination of both Pound and Maxim with one of the most seductive aspects of the natural historian's work, the construction of a whole range of information from what was, to the layman, a minute and seemingly insignificant piece of evidence. Maxim wrote: 'The great naturalist requires but a few pieces of bone from any prehistoric monster in order to ascertain whether it was herbivorous or carnivorous, reptile or mammal, or even to construct a counterpart of its entire skeleton' (p. ix). It was this ability that remained axiomatic for Pound's critical prose, from the notion of the 'luminous detail' in 1911 to the teaching methods of Louis Agassiz and to his admiration for the Kulturmorphology of Leo Frobenius in the 1930s and 1940s:

> He brought the living fact to bear on the study of dead documents. It began – *incipit vita nova sua* – with his hearing that certain railway contractors were in conflict with some local traditions. A king and a girl had driven into the ground where there was a certain hillock: they ought not to make a cutting through the sacred place. The materialist contractors took no notice and went ahead – and unearthed a bronze car with effigies of Dis and Persephone.
>
> Later he wrote, 'Where we found these rock drawings there was always water within six feet of the surface.'

Thought, always to Pound 'organic', needed such 'gristly facts'.[61]

Maxim's most insistent concern was with the 'economizing' power of the poetic imagination; his definition of this power was to be one of his most significant contributions to Pound's theories:

> Poetry obeys the law of conservation of energy. By poetry a thought is presented with the utmost economy of word sym-

bols. .... To beckon with the hand is more potent than the words
'Please come here', because the words, which are mere arbitrary
signs of ideas, can enter consciousness only by the roundabout
process of interpretation, while a beck of the hand expresses the
idea whole at a stroke, by a single symbolic motion. This is what
poetry tends to do, and it thereby economizes in the use of word
symbols by selecting only those most pregnant with meaning;
and this conserved energy is utilized by the hearer in perceiving
the thought with unusual force and vividness. Any surplusage of
word symbols in a line weakens the line by diluting it. (pp. 36–7)

The correlation between 'the law of conservation of energy' and
creative activity had its main source in Pearson's *The Grammar of
Science* and Poincaré's *Science et méthode* (1909), but Maxim
chose to articulate it through Herbert Spencer's little-known essay
'The Philosophy of Style' of 1852. Spencer, for obvious historical
reasons, was unable to postulate the law of 'conservation' within
the vocabulary of physics and mechanics available to Maxim, but
simply as 'Regard for economy of the recipient's attention'. He,
too, wanted to codify the rules of composition and advocated the
need for 'something like scientific ordination'; his premiss in evalu-
ating these rules relied on the importance of economizing the
reader's attention, and he offered this saving of unnecessary mental
effort as a primary standard of judgement in critical procedure:

> Regarding language as an apparatus of symbols for the convey-
> ance of thought, we may say that, as in a mechanical apparatus,
> the more simple and better arranged its parts, the greater will be
> the effect produced ... the more time and attention it takes to
> receive and understand each sentence, the less time and attention
> can be given to the contained idea; and the less vividly will that
> idea be conceived. .... How truly language must be regarded as a
> hindrance to thought, though the necessary instrument of it, we
> shall clearly perceive on remembering the comparative force with
> which simple ideas are communicated by signs. To say, 'Leave
> the room', is less expressive than to point to the door.[62]

Maxim thus reiterated Spencer's dictum virtually wholesale;
but later in the book, when he paraphrased the crux of Spencer's
argument ('language, considered as an apparatus for conveying
thought ... is most nearly perfect when it is of the simplest con-

struction and does its work with the least expenditure of energy'),
he saw that it fell somewhat short and so added, 'that language is
best which utilizes the powers of utterance to the best advantage'
(p. 78). The importance of Maxim's dissatisfaction with Spencer
became clear as he amplified his own position: 'Besides being a
vehicle of thought, an apparatus for conveying ideas, language is
also an instrument for the conversion of energy into pleasurable
emotions, which serve to energize perception' (p. 79). This ampli-
fication was important because it suggested a real engagement with
the possibilities of language that prevented the principle of
economy from remaining at a purely theoretical level. Language
now had not only to economize but to 'energize the mind of the
hearer' (p. 85); Maxim sought explication from the mathematical
sciences:

> The study of physics, mechanics, arithmetic, geometry and the
> higher mathematics requires alertness and a wakeful, questioning
> state of the mind; while the inculcation of creeds requires an
> unquestioning and somnolent state of the critical faculties of the
> mind. Suggestive speech *impresses* belief upon the hearer. It
> introduces conviction without examination, while reflective
> speech appeals to the intellect. (p. 81)

In 'The Wisdom of Poetry', the essay that began by referring to
Maxim's treatise merely as 'A book which was causing some clatter
about a year ago', Pound borrowed his terminology from Spinoza
to conceal his paraphrase of this exact point made by Maxim: 'The
function of an art is to free the intellect from the tyranny of the
affects . . . to strengthen the perceptive faculties and free them from
encumbrance'.[63] More famously, two years later in the first issue of
Blast, Pound distinguished between the artist as 'the TOY of circumstance, as the plastic substance RECEIVING *impressions*' and as
'DIRECTING a certain fluid force against circumstance, as CON-
CEIVING instead of merely observing and reflecting'; and in 1919,
within a different system of science, that of Remy de Gourmont, he
wrote of the dissociations 'between the aesthetic receptivity of
tactile and magnetic values, of the perception of beauty in these
relationships and the conception of love, passion, emotion as an
intellectual instigation'.

Maxim's definition, that 'Poetry is pregnancy of meaning – the
pregnancy of meaning in words, their pregnancy of the thought

exprest' (p. 40), clearly looked forward to Pound's assertion in the *ABC of Reading* that great literature was 'simply language charged to the utmost degree'; for both, these definitions belonged to a view of poetry as metamorphic. Maxim wrote: 'Poetry-making is an act of metamorphosis or transfiguration, an act of creating comprehensible tangibility from chaotic intangibility'. Revealingly for Poundian interests, Maxim's notion of 'metamorphosis' was essentially a notion of 'visualization': 'Poetry is largely an act of visualization. The insubstantial is given substance that it may be realized in consciousness, which can be done only by metamorphosis into the sensuous' (p. 41). Here, poetry was always conceived by an act of 'invention', where the 'inventor', understood in technological terms, became fused with the 'explorer' to offer a wholly apposite figure for both the creative and the critical activity; neither the artist nor the critic, no less than the scientist, could afford to work in a historical vacuum:

> An explorer entering a new territory must study the footprints of previous pioneers and learn where and how far they go in order to determine the merits of his own discoveries. The inventor must study the state of the art in order to determine the value of any invention. (p. 117)

Pound, castigating America in 1912, demanded the same cognition:

> It is not enough that the artist have impulse, he must be in a position to know what has been done and what is yet to do. He must not be like the plough-boy on the lonely farm who spent his youth devising agricultural machinery and found when he went out into the world that all his machines had been invented and patented long before he was born.[64]

If Maxim's advocacy of the economizing and energizing powers of poetry was his first most significant contribution to Pound's aesthetics, then the second was his exposition of an action-biased poetry that uses the verb as its major linguistic unit:

> the greatest forms of poetic expression must be verbal. Altho the effect may be much heightened by proper use of adjectives and adverbial modifiers, and lines of real beauty may be made up mainly of modifiers and qualifiers, still poetry must always be greatest when it exists in action. (p. 181)

Maxim's conception of poetry 'in action', with its concomitant reliance on verbal as opposed to adjectival modes of description, predicted exactly that of Fenollosa, whom Pound read three years later. The notion of poetry as essentially verbal elaborated (as in Fenollosa) an epistemology of action, of relationship, rather than of qualities (again, echoing reductionist thought): 'As knowledge of things depends absolutely upon the character of their activities, it is a far more important function of language to predicate their activities than to name or qualify things' (p. 182). This epistemology was expressed through analogies from physics, centred on the idea of 'interactivities', Maxim's version of the more familiar 'lines of force' in Fenollosa, the lines of relation that, for the scientist, were more significant than the *relata* terminating those lines:

> Our acquaintance with the environment is made up of conceptions of matter, time, space, force and motion. All energy is manifested through motion. Heat, light, electricity, are modes of motion. . . . Our acquaintance with the environment is that of interactivities, action and re-action between the things with which we are acquainted. (pp. 181–2)

Maxim's epistemology of 'interactivities' thus provided a specific view of the cognitive function of language in a passage that, more than any other, duplicated the argument that Pound was to find in Fenollosa:

> Adjectives, which acquaint us with the characteristics or properties of the subject, are less important than the activities of the subject expressed by the verb; and as the nature of the action means more to us than the nature of the subject, adverbs, which modify the verb, and tell us when, where and how the action is performed, are more expressive than are adjectives, and for the same reason participial adjectives that participate in the properties of verb and adjective are more expressive than mere qualifying adjectives. The words *running horse* are more expressive than the words *red horse*. Adjectives like *wicked*, *wilful*, *playful*, and the like, which indicate qualities dependent upon activities, are more expressive than are adjectives like *black*, *white*, *red*, *large*, which relate merely to properties; for it concerns us more to know about the active properties of things than about the passive. (p. 182)

It is quite extraordinary that Pound made no acknowledgement of Maxim's understanding of verbal language coded so distinctively by contemporary science. His reading of Maxim predated by only three years his acquisition of the Fenollosa manuscripts and his own programme for a poetry testifying to ideas going into action; indeed, his memory of Maxim in 'The Wisdom of Poetry' of 1912 would seem to beg an association with Fenollosa in the following year. The reasons for Pound's disregard must remain purely speculative, but one is tempted to guess that it was primarily because he considered Maxim's style to be laboured, repetitive and extremely tedious, easily consigned to oblivion by the incisive vigour and ideographic sparkle of Fenollosa's syntax. The book may perhaps best be understood as an essential part of the preparation that enabled Pound to respond so fully to the similar propositions he discovered in Fenollosa's notes.

Pound's view of *The Science of Poetry* was double-edged: he admired Maxim's 'vigorous mind' but was disturbed by his ignorance and lack of taste; Maxim's commonsense attitude in talking about art was applauded ('one feels that with such a fool-killer abroad there is a chance for the oldest of the arts, even here in America'), but this common sense, felt Pound, was wasted by its excess:

> if Mr Maxim had confined himself to one-third the space, and given nothing but constructive theory, he might have produced a high-school manual of rhetoric which would be useful. The book as it stands is a curiosity. A vigorous mind, some sound pedestrian thought, warped by a colossal conceit, bad taste and an execrable style, backed up by flamboyant advertising. It all seems such a waste, in a way pathetic, because there is much worth reading in the book.[65]

The tenor of the review thus consisted of a guarded approbation ('I would rather have my own poetry read by someone who had read Maxim than by someone who had read no criticism of poetry') supported by a willingness to note the 'sane things' in the book, isolating and quoting for particular attention Maxim's remark on the 'economizing' nature of poetry ('By poetry a thought is presented with the utmost economy of symbols'[66]) and referring to his comments on 'dead metaphors':

By long use, many metaphors have entirely lost their original material significance. . . . The metaphoric use of the word *sweet* has been so much abused that it has lost nearly all its sensuous meaning. . . . When a figure has become so use-worn and hackneyed as no longer to awaken any awareness of the fact that it is a metaphor, then it has ceased to be a figure of speech, and has become literal. When a metaphor no longer enlists the imagination and requires translation in the mind from the figure to the literal, then it has become literal.[67]

For Pound, the 'best chapter in the book' was chapter 3, and it is this chapter that I have drawn on for most of my material, since it was there that Maxim established the major principles of economy and metamorphosis; the chapter concludes with a definition:

Poetry is the expression of imaginative thought by means only of the essentials to the thought, conserving energy for thought-perception, to which end all animate, inanimate and tangible things may assume the properties and attributes of tangible, living, thinking, and speaking things, possessing the power of becoming what they seem, or of transfiguration into what they suggest.[68]

Pound admired the definition and cited the first clause ('Poetry . . . essentials of [Pound's version] thought'). It is interesting that he omitted the rest of the passage, since he went on to talk of how the first clause applied to 'painting, sculpture and the equations of analytical geometry', noting that these equations were 'much nearer to poetry in their essential nature than anything Mr Maxim succeeds in defining, and it seems strange that a scientist should not have noted the difference'.[69] It seems equally strange that Pound omitted a version of 'transfiguration' which was directly applicable to the mythic interests of his current verse, interests that in turn were to be reconstructed into the geometrical shapes of vorticist theory.

The omission was rectified eighteen months later when Pound wrote 'The Wisdom of Poetry' (the occasion for a different form of omission, that of Maxim's name and the title of his book) and quoted the passage in full. In fact he emphasized the notion of 'transfiguration' by opening the essay with a parallel definition by Maxim: 'Poetry is the expression of insensuous thought in sensuous terms by means of artistic trope'. Pound derided the ambition here of the 'first "scientific and satisfactory definition of poetry"', but he admitted agreement 'with the dogma of trope'.[70] His attitude towards Maxim had hardened considerably since his original review,[71] but what is interesting about the essay is that it demonstrated the way in which Maxim coloured the palette of Pound's mind with certain receptivities, certain characteristics of vocabulary. Pound began the second half of the essay by anticipating the predominant concern of 'The Serious Artist' of the following year: the problem of whether the artist (formerly of use as historian, genealogist, religious functionary) had 'any permanent function in society'. He proposed two 'scientific answers'. The first was to become a permanent battle-cry, the health of the language: 'Thought is perhaps important to the race, and language, the medium of thought's preservation, is constantly wearing out. It has been the function of poets to new-mint the speech, to supply the vigorous terms for prose.' Pound's second answer postulated an agnosticism that in 'The Serious Artist' was to be recoded as a basis for the morality of science's cognition:

> The poet is consistently agnostic in this; that he does not postulate his ignorance as a positive thing. Thus his observations rest as the enduring data of philosophy. He grinds an axe for no dogma. Now that mechanical science has realized his ancient dreams of flight and sejunct communication, he is the advance guard of the psychologist on the watch for new emotions, new vibrations sensible to faculties as yet ill understood.[72]

We have here, in embryonic form, the famous principle that artists are the 'antennae of the race' and have an ethical responsibility such as was illustrated in Pound's constantly reiterated quotation from Flaubert concerning the Franco-Prussian War: 'If they had read my *Éducation sentimentale* these things would not have happened.'

In 1912 we are dealing with the beginnings of a permanent attitude and with Pound's postulation of a distinctive vocabulary for its expression; art, like science, could not be evaluated in terms of an immediate pragmatism, just as Plarr developed purely for their intrinsic interest the functions of an 'obscure sort of equation', which were merely 'arbitrary symbols' in the contemporary state of knowledge, but 'without which we should have no wireless telegraph'. This general recognition suggested to Pound the germ of one of his most characteristic figures for the artist: 'the poet's true and lasting relation to literature and life is that of the abstract mathematician to science and life. . . . What the analytical geometer does for space and form, the poet does for consciousness.' We see here the first elaboration of a use for analytical geometry that was, as I have suggested, to provide the fulcrum for Pound's vorticist tracts within the next two years. He ended the essay by considering 'the nature of the formulae of analytics':

By the signs $a^2 + b^2 = c^2$, I imply the circle. By $(a-r)^2 + (b-r)^2 = (c-r)^2$, I imply the circle and its mode of birth. I am led from the consideration of the particular circle formed by my ink-well and my table-rim, to the contemplation of the circle absolute, its law; the circle free in all space, unbounded, loosed from the accidents of time and place.

But, unlike the assured manipulation of this figure that we find in the propaganda for vorticism, here Pound was unwilling to allow it to stand on its own; it had to be deconstructed within more familiar modes of discourse:

Is the formula nothing, or is it cabala and the sign of unintelligible magic? The engineer, understanding and translating to the many, builds for the uninitiated bridges and devices. He speaks their language. For the initiated the signs are a door into eternity and into the boundless ether.[73]

The substance of Pound's argument was a reiteration of the late Romantic, symbolist view of the artist's endeavour to arrive at a point where the factual limitations of the material world could be dispensed with and a form of 'eternity' approached. Pound's mixed vocabulary, a sifting of terms from technology, religious mysticism and Platonic idealism in order to focus the reference of his analogy from geometry, suggest the problematic of his discourse, a provisional questing for the modernity he found in that analogy for his vorticist programme in 1914–16. The 'Vorticism' essay of September 1914[74] and the reconstruction of Whistler in the memoir of Gaudier-Brzeska of 1916 displayed no such speculative mixing of terminology, but prescribed the consistently realized analogy of Cartesian geometry in a manner exhibiting none of the need to explicate his analogy within more familiar frameworks.

The distance between these essays illustrates in part Pound's increasing confidence in the vocabulary and methodology that he sought to determine as the function of aesthetic criticism. His willingness to experiment with new forms of terminology most obviously resulted in his scientific 'defence' of poetry in 'The Serious Artist' of 1913, but that same year witnessed his satire on this new criticism in a witty piece of comic distortion published anonymously in *The New Freewoman*. He began his satire quite seriously by discussing the limitations of literary reviews in general:

> There can be little doubt that we, we the reviewers, we the readers, we the voice of rumour, *on dit* etcetera, that the aforesaid we spend a deal too much of our time both in reading and in writing reviews. A single review in any single mentionable paper gives out no more than the puny preference of the puny and individual reviewer or at most the creaking and habitual voice of his organ.

As an alternative to the wrong kinds of individualism and traditionalism, Pound comically proposed the 'scientific norm':

> After years of assiduous study, after hours of patient comparison we are led to believe that there are only a certain number of things that can be said about a book, or at least about any work of fiction, poetry or belles lettres. I neglect certain nuances and variants for there are, even in the exact science of mathematics, certain nuances and fractions which we are permitted to neglect when we make practical computations of certain sorts. . . . Not only do we believe that there are only a limited number of remarks that can be made about any given literary creation but we believe that they are, in actuality, made about so vast a percentage of the works actually published that we will save the reader considerable time by presenting him with the following table of opinions.

The 'table of opinions' of 'normative' evaluations that could be made about a given work consisted, of course, in a list of criteria covering almost every variety of bad criticism. It included the standard journalese: '13. The "Spectator" says: "The author goes from strength to strength"'; the false scholarship: '9. Mrs Beatrice Hastings says this work is unadulterated rott (sic), besides the phrase "blue ships" on p. 421 is weak in comparison with the "Black ships" of Homer (vide Butcher and Lang, book 11)'; the evasion of direct responsibility to the text: '3. Mr Yeats believes the author to be meritorious and possibly excellent, he regrets that he has not had time to read the work in question and refers the reader to Mr T. Sturge Moore for a lucid opinion'; the false standards of comparison: '6. Mr Figgis considers that the merits of this author, while approaching those of Frank Harris, Abercrombie and Shakespeare, do not in all points attain those of Mr Abercrombie.' The most amusing of all were of a more personal nature: '1. Mr Henry James has never heard of this author' and '7. Mr Ezra Pound says that someone else has praised this book and that therefore it must be bad.' The absurd logic reached its highpoint as Pound concluded by advocating its possibilities for a ludicrous economy:

> It will be seen that we have here the opinions if not of all the leaders of thought at least of leaders who are typical of all the brands of thought now thought in England. As the number of clauses which apply to any given possible book is very greatly in excess of the number of those which do not apply, the reviews will consist simply of the numerals belonging to the clauses which do NOT apply.[75]

With economy and wit, Pound satirized not only contemporary conventions of literary criticism but also his own ambitions for a scientific method, what he referred to later as the need to establish 'measuring rods' and 'axes of reference'. His satire showed how far his confidence in such a method had developed, in that he could lampoon it so witheringly, and, more importantly, it showed his realization of its limits.

'The Wisdom of Poetry' marked Pound's first public attempt to use mathematics as an analogy and as a model for the procedures of criticism, but this was prefigured in *The Spirit of Romance* (1910). Here his attempt displayed nothing like the assurance of 1913 and consisted primarily in a series of illustrative aphorisms, but it did point forward to the more systematic discourse of later years. Pound tentatively offered a definition: 'Poetry is a sort of inspired mathematics which gives us equations, not for abstract figures, triangles, spheres, and the like, but equations for the human emotions.'[76] In 1914 this definition was modified and particularized by his confidence in the ability of Cartesian geometry to describe the 'image':

Great works of art contain this fourth sort of equation. They cause form to come into being. By the 'image' I mean such an equation; not an equation of mathematics, not something about *a*, *b*, and *c*, having something to do with form, but about *sea*, *cliffs*, *night*, having something to do with mood.[77]

Pound's definition of 1910 shared the problematic of vocabulary that is evident in 'The Wisdom of Poetry'; he completed the definition with a proposal from an alternative system of knowledge: 'If one have a mind which inclines to magic rather than to science, one will prefer to speak of these equations as spells or incantations; it sounds more arcane, mysterious, recondite.' The conjunction of mathematics and magic was, as I shall show later, crucial to the epistemology of Pound's modernity; its force was to offer these two systems of discourse as complementary, each defining the programme of the other. This conjunction was to be the centre of Pound's aesthetics, and the means whereby he gave modernity to areas of experience customarily understood to be 'arcane, mysterious', retaining elements of eternal truth that had hitherto resisted the vocabulary necessary for announcing their contemporary correspondence. Such correspondence was essential for a poet whose residual tastes always sought sustenance from the mystifications of Provençal and medieval poetics of love, from works that testified to the vitality of a divinely ordered world which hitherto had had only myth, magic and metaphor as its modes of articulation. Pound explicated this correspondence in 1910 by using the four stages of mathematical procedure to demystify the esoteric planes on which Dante's *Commedia* operated:

> The 'Commedia' . . . is written in four senses; the literal, the allegorical, the anagogical, and the ethical. For this form of arcana we find the best parallel in the expressions of mathematics. Thus, when our mathematical understanding is able to see that one general law governs such a series of equations as $3 \times 3 + 4 \times 4 = 5 \times 5$, or written more simply, $3^2 + 4^2 = 5^2$ . . . one expresses the common relation algebraically thus, $a^2 + b^2 = c^2$. When one has learned common and analytical geometry, one understands that this relation, $a^2 \times [sic] b^2 = c^2$, exists between two sides of the right angle triangle and its hypotenuse, and that likewise in analytics it gives the equation for the points forming the circum-

ference of any circle. Thus to the trained mathematician the cryptic $a^2 + b^2 = c^2$ expresses:

> 1st. A series of abstract numbers in a certain relation to each other.
> 2nd. A relation between certain abstract numbers.
> 3rd. The relative dimensions of a figure; in this case a triangle.
> 4th. The idea or ideal of the circle.

> Thus the 'Commedia' is, in the literal sense, a description of Dante's vision of a journey through the realms inhabited by the spirits of men after death; in a further sense it is the journey of Dante's intelligence through the states of mind wherein dwell all sorts and conditions of men before death; beyond this, Dante or Dante's intelligence may come to mean 'Everyman' or 'Mankind', whereat his journey becomes a symbol of mankind's struggle upward out of ignorance into the clear light of philosophy. In the second sense I give here, the journey is Dante's own mental and spiritual development. In a fourth sense, the 'Commedia' is an expression of the laws of eternal justice.[78]

Pound's model mimed what he saw as the great strength of Dante's work; for Dante and for Richard St Victor, Hell, Purgatory and Paradise were conceived, as part of the 'esoteric and mystic dogma', to be 'states, and not places', but for the purpose of 'art and popular religion' it was more convenient to 'deal with such matters objectively', particularly in an age when it was natural 'to personify abstractions'.[79] The equations of mathematics were ideal for such explication in that they themselves partook of both the concrete and the abstract, expressing the movement from the relation between numbers ('the literal') to the 'ideal' of the equation for the circle ('the ethical'). The problematic of vocabulary that we noted in 'The Wisdom of Poetry', operating at the level of theory, was here eliminated by the focus of a specific text, but the crisis of language remained clearly manifest in another essay of 1912, 'Psychology and Troubadours'. That essay ended with another attempt to explicate mystical dogma, here by means of analogies from electromagnetism rather then from mathematics, analogies that Pound exhibited as 'an assistance to thought'. It was here that Pound proposed to consider the body as 'pure mechanism' in order to decipher the 'psychic experience' accumulated in the Greek myths, which celebrated 'our kinship to the vital universe, to the tree and the living rock'. He famously defined two forms of consciousness, the 'phantastikon' and the 'germinal', the latter known significantly 'by its signs of gods and godly attendants and oreads'.[80]

Greek stories of the gods survived in Provence, discernible in 'the history of the various cults or religions of orgy and ecstasy', in stories that testified to 'the whole and the flowing' predominantly in terms of sexual force perceived as tensile energy: 'when we do get into contemplation of the flowing we find sex, or some correspondance to it, "positive and negative", "North and South", "sun and moon", or whatever terms of whatever cult or science you prefer to substitute.' Pound chose to illustrate this sexual force by electromagnetism:

> 1st, the common electric machine, the glass disc and rotary brushes; 2nd, the wireless telegraph receiver. In the first we generate a current, or if you like, split up a static condition of things and produce a tension. This is focussed on two brass knobs or 'poles'. These are first in contact, and after the current is generated we can gradually widen the distance between them, and a spark will leap across it, the wider the stronger, until with the ordinary sized laboratory appliance it will leap over or around a large obstacle or pierce a heavy book cover. In the telegraph we have a charged surface – produced in a cognate manner – attracting to it, or registering movement in the invisible aether.[81]

These analogies elaborated Pound's initial distinction between the two forms of consciousness via these varieties of sexual force, the 'sun and moon' that each man has within him:

> there are at least two paths . . . the one ascetic, the other for want of a better term 'chivalric'. In the first the monk or whoever he may be, develops, at infinite trouble, and expense, the secondary pole within himself, produces his charged surface which registers the beauties, celestial or otherwise, by 'contemplation'. In the second, which I must say seems more in accord with 'mens sana in corpore sano' the charged surface is produced between the predominant natural poles of two human mechanisms.

Sexual force thus had 'a double function and purpose, reproductive and educational', or, to switch analogies, 'as we see in the realm of fluid force, one sort of vibration produces at different intensities, heat and light'.[82] The aggressiveness of this bipartite force (what Pound later referred to as 'the phallus or spermatozoid charging, head-on, the female chaos' discernible in the Greek rites[83]) provoked the tensile energy of sex where the lady served as a 'mantram' before whom the lover stood 'ever in unintermittent imagination' ('co-amantis'). This tensile energy was made possible only through the woman as a source of visions (the 'coitu inluminatio' of Cantos XXXVI and LXXIV), and it was particularly available during the time of the troubadours: 'The electric current gives light where it meets resistance. I suggest that the living conditions of Provence gave the necessary restraint, produced the tension sufficient for the results.'[84] Pound's comparison between sexual gnosis and electromagnetism was arguably his most vivid and fertile use of scientific analogy, for the simple reason that it instigates new and suggestive ranges of perception. Pound offered it, however, quite deliberately at the level of simile, as the 'handiest' illustration. This device of rhetoric obviously militates against the possibility of an idealist synthesis; it both illuminates and limits its mode of analogy so that the rightness of the simile coexists with a scepticism about its own procedure. The two are not mutually exclusive (just as, in Pound's Provence, scepticism and faith seemed natural partners) but interfere with each other to suggest both a primitive trust and an urban worldliness. Pound's deciphering of early medieval sexual mysticism via contemporary electromagnetism thus not only defined his pagan religiosity but was properly the metamorphic vision of the savage in the city which marked primary interstices of psychic and sensual experience.

2 The seriousness of the artist

That it should exist, this school, this bulk of work, is the first necessity of the State, for it would be the symptom of national health.

(Ford)

A writer's freedom

Walter Pater defined the ontology of the art-product in his Preface to *The Renaissance*: 'The objects with which aesthetic criticism deals . . . are indeed receptacles of so many powers or forces; they possess, like the products of nature, so many virtues or qualities.' Confronted by such 'virtues', the critic's function was to disengage their potency 'as a chemist notes some natural element' and to avoid the metaphysics of critical discourse by asking quite simply 'What effect does it really produce on me?' Thus the critic was to share the scientist's honesty; the answers to his question constituted his responsibility to the world at large, a responsibility that began with honesty to the self: the answers were 'the original facts with which the aesthetic critic has to do; and, as in the study of light, of morals, of number, one must realize such primary data for one's self, or not at all.'[1] The worlds of physics, ethics and arithmetic were thereby paralleled to that of aesthetics; in each, the 'virtue' of its material had to be isolated and then explicated according to the standards of a public responsibility that relied initially on this special sense of personal integrity. Pound in 1912 preferred the term *virtù* to describe what Pater meant by 'powers or forces', and he chose a more precise, and vividly contemporary, metaphor from science to express it:

La virtù is the potency, the efficient property of a substance or person. Thus modern science shows us radium with a noble virtue of energy. Each thing or person was held to send forth magnetisms of certain effect. . . . It is a spiritual chemistry, and modern science and modern mysticism are both set to confirm it.[2]

Pound was concerned to suggest modernist confirmations (radium understood as exhibiting the same magical powers as women's names in alchemical equations) rather than to share the ethical burden of Pater's analogy.

A few months previously, in the 'Osiris' series, Pound did recognize the scientist's moral function when he coded the notion of *virtù* as part of the 'new' method in scholarship, the 'luminous detail'. Details that were 'luminous' were 'interpreting' details that, in embryonic form, predicated knowledge of an entire range of cultural values, resuming a complete social, historical or aesthetic complex in order to instigate 'intelligence of a period'. Pound sought an analogy in electricity to demonstrate these details' function – to 'govern knowledge as the switchboard governs an electric circuit' – and it was the search for such details that characterized the scientific morality of the method: 'The artist seeks out the luminous detail and presents it. He does not comment. His work remains the permanent basis of psychology and metaphysics.'[3] Over two decades later, Pound was to cite Leo Frobenius as the great expositor of such detail: 'Hence the yarn that Frobenius looked at two African pots and, observing their shapes and proportions, said: if you will go to a certain place and there digge, you will find traces of a civilization with such and such characteristics.'[4] More immediately, the practical operation of the 'luminous detail', its economical selection from 'a great array of facts of the other sort' (the method of 'multitudinous detail'), was a result of a similar insistence on economy by Hudson Maxim and by the reductionist theory of scientific language. In stressing the place of 'imagination' in science for the purposes of 'discovery' (another crucial term for Pound's practical science), Karl Pearson quantified the scientific nature of aesthetic judgement by emphasizing its capacity for economy:

> Is it not because we find concentrated into a brief statement, into a simple formula or a few symbols, a wide range of human emotions and feelings? . . . Does not the beauty of the artist's work lie for us in the accuracy with which his symbols resume innumerable facts of our past emotional experience? . . . If this

account of the aesthetic judgement be at all a true one, the reader will have remarked how exactly parallel it is to the scientific judgement.

It was the ambition of Pearson's science to offer 'a mental résumé of the universe', an ambition he saw (significantly for Poundian purposes) as a contemporary version of primitive anthropomorphism:

> There is an insatiable desire in the human breast to resume in some short formula, some brief statement, the facts of human experience. It leads the savage to 'account' for all natural phenomena by deifying the wind and the stream and the tree. It leads civilized man, on the other hand, to express his emotional experience in works of art, and his physical and mental experience in the formulae or so-called laws of science.[5]

These notions informed Pound's position in the 'Osiris' articles at the level of practical workmanship; he was concerned to emphasize the importance of learning rhyme 'with the least waste of energy' and so preached the 'sane' course suggested by mathematics: the apprentice should study 'in the work not of its greatest master, but of the man who first considered it critically, tried and tested it, and controlled it from the most diverse angles of attack.'[6] This workmanlike attitude sought its most satisfactory expression in technology; he described the critic's procedure by comparing him with a man who, ignorant of painting, was shown into a room full of masterpieces:

> His feelings are not unlike mine when I am taken into the engineering laboratory and shown successively an electric engine, a steam-engine, a gas-engine etc. I realize that there are a number of devices, all designed for more or less the same end, none 'better', none 'worse', all different. . . . They all produce 'power' – that is they gather the latent energy of Nature and focus it on a certain resistance. The latent energy is made dynamic or 're-vealed' to the engineer in control, and placed at his disposal.[7]

Pound used technology here as a version of practical science not only to stress the necessity for a workmanlike attitude but also to insist on the notion, familiar from 'The Serious Artist' onwards, that conventionally moralistic literary criticism is meaningless; just as the varieties of engine were neither 'better' nor 'worse' than each other, simply having a different mode of operation, so too was the only 'bad' art (and the only 'immoral' art) one that failed in its technique or its standards of truth. It made as little sense to talk of the immorality of *Ulysses* as to talk of the immorality of a threshing machine; the value of both resided in the efficiency of their function.

The gritty practicality that Pound advocated here reflected a recent voice in American literary debate which began its most popular life with the ambition of the critic E. C. Stedman in 1892 to establish the societal function of the arts, which 'belong as much to the order of things, and indirectly make as much for wealth, as the science of economics, and they make as much for social happiness as the science of sociology'.[8] Stedman's ambition had its root, of course, in the European discussions of, and sanctions for, the realism of the novel, but it distinguished itself from such discussions by its engagement at the level of theory. The first instalment of Pound's important essay of 1913, 'The Serious Artist', was offered self-consciously as a 'Defence of Poesy' and showed itself to be irritated precisely by those sorts of questions, 'in the age of Gosse', concerning the social function of the arts that were a product of the realist debate. Such questions, for Pound, simply had no place in aesthetics: 'we are asked if the arts are moral. We are asked to define the relation of the arts to economics, we are asked what position the arts are to hold in the ideal republic.' Of course Pound, as his entire career abundantly demonstrates, believed profoundly in the importance of these very questions, but in 1913 his irritability, exacerbated perhaps by the clinging air of the nineties, was rasped by their utilitarian overtones and by the very fact that the present state of letters should require such questions to be reiterated. So he snapped out his answers, claiming the scientist's prestige ('The arts, literature, poesy, are a science, just as chemistry is a science') and the value of his cognition ('a great percentage of the lasting and unassailable data regarding the nature of man'), grumbling all the while that 'I take no great pleasure in writing prose about aesthetic. I think one work of art is worth forty prefaces and as many apologiae.'[9] That these matters – belonging as they did to the 1860s and the 1870s, to the period castigated (for Pound, once and for all) by the Prefaces of the brothers de Goncourt – had to be revived in the year of modernity, 1913, meant that the state of progress in the arts had to be put back by forty years. Nevertheless, despite his

irritation, Pound was obliged to restate the artist's functional responsibility, primarily by replacing the technological focus of the
'Osiris' articles with a more sweeping scientific coding of art's
special morality: 'Bad art is inaccurate art. It is art that makes false
reports. If a scientist falsifies a report either deliberately or through
negligence we consider him as either a criminal or a bad scientist
according to the enormity of his offence.' This was a predominantly
public gesture, designed to defend the status of the artist to the
world at large by demanding for the artist the seriousness with
which the work of the scientist was received:

> One does not need to read black print to learn this ethical fact
> about physicians. Yet it takes a deal of talking to convince a
> layman that bad art is 'immoral'. And that good art however
> 'immoral' it is, is wholly a thing of virtue. Purely and simply that
> good art can NOT be immoral. By good art I mean art that bears
> true witness, I mean the art that is most precise.

Switching analogies again, Pound saw in medicine the ideal
figurability for his point; the surgeon's 'diagnosis' became in the
transposition the 'hygiene' of 'beauty', and his 'cure' became
'satire', a matter of 'insertions and amputations'.[10] Pound's medical
analogies in 'The Serious Artist' and his sense of the paucity of the
writer's public status found a more specific focus as the work of
Joyce began to disturb the state of letters. In three essays, written
between 1916 and 1922, Pound instigated an analysis of the situation of the contemporary novel in general, and that of Joyce in
particular, by means not of Zola or Balzac but of the Goncourts'
Preface to *Germinie Lacerteux*; in 1918 he justified the necessity for
turning the clock back by wearily claiming:

> I am tired of rewriting the argument for the realist novel; besides
> there is nothing to add. The Brothers de Goncourt said the thing
> once and for all, but despite the lapse of time their work is still
> insufficiently known to the American reader. The programme in
> the preface to *Germinie Lacerteux* states the case and the whole
> case for realism.

Pound quoted the Preface in its entirety to sanction his claims for
the artist's scientific seriousness and to remind his audience of the
impasse in the condition of literature that needed such a reminder;
my redaction isolates its main argument:

Le public aime les romans faux: ce roman est un roman vrai.

Il aime les livres qui font semblant d'aller dans le monde: ce livre vient de la rue.

Il aime les petites œuvres polissonnes, les mémoires des filles, les confessions d'alcôves, les saletés érotiques, le scandale qui se retrousse dans une image aux devantures des libraires, ce qu'il va lire est sévère et pur. Qu'il ne s'attende point à la photographie décolletée du plaisir: l'étude qui suit est la clinique de l'Amour.

Le public aime encore les lectures anodines et consolantes, les aventures qui finissent bien, les imaginations qui ne dérangent ni sa digestion ni sa sérénité: ce livre, avec sa triste et violente distraction, est fait pour contrarier ses habitudes et nuire à son hygiène. . . . . Aujourd'hui que le Roman s'élargit et grandit, qu'il commence à être la grande forme sérieuse, passionnée, vivante, de l'étude littéraire et de l'enquête sociale, qu'il devient, par l'analyse et par la recherche psychologique, l'Histoire morale contemporaine, aujourd'hui que le Roman s'est imposé les études et les devoirs de la science, il peut en revendiquer les libertés et les franchises.[11]

Pound emphasized his point by reprinting the Preface again two months later, on its own, with a brief introductory note.[12] He was certainly aware of more sophisticated ways of talking about the novel; 1918 was also the year in which he published six essays on Henry James, and the arguments for realistic fiction (with the vocabulary from science that was used to explicate those arguments) were, as Pound acknowledged, long familiar. His anachronism in a decade of intense modernity was necessitated partly by his sense of an American audience and partly by the romanticized expectations of the reading public in general. The reception of *Ulysses* brought out this necessity; Pound's essay on Joyce's novel in 1922 demonstrated that his response to the Goncourts' Preface was primarily a response to a demand for the artist's freedom, which for Pound was the most important corollary to the seriousness that he had maintained for literature's reception in 1913. He paraphrased the Goncourts' argument, retaining their model of scientific research, as the situation of *Ulysses* revived the need for a public defence of literature:

Ought the people to remain under a literary edict? Are there classes unworthy, misfortunes too low, dramas too ill set, catastrophes, horrors too devoid of nobility? Now that the novel is augmented, now that it is the great literary form . . . the social inquest, for psychological research and analysis, demanding the studies and imposing on its creator the duties of science . . . seeking facts . . . whether or not the novelist is to write with the accuracy, and thence with the freedom of the savant, the historian, the physician?[13]

Freedom was a product not so much of the artist's autonomy as of his scientific responsibility; in the terms of 1912, of not playing up to 'the law of supply and demand', a refusal coded by the model of 'the chemist experimenting' where, as the artist 'paints the thing as he sees it', he must be 'as free as the mathematician'.[14] By 1915 Pound's increased sense of public pressure on the artist again provoked claims for a release from this pressure, such as was enjoyed by the scientist:

It is as futile to expect a poet to get the right words, or any sort of artist to do real work, with one eye on the public, as it would be to expect the experimenter in a chemical laboratory to advance the borders of science, if he has constantly to consider whether his atomic combinations are going to flatter popular belief, or suit the holders of monopolies in some over-expensive compound.[15]

In the following year, another of Pound's essays on Joyce attacked the climate that rendered the publication of books such as *A Portrait of the Artist as a Young Man* or *Ulysses* difficult and often impossible. Here he quoted from Edmond de Goncourt's additions to the original Preface for the 1877 edition of *Germinie Lacerteux*. These additions, rather than stressing the content of literature, argued more forcefully for the freedom of the writer in the role of social anatomist and for the status of his work:

It has been impossible, at times, not to speak *as a physician, as a savant, as a historian* [Pound's emphasis]. It would be insulting to us, the young and serious school of modern novelists, to forbid us to think, to analyse, to describe all that is permitted to others to put into a volume which has on its cover 'Study', or any other grave title. You cannot ask us at this time of day to amuse the young lady in the rail-road carriage. I think we have acquired, since the beginning of the century, the right to write for formed men, without the depressing necessity of fleeing to foreign presses.[16]

One of the reasons for these revisions is apparent from the title of Grant Allen's *Physiological Aesthetics*, published in the same year; Allen wrote of his choice of title:

> I have been influenced in the choice of that name which now appears on the title-page by the fact that it will most clearly explain to ordinary readers the nature of my design. The subject of Aesthetics has so long been given over to transcendental rhetoric and vague poetical declamation, that the name alone upon a cover is sufficient to deter most scientific readers. I have therefore qualified it by an epithet which at once exhibits the positive point of view from which the present volume is written.[17]

Allen was talking about a different topic, but the principle was transposable; in 1877, for either a novel or a treatise on aesthetics to be received with serious attention, it was obliged to assume the grave persona of science. For Pound, the state of letters in 1913–22 remained parallel, and in a post-Jamesian era, he picked up the hint of Edmond de Goncourt's revisions in order not to defend the content of a novel but to claim for the writer the scientist's freedom:

> if one can't, *parfois*, write 'as a physician, as a savant, as a historian', if we can't write plays, novels, poems, or any other conceivable form of literature with the scientist's freedom and privilege, with at least the chance of at least the scientist's verity, then where in the world have we got to, and what is the use of anything, *anything*?[18]

Pound's claim relied ultimately on an analogy with the physician, specifically on the vocabulary of 'diagnosis'; it was here, precisely, that the writer earned freedom as a necessary corollary of responsibility. At the close of the First World War, Pound wrote:

> As Armageddon has only too clearly shown, national qualities are the great gods of the present and Henry James spent himself from the beginning in an analysis of these potent chemicals; trying to determine from the given microscopic slide the nature of Frenchness, Englishness, Germanness, Americanness, which

chemicals too little regarded, have in our time exploded from want of watching. They are the permanent and fundamental hostilities and incompatibles.[19]

The Jamesian 'diagnosis', more appropriate to chemistry, did not quite provide the edge that Pound needed for his polemic; the medical analogies that he picked up from the Goncourts required the more extreme case of Joyce. Pound saw Flaubert as the most meaningful ancestor of Joyce, and in another essay published in the same month as that praising the Jamesian 'chemicals' he wrote of *L'Éducation sentimentale*: 'If it is the business of the artist to make humanity aware of itself; here the thing was done, the pages of diagnosis.'[20] A year earlier, the function of 'diagnosis' provided the means whereby Pound elaborated Joyce's novelty and his ancestry:

I doubt if a comparison of Mr Joyce to other English writers or Irish writers would much help to define him. One can only say that he is rather unlike them. *The Portrait* is very different from *L'Éducation Sentimentale*, but it would be easier to compare it with that novel of Flaubert's than with anything else. Flaubert pointed out that if France had studied his work they might have been saved a good deal in 1870. If more people had read *The Portrait* and certain stories in Mr Joyce's *Dubliners* there might have been less recent trouble in Ireland. A clear diagnosis is never without its value.[21]

The case of James was acknowledged by Pound for similar virtues, but it was a much calmer affair; he wrote of James in 1912, for example, that 'Much of the real work of the world is done, and done almost solely by such quiet and persistent diagnoses as his are', and in 1918 with optimistic topicality he judged 'Pandora' as 'another synthesis of some of the million reasons why Germany will never conquer the world': James was not the swingeing satirist, the violent disrupter that Pound's defence needed, but 'the great true recorder'.[22] We cannot imagine James provoking the level of response that *Ulysses* instigated:

The katharsis of *Ulysses*, the joyous satisfaction as the first chapters rolled into Holland Place, was to feel that here was the JOB DONE and finished, the diagnosis and cure was here. The sticky molasses-covered filth of current print, all the fuggs, all the foetors, the whole boil of the European mind, had been lanced.[23]

Cosmopolitan diagnoses

The history of Pound's campaign for Joyce illustrates the rarity, particularly in America, of such a willingness to recognize the special Joycean realism. At the same time, however, James Huneker, 'Critic of the Seven Arts', iconoclastic defender of the avant-garde and supreme expositor of cosmopolitan standards, conducted a parallel campaign from New York. It is extraordinary that Pound had no substantial comment to make about Huneker, since the battles he fought in America were virtual replicas of Pound's campaigns in London. If Pound was seeking the indigenous reassurance that his exile so frequently seemed to need, if he was seeking an American partner in his struggle for the seriousness of literary behaviour against parochial values, against a puritan mentality, against nationalist prejudice and against trivial critical debate, then Huneker would have been the ideal ally and a worthy inhabitant of Pound's ideal metropolis in the composite 'Paris and Rome'.

From the 1890s onwards Huneker was in the vanguard of the movement to introduce contemporary European literature to America; his bohemian cosmopolitanism was distinctly at odds with the mainstream line of American literary criticism, which was concerned to shore up its national product specifically against foreign influences. Huneker's range, perhaps his most characteristic feature, was impressively wide; one recent commentator has noted: 'Huneker's versatility in the arts was unique in America. Primarily a student of music, he had added the other six arts to his province; his theories blended music, the plastic arts, and literature.'[24] His championship of Flaubert, Gourmont and Joyce, the new and the unknown, French poetry, Strindberg and Nietzsche, anticipated the positions of the little magazines with which Pound was associated, and as a critic in New York, as Van Wyck Brooks has said, 'he was to contribute as much as any one, possibly more than any one else, to the cosmopolitan growth of the city'. Brooks, an observer of that contribution, summarized it well:

He was a symbol of the generation during which Americans so generally turned from their Anglo-Saxon past towards an inter-racial future, when the 'new cosmopolis' of Huneker's phrase replaced beyond recall what he also described as 'our staid Quakerish old New York'. Huneker spread the influence of many of the writers who were largely to form the outlook of the coming generation and who supplanted at every turn the traditional American optimism that was on the wane already in the eighteen-nineties. . . . In a day of 'uncritical parochialism' that made American criticism a 'cemetery of clichés', as Huneker put it, he widened immeasurably its consciousness of the great world outside. He left it broad awake to modernity elsewhere.

And in Huneker's celebrated role as instructor Brooks compared him with the figure joined by Pound with Confucius as an imparter of knowledge, Louis Agassiz: 'In some ways like Ticknor with his new learning at the Harvard of three generations before, or like Agassiz, the Johnny Appleseed of science, Huneker the showman, with his wholesale methods, shovelled into the minds of the young precisely what they did not learn in college.'[25] Brooks's account suggests the synthesis that made Huneker such an excellent model for Pound's programme between 1910 and 1920. Above all, it was his modernity that would have sealed his appeal; Eliot began his review of Huneker's *Egoists* in 1909 by stressing Huneker's modernist sensibility: 'Now that Arthur Symons is no longer active in English letters, Mr James Huneker alone represents modernity in criticism. Few critics are possessed of so much erudition, yet there are few so determined to consider subjects only of the most modern interest.' Eliot noted the rarity of this sensibility in America:

In fact, he is far too alert to be an American; in his style and in his temper he is French. Then, too, he is a musician; plays himself, and has written an interesting life of Chopin; has written also a volume on contemporary European drama, and can speak intelligently of art. All this, in an American (or English) critic of literature, is quite unusual.[26]

Huneker's style, frequently similar to the distinctive acerbic tenor of Pound's prose, also occasioned Eliot's interest:

Huneker's style may impress us as unpardonably hasty, crammed, staccato; a note-book and journalistic style. But (among American writers, still further distinction) a style it decidedly is, and shares with that of Mr Henry James (from which, we need not add, it differs in almost every other respect) what I should call conversational quality; not conversational in admitting the slipshod and maladroit, or a meagre vocabulary, but by a certain informality, abandoning all the ordinary rhetorical hoaxes for securing attention.[27]

Despite the fact that it was rather odd for Eliot to respond so positively to a style that worked against all we customarily find in his own prose, his description pointed exactly to an element of the provisory that I have suggested as constituting the fulcrum of Pound's interest in Whistler and Whitman. Much later, Pound asserted James's 'conversational quality' to be the essence of 'an American form':

> I'll tell you a thing that I think *is* an American form, and that is the Jamesian parenthesis. You realize that the person you are talking to hasn't got the different steps, and you go back over them. . . . That I think is something that is definitely American. The struggle that one has when one meets another man who has had a lot of experience to find the point where the two experiences touch, so that he really knows what you are talking about.[28]

The verbal pattern that Pound described here was precisely that of his own broken syntax, the prose formed under the pressures of the London experiments, of maintaining a Whistlerian openness, of Making It New, of walking 'sheer into nonsense' with his gristly explications of gods and myths, of finding 'a language to think in'.

Huneker was most obviously available to Pound through his campaigns for figures close to Pound himself. The most significant of such figures were Gourmont (to whom I shall return in a later context) and Joyce. Huneker's review of *A Portrait of the Artist as a Young Man* for the *New York Sun* in 1917 was one of the first in America to make claims for Joyce. In case Pound missed it, John Quinn asked B. W. Huebsch to send him a copy, and Joyce himself mentioned the 'very favourable' notice to Pound.[29] Huneker's review concentrated on Joyce's particular 'realism':

> James Joyce, potentially a poet, and a realist of the De Maupassant breed, envisages Dublin and the Dubliners with a cruel scrutinizing gaze. He is as truthful as Tchekov. . . . Joyce is as implacably naturalistic as the Russian in his vision of the sombre, mean, petty, dusty commonplaces of middle-class life, and he sometimes suggests the Frenchman in his clear, concise, technical methods.[30]

Joyce's 'well-nigh perfect' portrait was of 'the House of Flesh in its most sordid aspects', avoiding the 'half-way house of reticence', yet achieving the scientific balance of *impassibilité*: 'Mr Joyce holds the scales evenly. He neither abuses nor praises.'[31] It was, of course, exactly such realism, recognizable and valuable only to a temperament familiar with the French novel, that occasioned its tardy public appreciation and necessitated Pound's struggle on Joyce's behalf; Huneker wrote: 'There is no denying that the novel is as a whole hardly cheerful. Its grip on life, its intensity, its evident truth, and unflinching acceptance of facts will make A Portrait disagreeable to the average reader.' What compounded the degree of the 'disagreeable' was the 'personal' voice that enforced the 'objectivity' of Joyce's work: 'No one may tell the truth with impunity, and the portrait of Stephen in its objective frigidity – as an artistic performance – and its passionate personal note, is bound to give offence in every quarter.'[32]

Huneker's criteria were those which for Pound constituted the scientific seriousness of literary endeavour. He too approached Joyce from a familiarity with the tradition of the French novel expounded by Flaubert and Maupassant, and similarly he found himself defending the 'sordid' aspects of A Portrait through a comparison with its European counterparts, claiming in 1918: 'The sordid is there in all conscience as you would find it in De Goncourt.'[33] Pound relied on the example of the French novelists not only to defend the 'sordid' in Joyce but to explicate the scientific basis for a realism that could incorporate such material truthfully and without sensationalism. This scientific basis was what Huneker implied by Joyce's 'objective frigidity', the coldness of impassioned experiment; in Pound's version, it was the Flaubertian 'exact presentation' that had early defined the meaning of the 'French scientific prose' which he expressed through technological example on behalf of Joyce: 'Mr Joyce writes a clear hard prose. He deals with subjective things, but he presents them with such clarity of outline that he might be dealing with locomotives or with builders' specifications.'[34] The French novel, the models of science and technology, and the precise clarity they shared, served to underwrite that seriousness around which Pound constructed his campaign for Joyce; again we witness the choice of a distinctive vocabulary as a result of specific pressure. The parity with Huneker's campaign may be illustrated by their shared reading of

Remy de Gourmont who established the basis of Flaubertian realism in *Promenades philosophiques* (1905–8): 'Être impersonnel c'est être personnel selon un mode particulier: Voyez Flaubert. On dirait en jargon: l'objectif est une des formes du subjectif.'[35]

Huneker's *Egoists* (1909), the occasion for Eliot's admiring review, summarized, in conjunction with his illuminatingly titled *Iconoclasts* (1905), the efforts of his periodical essays to inject European literature into American culture. The peak of that literature was to be found in France, where the finest literary craftsman was Flaubert, whom Huneker, in an essay called 'The Real Flaubert', acclaimed as 'the patron-saint of all true literary men', and who, in *L'Éducation sentimentale*, was 'the supreme exemplar of realism in fiction'.[36] Huneker's essay provided a literalness for Pound's admiration of the Flaubert he received from Ford Madox Ford, the Flaubert of 'French scientific prose'; Flaubert's grandfather was a surgeon, and Huneker commented:

> From him Gustave inherited his taste for all that pertained to medicine and science. Recall his escapades as a boy when he would peep for hours into the dissecting-room of the Rouen hospital. . . . He knew more about the theory and practice of medicine than many professional men. An air of mortality exhales from his pages. He is in Madame Bovary the keen soul-surgeon.[37]

Huneker's pun, his shift from literal biography to the surgical metaphor of that biography, anticipated Pound's use of the same metaphor throughout his discussions of Flaubert's Irish inheritor. For both Pound and Huneker this metaphor, open and hidden, coded their appreciation of the realism exhibited by Flaubert and Joyce; the figure of the 'scales' that Huneker was to use in 1917 to describe Joyce's realism was implicit in his response to Flaubert: 'The distinguished writer is a sober narrator of facts. His is not a domain of delicate thrills. His women are neither doves nor devils. He does not paint those acrobatics of the soul so dear to psychological fiction.' The opposition between the 'sober narrator of facts' and the diluters of popular fiction was grounded in the scientific struggle for style:

The tormented desire . . . for perfection, for the blending of idea and image, for the eternal pursuit of the right word. . . . It was always O *altitudo* in art with Flaubert. . . . He had set himself an impossible standard of perfection. . . . He would annotate three hundred volumes for a page of facts.[38]

This 'page of facts' was to be the issue of Pound's biological 'Serious Artist':

That is to say a good biologist will make a reasonable number of observations of any given phenomenon before he draws a conclusion, thus we read such phrases as 'over 100 cultures from the secretions of the respiratory tracts of over 500 patients and 30 nurses and attendants'.

The mode of realism that Pound determined here was that of Flaubert and Joyce, their 'objective frigidity': 'The serious artist is scientific in that he presents the image of his desire, of his hate, of his indifference as precisely that, as precisely the image of his own desire, hate or indifference.'[39]

Pound's vocabulary of 'diagnosis' and 'antisepsis' was not confined to the immediate pressures of the state of the novel but extended throughout the more general spectrum of his attitudes towards current epistemologies. In an essay of 1915 on Remy de Gourmont, he distinguished what he saw as characteristic French and Teutonic procedures of thought: 'the whole difference between the French and Tedescan systems: a German never knows when a thought is "only to be thought" – to be thought out in all its complexity and its beauty – and when it is to be made a basis for action.' Hence he saw Germany as having 'got decidedly and disgustingly drunk' on ideas, whereas 'Paris is the laboratory of ideas; it is there that poisons can be tested, and new modes of sanity be discovered. It is there that the antiseptic conditions of the laboratory exist.' The function of Paris was shared by Gourmont who had 'this absolute fairness, the fairness of a man watching his own experiment in a laboratory'.[40] Gourmont's 'absolute fairness' was understood as an 'absolute openness to all thought', the openness that Pound was currently admiring in Whistler and that was allied to the 'sincerity' of the artist on which the 'health' of literature ultimately depended. It was here that Pound prescribed his favourite line from Gourmont, 'Franchement d'écrire ce qu'on pense, seul plaisir d'un écrivain', for its function 'as much the basis of a clean literature . . . as is an antiseptic method, the basis of sound surgical treatment', and he placed Gourmont's significance deliberately within a programme for antisepsis: 'He never abandoned beauty. The mountain stream may be antiseptic as the sterilized dressing.'[41]

The placing of Gourmont's 'openness' within the complex of terms defining Pound's notion of scientific realism situates the final area of reference for the vocabulary of 'diagnosis'. Pound gave his most succinct definition of literary criticism in 1918: 'Criticism is not a circumscription or a set of prohibitions. It provides fixed points of departure.'[42] This definition was a rephrasing of Matthew Arnold's dictum that he had used as an epigraph three years earlier, 'All criticism is an attempt to define the classic',[43] where 'classic' was to be understood in the sense of 'the very best'.[44] The Arnoldian 'touchstone' whereby the 'real estimate' of literature was formed became the Poundian 'masterwork' that, within an open system of critical debate, provided the necessary 'fixed points of departure'. As such, the importance of the 'masterwork', the 'classic', included its function of diagnosis; in 1917, Pound claimed that

> What we know of any art is mostly what some master has taught us. We may not know him in the flesh, but the masterwork, and only the masterwork, discontents us with mediocrity, or rather, it clarifies our discontentment; we may have suspected that something was wrong, been uninterested, worried, found the thing dull; the masterwork diagnoses it.[45]

In a letter to Margaret Anderson he argued forcefully: 'The classics "ancient and modern", are precisely the acids to gnaw through the thongs and bull-hides with which we are tied by our schoolmasters. They are the antiseptics.'[46]

The vocabulary that Pound derived from medicine was extreme; its technical reference was a necessary instrument against what he saw as the almost physiological tyranny that contemporary puritanism exercised over the state of letters. His vitriolic attacks on puritanism adopted two levels of discourse: the first took the form of a Menckenian grouse against the general suppression of serious literature, usually focused by a contempt for the cowardice and fake morality that he lumped together as 'Comstockery', the old-

maidenly prudishness that caused, to take but one example out of
the literally hundreds of pages he wrote on the subject throughout
his London years, the suppression for supposed 'immorality' of
Dreiser's The 'Genius' in 1916: 'The general *louche*ness and crapu-
larity of the New York Sunday-school grafters is made rather more
manifest by their attack on Dreiser.' This suppression was laid
firmly at Comstock's door:

> America has ceased to matter and there is no particular use in
> elaborating the expression of one's disgust with her farcical
> attempts at what the organized Comstockians call 'morality'.
> The place is the sort of sink where a Comstock is possible, where
> a worse than Comstock succeeds to a dead Anthony. It is the
> business of the people who have to live in the country to decide
> whether the sinkiness is to remain and thicken, or whether the
> country is to retain any vestige of personal freedom.

Pound was by now rather weary of the necessity to enter the lists
yet again, as his disgust included not only the Comstockians but
also those who were protesting against Dreiser's suppression:

> If they cannot maintain the freedom of Dreiser they will be ad-
> judged a nation of cowards, of very indolent cowards, of very
> 'tacky' and cranky cowards; they will, as the protest indicates,
> receive the contempt of the civilized world, but they will not
> receive what the protest entitles, the 'ridicule' of the world. The
> joke is already too stale.[47]

The immediate context of Pound's note was his reprinting of
a 'Protest' from the Authors' League of America against the
attempted suppression of Dreiser's novel. Pound's tone occasioned
a response from an anonymous (inevitably damning him from the
start) member of that League, offering bourgeois arguments for
restraint and for the anaesthetizing comfort of historical pre-
cedents:

> I hope we shall not run blubbering into the street and begin calling
> every one names. If *we* fail some one else will carry on the work.
> A country which has produced a Whitman and an Alexander
> Hamilton can surely produce other titans and finally accept
> them. The public gradually forgets the battle, and works of art
> which were assailed in times gone by now occupy permanent
> niches in the halls of fame. . . . So it will be with Dreiser.[48]

Such arguments, with their bland acceptance, and indeed insistence, on the *status quo*, demonstrated exactly why Pound's anger was directed as much against the protesters as against the Comstockians. The attitude expressed in this rejoinder summarized everything that Pound had been fighting against since 'Sestina: Altaforte': 'Hell grant soon we hear again the swords clash! / Hell blot black for always the thought "Peace"!'[49] Pound replied in another letter, condemning the League because, out of a total of sixty, only seventeen members had in fact signed the 'Protest':

> I beg the reader to witness the number of professional 'red-bloods', and of writers of the sentimental-suggestive, boudoir-and-delicious caresses type of novel, who have NOT supported the Dreiser protest. These leading lights of American Democracy are banded together presumably for the protection of the rights of authors and of literature. Many of them have not only failed to support Dreiser's fearless and unexaggerated realism, but cowering before the successor to Anthony Comstock of foul and ridiculous memory, the majority of them have combined together and DISMISSED the former secretary of their society BECAUSE he showed himself too active in organizing the protest against the suppression of Dreiser's book.

His indictment therefore exacerbated the tone of his original note:

> O *patria mia, vedo le mura e gli archi* as usual, and the cowardice of a servile democracy, also as usual, and the pusillanimity of America's popular writers, also as usual, and the inactive timidity of America's 'elder generation of literati', also as usual, and my contempt for these national characteristics remains unaltered – as usual.[50]

Pound's exaggerated weariness was of the most stultifying kind, a product of that special variety of cultural paralysis where the contradiction of seemingly conflicting forces merely flattened out conflict's sharp possibilities for change; the 'paralysis' in which Joyce included both the subject of *Dubliners* and its entry into the world scored by that 'barometer of English opinion', the printer used by Grant Richards's publishing house in 1906.[51] Such paralysis anaesthetized potential for action; to adopt Pound's electromagnetic figure from 'Psychology and Troubadours', it failed to energize the necessary poles of resistance and so collapsed into a somnolent reflectivity or mere inertia. It required a more violent level of discourse to 'charge' these poles, a discourse that exhibited the major resource for Pound's vocabulary of diagnosis and antisepsis. This was the discourse of scatology that famously found its expression not within the decorum of his prose but in Cantos XIV and XV. The reading experience of these cantos has usually refused to permit specific discriminations; faced with a blanket condemnation of contemporary civilization as usurously and irredeemably awash with filth and excrement, the reader has difficulty in remaining anything other than swamped by the plethora of Pound's vitriol into either acceptance or disgust. But in the midst of this modern/medieval Hell, it seems to me that the basis of the whole affair is situated in those lines about speaking towards the end of Canto XIV: 'and above it the mouthing of orators, / the arse-belching of preachers.'[52] Corruption in Pound's Hell, as we know, is manifest at all levels, but to locate it in voice, where we have not 'speaking' but 'mouthing', and 'mouthing' conceived as farting, directs us to a distinct problematic of discourse, that of the status and function of voice itself. This was the problematic also of Joyce whose *Ulysses* prepared the way for so much in the early *Cantos*.[53] Richard Godden has explicated this problematic in his discussion of Molly's soliloquy:

> her 'voice' shares the section with conspicuous emissions from all other orifices. Vaginal discharge, menstrual blood, milk, semen and excrement (often linked to eating) are thematic focal points for Molly's imagination. It is clear from Joyce's love-letters to Nora that the relation between writing and excremental functions intrigued him; a proximity between language and human emission is constant in 'Penelope'.

The intimacy between talking and emission that Godden suggests serves to centre an essential ambition of modernist language:

> dirt must threaten all decorums (literary, social and linguistic) because it is matter out of place. Naming and meaning are intimately connected with the mental process of setting things in order. Dirt – so difficult to categorize, particularly when it involves a confusion of orifices – challenges the capacity for order. So Molly's flow, being at least as excremental as it is vocal, threatens the very materials of the voice.[54]

Of course, immediately prior to Pound's medievally excremental catalogue of civilization in Canto XIV, he gives his equally famous celebration of Confucian order as a potential counter to the confusions that follow: 'If a man have not order within him / He can not spread order about him',[55] order that depended at base, in the *Ta Hsio*, on linguistic order, 'precise verbal definitions'.[56]

Our experience in reading the excremental cantos is apt to be amorphous because, as Godden argues, the vocabulary of emission threatens the very materiality of voice, not only because excrement is 'matter out of place' but also because urine, faeces and farts lack discernible shape, or, in the case of faeces, lack a shape that may be assimilated into any other matrix. This loss of materiality poses the large contradiction of Pound's enterprise; he engaged in the discourse of excrement not simply as a means of castigating contemporary culture but as a means of offending the decorum of that culture, a tactic of shock that should destroy 'paralysis' (for Pound, the root evil) by restoring the antinomies that 'paralysis' had domesticated. Richard Sieburth has written well of Pound's Voltairian distrust of Protestant monotheism as a pervasive source of linguistic and social tyranny. Sieburth claims that such monotheism substitutes 'a single abstract ideological principle for the sensuous immediacies of the gods'. This substitution, accompanied by its denial of the sexual nature of *mœurs contemporaines*, becomes equated with usury and capitalism in the economic sphere and, in the linguistic sphere, instigates the dissociation of words from their objects that results in abstraction and in a tyranny of ideas.[57] Sieburth's argument is a good one because it is well informed and undeniably right at a certain level of detail, but it tends to resolve itself into familiar antitheses that are too comfortable: monotheism *v.* polytheism, fixity *v.* multiplicity, abstraction *v.* materialism. His resolution is ultimately misleading because its satisfying comfort absolutely belies the problematic of Pound's discourse by miming Pound's own resources, coded heavily (as Sieburth amply illustrates) by what Pound called Remy de Gourmont's 'sexual intelligence', for his battles against the false Comstockian 'morality'. Pound quoted from Gourmont's *Songe d'une femme* to illustrate this 'intelligence' – 'La virginité n'est pas une vertu, c'est un état; c'est une sousdivision des couleurs'[58] – and he would have thoroughly approved Pater's praise for the moral and religious rebellion of medieval antinomianism: 'In their search after the pleasures of the senses and the imagination, in their care for beauty, in their worship of the body, people were impelled beyond the confines of the Christian ideal.'[59] To claim with Sieburth that such 'intelligence' argued for an 'ecological totality and reciprocity of natural forces' (in order to displace the Victorian teleology of progress with its primacy of man and, quoting Gourmont, to consider 'human love as one form of numberless forms' and to evaporate the 'Christian dichotomy between man and nature')[60] is to accept an idealist model of totality that, as I shall show when I discuss Pound's notion of 'tradition' in a later chapter, concealed Pound's authoritarianism in its most dangerous form. The resolution that Sieburth offers can in the end only reflect the paralysis that Pound was concerned to resist in the first place.

Sieburth is right to attend to the theological bias of Pound's rhetoric; in employing the vocabulary of excrement, Pound sought to explode contemporary paralysis by restoring energetic antinomies. Norman O. Brown has shown that Lutheran theology relied on exactly such vocabulary in order to situate the Devil as a positive counterpart to God: for the medieval mind, such polarities pervaded every area of the ordinary world; the strengths of their opposition were potent and real. Such opposition was muted by the liberalism of nineteenth-century theology, which did not admit of any true battle between the two and hence would not admit the full force of transformation.[61] This was the monotheism that Sieburth describes so well, and it is in the nature of monotheism that it cannot incorporate any such clash. For a bourgeois theology, flesh belongs to the Devil and is thus relegated to a secondary role in human affairs; both have to be denied, but their denial can have no energy in the oppositions that Pound sought to restore. The potential of these oppositions was, of course, that they should be cathartic by instigating a series of further energies for the necessary poles of resistance and restraint. In Poundian terminology, these oppositions ordered his vocabulary of antisepsis on behalf of Flaubert and Joyce as a challenge to a state of letters figured by excrement and mess, and established his permanent faith in the world of the Provençal and Tuscan poets:

They are opposed to a form of stupidity not limited to Europe, that is, idiotic asceticism and a belief that the body is evil. This more or less masochistic and hell-breeding belief is always accompanied by bad and niggled sculpture. . . . This invention of hells for one's enemies, and mess, confusion in sculpture, is always symptomatic of supineness, bad hygiene, bad physique (possibly envy); even the diseases of mind, they do not try to cure as such, but devise hells to punish, not to heal, the individual sufferer.

Pound's entire hatred for a paralysed theology is centred in his final point here, the invention of hells to 'punish' and not to 'heal', and he suggested what was the most important single system of opposition for his aesthetics: 'Against these European hindoos we find the "mediaeval clean line", as distinct from mediaeval niggle', designs for 'ornament flat on the walls, and not bulging and bumping and indulging in bulbous excrescence . . . the architectural ornament of bigotry, superstition, and mess.'[62] The antiseptic diagnoses of the contemporary novel belonged to this order of things; the vocabulary of antisepsis provided a literal and metaphorical antinomy to that of excrement.

As we recognize the appropriateness of this antinomy, however, we also recognize its contradiction. While Pound's metaphor of excrement includes a potential for catharsis, that potential is not realized; we read in Canto XV:

> the great scabrous arse-hole, shitting flies,
> 　　　rumbling with imperialism,
> ultimate urinal, middan, pisswallow without a cloaca,
> . . . . . .r less rowdy, ... Episcopus,
> . . . . .sis [63]

The absence of the 'cloaca' suggests the diffusion of catharsis, the uncontrollable spilling over of the excrement (truly 'matter without place', without the office for its disposal), which is then immediately transferred to the confusions of writing itself in a typography that cannot be assimilated. Materiality at both levels is wholly denied for a spoiled/soiled mouth ('arse-belching'). This soiling of voice, and hence of the capacity of voice for proper utterance, 'precise verbal definitions', was, of course, the major crisis of language for modernism: the loss of word meant loss of world, the diffused materiality of the one resulted in the insubstantiality of the other, with the concomitant absence of order and hence of control, the absence signified by the typography of Canto XV. Pound tried to restore that control here within a metaphoric system that was deliberately asocial, not available for customary intercourse (an escalation of the more coy ambition of 1913 for his poems to 'Dance and make people blush, / Dance the dance of the phallus / and tell anecdotes of Cybele! / Speak of the indecorous conduct of the Gods! // Ruffle the skirts of prudes, / speak of their knees and ankles'[64]), and a deliberate act of private authoritarianism. At the beginning of the story that began Joyce's first attempt to 'lance' the paralysis of Dublin, the anonymous narrator looked up at a window concealing possible death:

> Every night as I gazed up at the window I said softly to myself the word paralysis. It had always sounded strangely in my ears, like the word gnomon in the Euclid and the word simony in the Cathechism. But now it sounded to me like the name of some maleficent and sinful being. It filled me with fear, and yet I longed to be nearer to it and to look upon its deadly work.

The association of 'paralysis' (itself having here both a literal and a metaphoric function) with words of geometrical determination and of ecclesiastical manipulation indicates the will to private, concealed power as a means to counter the amorphous nature of paralysis and excrement. The privileged vocabulary that constitutes the discourses of Joyce, Pound and Eliot exhibits precisely the fear of their contemporary situation and the fascination of modes of control.[65] Their vocabulary, whether it be that of erudite reading or, in our immediate case, that of excrement, insists on its removal from available social matrices and thus on its secretive usage, control of which is accessible only to those who are in on the secret.

The art of the practical: workmanship

'The Serious Artist' was published in three instalments; the issue of *The New Freewoman* in which the second instalment appeared also included a leader-article, 'The Art of the Future', which complemented much of Pound's argument. The anonymous author (almost certainly the editor, Dora Marsden) drew attention to the discrepancy in attitudes towards the artist and the scientist and, while her tone was not that of Pound's public justification, she also sought to establish an equivalence between the two. The article was directed primarily against the looseness of aesthetic discourse and the weaknesses of contemporary literature, adopting the models of science and technological craftsmanship as paradigms for literary procedure, and it began by pointing to the vague incoherence characteristic of artists talking about art:

> There is, about artists when asked to define their business, a coyness which would be exquisitely ludicrous if it were evinced by chemists or mathematicians, by carpenters or brick-layers. This coyness, and the vague waving of hands to give the expression of helplessness, in-a-sort, in the grip of some high force, which if not divine, is at least too much above the common level to be comprehended by the Philistine, or common-sense man — these are quite sufficient to place art as we know it, in its subconscious period. There is nothing to be gained by calling out against artists: their lack of comprehension as to what they are about, is a matter for regret rather than reprehension. They are in the position the alchemists and astrologers were, before alchemy became chemistry, and astrology astronomy.

The image of the artist offered here was deliberately out of date; it was inappropriate to a magazine that was consciously 'new', in an issue that included contributions from Pound and from Remy de Gourmont. The image was deliberately arcane because such a presentation provided an excellent way of emphasizing a renewal of critical language for 'the art of the future', of proclaiming that the sphere of Art was to be understood and received as 'the complement of Science'. The article thus offered itself as an announcement of modernity in reaction to the vagueness of the preceding period, and defined its method: 'If science is the knowledge gained by applying to non-vital phenomena, the method of accurate description as opposed to that of imaginative interpretation, art is the product of the same method applied to vital (and mainly humanly vital) phenomena.' The triumph of science, as opposed to the 'charlatans' and 'dullards' of literature, was found in those familiar Poundian axioms, a willingness to experiment, a concern with the objects under observation, and an unbiased fidelity to those objects:

> Science has made its advance chiefly in the last three hundred years, because during this period it has trusted to the results of

unprejudiced observation of the 'thing'. Before, as now in art, save for one or two outstanding geniuses, it had guessed about things, and its guesses made a pile of useless words and ideas, unproved and incapable of proof. The energy of the greatest as well as the least of investigators was wasted in spinning these futile guesses. But the experiment, i.e., the essaying of what could be done to a thing and what could be done with it, put an end to all that. Experiment broke the dominion of the guess – the imaginative interpretation. The idea broke upon the perception of the fact. Thought was bridled by knowledge of the 'thing'; thought's utmost reach attained only to a 'suggestion'; the hypothesis holding tentative existence only until the experiment should dissolve it into error or fact.

By comparison, there was the record of the 'charlatan artists', of those who 'pretend they follow the motions of the soul, but who merely follow the idea; of those who speak with the certainty of knowledge concerning that of which they have made a bold guess',[66] those who perpetuated the tyranny of abstract ideas.

Consequently, contemporary literature was seen as a literature merely of ideas and 'verbal conceptions' which had ousted the 'thing'. In the theatre 'The conflict is one of words not of living moments': the task of the genuine dramatist was to 'gauge the measure of human forces', whereas the dramatist of the 'drama of ideas' had merely 'to direct words'; the one manipulated 'living forces', the other only 'verbalities'. Salvation for the modern artist lay in emulating the scientist or the craftsman:

If progress is to be made in Art, as it has been made in science, artists will have to put off their agnosticism and the vague waving of hands as to what their business is, and come to their tasks with as much sense of purpose as the carpenter who lays down a floor, or puts in window-frames. . . . The artist must be prepared to begin humbly with matter which lies to hand: as Archimedes began with the physics observable in his bath, or Newton watching an apple fall, or Watt the spluttering of a tea-kettle.[67]

These arguments (as with Pound) were not new; novelty inhered in the vocabulary of science and craftsmanship that underwrote them, a vocabulary that tonally proclaimed its modernity and technically solidified and sharpened the language available for talking about literature. For Pound, in the first instalment of 'The Serious Artist', the distinction between the 'scientist' and the 'charlatan' was equivalent to that between the 'serious artist' and the 'theorist'; while the latter was 'empiric in the mediaeval fashion', the former was 'scientific' in that he was like the 'good biologist' who essayed a number of observations before announcing a law and, crucially, in that he was dispassionate: 'the theorist constantly proceeds as if his own case, his own limits and predilections were the typical case, or even as if it were the universal.'[68] Five years earlier, Pound had announced this latter point through the vocabulary of medicine in a letter to William Carlos Williams: 'I record symptoms as I see 'em. I advise no remedy.'[69] The 'empiric' theorist's extrapolation from the self to the universal was countered by the sincerity of the serious artist which incorporated no such pretence and exhibited a far more radical epistemology of the 'thing'.

The positions advocated by 'The Art of the Future' again reflected the fundamental propositions about scientific language instigated by the reductionist school. Karl Pearson's Introduction to the second edition of The Grammar of Science in 1900 established the importance of a 'tribal consciousness' as opposed to a private interest, and he defined the judgement of the 'ideal citizen' as one that was free from personal bias, from the interposition of preconceived ideas between the observer and his objects, and that recognized the 'sequence' of those objects, their modes of relation:

it is obvious that it can only be based on a clear knowledge of facts, an appreciation of their sequence and relative significance. The facts once classified, once understood, the judgement based upon them ought to be independent of the individual mind which examines them. . . . The classification of facts and the formation of absolute judgements on the basis of this classification – judgements independent of the individual mind – essentially sum up the *aim and method of modern science*. The scientific man has above all things to strive at self-elimination in his judgements, to provide an argument which is as true for each individual mind as for his own. *The classification of facts, the recognition of their sequence and relative significance is the function of science*, and the habit of forming a judgement upon these facts unbiased by personal feeling is characteristic of what may be termed the scientific frame of mind.

Pearson's 'habit of dispassionate investigation'[70] required a restatement of its hallmarks, the clarity of definition and of observation; he wrote of the aim of his book that 'The object of the present "Grammar" has been chiefly to show how a want of clear definition has led to the metaphysical obscurities of modern science',[71] and in 1911 Whitehead added the weight of mathematical philosophy to the question: 'A symbol which has not been properly defined is not a symbol at all. It is merely a blot of ink on paper which has an easily recognizable shape.'[72]

The emphasis placed on the quiddity of 'things' by the author of 'The Art of the Future' coincided with what Pound had learned from T. E. Hulme and Ford Madox Ford, a lesson that was to be reinvigorated by his reading of Ernest Fenollosa. The argument of the article was anticipated in the 'Views and Comments' section of the preceding issue of *The New Freewoman* (the issue including the first instalment of 'The Serious Artist'), where the notion of 'things' was expressed through a vastly more significant vocabulary drawn from electricity. The anonymous author (again, almost certainly Dora Marsden) was again concerned to battle against the 'verbalism' of contemporary literature:

> We shall have gone far towards rounding the Verbal Age to finality when we recognize that there exists nothing save things and the relations between things, and that all words which purport to express anything other – any 'thought' – avail for nothing but gratuitous illusion and irrelevance.

By insisting not only on 'things' but on 'the relations between things', the writer illustrated the line of development from what Pound had heard from Hulme to what he was taught by Fenollosa's notes. The vocabulary from electricity in what was the editorial platform of *The New Freewoman* predated the 'lines of force' used by Fenollosa to describe these 'relations'; the writer discussed the soul, 'the life within ourselves', as the 'first thing of which we have any knowledge':

> The soul is not a thought, and has nothing to do with thought. It is a 'thing' as electricity running along a wire is a thing, with movements, consciousness, repulsions, attractions, making ex-

cursions and returning to its shell through the apertures for entry and exit it has made; a thing which forages, feeds, dissipates or grows, by means we can learn if we keep watch.

This fusion of terminologies whereby the contemporaneity of electricity explicated the arcane metaphysic of the soul was, as we shall see in a later chapter, a large part of the vocabulary that Pound designed to articulate his modernity. More immediately, Pound's argument eleven months later that the difference between art and analytical geometry was a difference in subject matter only was prefigured in this editorial of 1913 where the 'scientific spirit' that art exercised was defined: 'The difference between science and art is not a difference of method, but of subject matter. Art is the scientific spirit applied to soul, observing, collating, noting.' At this point, the writer put forward Pound's claim that it was the function of art to 'bear true witness' by its impartiality and defined this function as that of science:

> It [art] is in a position analogous to that in which science was, when astronomy was astrology, chemistry alchemy, and mathematics witchcraft, that is, when scientists looked at facts but with a pre-conceived idea, or thought, interpolated between facts and their intelligence of them. So inferior artists look at the soul . . . with a notion interposed between it and them.

Hence, as in 'The Serious Artist', the canon of sincerity was offered as scientific and, thus clothed, provided the cognitive basis for art's sole morality, as the scientific 'thing' displaced conceptualized 'verbalism': 'art comes as a flail to a concept-based morality'.[73]

It was in the first instalment of 'The Serious Artist' that Pound deployed his aggressive programme for a scientific basis for the arts, after which, the irritation of public defence having been eased, he proceeded to establish a series of strictures on writing that particularized his theoretical affirmations of the artist's seriousness. These strictures boiled down to a purposive attitude towards the technique of the craft, an attitude of what Pater had termed 'manliness' in his 1893 essay on Plato's aesthetics:

> a full consciousness of what one does, of art itself in the work of art, tenacity of intuition and of consequent purpose, the spirit of construction as opposed to what is literally incoherent or ready

to fall to pieces, and, in opposition to what is hysteric or works at random, the maintenance of a standard.[74]

The sense of 'art itself in the work of art', of 'the spirit of construction', instigated the entire vocabulary of the practical that Pound derived from his scientific analogies, in, for example, his understanding of 'poetry' itself: 'On closer analysis I find that I mean something like 'maximum efficiency of expression'; I mean that the writer has expressed something interesting in such a way that one cannot re-say it more effectively.'[75] Pound's letters during this time proliferated with his insistence on craftsmanship and the perfection of its technique;[76] he always operated according to the Aristotelian classification of cognition, which began with 'teXne, skill in an art, in making things'[77] and which precipitated the broader, workmanlike proposition: 'It is not enough that the artist have impulse, he must be in a position to know what has been done and what is yet to do.'[78] Pound's permanent interest in practice requires little reiteration here, but we may note that, for the reductionist theoretician of science, clarity of observation and description was an inevitable result of practical engagement with the subject. Karl Pearson argued for the necessity of 'a scientific theory of observation and description' and, although he did not, in fact, give a technical account of such a theory, he suggested its practical bias in a footnote: 'One of the best practical trainings . . . is that to be obtained by a clinical clerk in a hospital ward. Another good training, I have noticed, is almost unconsciously acquired by the careful sketcher or painter of flowers and trees.'[79]

Pearson's suggestion of the necessity for practical training was obviously crucial for a poetics deeply committed to 'facts' and to 'things'. I use 'practical' here in the Kantian sense – that a 'practical' method is one leading to action of some kind – the sense to which T. H. Huxley referred in a lecture of 1876 when he claimed that 'the scope of all speculation is the performance of some action or thing to be done'.[80] It was the absence of the practical sense that, for Pearson, led to an opposition between the 'scientific' and the 'philosophical' method, where the latter was seen as limited by the mysteriousness of its procedure and its individualistic bias, thereby failing to lead to any 'practical unanimity of judgement'.[81] Manual experience was therefore the major prerequisite for science's restriction of the abstract tendencies of deduction in its striving after

facts.[82] Huxley was perhaps one of the most influential popu-
larizers of science who stressed the importance of practical work; in
a particularly interesting passage he anticipated one of Pound's
most famous lessons to the aspiring writer (that if we want to find
out about an automobile we should not read books about it but go
to someone who actually builds automobiles) in his proposals for a
'method' in the study of biology:

> since Biology is a physical science, the method of studying it must
> needs be analogous to that which is followed in the other
> physical sciences. It has now long been recognized that, if a man
> wishes to be a chemist, it is not only necessary that he should
> read chemical books and attend chemical lectures, but that he
> should actually perform the fundamental experiments in the
> laboratory for himself, and thus learn exactly what the words
> which he finds in his books and hears from his teachers, mean. If
> he does not do so, he may read till the crack of dawn, but he will
> never know much about chemistry.

Huxley was, of course, defending biological science during the
period in which it was still overshadowed as a respectable discipline
by the positivism of the exact sciences, physics and chemistry; in the
1870s these disciplines seemed to offer all the certainty and pre-
dictability that biology, in its nascent years, could not. He too
found it necessary, as Pound was to do with regard to literature
during what he felt was a time of crisis, to request parallels with
stronger epistemologies, and he relied on the principle of practical
work to answer the perennial question, deeply significant for
Pound, of an adequate system of terminology:

> Nobody will ever know anything about Biology except in a
> dilettante 'paper-philosopher' way, who contents himself with
> reading books on botany, zoology and the like; and the reason
> for this is simple and easy to understand. It is that all language is
> merely symbolical of the things of which it treats; the more
> complicated the things, the more bare is the symbol, and the
> more its verbal definition requires to be supplemented by the
> information derived directly from the handling, and the seeing
> and the touching of the thing symbolized. . . . If you want a man
> to be a tea merchant, you don't tell him to read books about
> China or about tea, but you put him into a tea-merchant's office

where he has the handling, the smelling and the tasting of tea. . . .
You may read any quantity of books, and you may be almost as
ignorant as you were at starting, if you don't have, at the back
of your minds, the change for words in definite images which
can only be acquired through the operation of your observing
faculties on the phenomena of nature.[83]

If any single phrase could locate the whole enterprise of Pound's
poetics, it would be this of Huxley's, the 'change for words in
definite images', the way in which words, properly composed,
always create a clear and definite picture, as a consequence of
practical engagement. Huxley's sense of figurability proposed a
specific picture for the necessity of the practical in a particular area,
that of the biologist's mode of 'selection':

What one of the general public walking into a collection of birds
desires to see is not all the birds that can be got together. He does
not want to compare a hundred species of the sparrow tribe side
by side; but he wishes to know what a bird is, and what are the
great modifications of bird structure, and to be able to get at that
knowledge easily. What will best serve his purpose is a comparatively small number of birds carefully selected . . . with their
different ages, their nests, their young, their eggs, and their
skeletons side by side.

This schema incorporated exactly the revolution in teaching
methods established by Louis Agassiz in the laboratories of Harvard and the Museum of Comparative Zoology at Cambridge,
those methods that Pound was to celebrate in his *ABC of Reading*.
Huxley's insistence on the 'change for words in definite images'
operated at every level of scientific training; he proposed this
method for a course teaching the techniques of dissection:

The purpose of this course is not to make skilled dissectors, but
to give every student a clear and definite conception, by means of
sense-images, of the characteristic structure of each of the leading
modifications of the animal kingdom . . . it then becomes possible for him to read with profit; because every time he meets with
the name of a structure, he has a definite image in his mind of
what the name means in the particular creature he is reading
about, and therefore this reading is not mere reading. It is not
mere repetition of words; but every term employed in the de-

scription, we will say, of a horse, or of an elephant, will call up this image of the things he had seen in the rabbit, and he is able to form a distinct conception of that which he has not seen, as a modification of that which he has seen.[84]

So Pound wrote in 1917: 'We need standards of comparison. All excellence has not risen out of one ant-hill.'[85]

Pound's sense of the practical was of obvious use in combating the 'dilletante' excesses he detested in contemporary letters. It was also, as I suggested in my discussion of Whistler, part of his distinctly American voice and habitually expressed itself – particularly in his later criticism during the 1930s, in *How to Read*, the *ABC of Reading* and the *Guide to Kulchur* – through metaphors not only from technology and the applied disciplines of manufacture, but from geography and architecture; such metaphors extended the practical to questions of place and of landscape, and, almost literally, shaped the *Cantos*. Here we may detect the wider ramifications of the practical as a way of looking at the world, as a particular ideology. These metaphors belonged to a lengthy tradition in American literature, a tradition of building and of making things that related to the pervasive concern of the nineteenth-century writer to suggest shape and definition for what was still a nebulous civilization. So we have Whitman's extensive use of artisans as the major figures in his poetry, the emphasis on building and on the cultivation of land in Thoreau, Emerson's admiration for the early industrial labours of Swedenborg, and the preoccupation in Hawthorne and Melville with the materiality of the act of writing itself. This tradition expressed above all the artist's commitment to the constructive duties of daily life, offering his craft as yet a further mode of productive labour to deny the intrusions (as we saw to be the case with Whitman) of a European élitism that separated the artist's function from the endeavours of ordinary life. F. O. Matthiessen has quoted Emerson to good effect: 'I like a man who likes to see a fine barn as well as a good tragedy'. Whitman also testified to a sensibility that refused to separate work and culture: 'I know that pleasure filters in and oozes out of me at the opera, but I know too that subtly and unaccountably my mind is sweet and odorous within while I clean up my boots and grease the pair that I reserve for stormy weather.'[86] American literature is filled with a specific attitude towards the building and acquisition

of houses and land which most completely expresses this sensibility; as Richard Poirier has said, '*Walden* is only one of the
examples of something like an obsession in American literature
with plans and efforts to build houses, to appropriate space to one's
desires, perhaps to inaugurate therein a dynasty that shapes time to
the dimensions of personal and familial history.' Poirier directs us
to the determinant ideology of his key phrase, 'to appropriate space
to one's desires':

> The building of a house is an extension and an expansion of the
> self, an act by which the self possesses environment otherwise
> possessed by nature. By an act of building . . . it is possible to join
> forces with the power of nature itself, to make its style your style.

The acquiring of unmediated space predicated, for the writer,
nothing like the solidity or completeness it would seem to offer;
indeed, the converse was true, for it predicated a further version of
the provisory that I discussed earlier: 'It is an aesthetic so devoted
to the *activity* of creation that it denies finality to the results of that
activity, its objects or formulations. Art is an action not a product
of action.'[87] Poirier's point is profoundly relevant to the Poundian
aesthetic, which was dependent on a series of 'sextants' and 'com-
passes' (the geographical equivalents of the scientific 'measuring
rods' and 'axes of comparison') to map out the topography of
world literature, and was permanently aware of a creative epistemology of action that ensured a provisional, unfinished art-
product.

The art of the practical was the art whereby, for Pound, the
necessarily gristly nature of literary behaviour could be salvaged
from the preciosity and dilettantism of contemporary letters as a
way of ensuring the 'real' and denying the abstractions of ideas. An
excellent model for this practicality, which was very close to Pound
during his London years, has been suggested by Hugh Kenner in his
proposal of the version of Homer most relevant to Joyce. This was
the Homer discovered by nineteenth-century archaeology, by
Schliemann's excavations in 1870 which posited the palpably real
for a series of ill-defined words:

> 'Troy' after Schliemann was no longer a dream, but a place on
> the map. As his discoveries persisted, more and more Homeric
> words came to mean something producible, something belonging

to the universe of the naturalistic novelist. Each such word is salvage from the vortex of mere lexicography, where of words we learn chiefly what company they keep.

Joyce's Homer, for Kenner (and for the present writer, who is wholly convinced by Kenner's argument and by *Ulysses* itself), was 'a real person in touch with the living details of real cities, real harbors, real bowls and cups and pins and spoons, real kings, real warriors, real houses . . . the poet using knowledge of an immediate and experienced world', the Homer recorded in Victor Bérard's *Les Phéniciens et l'Odyssée* (1903) and in Samuel Butler's *The Authoress of the Odyssey* (1897).[88] Pound's Homer in 1912 was a man 'conscious of the world outside him',[89] and in 1919, thinking of Homer to focus Aeschylus, Pound wrote: '"Damn ideas anyhow." An idea is only an imperfect induction from fact. . . . The solid, the "last atom of force verging off into the first atom of matter" is the force, the emotion, the objective sight of the poet.'[90] His Homer was always the Homer of the 'real'; he appreciated Hugues Salel's 1545 translation of the *Iliad* because 'he has authenticity of conversation as would be demanded by an intelligent audience not yet laminated with aesthetics; capable of recognizing reality', and he noted, as one of Homer's two qualities that 'remain untranslated', 'the authentic cadence of speech; the absolute conviction that the words used, let us say by Achilles to the "dog-faced" chicken-hearted Agamemnon, are in the actual swing of words spoken.'[91] Pound's response to Homer was of a sensibility accustomed to expressing itself through metaphors of science, technology and architecture, a sensibility that saw fit in 1915 to append an explanatory note to 'The Jewel Stairs' Grievance'[92] and to praise Arnold Dolmetsch's manufacture of ancient instruments as a means of access to the truth of the mythic past.[93]

It was this practical approach to the reappropriation of the 'real' that distinguished the Homeric scholarship of Samuel Butler, a figure who, as I shall show in a later chapter, was important in a further context for Pound. We need not duplicate Kenner's argument for Butler's study but merely remind ourselves of the mode of debate in which Butler engaged. The second half of *The Authoress of the Odyssey* (chapters 8–13) sought to 'map' Ithaca by situating it as Trapani on the west coast of Sicily, but it was the kind of detail established by Butler concerning the particulars of the *Odyssey* that are of most interest: his gritty observations on the siting of Ulysses' house, the actual locations of rooms, halls and courtyards, which explicated his plan of the house,[94] and especially the details of narrative action that he questioned in his commentary on the text itself; he wrote, for example, of the fight between Ulysses and Irus at the beginning of Book XVIII that 'They might very well fight in the middle of an open court, but hardly in a covered hall. They would go outside.'[95] Butler's practicality was usually occasioned by a sturdy scepticism: he noted of Alcinous' promised gift to Ulysses that 'Alcinous never seems to have got beyond saying that he was going to give the cup; he never gives it, nor yet the talent', and of varying proposals for the siting of the land of the Cyclopes that

> Dwellers on the East coast of Sicily believe the island here referred to to be Acitrezza, between Acireale and Catania. I have been all over it and do not believe that it contains more than two acres of land on which any goat could ever have fed. The idea that the writer of the 'Odyssey' would make Ulysses and his large body of men spend half a day in killing over a hundred goats on such a site need not be discussed seriously.[96]

Butler's mode of scepticism served always to reveal, in Kenner's phrase, the 'sticks and stones' of his subject; he wrote of the famous trial of the bow in Book XXI that

> If Telemachus had never seen anything of the kind before, so probably, neither had the writer of the 'Odyssey'. . . . It looks as though the axe heads must have been wedged into the handles or so bound on to them as to let the hole be visible through which the handle would go when the axe was in use. The trial is evidently a double one, of strength as regards the bending of the bow, and accuracy of aim as regards shooting through a row of rings.

He marked the divergence of his method from that of other commentators in his description of the room prepared for Ulysses after the defeat of the suitors:

> This room was apparently not within the body of the house. It was certainly on the ground floor, for the bed was fixed on the stump of a tree; I strongly suspect it to be the vaulted room, round the outside of which the bodies of the guilty maids were still hanging, and I also suspect it was in order to thus festoon the

room that Telemachus hanged the women instead of stabbing them, but this is treading on that perilous kind of speculation which I so strongly deprecate in others.[97]

It is especially significant that Butler's practical temperament should attend to this particular passage towards the end of Book XXIII, since this is the moment when Penelope is finally convinced of Ulysses' identity. She instructs Euryclea to remove Ulysses' bed from its proper room; Ulysses is angered by this since he knows that the bed could not be moved without cutting down the stem of a growing olive tree, on the stump of which the bed had originally been built. This scene belongs to that earlier recognition scene, in which Euryclea knew Ulysses by his scar, as an immensely vivid moment of literary realism which achieves its vitality solely by means of a clearly seen relationship with the reality of the world conceived in practical terms. But its practicality disguises its other resource as effective writing: the mode of recognition here is realized through an act of intimate privacy, the secret of the bed shared only by Penelope and Ulysses and unavailable, by its very nature, to others. The advertised schema of the practical temperament, a deconstruction of the barriers between the world of ordinary life and that of literature, here relies at root on an order of privacy which in itself permits no access to any wider matrix. The detail of the bed suggests the wider contradictions of the ways in which the advertisement of realism actually works. The art of the practical acknowledges the activities shared by literature with other modes of work but has the *effect* of again displacing those shared activities from available norms. The synthesis of self and environment, potential within this art (figured in acts of writing, acts of building, acts of topography), thus includes the danger of a special alienation in that, as Poirier suggests, it is only possible 'if the imagination and space are freed from the possessive power of all that is not nature: from systems of any kind that derive from society and history'. This alienation carries its own privileged authority implicit in its distinctive individualism: 'To be creative is to discover one's affinity with "God" and thereby one's superiority to the works of men.'[98] The complex of ideas with which we are concerned – the discourses of science and technology which announce the functions of a poetics of 'action' to be the provisory and the practical – thus includes the implicit contradiction that an epistemology for open access to the 'real' in effect conceals a private, secret willingness for control over such access, for appropriation at the metaphorical and the literal level. The discourse of science was especially purposive for an epistemology of concealment since, with the advent of field theory, wave theory and quantum theory, its possibilities for radically dematerializing the apparent solidity of the world both testified to a different, and more accurate, version of the 'real', showing it to be indeed in a state of flux and movement, and, with its increasing sophistication, clearly suggested an order of cognition that was not generally available. Pound's topographical metaphors for the acquisition of important moments in literature during the 1930s were alternative versions of the appropriation and control that had instigated his scientific metaphors during the London years; the language of the 'road map' was simply more in accord with the traditional exercise of American writing.

The little magazines

With an occasional exception, the platforms for modernist aes-thetics, the little magazines, rarely printed arguments for the arts that relied on the sanctions of science to anything like the same extent as those of Pound. *The Little Review*, for example, published lively debates on those areas of the arts for which Pound used metaphors from science – the questions of tariff and censorship, complaints about the lack of seriousness accorded to the status of the arts, criticism of the ignorance of technique and craftsmanship displayed by practising writers, especially in America – but these debates were conducted with hardly any reference to the models of science. Scientific reference, when it did occur, was usually loosely employed merely to support a more positive, systematic approach to aesthetics. Harriet Monroe, for example, pleaded in a 1913 issue of *Poetry* for a 'more scientific knowledge' of the subject of rhythm in order to free discussion of rhythm from its current inhibiting categories: 'Poetic technique is still a mediaeval province un-illumined by modern scientific research.'[99] *The Little Review* permitted more detailed analogies, usually derived from French realist arguments; George Soule wrote of Wells in 1914:

> Wells . . . is not a preacher, but a scientist. He starts with the conviction that, through lack of impartial investigation, we don't

really know what the eternal verities are, or what power can be derived from them. His attitude is as far from the old writers' as is Mme Curie's from the old alchemists'. He attempts to free his mind from every prejudice. Then he begins his experiment, puts his characters in their retort under 'controlled conditions', and *watches what happens*.[100]

The same magazine witnessed some cynicism towards the terms of this kind of appreciation; a year later an anonymous reviewer wrote of Willard Huntingdon Wright's *Modern Painting*:

> It is a hard book, brothers-dilletanti. It gives us a merciless thrashing, we who love without being able to state why and wherefore. We are ordered to go back to school, children, to study chemistry and color, to approach a work of art as scientifically equipped as a surgeon venturing to operate on a human body.[101]

The witty edge of this cynicism was not shared by Huntley Carter who, in the magazine most willing to incorporate the discourse of science, *The Egoist*,[102] clearly felt the pressure of such modernist terminology: 'I feel that I ought to add to my mystic and metaphysical explanations of Drama a mathematical and mechanical explanation of the drama and the theatre.'[103]

We need to recognize, of course, that certain uses of scientific discourse were quite commonplace in literary discussions around the turn of the century[104] and tended to emerge either as a modish display of rhetoric or, more systematically, as an attempt to formalize literary criticism by means of scientific analogy. The latter attempt divided itself into familiar categories: the critic as an analyst with extensive technical knowledge ('the science of any art can be nothing but the body of large facts which presents itself upon assembling all the observed small facts of that art and classing together such as are substantially alike');[105] the critic as expositor of the 'new' science of the mind ('Criticism is a complex development of psychological science');[106] the critic as evolutionist, the explicator of, for example, Elizabethan drama, who 'regards the totality of the phenomena presented as something necessitated by conditions to which the prime agents in the process, Marlowe and even Shakespeare, were subordinated. For him this type of art exhibits qualities analogous to those of an organic complex undergoing successive phases of germination, expansion, efflorescence, and decay, which were independent of the volition of the men who effected them.'[107]

The general absence of a programme for scientific discourse in the literary magazines pointed up Pound's usage and, to an extent, that of T. S. Eliot towards the end of Pound's London period. We know from letters of March and September 1917 that Eliot had been reading in biology and preparing courses of lectures that included men of science (Huxley, Spencer and Butler) and men of letters (Emerson, for example) who were deeply knowledgeable in science.[108] But Eliot's reading, on those few occasions where he offered scientific analogies, did not seem to equip him to do much more than reflect the usage we find in Pound. His most famous analogy – that of catalytic action on a filament of platinum to describe the notion of 'depersonalization', the condition in which 'art may be said to approach the condition of science'[109] – was not allowed to retain its specificity; he reiterated the scientific basis for 'depersonalization' in a review published during the following month as part of a debate more akin to Arnold or Pater than to the contemporary scientist: 'In the man of scientific or artistic temper the personality is distilled into the work, it loses its accidents, it becomes, as with Montaigne, a permanent point of view, a phase in the history of mind.'[110] I shall discuss the occasion of Eliot's analogy in Chapter 5; here I want to argue that Eliot's use of science was wholly imitative of Pound's by looking at the essays incorporating that use that he published in *The Egoist* during the year prior to 'Tradition and the Individual Talent'.

Eliot's essay on James in January 1918 made virtually all the general points that concerned Pound's essay on James in the same issue, predominantly the notions of metropolis and the cosmopolitan nature of good writing. Eliot used science to isolate Jamesian subtleties of intercourse – 'It is in the chemistry of these subtle substances, these curious precipitates and explosive gases which are suddenly formed by the contact of mind with mind, that James is unequalled'[111] – while Pound wrote of the 'instruments' of Jamesian sensitivity: 'Interest in a writer being primarily in his degree of sensitization . . . what interest can we take in instruments which must by nature miss two-thirds of the vibrations in any conceivable situation?'[112] Eliot's echoing of Pound may be seen most clearly in his more theoretical pronouncements on aesthetics and criticism. Five months later, he stressed the importance of a cosmopolitan attitude with a model from biology:

> A poet, like a scientist, is contributing toward the organic development of culture: it is just as absurd for him not to know the work of his predecessors or of men writing in other languages as it would be for a biologist to be ignorant of Mendel or De Vries. It is exactly as wasteful for a poet to do what has been done already, as for a biologist to rediscover Mendel's discoveries. The French poets in question have made 'discoveries' in verse of which we cannot afford to be ignorant, discoveries which are not merely a concern for French syntax. To remain with Wordsworth is equivalent to ignoring the whole of science subsequent to Erasmus Darwin.[113]

Eliot's citation of Mendel and de Vries had, of course, a special significance of its own; it was their theories of development by modification and mutation that were to inform his notion of tradition just over a year later: 'The existing monuments form an ideal order among themselves, which is modified by the introduction of the new (the really new) work of art among them.'[114] But apart from this specialized use of biological development, Eliot's statement was in essence no more than a shadow of the argument Pound had been advancing since 1912 for the poet's necessary apprenticeship in the study of what had already been achieved;[115] as he wrote in 1913, 'The scientist does not expect to be acclaimed as a great scientist until he has *discovered* something. He begins by learning what has been discovered already. He goes from that point onward.'[116] Eliot continued his diatribe against the wastage of effort consequent upon not knowing what has gone before in October 1918: 'What we find are discoverers of methods whose methods remain unstudied. . . . We are justified in reprobating such wasted energy.' He restated French realist arguments for replacing the conventional terms of critical language with the vocabulary of scientific method:

> The work of the critic is almost wholly comprehended in the 'complementary activities' of comparison and analysis. The one activity implies the other; and together they provide the only way of asserting standards and of isolating a writer's peculiar merits. In the dogmatic, or lazy, mind comparison is supplied by judge-

ment, analysis replaced by appreciation. Judgement and appreciation are merely tolerable avocations, no part of the critic's
serious business. If the critic has performed his laboratory work
well, his understanding will be evidence of appreciation; but his
work is by the intelligence not the emotions.

The principle of 'comparison and analysis' was, for Pound, only
possible in a cosmopolitan culture; so Eliot enlisted further scientific reference to support an argument for international standards:

> Criticism, like creative art, is in various ways less developed than
> scientific research. For one thing, scientific research, in Europe
> and America, would not have reached its present stage had it not
> been pretty thoroughly internationalized: if the results of any
> important experiment in one country were not immediately
> taken up, tested and proceeded upon in every other.[117]

Having argued in 1915 that 'The arts and sciences hang together.
Any conception which does not see them in their interrelation be-
littles both', Pound announced his first line of attack on the current
literary malaise: 'First, that we should develop a criticism of poetry
based on world-poetry, on the work of maximum excellence.'[118]
The final gesture towards science in Eliot's essay was based on the
materialism of Remy de Gourmont's discussion of metaphor in *Le
Problème du style*, the resource for much of Pound's thinking on the
same subject, as part of an attack on the 'hackneyed phrases' of
'dead language':

> All thought and all language is based ultimately upon a few
> simple physical movements. Metaphor is not something applied
> externally for the adornment of style, it is the life of style, of
> language. . . . The healthy metaphor adds to the strength of the
> language; it makes available some of that physical source of
> energy upon which the life of language depends . . . in most good
> metaphor, you can hardly say where the metaphorical and the
> literal meet.[119]

We should note the bias of Eliot's conclusion, that in 'most good
metaphor, you can hardly say where the metaphorical and the
literal meet', since it marks a significant alteration to that fine
phrase of Huxley's 'the change for words in definite images', which

seems to me to posit the entire ambition of modernist epistemology. What Eliot is doing here is to offer yet a further mode of concealment belonging to that particular category of materialist idealism which Gourmont shared with the American transcendentalists. By disguising the necessary distinctions between the metaphoric and the literal, Eliot implicitly argues for the order of control that is the inevitable result of diffusing the separation of categories, of denying difference. As Paul Ricœur has suggested, metaphor constitutes a function of displacement, an order of substitution that aims at persuasion, 'the rhetorical process by which discourse unleashes the power that certain fictions have to redescribe reality'.[120] Metaphor thus promises a plenitude of energy to Make It New, but as its own procedure becomes blurred, in Eliot's formulation, it includes the threat of hidden manipulation by sustaining the mystery of that procedure, the 'swift and unanalysable process' Pound had characterized as the 'undeniable tradition of metamorphoses' in 1915.[121]

Eliot's essays of 1918 and 'Tradition and the Individual Talent' of the following year mark the extent of his willingness during the period in which he was most under Pound's influence to cite contemporary science on behalf of the modernist programme. The present context is inappropriate for speculating about Eliot's unwillingness to avail himself of Pound's characteristic modernist gesture, but it is worth noting as a partial explanation Eliot's scepticism towards one of the main assumptions behind Pound's gesture, the confirmation by science of supposedly mystical experience. In reviewing Clement C. J. Webb's *Group Theories of Religion and the Religion of the Individual* in 1916, Eliot suggested that 'the growth of the scientific spirit has been unfavourable to mysticism, and that mysticism has had an obscurantist effect in science'.[122] For Pound, as I shall show in my discussions of tradition and the vortex, exactly the converse was true. In 1958, however, in his Introduction to a collected edition of Valéry's works in translation, Eliot offered exactly that conjunction between the scientific and the modern that Pound had persistently laboured; he claimed of Valéry's 'Sur la technique littéraire' (1889): 'What it announces is no less than a new style for poetry. The satanist, the dandy, the "poète maudit" have had their day: eleven years before the end of the nineteenth century Valéry invents the role which makes him representative of the twentieth.' Eliot defined this 'role':

Valéry in fact invented, and was to impose upon his age, not so much a new conception of poetry as a new conception of the poet. The tower of ivory has been fitted up as a laboratory. . . . The poet is comparable to the mathematical physicist, or else to the biologist or chemist. He is to carry out the role of scientist as studiously as Sherlock Holmes did. . . . Our picture of the poet is to be very like that of the austere, bespectacled man in a white coat, whose portrait appears in advertisements, weighing out or testing the drugs of which is compounded some medicine with an impressive name.[123]

Eliot's references to 'Sherlock Holmes' and to the scientist as 'the austere, bespectacled man in a white coat' have a vagueness of conception that detracts from his point; it is not a very impressive claim and could have little relevance from the retrospect of 1958. Eliot also exaggerated the essay; Valéry's concern was with the labour and preparation of being a poet, with the craftsmanship of the job, and his analogy from science was not of the size that Eliot suggested. In offering 'a totally new and modern conception of the poet' against customary mythologies, Valéry wrote:

He is no longer the dishevelled madman who writes a whole poem in the course of one feverish night; he is a cool scientist, almost an algebraist, in the service of a subtle dreamer . . . everything he has imagined, felt, dreamed, and planned will be passed through a sieve, weighed, filtered, subjected to *form*, and condensed as much as possible so as to gain in power what it loses in length.[124]

Eliot's exaggeration was compounded by the fact that, despite Valéry's extensive knowledge of contemporary science, that knowledge rarely emerged in print in the form it took here; it was more usually expressed in his private notebooks,[125] and not until the 1920s and 1930s did his published essays exhibit such analogies. Eliot's late version of Valéry's modernity can, in a sense, tell us something, retrospectively, about his own use of science in 1918 and 1919; his vulgarization of Valéry and his tardy celebration of Valéry's modernity cannot help but raise doubts as to the seriousness of his analogies in the earlier essays: that they were nothing more than shadows of Pound's analogies and that they were embarrassedly modish.

Lessons in looking

Pound's reprinting of the Goncourt Preface was a resurrection of the period of what he called 'French scientific prose'. He learned the value of such prose from Ford Madox Ford, and it depended for its 'scientific' status fundamentally on an unequalled accuracy of perception. Shortly after the publication of 'The Serious Artist' and prior to the reprinting of the Preface, an essay by Edith Wyatt appeared in *The Little Review* which had the rare distinction of drawing attention precisely to the accuracy of nineteenth-century French fiction. This essay, too, was directed towards an American audience, and as Pound was to cite the Goncourts' example, so Wyatt reprinted much of Maupassant's Preface to *Pierre et Jean* which for her evinced a seriousness towards literature, lacking in America, and which 'expresses the clear fire of attention our American habits lack'. She quoted that part of the Preface where Maupassant gave the famous account of the lesson in perception that he received from Flaubert:

> Flaubert compelled me to describe in a few phrases a being or an object in such a manner as to clearly particularize it, and distinguish it from all other beings or all other objects of the same race, or the same species. 'When you pass', he would say, 'a grocer seated at his shop door, a janitor smoking his pipe, a stand of hackney coaches, show me that grocer and that janitor, their attitude, their whole physical appearance, including also by a skilful description their whole moral nature so that I cannot confound them with any other grocer or any other janitor: make me see, in one word, that a certain cab-horse does not resemble the fifty others that follow or precede it.'[126]

Pound used the anecdote himself for the first time over two years later as part of his instructions on composition to the aspiring Iris Barry.[127] It was this lesson in looking that centred his interest in the 'prose tradition' he derived from Ford with its twin values of craftsmanship and 'scientific' procedure, and it was Ford who consistently relied on analogies from science to sustain the meaning of that 'tradition'. Ford's scientific analogies were rooted, as were Pound's, in a concern with the status and the public acknowledgement of the writer's situation, predominant interests of Pound's modernity. Pound's understanding of that situation was most obviously determined by his own experiences in literary London, his battles with the publishing system, with the fake standards of contemporary criticism, with the struggle to create a proper audience for Joyce, but he found a major resource for the expression of its propaganda in Ford's diatribes.[128] Their shared vocabulary of science was rooted in a criticism of current opinion about the writer; Ford's *Ancient Lights* made the case, shortly after the first meeting between the two in 1909, by noting the feeling that 'a man of letters is regarded as something less than a man', and as 'at least effeminate if not a decent kind of eunuch'.[129] The societal problem that Ford suggested would have been particularly acute for the early confusions of Pound's exile, which were social as well as aesthetic; Donald Davie has given a good account of these confusions:

> Pound, it seems clear, was acutely conscious of his situation as an American artist in London, and of the sheerly social embarrassment and uncertainties which that let him in for. For what he felt as his disabling 'colonialism', or for the disqualifications of that sort which he imagined his British associates imputing to him, he over-compensated with aggressive affectations of dress and behaviour, a calculated outrageousness which he seems to have concocted on Whistler's model.[130]

Pound's social unease would have been exacerbated by the romantic and medieval tendencies of his own work, his admiration for the glamour of the early Yeats and the nineties in general (factors that contributed to Ford's image of the writer), and by his simultaneous ambitions for modernity where his American temperament, to his mind, left him ill-equipped: he thus had to fight on all fronts, and Ford's image compounded the urgency to react through a public 'propaganda'. Ford's account saw public opinion as the result not simply of an outmoded response to aestheticism but of specific misunderstandings about the craft of writing itself:

> A book has outlines, has architecture, has proportion. These things are called in French technique. It is significant that in English there is no word for this. It is significant that in England a person talking about the technique of a book is laughed to scorn. The English theory is that a writer is a writer by the grace of God. He must have a pen, some ink, a piece of paper and a table. Then he must put some vine-leaves in his hair and write.[131]

His counters to this opinion were the axioms whereby the 'prose tradition' became important for Pound, the axioms of contemporary idiom and clear language. In Ford's canon, the model for these axioms in poetry was Christina Rossetti, whom he saw as 'seeking almost as remorselessly as did Flaubert himself and just as solitarily, for correct expression', as exhibiting the hallmark of modernity: 'one symptom of the gulf that separated Christina Rossetti as a Modernist from Ruskin and the old Pre-Raphaelites. The very last thing that these, the last of the Romanticists, desired was perfection.' As Pound celebrated the 'realism' of medieval poetry (substantially in *The Spirit of Romance*, 'Near Perigord', 'Provincia Deserta', 'Sestina: Altaforte', and in his admiration for Bertran de Born), Ford recognized a correspondence between the 'modernity' of Rossetti and her 'mediaeval' attitude, a correspondence characterized by a particular form of 'empiricism':

Christina Rossetti's nature was mediaeval in the sense that it cared for little things and for arbitrary arrangements. In the same sense it was so very modern. For the life of today is becoming more and more a life of little things. We are losing more and more a sense of a whole, the feeling of a grand design, of the co-ordination of all Nature in one great architectonic scheme. . . . And if in outside things we can perceive no design but only the fortuitous materialism of a bewildering world, we are thrown more and more in upon ourselves for comprehension of that which is not understandable and for analysis of things of the spirit. In this way we seem again to be returning to the empiricism of the middle ages and in that way, too, Christina herself, although she resembled the figure of a mediaeval nun, seems also a figure very modern amongst all the romantic generalizers who surrounded her, who overwhelmed her, who despised and outshouted her.[132]

The final cause, claimed Ford, of the refusal to recognize 'technique', of the view of the artist as 'effeminate', of the rejection of the 'mediaeval' modernity of Christina Rossetti by 'romantic generalizers', was the insularity of English letters, the absence, in Poundian terminology, of the 'metropolis'. Ford wrote of Turgenev and Flaubert:

They lived and unfolded their unprecedented talents in the same years, in the same city, in the same circle, filled with the same high ideals and high enthusiasms. And this is a very striking proof of how high effort in the arts flourishes by the mere contagion of contact.[133]

Ford's main lines of support for the modernist 'prose tradition' and for the seriousness of literary activity in general were sought in his analogies to the procedures of science. They were announced primarily in his essays for *The English Review* in 1909–10 (collected as *The Critical Attitude* in 1911), which propagated the dominant themes of Pound's 'The Serious Artist'. Ford reiterated his sense of an audience unsympathetic to the production of literature:

Our public being strictly utilitarian, it cannot be proved that reading imaginative literature ever led to the invention of the steamboat, the gaining of a new colony for the British Crown, the improvement of the morals of Society, or the extension of the Franchise. In short, in the minds of engineers, empire-builders and moral or social reformers in this country, imaginative literature occupies no place at all.[134]

The utilitarianism that was blind to the seriousness of literature also made it difficult for the artist to go about the ordinary business of living and to fulfil his proper function: 'With the standard and cost of living increasing daily and with the contempt for the imaginative writer daily increasing too, it becomes almost impossible for the novelist to remain the stern scientist that he should be' (p. 105). To justify the seriousness of imaginative enterprise, Ford stressed the scientific *use* which that enterprise serviced:

For, if the arts have any function at all, that function is truly educational – nay, it is truly scientific. The artist today is the only man who is concerned with the values of life; he is the only man who, in a world grown very complicated through the limitless freedom of expression for all creeds and all moralities, can place before us how those creeds work out when applied to human contacts, and to what goal of human happiness those moralities will lead us. (p. 27)

By the 'scientific' function of the arts, Ford meant a function of cultural diagnosis: 'that it should exist, this school, this bulk of work, is the first necessity of the State, for it would be the symptom of national health' (pp. 30–1). He thus claimed of the theatre, 'The Drama, moreover, is a very interesting thermometer of the state of public desires and necessities' (p. 73), and reiterated that statement by Flaubert which Pound was to quote so often: 'Nothing was more true than the words of Flaubert, when he said that, if France had read "Education Sentimentale", she would have been spared the horrors of the Franco-Prussian War' (p. 29).

The artist's diagnostic function was the broad base of Ford's justification for the writer in the *res publica*; that function depended upon the notion of authorial expression that Ford had learned from the French novel:

> His actual and first desire must be always the expression of himself – the expression of himself exactly as he is, not as he would like other people to think him, the expression of his view of life as it is, not as he would like it to be.
>
> It is for this reason that the work of a really fine renderer of the life of his day is of such great value to the Republic. For whatever his private views may be, we have no means of knowing them. He himself will never appear, he will never buttonhole us, he will never moralize. (pp. 32–3)

Such 'expression' was the basis of a writer's 'sincerity': 'the poet has become more sincere: he writes, that is to say, along the lines of his own personality and of his own personal experience' (p. 175); this 'sincerity' made possible the claims for a diagnostic literature that expressed the artist's function as scientist. Ford distinguished 'the difference between the more insular and amateur and the more cosmopolitan and scientific schools of writers', exemplifying the former by the 'school' of Wells and Kipling who had no 'canons of Art', and the latter by the 'school' of James, Conrad, Moore and Galsworthy who were 'wholly concerned with their Art' (p. 89). It was this latter 'school' that merited the analogy of science as a substantiation of their seriousness and their modernity:

> Their method is one of the production of what a barrister would call 'cases'. They do not obtrude their personalities: they state as well as they can the definite facts of a story, leaving to the reader

the task of adopting what moral attitude he will towards a given set of circumstances. This is the modern canon. It will be observed that this elevates the novelist of this school to the rank of a scientific observer.[135]

Ford's proclamation of a 'diagnostic' function for literature was part of his famous ambition to 'register my own times in terms of my own times'. This was a matter of diction and of choice of material; fiction could only be 'diagnostic' if it were up-to-date. Ford's most succinct statement on the matter was made in 'The Poet's Eye', an essay published in the same journal at the beginning of the same month as Pound's 'The Serious Artist' and that provided most of the material for Ford's better-known Preface to his *Collected Poems* in 1916. His arguments were against conventional views of the acceptability of certain materials for poetry to the exclusion of others, against the confinement of English poetry by its own literariness ('If we cannot use the word "procession" we are apt to be precluded from thinking about processions'), against the sentimentalism of 'the sure cards of the poetic pack' whereby 'the comfrey under the hedge may seem a safer card to play for the purposes of poetry than the portable zinc dustbin left at dawn for the dustman to take', sentimentalism that obscured the true purpose of poetry, the 'putting of certain realities in certain aspects'.[136] For Ford, diction explicitly displayed an epistemology; a concern with the 'realities' of contemporary language was a sure sign of a writer's willingness to present a picture as he saw it and hence a diagnosis. His major work of 1913 was *Henry James: A Critical Study*, a continuation of his campaign for seriousness which, particularly in its second chapter, anticipated virtually all that Pound was to admire in James in his essays of 1918. Ford recognized the 'impersonal' quality in James's work, surpassing even that of Flaubert, and James's function as 'historian': 'His greatness, to put it succinctly, is that of the historian – the historian of one, of two, and possibly of three or more, civilizations'.[137] For Pound, James was to be 'the great true recorder',[138] and for both Ford and Pound his work was distinguished by its detailed accuracy; Ford wrote of *The American Scene*:

When you close the book – at that very moment a sense of extraordinary reality overwhelms you. You will find that you have actually been in New York whose note is the scream of

trolley wheels upon inefficiently laid granite streets; you will find
that you have actually been at Manhattan Beach, where ladies, so
lacking in elusiveness, say and do the odd, queer things in the
high queer voices. (p. 21)

This was, at the time, an unusual response to James; it was shared
by Pound, who chose *The American Scene* with *Washington Square*
and *The Europeans*, without quite the novelist's eye for naturalist
detail, as giving America 'our peculiar heritage' and as 'so autoch-
thonous, so authentic to the conditions'.[139] Ford emphasized the
limits of James's observations as a key factor in his scientific
attitude:

> It is perfectly true that his hunting grounds have been almost
> exclusively 'up town' ones. . . . But a scientist has a perfect right
> – nay more, it is the absolute duty of the scientist – to limit his
> observations to the habits of lepidoptera, or to the bacilli of
> cancer if he does not feel himself adapted for enquiry into the
> habits of bulls, bears, elephants or foxes. (pp. 48–9)[140]

James was celebrated primarily for his diagnostic value ('bacillus'
and 'virus' were the terms Ford often used to describe the atmosphere of James's material), and this, essentially, was what Ford
meant by James's 'artistry' (pp. 64–5). Ford persistently argued
that the relationship of literature to the world of affairs was symptomatic (pp. 50–1), seeing James as 'the only unbiased, voluminous
and truthful historian of our day' (p. 66), as a manifestation of the
dependence of the health of a nation upon the health of its language
and literature: 'the race that cannot either in allegories [for Ford,
James's dominant mode] or in direct speech think clearly is doomed
to fall before the nations who can' (p. 172).

Ford's principles and the scientific analogies through which he
expressed them were rare among Pound's contemporaries; his concern for the status and function of writing and the vocabulary of
that concern profoundly informed Pound's similar campaign
during the London years. Eric Homberger's work on the relationship between Pound and Ford summarizes the account I have given
of Pound's campaign for the seriousness of literature[141] but, in
company with most commentators on Pound, offers only a very
general view of what he somewhat disparagingly calls Ford's
'scientism' (supported by a single citation), and offers this view very

much as a sideline, refusing to recognize the extent of scientific usage in Pound's modernist programme. Homberger's interests lie in other directions, towards which Pound's scientific analogies are merely stepping-stones:

> To see the artist as a scientist, solely preoccupied with the 'constatation of fact', is to protect him against the judgement of conventional morality. It was the analogical force of the scientist who remained faithful to his own standards, no matter what society wanted, which propelled Pound toward becoming a social critic.

There is, of course, a rightness to this argument, but it is also certain that the 'analogical force of the scientist' was considerably more complicated and considerably more germane to the vocabulary of modernism than merely the 'constatation of fact'. Because Homberger does not give full documentation of the scientific analogies of either Pound or Ford, I find his conclusion (following, misplacedly, a good discussion of the adverse reaction to Pound's 'Contemporanea' poems) particularly misleading:

> In attempting to follow his conscience as to his responsibilities as an artist, Pound succeeded in alienating whatever kindness might have been directed towards him. By 1916 he was an isolated figure. . . . The consequences of the 'prose tradition', the scientism and social responsibility inherent in Ford's doctrine disturbed and eventually destroyed the easy security of Pound's relations with Edwardian England. He had to turn away from the conventional view of the 'poetic' to prose, and from the poet to the scientist, to overcome the 'disease of Dilletantism': in doing so he suffered the inevitable consequence. He had to become a pariah in order to be a 'modern' artist.[142]

It is right to attend to Pound's isolation and to suggest Ford's influence as a contributing factor, but the argument is really no more than a restatement of the late Romantic artist's removal from the world of process, classically circumscribed by Kermode's *Romantic Image*. Furthermore, Homberger's categorization of Pound as 'pariah' implicitly reiterates exactly Ford's comment on the writer's social standing ('in England all writers being well aware that they are not regarded as gentlemen'),[143] thereby miming the judgement of Edwardian society itself, the judgement that Pound was later to satirize in *Hugh Selwyn Mauberley*. Homberger's tone suggests that Pound's isolation is merely a matter for biographical regret, but Pound was not Yeats, and the modernist programme specifically incorporated a mode of alienation as a necessary tactic; Pound's voice, like that of Whistler, was calculated to alienate, and the cultivation of a new discourse for literary debate involved a deliberate abrasiveness, which would hardly expect, in the nature of things, to be free from painful consequences. For Pound, isolation was not a negative but a positive and, indeed, an inevitable gesture. His reliance on Ford for the status and epistemology of the artist was as positive and significant in his struggle towards modernism as was his reliance on Fenollosa, the other major arbiter of Pound's early aesthetics, sustaining him throughout his London years and providing crucial ammunition for the battles on behalf of Joyce.

3 Correspondences: modes of idealist science

> Observe the phenomena of nature as one in whom the ancestral voices speak, don't just watch in a mean way.
>
> (Confucius)

Dry things

The schoolboy T. E. Hulme quarrelled with his headmaster over Karl Pearson's *The Grammar of Science*.[1] We do not know the occasion or the nature of the quarrel, but Hulme's attitude towards science demonstrates the truth of Herbert Schneidau's accurately dismissive conclusion that Hulme's poetics 'leads only to a subjective, self-asserting toying with unsatisfactory, untrustworthy words: poetry "absolutely removed from reality"'.[2] To an extent shared only by Ford and Fenollosa among sources contemporary to Pound, Hulme elaborated his poetics through models from science, but, in distinct contrast to all three, Hulme was unable to recognize the figurative potential of such models. Hulme's central argument for a poetry of 'small dry things' as opposed to abstract ideas was, of course, shared by Ford, Fenollosa and Pound, but the vocabulary of that argument was diametrically opposed to the scientific analogies whereby theirs were sustained. At the end of his most famous essay, 'Romanticism and Classicism', Hulme argued an analogy between 'prose' and 'algebra' to show how both consisted in fixed 'counters', subject to 'rules' whose 'automatic' movement denied visualization; the 'X's and the 'Y's were returned to the realm of the physical only at the end of the process. By comparison, poetry was not a 'counter language' but 'visual' and 'concrete', expressing a 'language of intuition' which would 'hand over sensations bodily'. Its energy lay in the novelty of its figurability whereby 'you continuously see a physical thing' as against jaded abstractions. 'Verse', he concluded, 'is a pedestrian taking you over the ground, prose – a train which delivers you at a destination.'[3] The banal metaphor of Hulme's argument, the 'pedestrian' versus the 'train', suggests his somewhat snobbish antipathy towards the utilitarian function of science, its ease of getting about. His urge to distinguish between creative activity and the more expositional agencies of the mind[4] led Hulme to misunderstand, or to misuse, the reductionist claim for science's provision of an alternative language in its descriptive account of phenomena. Sir Arthur Eddington wrote of this claim that 'Science aims at constructing a world which shall be symbolic of the world of commonplace experience', a world in which 'we watch a shadowgraph performance of the drama of familiar life.'[5] Eddington's terms 'symbolic' and 'shadowgraph' suggest, of course, a view that would have been anathema to the Bergsonian intuitionism of Hulme that habitually rejected, at the level of theory, any such threat of removal from the world of ordinary discourse. Hulme's sense of the prosaic function of science's 'counter language' clearly seems to have assumed a mode of procedure whereby phenomena were given a reductionist representation; Eddington wrote of the schema for replacement that this involved:

> The whole subject matter of exact science consists of pointer readings and similar indications . . . although we seem to have very definite conceptions of objects in the external world, those conceptions do not enter into exact science and are not in any way confirmed by it. Before exact science can begin to handle the problem they must be replaced by quantities representing the results of physical measurement.

The reductionist ideology of replacement advertised itself exactly as such, as no more than an alternative system of measurement with no pretence to the plenitude of 'explanation'; Eddington offered a carefully circumscribed tripartite structure for science's descriptions:

(a) a mental image, which is in our minds and not in the external world;

(b) some kind of counterpart in the external world, which is of inscrutable nature;

(c) a set of pointer readings, which exact science can study and connect with other pointer readings.[6]

As I argued earlier, this was precisely the strength of the reductionist position; by proposing itself as a partial lexicon, it avoided the increasingly impossible situation that the determinist burden of Victorian science had created. Hulme, however, was unwilling to translate the measurements of scientific symbols into anything other than a system of crude substitution; his view that 'counters' were only definable and meaningful in terms of other 'counters' within the same field[7] made impossible for him the Poundian recognition of the potential within the equations of analytical geometry. For Pound, the reductionist view of science's function for translation provided an excellent model for the critic's procedure, but for Hulme, who was little concerned with the utilitarian questions of criticism, science's mode of translation was, as translation, simply deadening for creativity because it was valuable only as a means of getting about and thus inevitably automatic and abstract. To see 'solid things' was impossible within the alternative discourse presented by science because we manipulate the algebraic symbols for those 'things' in a formalistic way so that they 'fall into well-known patterns' which we accept 'without thinking of their meaning'.[8] Science was thus conducive not only to a kind of lexical incest (a breeding, as it were, of words among themselves in which they translate each other unproblematically and function solely as mirrors of each other) but also to mental laziness; Hulme castigated 'prose' as 'something resembling reflex action in the body', merely an 'economy of effort'.[9] The need for mental and imaginative economy constituted for Pound, as we have seen, a major lesson from science; for Hulme it was only a 'reflex' aid, useful but thoughtless. Pound understood 'economy' in its rigorous sense of a right method whereby the mind (with, indeed, large 'effort') avoided clutter as a result of necessary apprentice work. Hulme equated 'economy' merely with finding the easiest way out, which of course required virtually no 'effort' at all. An important part of Hulme's ideology was, however, to remain directly pertinent for Pound; Hulme emphasized the difference between Bergson's style of lecturing to the Philosophical Congress at Bologna in 1911 and that of the German delegation:

It appeared as if in the confused flux of things he was able by great attention to just see a certain curve, and that he was carefully choosing his words and picking out metaphors and illustrations in order to make sure he was conveying over to one just the exact shape of the curve he saw and no other. . . . The Germans presented a tremendous contrast to that. . . . They expressed not the attitude of a man who with difficulty sees a new shape, but on the contrary gave one the certain conviction that they saw nothing at all. There was no question of vision. Vision breeds dissatisfaction with ready-made phrases and an attempt to supplement the inadequacies of language by new metaphors. It was perfectly plain that no glimmering of the inadequacy of language had ever struck them. The concepts which they perpetually arranged in different orders, like a set of counters, were perfectly adequate to them for the representation of all the mysteries of thought.[10]

Here, in one of the few honest moments of his entire *œuvre*, Hulme established the discrimination that Pound was to draw later between French and Teutonic modes of thought, between a France where 'the antiseptic conditions of the laboratory exist' and a Germany which had 'got decidedly and disgustingly drunk' on ideas.[11] Pound's rephrasing of Hulme's discrimination within the models of science revealed his distance from the deeper Hulmean ideology which merely perpetuated a familiar reaction against the mechanism of the nineteenth century, condemning scientists for having 'turned the world into the likeness of a mechanical toy' by their aim 'to reduce the complex and inevitably disconnected world of grit and cinders to a few ideal counters, which we can move about and so form an ungritlike picture of reality – one flattering to our sense of power over the world.'[12] The sciences distorted the world because they 'all resolve the complex phenomena of nature into fixed separate elements changing only in position', because the analytical intellect guiding their research persisted in 'unfolding things out in space. It is not satisfied unless it can see every part.'[13] The antinomy of such distortion was of course the Bergsonian 'intuition', and Frank Kermode has suggested that this opposition was essentially commonplace:

it is fundamentally a new statement of the old defense of poetry against positivism and the universe of death. It is a revised form of the old proclamation that poetry has special access to truth, and is not merely light entertainment for minds tired out by physics. Poets, excluded from action, are enabled to achieve the special form of cognition and pierce the veil and intuit truth.[14]

Hulme's view of science was, however, rather more complex and involved a more particular attitude to the notion of 'action'. In the essay that went furthest towards establishing his conception of scientific method and its areas of operation, 'Humanism and the Religious Attitude', Hulme demanded that philosophy be seen as a twofold discipline, both as a *Weltanschauung* and as a 'science'. Here he recognized the 'solid growth' of science, the value of its impersonality and exactitude; it was only when it was misapplied in an attempt to bring the 'absolute' to bear on the 'relative', or to use the *Weltanschauung* as an 'exact' method, that confusion and distortion arose. The assumption here was of the difference between the 'objective' and 'impersonal' qualities of science and the functions of 'logic' which 'confine us to the use of flat counter-images only'.[15] Karl Pearson had, ironically, also argued against scientific confusion by distinguishing between the 'philosophical method' and that of science; the former, he wrote,

> seems based upon an analysis which does not start with the classification of facts, but reaches its judgements by some obscure process of internal cogitation. It is therefore dangerously liable to the influence of individual bias; it results, as experience shows us, in an endless number of competing and contradictory systems . . . the so-called philosophical method does not, when individuals approach the same range of facts, lead, like the scientific, to practical unanimity of judgement.[16]

While Pearson opposed the confusions of philosophy, Hulme opposed those resulting from science's interference with philosophy; ultimately, it was science's logical equipment that bothered him as it bothered Bergson, who had also castigated analytical procedure for its function of 'translation', its 'development into symbols'.[17] But Hulme was not the clearest of thinkers; although he made concessions to the necessary exactitude of science and recognized its role for philosophy, in practice he invariably used science and science's logic as interchangeable topics for condemnation. This was as a result of his adoption of Bergson's notion of 'action', which he saw as one of the two most important aspects of Bergson's philosophical position for aesthetics and which, crucially, marks an essential distinction from Pound's attitude:

> Man's primary need is not *knowledge* but *action*. The character-istic of the intellect itself Bergson deduces from this fact. The function of the intellect is so to present things not that we may most thoroughly understand them, but that we may successfully act on them.[18]

It was Bergson's understanding of man's dominance by the 'ne-cessity of action' that structured his antipathy towards conceptual cognition:

> We do not aim generally at knowledge for the sake of knowledge, but in order to take sides, to draw profit – in short to satisfy an interest. We inquire up to what point the object we seek to know is *this* or *that*, to what known class it belongs, and what kind of action, bearing or attitude it should suggest to us. These different possible actions and attitudes are so many *conceptual directions* of our thought, determined once for all; it only remains to follow them: in that precisely consists the application of concepts to things.[19]

For Hulme, it was the action-biased intellect that limited creative perception, and the artist was the person that was emancipated from action-orientated modes of visualizing;[20] hence his distrust for a 'vital' or 'representative' art which was, necessarily, too closely allied to the impulse towards action, towards a standardized, or communal, series of perceptions.[21] The artist's removal from 'action' in this way precipitated, of course, the particular insidious-ness of Hulme's politics, more in accord, as Samuel Hynes and Herbert Schneidau have suggested, with those of Eliot than with those of Pound.[22] We may remember Pound's translation of Gourmont's 'Dust for Sparrows' (1920): 'The most terrible tyrants have been those who had the horror of action, those who could not shed blood themselves; who never laid eyes on their victims, but had them coldly eliminated; as if making mental operations which dealt with abstractions only.'[23]

With these discriminations in mind, we should note the figure Hulme chose in order to demonstrate the paucity of analytical procedure:

Logical reasoning is simply a means of passing from a certain premise to certain conclusions. It has in itself no motive power at all. It is quite impotent to deal with those first premises. It is a kind of building art; it tells you how to construct a house on a given piece of ground, but it will not choose the ground where you build. That is decided by things outside its scope altogether.[24]

Ernest Fenollosa also chose a figure from building to describe 'the tyranny of mediaeval logic' whereby 'thought is a kind of brick-yard' and 'baked into little hard units or concepts'. Within this system 'pyramids' were built up for each 'thing' in ever-increasing abstraction towards the apex, while at the base the 'things' lay 'stunned'. Fenollosa pointed to the sheer waste of such a system, the impossibility of 'bringing together any two concepts which do not happen to stand one under the other and in the same pyramid', the impossibility of representing 'growth' or 'change' or of dealing 'with any kind of interaction or with any multiplicity of function'. Fenollosa's emphasis on 'growth', 'change', 'interaction' and 'multiplicity of function' significantly suggested the alternative procedure of biology, the observation of a phenomenon through all the interactivities of its various stages of development. It was this understanding that emphasized not only 'things' but the relations between them, and so 'science' was seen in opposition to 'logic' and famously as a partner for 'poetry':

Science fought till she got at the things. All her work has been done from the base of the pyramids, not from the apex. She has discovered how functions cohere in things. . . . In diction and in grammatical form science is utterly opposed to logic. . . . Poetry agrees with science and not with logic. . . . The more concretely and vividly we express the interactions of things the better the poetry.[25]

Fenollosa understood 'classification' in the scientific sense of comprehensiveness, while Bergson and Hulme understood the term in its logical sense of categorization; Fenollosa recognized science as the best means for coming to terms with natural process, whereas Bergson, committed to the view of scientific method as purely conceptual, saw it as distortive in accounting for the elements of flux and duration. Bergson wrote of the 'stationary' quality of concepts in their attempts to 'fix' the elements of the 'invariable' and maintained that our customary habit was to seek to explain the 'mobility' of the world in terms of static, immobile concepts as the mind sought 'solid points of support', concluding aphoristically that 'analysis operates always on the immobile, whilst intuition places itself in mobility.'[26]

By means of different systems of vocabulary, both Hulme (echoing Bergson) and Fenollosa emphasized the 'real' as a mode of activity against the stasis of conceptual thought. Hulme juxtaposed the mechanist picture of the world with an organic account of Bergson's 'real time', a 'continuous growth in creation. A becoming never the same, never repeating itself, but always producing novelty, continually ripening and creating.'[27] In a sense, this was the lesson Pound was to celebrate (at the beginning of the *ABC of Reading* in his testament to Agassiz's teaching methods), the observations of a fish throughout its various stages of decay. But Hulme's emphasis lay on what is ultimately an unsatisfactory notion of 'novelty' – unsatisfactory for Poundian purposes because its insistence on 'never repeating itself' was at variance with the theory of development that both Fenollosa and Pound adopted from the idea of recapitulation, the major alternative to Darwinian evolution for the nineteenth-century biologist and the most famous defender of which was Louis Agassiz. An argument for 'novelty' relies fundamentally on an attention to the quiddity of phenomena centred in a series of changes of 'becoming never the same', in the separateness that those changes inevitably impose by inscribing their difference from previous changes. It is an argument that, in its concern with *relata*, is thus unable to incorporate the relational nature of phenomena that lay at the centre of Fenollosa's poetics, the 'lines of force' expressing interaction rather than novelty. At the level of theory, Hulme's position appeared to advocate the art of the 'real', but at the level of practice the 'real' was always apprehended from the remove of a poorly assimilated philosophy; for all his talk about the false order imposed by conceptual thought, Hulme's vulgarization of Bergson postulates nothing more than the order implicit in a different sort of ideal, removed world. His pervasive denial of 'plain speech', his view of all language merely as a debased 'compromise' and the paranoid disgust that sees reality as uncontrollable 'cinders': all suggest an ideology of denial. Language is irredeemably divorced from its productive forces to become a mystification – self-sealing and apprehendable only to Hulme himself – of all that lies beyond the potential of available discourse. For Hulme, to touch the 'real' is, in practice, to be contaminated.

Intelligent seeing

While Hulme denied science in order to assume a mode of privacy particular to himself, Fenollosa celebrated science's function to sustain a theory of language whose hallmark was its availability to the public sphere; as Pound noted in 1934, 'The Chinese "word" or ideogram for red is based on something everyone KNOWS.'[28] The ideogram was structured not along the lines of restrictive grammar but from a series of pictures that were communally accessible, violating 'the celibacy of subject, agent, and object which Western grammar holds as sacrosanct'.[29] Such accessibility avowedly ensured concreteness against abstraction and maintained the truth of Pater's dictum: 'To define beauty, not in the most abstract but in the most concrete terms possible, to find not its universal formula, but the formula which expresses most adequately this or that special manifestation of it, is the aim of the true student of aesthetics.'[30] It was this availability, coded by the 'liberation' of science, which above all differentiated the sense of reality's concreteness in Pound and Fenollosa from that in Hulme. This complex of concerns was to provide the main arguments for Pound's accumulative strictures on aesthetics in the 1930s; the ambition of the *ABC of Reading*, a study in 'the development of language as a means of registration', was originally discerned by Pound in Fenollosa's notes for *The Chinese Written Character as a Medium for Poetry*, where he found the 'first definite assertion of the applicability of scientific method to literary criticism'.[31]

The relationship between Pound and Fenollosa is familiar from most commentaries; the most useful perspective is Hugh Kenner's: that Fenollosa's notes, while adding nothing radically new to Pound's theories about art, had the effect of a codifying influence over many of Pound's rather disparate ideas; their main value was to synthesize a position Pound had already been moving towards. Things Japanese and Chinese had been familiar to literary London since Whistler's introduction of Japanese paintings in the 1860s.[32] There was nothing novel about Pound's reception of oriental aesthetics; such things were simply very much in the air. The *Poetry* issue of November 1915, for example, included Alice Corbin

Henderson's review of Yone Noguchi's *The Spirit of Japanese Poetry* and of Lafcadio Hearn's translation, *Japanese Lyrics*. This review indicated very broadly the kind of contemporary interest in the art of Japan that reflected Pound's own concern with practical poetics, at a time when he was responding to a new dynamics for writing in the energies of vorticism. Mrs Henderson's essay contained much that was directly relevant to Pound's current preoccupation with the 'image'. She began by noting that 'Japanese poetry is never explanatory, its method is wholly suggestive. . . . Brevity is occasioned by intensity', and she quoted illuminatingly from Fenollosa's *Epochs of Chinese and Japanese Art*:

> That such a doctrine (Zen) should become a powerful adjunct of poetry . . . is due to its keen perception of analogies. All real poetry is just this underground perception of organic relation of things which custom classifies as different. . . . Nature was so plastic and transparent to the eye of early man that what we call metaphor flashed upon him as a spiritual identity to be embodied at once in language, in poetry and in myth. Zen only tried to get back to that primitive 'éclaircissement'.

The important dichotomy between 'organic relation' and 'custom' incorporated a primitivist and transcendentalist view of the value of Chinese language for poetry: 'So in Chinese poetry every character has at least two shades of meaning, its natural and its spiritual, or the image and its metaphorical range.'[33] It was clearly but a short step to Pound's frequently offered quotation from Aristotle: 'But the greatest thing by far is to be a master of metaphor. It is the one thing that cannot be learned from others; and it is also a sign of genius, since a good metaphor implies an intuitive perception of the similarity of dissimilars.'[34] From these premises, the next stage, as Mrs Henderson noted by her quotation from Mallarmé, was 'To be instituted, a relation between images, exact; and that therefrom should detach itself a third aspect, fusible and clear, offered to the divination.' We are given here what was missing in the theories that Pound had learned from Ford, that sense of interaction between poem and reader often neglected by Ford's formal propositions. Ford's teaching provided much of the structure for the writing of verse, but Pound discovered the realization of the process in the art of the Orient. This sense of interaction is conveyed by Mrs Henderson's quotation from Noguchi:

The real hokkus are a running living water of poetry where you can reflect yourself to find your own identification. . . . A great hokku poem never makes us notice its limitations of form, but rather impresses us by the freedom through mystery of its chosen language, as if a sea-crossing wind had blown in from a little window.

There is a certain mystification here, not to say a preciosity and a naïvety, that would have irritated a Pound whose interest lay in a 'language beyond metaphor', epithets of 'primary apparition' that offered a concrete suggestiveness, a sensory mode of apprehension.[35] Noguchi's 'freedom through mystery of its chosen language' has too much of the obscure and the indefinite about it, but while it was not Pound's 'sudden sense of freedom which we feel in the presence of great works of art', not the scientific 'liberation' of Whistler that I discussed earlier, it was 'freedom' nevertheless and was consequently formulated into a proposition that was paramount for the vorticist Pound:

When our Japanese poetry is best, it is, let me say, a searchlight or flash of thought or passion cast on a moment of life and nature which, by virtue of its intensity, leads us to the conception of the whole; it is swift, discontinuous, an isolated piece.[36]

For Fenollosa, Noguchi's 'searchlight or flash' expressed itself as the 'flash of lightning' that was the sentence at work in nature; the notion of the 'swift, discontinuous' moment, whose 'intensity' led to a 'conception of the whole', illustrated how, for the post-Paterian modernist, actuality was experienced and became a theme for art: it formed a means of synthesis in poetry through the ideogram, and in prose and literary criticism a means of diagnosis through the 'luminous detail'.

Fenollosa's notes instigated for Pound not so much ideas as an attitude; oriental aesthetics were not new, but their inclusion within a model of science was the radical confirmation of a mode of modernist poetics that Pound needed at that particular moment. Pound's response to Fenollosa's work is best suggested in a note indicating his understanding of the *Confucian Analects*:

It is an error to seek aphorisms and bright sayings in sentences that should be considered rather as definitions of words, and a number of them should be taken rather as lexicography, as ex-

 amples of how Kung had used a given expression in defining a
man or a condition.

Points define a periphery. What the reader can find here is a set
of measures whereby, at the end of a day, to learn whether the
day has been worth living.[37]

Pound summarized here not only the ethical strength of the
Analects but also the end-product of scientific method as he understood it – the provisory suggestion of 'measures' or 'points' to
specify the area of experience with which they were concerned –
and, in this, such method could not help but be poetic. The most
immediate effect on Pound of Fenollosa's theories was that, for
him, they expressed all the uneasiness he felt about the current
formulations of imagism, its stasis, its lack of dynamism, its
tendency towards a poetry of aphorism that indicated a failure to
recognize the intimate relationship between descriptive language
and the world to which it was responsible. Above all, Fenollosa
advocated a triumph of the sensory imagination over abstraction,
appealing to the emotions with 'the charm of direct impression'.[38]
The disregard of the Chinese language for the hegemonic directives
of Western grammar permitted a mode of registration that was
directly of the senses: Pound's editorial note directed the reader
back to the 'primary apparition' of *The Spirit of Romance*, that
which is 'actually presented to the sense or vision' (p. 22). The
description of phenomena was to be modelled on that employed by
the scientists, 'a vivid short-hand picture of the operations of
nature' that followed 'natural suggestion' in its concreteness (pp.
8–9), a descriptive theory that distinctly involved a fleshing-out, as
it were, of the reductionist ambition to provide 'a résumé in mental
shorthand, which replaces for us a lengthy description of the
sequences among our sense impressions'. Karl Pearson wrote of
science's descriptive artefacts:

Geometrical surface, atom, ether, exist only in the human mind,
and they are 'shorthand' methods of distinguishing, classifying
and resuming phases of sense-impressions. They do not exist in
or beyond the world of sense-impressions . . . the scientist postulates nothing of the world beyond sense; for him the atom and
the ether are – like the geometrical surface – modes by aid of
which he resumes the world of sense.[39]

Part of the necessity for the reductionist philosophy of scientific language was an increasing scepticism towards science's claims to account for a world rapidly being revealed as constituted by flux and movement rather than by the solidity proposed by classical physics; the relatively 'new' science of biology was making mechanist accounts particularly uncomfortable. So, too, Fenollosa's poetics was designed to deal precisely with the problem of lexical mobility and thus attended to the peculiarly active function of the ideogram, its 'verbal idea of action' whereby even the seemingly primitive characters ('what grammar calls nouns') were in fact 'shorthand pictures of actions or processes' (p. 9). The isolation of objects was meaningless because it was inevitably an abstraction, a denial of synthesis and relation, whereas in the Chinese conception 'The eye sees noun and verb as one; things in motion and motion in things' (p. 10). It was here that Fenollosa made his scientific analogy explicit: 'Valid scientific thought consists in following as closely as may be the actual and entangled lines of force as they pulse through things. Thought deals with no bloodless concepts but watches things move under its microscope.' These 'lines of force' were expressions of what, for Fenollosa, constituted the 'transference of power', which was the fundamental activity of nature: 'Light, heat, gravity, chemical affinity, human will, have this in common, that they redistribute force.' By contrast, the abstractive tendency of logic 'despised the "thing" as a mere "particular" or pawn', rather 'as if Botany should reason from the leaf-patterns woven into our table-cloths' (p. 12). The Chinese transitive sentence was thus celebrated because it brought 'language close to *things*' and because 'in its strong reliance upon verbs it erects all speech into a kind of dramatic poetry' (pp. 12–13).

To say that such a sentence in an uninflected language follows the 'natural order' was partly to subscribe to an idealist lexicography (to which I shall return) and partly to suggest possibilities for gristly observation which evades grammatical conventions: 'Outside grammar the word "state" would hardly be recognized as scientific. Who can doubt that when we say "The wall shines", we mean that it actively reflects light to our eye?' (p. 14). And Pound remembered the metaphoric act whereby a small girl asked if she could 'open the light'; like nature, Fenollosa argued, 'Chinese words are alive and plastic because *thing* and *action* are not formally separated' (p. 17). Science thus denied grammar's abstractions, which insisted exactly on such separation; the vitality of 'primitive metaphors', forced upon early man by nature, was made possible by their following 'objective lines of relations in nature herself', and those 'lines' were 'more real and more important than the things which they relate' (p. 22). It was essentially to this complex of ideas that Fenollosa applied the prescription of science; his 'lines of force' were a version of the 'correspondence' ('The continuous adjustment of internal relations to external relations') that Herbert Spencer had maintained as the 'broadest and most complete definition of life': 'Immediately or mediately proximately or remotely, every trait exhibited by organic bodies . . . must be referable to this continuous adjustment between their actions and the actions going on around them.'[40] A form of Spencer's 'correspondence' was important for reductionist theory; Ernst Mach argued: 'The aim of research is the discovery of the equations which subsist between the elements of phenomena.' By 'equations', Mach meant 'functions', a better term in that it suggested the relation not of static but of kinetic properties: 'Instead of equations between the primitive variables, physics gives us, as much the easiest course, equations between *functions* of those variables', 'functions' that illustrated the 'interdependence' of the world that science revealed.[41] These 'functions' were the product of a particular procedure, that of 'comparison', which 'as the fundamental condition of communication, is the most powerful inner vital element of science. The zoologist . . . compares . . . the embryos of different organisms with one another, and the different stages of development of the same organism with one another.'[42] As products of this kind, 'functions' displaced the rigidity of traditional causality:

> The connections of nature are seldom so simple, that in any given case we can point to one cause and one effect. I therefore long ago [1872] proposed to replace the conception of cause by the mathematical conception of function, – that is to say, by the conception of the dependence of phenomena on one another, or, more accurately, the dependence of the characteristics of phenomena on one another.[43]

Mach's 'functions' and Spencer's 'correspondence' were forms of the larger ideology of biological idealism, which characterized so much of nineteenth-century American thought, and which we associate primarily with Louis Agassiz. It was an idealism constituted by those theories of biology that viewed their material in essentially transcendentalist or quasi-mystical terms, seeing nature, for example, as the intelligent expression of divine composition or as the single manifestation, in a variety of forms, of one idea. At the very end of the century J. Arthur Thomson assessed its progress in biology and noted part of the difference between its mainstream development and the position of figures like Agassiz who, in important senses, stood outside that development; he noted how the search for 'natural affinities', which characterized the work of Agassiz and of Agassiz's only acknowledged master, Georges Cuvier, had tended to become replaced by the evolutionists' 'record of pedigrees'. It was Cuvier who offered the first significant opposition to the notion of *scala naturae*, the arrangement of species in a linear order from the highest to the lowest, and instead suggested the principle of *embranchements*. His pioneering work in palaeontology instigated Agassiz's own researches into extinct forms and postulated a biological version of what Pound perceived as the 'luminous detail' and what Fenollosa chose to call 'lines of force':

> The work of Cuvier must always be associated with the idea of the 'correlation of parts' – that the organism is a morphological unity. Certain characters are invariably correlated, others invariably exclude one another; in short, the part is of a piece with the whole.[44]

Pound's recognition of Fenollosa's contribution to the *forma mentis* of modernism involved considerably more than his celebration of Fenollosa's 'essay on verbs' and the revitalizing of the ideogram. Fenollosa's unique position in relation to the intellectual history of New England and Japan produced his distinctive attitude towards science, poetics and the teaching of art. Himself a graduate of Harvard, Fenollosa left in 1878 to teach political economy, philosophy and logic at the University of Tokyo where the Professor of Zoology was Edward Morse, also from Harvard where he had been 'An assistant of Agassiz in conchology'. While Morse was lecturing on evolution, Fenollosa was lecturing on Hegel and Spencer; Van Wyck Brooks has noted: 'As one of the new professors himself who was also teaching Darwinism, – which, he said, went well with Shintoism, – he was doing for science in Japan, for biology, botany and archaeology, what Fenollosa was to do for art.' The community of activity that Morse perceived between the world revealed by contemporary biology and that revealed by Shinto religion was possible only for a temperament trained not only by Agassiz but by Emerson's arguments for the contiguity of the spiritual and the material. Morse was not alone among Fenollosa's fellow expatriates in this respect; a later arrival in Tokyo in 1890 was Lafcadio Hearn: 'In Spencer, Hearn discovered the doctrines of Eastern philosophy on which he based so many imaginative visions, – the idea of Nirvana, metempsychosis, Karma, – remarking that Shinto, Buddhism and the thinking of Spencer did not merely "mix well" but "rushed together".'[45] The painterly eye of John La Farge, who visited Japan with Henry Adams, perceived a further mode of continuity that was to be vital for Pound's aesthetics, discovering in the Buddhist and Shinto religions the 'soul-informed rocks of the Greeks': 'The great Pan might still be living here, in a state of the world which has sanctified trees and groves and associated the spirit-world with every form of the earthly dwelling-place.'[46] In Japan, the speculations of New England transcendentalism, deeply marked by earlier versions of the scientific imagination, found new ground for exploring intuitions of spiritual and material conjunction. The mind of Fenollosa responded richly to such intercourse; in a diary entry for 1897 his wife reflected on their joint thinking informed by Hegel and Emerson, models for a specific education in practical science:

> What a privilege to study and learn – not to hoard up in dusty piles but to use as daily nutriment and strength. Not mere abstract speculation, but concrete experiment. It is the difference between painted sunlight and the chemical effects of the real sunlight on plant growth, between a long description of a laboratory experiment and the vibrations of early spring sap.

Three years earlier, in *Imagination in Art*, Fenollosa had written: 'Every element that enters into an imaginative group must be plastic and sensitive, full, as it were, of chemical affinities'.[47] These 'chemical affinities' sustained a notion of the 'image' which has a self-evident importance for Pound's famous account in 1913:

> In art, imagination is the faculty of thinking and feeling in terms of a single image. It implies the integrity, the wholeness and purity of the image. Imagination comes from the word 'image', not a fancy, not a dream, not a vague blur of consciousness, but a

clear, unbroken image. It is a visible integer. . . . Visual art is to be distinguished from ordinary sight, from vague revery, and from imperfect phantasy, in this, that the artistic image has persistence, congruity, natural limits, a kind of organization within itself. In strong imagination it is singular and complete, a group of parts, lines and proportions, which lacks nothing essential to make its wholeness clear, which admits nothing which tends to distort the image, or disturb its integrity.[48]

Fenollosa's scientific education was employed most importantly in *The Chinese Written Character as a Medium for Poetry*, but it also played a major role in his theories of education. Agassiz was celebrated throughout the latter half of the nineteenth century and consequently by Pound himself as the arbiter of lessons in *looking* at nature;[49] Fenollosa in turn claimed: 'There is no education like intelligent seeing.'[50] Within the tradition of Agassiz, Fenollosa's theories of art education involved principally a freedom from standardized perception and an opposition to utilitarian and didactic theories; he emphasized the spiritual quality of art against criteria of representationalism much in the manner of Whistler.[51] Lawrence Chisholm has described Fenollosa's performance at the International Congress of Education at Chicago in 1893:

Asked to discuss the question of the value of copying and modeling in training an artist, Fenollosa replied that an artist must turn to art rather than to nature for his instruction, that great works of the past constitute an invaluable aid in developing originality so long as art is not frozen to past standards. The artist inherits 'unlimited possibility' and should recast the possibilities of line and light into new relations.

His stance was revolutionary by current standards. Chisholm comments: 'The ensuing addresses and discussions assumed that art should represent noble themes and that the higher forms of painting, namely figure and landscape, required the traditional studies of anatomy, perspective, lighting and costume.'[52] Against such conventions Fenollosa was virtually a solitary voice, inheriting the examples of Agassiz who revolutionized the study of biology by insisting that students should work from actual specimens rather than from illustrations in books, and of Whistler who substituted 'harmonies' and 'arrangements' for 'representations'. Both examples maintained the primacy of contact with the materials of their discipline, again an insistence on practicality and firsthand knowledge. Fenollosa's practicality and sense of craft were due in part to his awareness of contemporary science; he wrote in an essay on 'The Fine Arts' in 1904:

> It was about a year ago that Professor Dewey and I were discussing the question whether it is possible to demonstrate that the order of progress in getting the power for an artistic creation in the mind of a single individual – and therefore the psychological order of development of the artist's powers – is practically identical with the historical order of the development of the art powers in the human race. If that could be shown . . . we should then get the broadest inductive basis for something like a scientific view of education.[53]

This proposal held the possibility for a 'scientific' basis of education because it expressed the doctrine of recapitulation, the doctrine – most famously expounded in America by Agassiz – that the life of an individual member of a species 'repeated', in the course of its own development, the developmental history of the species as a whole. This special mode of repetition, incorporating Cuvier's *embranchements* rather than the Darwinian 'record of pedigrees', offered, as I shall show later, an apposite model for modernist traditionalism.

Fenollosa's transcendentalist temperament, his radical lessons in 'intelligent seeing', sustained by his acquaintance with contemporary science, made him a far richer source for the modernist poetics of the 'real' than the negative view of science that Hulme's 'small dry things' resisted. His opposition to abstraction and absolutism was based on a much wider inheritance of science than Hulme, limited by a misunderstanding of science's mechanism, could ever conceive. The result was a theory of language that could lay claim to the designs of natural process because it was, in Poundian terminology, a theory of a 'condensed' language, of words 'charged with meaning to the utmost degree'. Fenollosa's version of this 'condensed' language was what he called the 'pregnant language' of 'synthetic thinking' in an essay on 'The Nature of Fine Art' in 1896:

> Synthetic thinking demands a pregnant language; rich, juicy, significant, full words, charged with intense meaning. . . . This is

poetry, the making a word stand for as much thought and feeling as possible, and that through the mutual modifications of the successive words.[54]

The Chinese ideogram was the most concrete exemplum of such 'pregnant language', the articulation of that mode of thought conceived as 'synthetic' only by a mind responsive to the New England of Agassiz and Emerson.

Strange sympathies

'Ere long', prophesied E. C. Stedman in 1873, 'some new Lucretius may care to reinterpret the nature of things, confirming many of the old prophecies, and substituting for the wonder of the remainder the still more wondrous testimony of the lens, the laboratory, and the millennial rocks.'[55] Stedman was reiterating an ambition that was both prospective and retrospective. In a letter of 1884 to Edward Morse, the author of two reminiscences of Agassiz, Sturgis Bigelow wrote shortly after Morse's departure of the small American community that Morse had known in Japan: 'Everything the same, even Fenollosa stretched out flat on his back reading Emerson'.[56] During his first visit to Europe in 1832–3 Emerson wrote in his journal after a visit to the Jardin des Plantes in Paris:

> Not a form so grotesque, so savage, nor so beautiful but is an expression of some property inherent in man the observer, – an occult relation between the very scorpions and man. I feel the centipede in me, – cayman, carp, eagle, and fox. I am moved by strange sympathies.[57]

Agassiz had worked in the same Jardin des Plantes; it provided a model for his Museum of Comparative Zoology at Cambridge, designed to illustrate the comprehensive morphology of the animal world and the unity of perspective that for Agassiz ensured an intelligible description of nature: in his capacity as Director, Agassiz wrote in the *Museum Report* for 1868 of a 'labyrinth of organic life' which assumed 'the character of a connected history'. For Elizabeth Cary Agassiz in her famous biography, this unity was symbolized by her husband's distinctive temperament:

> The ability, so eminently possessed by Agassiz, of dealing with a number of subjects at once, was due to no superficial versatility.

To him his work had but one meaning. It was never disconnected in his thought, and therefore he turned from his glaciers to his fossils, and from the fossils to the living world, with the feeling that he was always dealing with kindred problems, bound together by the same laws.[58]

Theodore Lyman, a pupil at Harvard, presented Agassiz's laboratory at the Jardin des Plantes as a concrete emblem of the vital interaction between past and present through the kind of detail usually to be found in a naturalistic novel:

> [Agassiz's] handwriting may be seen on the labels, besides that of Valenciennes and De Blainville and of the great Lamarck. . . . The spirits of great naturalists still haunt the corridors and speak through the specimens their hands have set in order . . . to bind past and present in unbroken reality.[59]

Emerson's 'strange sympathies' were, of course, to become a testament to the unity of phenomena throughout nature; what is notable here is the basis for those 'sympathies', a recognition of empathy arising not from metaphysical speculation but from direct observation of the order of natural objects in the 'cabinet' of science. This proposition of empathy became, three years later, the opening question of *Nature*: 'The foregoing generations beheld God and nature face to face; we, through their eyes. Why should not we also enjoy an original relation to the universe?' The lesson of direct observation in the Jardin des Plantes continued: 'The greatest delight which the fields and woods minister, is the suggestion of an occult relation between man and the vegetable. I am not alone and unacknowledged. They nod to me, and I to them.' The lesson's point was the 'totality' of nature: 'Nothing is quite beautiful alone; nothing but is beautiful in the whole. A single object is only so far beautiful as it suggests this universal grace.'[60] Fenollosa went further, arguing that a noun, an 'isolated thing', did not, by virtue of its isolation, even exist in nature.[61] Emerson's unity of the 'totality of nature' was based in part on early evolutionist theory; as Harry Hayden Clark has pointed out, Emerson delivered his lecture 'On the Relation of Man to the Globe' in December 1833, five months after his visit to the Jardin des Plantes:

> man is no upstart in the creation, but has been prophesied in nature for a thousand ages before he appeared; from times in-

calculably remote, there has been a progressive preparation for him, an effort to produce him; the meaner creatures containing the elements of his structure and pointing at it from every side. . . . His limbs are only a more exquisite organization – say rather the finish – of the rudimental forms that have been already sweeping the sea and creeping in the mud: the brother of his hand is even now cleaving the Arctic Sea in the fin of the whale, and innumerable ages since was pawing the marsh in the flipper of the saurian.[62]

The unity intuited by Emerson's 'sympathies' was the morphological correspondence through all ages and all types revealed by the evolutionists; the attraction of science for Emerson was its provision of a material vocabulary for what was otherwise a familiar line of theological metaphysics: it was a discourse of confirmation, exhibiting the truth of ancient prophecies. For Louis Agassiz, the unity predicated by this discourse was to be expressive of a divine plan:

> Investigators only read what they see, and, when they compare their results, it is found that they all tell the same story. He who reads most correctly from the original is the best naturalist. What unites all their investigations, and makes them perfectly coherent with each other, is the coincidence of thought expressed in the facts themselves.

This 'coincidence of thought' was possible because the 'facts' of the material world were simultaneously 'signs' of intelligent order:

> we must believe that these structures are the Creative Ideas in living reality. In other words, so far as there is truth in them, our systems are what they are, not because Aristotle, Linnaeus, Cuvier or all the men who ever studied Nature, have so thought and expressed their thought, but because God so thought and so expressed his thought in material forms when he laid the plan of Creation.

Hence, classification, the main task of the naturalist, was defined as the discerning of 'the creative plan of God as expressed in organic forms' and the function of scientific investigation as 'interpreting the purposes of the Deity in creation, and the relation of man to all the past'; the animal kingdom itself was thus conceived as 'a single complete work of one Creative Intellect'.[63] Agassiz's faith in the divine plan, sustained by his researches in all branches of natural science, ensured his opposition to Darwin and, as Theodore Lyman remembered, became integral to his descriptions of the phenomenal world:

> Last, and above all, Agassiz was a man of inborn spiritual belief, which made a primary element in his nature, and which entered into all his interpretations of the outer world. That material form was a cover of a spirit appeared to him a truth fundamental and almost self-evident.[64]

Agassiz's testimony to a special interaction of the material and the spiritual was similarly fundamental to Emerson's acknowledgement of science as an essential part of his practicality; he wrote of Swedenborg's *Animal Kingdom* that it was 'written with the highest end, – to put science and the soul, long estranged from each other, at one again'. He began his essay on 'Swedenborg; or, The Mystic' by emphasizing Swedenborg's 'practical labours' in engineering prior to his devotion to theological matters in the later part of his life, and he stressed the scientific and practical foundations for the more familiar areas of Swedenborg's reputation:

> The genius which was to penetrate the science of the age with a far more subtle science; to pass the bounds of space and time; venture into the dim spirit-realm, and attempt to establish a new religion in the world – began its lessons in quarries and forges, in the smelting-pot and crucible, in ship-yards and dissecting-rooms. . . . It seems that he anticipated much science of the nineteenth century; anticipated, in astronomy, the discovery of the seventh planet . . . the views of modern astronomy in regard to the generation of earths by the sun; in magnetism, some important experiments and conclusions of later students; in chemistry, the atomic theory; in anatomy, the discoveries of Schlichting, Munro and Wilson; and first demonstrated the office of the lungs.

The scientific training Swedenborg was to bring to bear on matters spiritual included a particular means of perception; he belonged to that tradition of 'intelligent seeing', always sustained by practical engagement, which Pound was to admire in Agassiz. Jules Marcou, one of Agassiz's early biographers, noted that Agassiz's insistence on factual observation placed him in the vanguard of science's efforts to resist metaphysics by means of the comparative method: 'True progress in natural history does not depend on fine theories, hypotheses and philosophy. What is wanted are new observations, new facts, new deductions well based on facts absolutely undeniable.' Marcou argued that Agassiz's insistence played a part in his reaction against Darwin and his followers who failed to meet the exacting demands of the new comparative methodology: 'Agassiz was unwilling to abandon the method of exposition of facts which he had found established in science, and to substitute in its place metaphysics and hypotheses; he clung to observation and experiment.'[65] Agassiz's principle of the close observation of individual morphology and the consequent tracing of developmental process was the cornerstone of his reputation to which all contemporary accounts testified. Theodore Lyman wrote of Agassiz's perennial distrust of material gathered at second hand:

A thing he never liked, and which troubled him quite as much in this country as in others, was book-learning. Text-books and 'school-series' exasperated him. . . . This turn of mind led him to gather what he considered the real books, animals of all sorts, preserved, so far as might be, in their natural state.[66]

Here was Agassiz's major lesson: 'Sooner or later, someone interviewing Agassiz was bound to ask, "What do you consider your greatest achievement?" And he would say, "I have taught my students to observe."'[67]

One of these students, Samuel Hubbard Scudder, gave the most famous celebration of Agassiz's lesson, the lesson that later opened Pound's *ABC of Reading*. Scudder told of how Agassiz gave him a species of fish to examine with the sole instruction to 'look at it', then leaving him alone for several hours: 'I might not use a magnifying glass; instruments of all kinds were interdicted. My two hands, my two eyes, and the fish; it seemed a most limiting field.' One aid was, however, permitted: 'At last a happy thought struck me – I would draw the fish; and now with surprise I began to discover new features in the creature. Just then the professor returned. "That is right," said he; "a pencil is one of the best of eyes."' The 'lesson in looking' that Scudder received from Agassiz provided the bulk of his reminiscence: 'for three long days he placed that fish before my eyes, forbidding me to look at anything

else, or to use any artificial aid. "Look, look, look," was his repeated injunction.' This for Scudder was 'the best etymological
lesson I ever had, – a lesson, whose influence has extended to the
details of every subsequent study.' Part of the importance of the
exercise was that it extended over several days, so that what was
being observed was not simply an accumulation of morphological
details but also the process of change and decay itself. The observation of process precipitated the next stage in Agassiz's programme, that of comparative study: 'The fourth day, a second fish
of the same group was placed beside the first, and I was bidden to
point out the resemblances and differences between the two;
another and another followed, until the entire family lay before
me.' Finally, there was the all-important synthesis of the data
gathered by observation and comparison: 'Agassiz's training in the
method of observing facts and their orderly arrangement was ever
accompanied by the urgent exhortation not to be content with
them. "Facts are stupid things," he would say, "until brought into
connection with some general law." '[68] Scudder's lesson illustrated
the major function of Agassiz's revolution in America; he was the
first to insist that all students be provided with their own specimens
to handle and examine during his expositions. And Agassiz himself
was capable of remarkable passages of structural description,[69]
providing a paradigm of an astonishing precision and clarity of
perception; his wife wrote, 'He said of himself that he was no artist,
and that his drawing was accurate simply because the object existed
in his mind so clearly',[70] and Jules Marcou in particular gave
numerous examples of his 'rare ability as an observer'.[71] In other
words, Agassiz's theorizing was also his essential practice, becoming an integral part of the *claritas* of his prose.

Emerson (a member, with Agassiz, of Boston's 'Saturday Club')
celebrated the practical training of Swedenborg's perception for
similar reasons: 'He had studied spars and metals to some purpose. . . . In the atom of magnetic iron, he saw the quality which
would generate the spiral motion of sun and planet.' This 'spiral
motion' was vortical movement and hence of particular relevance
to the figures chosen by Pound to illustrate his own aesthetics, as I
shall show later. Emerson's point was to offer Swedenborg not
merely as a metaphysician but as a thinker whose spiritual speculations were thoroughly grounded in the practice of science:

The thoughts in which he lived were, the universality of each law in nature; the Platonic doctrine of the scale or degrees; the version or conversion of each into other, and so the correspondence of all the parts; the fine secret that little explains large, and large, little; the centrality of man in nature, and the connection that subsists throughout all things. . . . In short, he was a believer in the Identity-philosophy, which he held not idly, as the dreamers of Berlin, or Boston, but which he experimented with and established through years of labour, with the heart and strength of the rudest Viking that his rough Sweden ever sent to battle.

Swedenborg's principles matched in many respects those of Emerson himself; Emerson supported Swedenborg's position with the discourse of botany to illustrate the contemporary relevance of identity-philosophy, the doctrine of unity through variety:

This theory dates from the oldest philosophers, and derives perhaps its best illustrations from the newest. It is this; that nature iterates her means perpetually on successive planes. In the old aphorism, *nature is always self-similar*. In the plant, the eye or germinative point opens to a leaf, then to another leaf, with a power of transforming the leaf into radicle, stamen, pistil, petal, bract, sepal, or seed. The whole art of the plant is still to repeat leaf on leaf without end.

Thus for Emerson did the discourse of science reconstruct the mystical proposals of earlier philosophies. Relations and repetitions, indeed, for it was exactly this process of reconstruction that defined the 'strange sympathies' uniting the diversity of phenomena, what Emerson called the 'rhymes' of nature:

Astronomy is excellent; but it must come up into life to have its full value, and not remain there in globes and spaces. The globule of blood gyrates around its own axis in the human veins, as the planet in the sky; and the circles of intellect relate to those of the heavens. Each law of nature has the like universality; eating, sleep or hibernation, rotation, generation, metamorphosis, vortical motion, which is seen in eggs as in planets. These grand rhymes or returns in nature . . . delighted the prophetic eye of Swedenborg.[72]

These 'rhymes' (manifest through the vortex that Descartes had suggested as the primary movement of matter and of creation itself and that Pound was to use as the primary cipher of modernism) were conflated with 'returns', the conflation described in Pound's famous letter of 1927, where the fugal structure of the *Cantos* was seen to incorporate the 'repeat in history' (Emerson's 'returns') and the compositional procedure of the 'subject-rhyme'.[73]

Repeats, indeed (the explicit characteristic of any idealist discourse), since Swedenborg's 'rhymes' in Emerson's version prompted the doctrine of correspondences: the ultimate fusion of material and immaterial, of word and object. Again, the relevance of the doctrine for Emerson lay in its scientific basis, that it was not 'idle' metaphysical lore, that it was based on the recognition that the same series of observable laws applied to the diverse phenomena of the universe, just as 'vortical motion' could be 'seen in eggs as in planets': 'Swedenborg first put the fact into a detached and scientific statement, because it was habitually present to him, and never not seen. It was involved . . . in the doctrine of identity and iteration, because the mental series exactly tallies with the material series.' Here were the grounds of a truly physiological symbolism, propounded in the *Animal Kingdom*, a book which, claimed Emerson, 'comes recommended by the hard fidelity with which it is based on practical anatomy'. Emerson provided a summary of Swedenborg's ambition by quoting his introductory remarks on the doctrine:

> In our doctrine of Representations and Correspondences, we shall treat of both these symbolical and typical resemblances, and of the astonishing things which occur, I will not say, in the living body only, but throughout nature, and which correspond so entirely to supreme and spiritual things, that one would swear that the physical world was purely symbolical of the spiritual world; insomuch, that if we choose to express any natural truth in physical and definite vocal terms, and to convert these terms only into the corresponding and spiritual terms, we shall by these means elicit a spiritual truth, or theological dogma, in place of the physical truth or precept. . . . This symbolism pervades the living body.

Emerson immediately pointed to the relationship of this physiological symbolism to literature and to language: 'The fact, thus explicitly stated, is implied in all poetry, in allegory, in fable, in the use of emblems, and in the structure of language.'[74] And Pound in 1907 wrote of Swedenborg's notion of 'the angelic language' as 'artistic utterance' for an art that included 'only so much of religion as is factive, potent, exalting', Blake's dictum of the 'triple bow' whereby we ascend 'to meet God in the air' and Coleridge's 'KALON quasi KALOUN' ('Kalon the Greek for "The Beautiful" as it were; Kaloun "a calling" to the soul'). His context was a specific definition of art: 'I am interested in art and ecstasy, ecstasy which I would define as the sensation of the soul in ascent, art as the expression and sole means of transmuting, of passing on that ecstasy to others.' This definition manifested its Swedenborgian gloss more explicitly in Pound's note on 'the great hero of the new things spiritual' for the prose-poem 'Malrin':

> To give concrete for a symbol, to explain a parable, is for me always a limiting, a restricting; yet, because some to whom this has already come have not seen into it, I will say this: that it arises from a perception how the all-soul of mankind is one and joineth itself wholly at some time and returneth to God as a bride.[75]

Emerson was properly sceptical about science's limitations, what he called in *Nature* its 'half-sight' which threatened to lose a sense of correspondence by its narrow attention to the 'means' of its own discipline:

> Empirical science is apt to cloud the sight, and, by the very knowledge of functions and processes, to bereave the student of the manly contemplation of the whole. . . . For, the problems to be solved are precisely those which the physiologist and the naturalist omit to state. It is not so pertinent to man to know all the individuals of the animal kingdom, as it is to know whence and whereto is this tyrannizing unity in his constitution, which evermore separates and classifies things, endeavouring to reduce the most diverse to one form.

In 1836 Emerson's contemporaries were unwilling to trace the relations that Swedenborg displayed, but, if their science had not yet achieved the syntheses of the Swedish mystic, it still retained a potential for those syntheses; as Agassiz was to assert that 'Facts are stupid things until brought into connection with some general law', so Emerson held faith in that potential:

When I behold a rich landscape, it is less to my purpose to recite correctly the order and superposition of the strata, than to know why all thought of multitude is lost in a tranquil sense of unity. I cannot greatly honour minuteness in details, so long as there is no hint to explain the relation between things and thoughts; no ray upon the *metaphysics* of conchology, of botany, of the arts, to show the relation of the forms of flowers, shells, animals, architecture to the mind, and build science upon ideas. In a cabinet of natural history we become sensible of a certain occult recognition and sympathy in regard to the most unwieldy and eccentric forms of beast, fish and insect.[76]

His faith resided in science's verification of this 'occult recognition and sympathy', impelled by the novelty, the making new of ideas and experiences from other sources of thought; he was persuaded by his sense of modernity, as Harry Hayden Clark has noted:

If science was always of secondary interest to Emerson, this fact should not prevent us from recognizing the important function of science in suggesting novel *reinforcement* for views which were primarily, I think, native, Christian, classical, Oriental, romantic, or transcendental. For he recognized very early that his 'own time' was the 'era of science'.[77]

This modernity permeated to Emerson's famous tripartite structure of language, which bore the impress of the doctrine of correspondence and its attendant physiological symbolism:

1 Words are signs of natural facts.
2 Particular natural symbols are symbols of particular spiritual facts.
3 Nature is the symbol of spirit.

It was the first of these propositions that anticipated in particular what Pound was to learn from the Chinese ideogram; Emerson explicated this proposition to argue:

The use of natural history is to give us aid in supernatural history; the use of the outer creation, to give us language for the beings and changes of the inward creation. Every word which is used to express a moral or intellectual fact, if traced to its root, is found to be borrowed from some material appearance.[78]

In an important essay of 1915 in *Poetry*, Alice Corbin Henderson (that rare creature, a contemporary critic whom Pound actually admired) adopted exactly these principles of Emerson's to describe the metaphoric nature of the Chinese written character:

> Nature was so plastic and transparent to the eye of early man that what we call metaphor flashed upon him as a spiritual identity to be embodied at once in language, in poetry and in myth. . . . So in Chinese poetry every character has at least two shades of meaning, its natural and its spiritual, or the image and its metaphorical range.[79]

And Ernest Fenollosa, too, continued Emerson's proposition:

> The Chinese language with its peculiar materials has passed over from the seen to the unseen by exactly the same process which all ancient races employed. This process is metaphor, the use of material images to suggest immaterial relations. . . . Metaphor, the revealer of nature, is the very substance of poetry. The known interprets the obscure, the universe is alive with myth.[80]

Emerson had also recognized the primitivist nature of such language, myth as the vehicle for metaphor in its function of translation, its announcement of material and immaterial connections, and the particular relation between noun and verb, characteristic of primitivist lexicography, which was to form the main argument of Fenollosa's essay:

> Most of the process by which this transformation is made is hidden from us in the remote time when language was framed; but the same tendency may be daily observed in children. Children and savages use only nouns or names of things which they convert into verbs, and apply to analogous mental acts.

Emerson gave examples of how words exhibited this 'transformation', the material base for their immaterial suggestion: '*Right* means *straight*; *wrong* means *twisted*. *Spirit* primarily means *wind*; *transgression*, the crossing of a *line*; *supercilious*, the raising of the *eyebrow* . . . words borrowed from sensible things, and now appropriated to spiritual nature.'[81] Similarly at the end of *The Chinese Written Character as a Medium for Poetry*, the reader was given a breakdown of a series of ideograms; the ideogram for the immaterial 'like', for example, consisted in two material components: 'woman' and 'mouth'.[82]

For both Emerson and Fenollosa, a philosophy of language was no purely linguistic affair; what made their theories possible was the human tendency to construct pictures, and this tendency relied on the emblematic power, as Emerson noted, not only of words but of natural objects themselves:

> It is not words only that are emblematic; it is things which are emblematic. Every natural fact is a symbol of some spiritual fact. Every appearance in nature corresponds to some state of mind, and that state of the mind can only be described by presenting that natural appearance as its picture. An enraged man is a lion, a cunning man is a fox, a firm man is a rock, a learned man is a torch.

Emerson insisted that the making of these pictures was not accidental but a necessary function of a willingness to construct relations:

> It is easily seen that there is nothing lucky or capricious in these analogies, but that they are constant and pervade nature. These are not the dreams of a few poets, here and there, but man is an analogist, and studies relations in all objects. . . . All the facts in natural history taken by themselves have no value, but are barren like a single sex.

Here was the key to a philosophy of language based on the making of pictures:

> Because of this radical correspondence between visible things and human thoughts, savages, who have only what is necessary, converse in figures. As we go back in history, language becomes more picturesque, until its infancy, when it is all poetry; or all spiritual facts are represented by natural symbols.[83]

So Fenollosa, recognizing that 'All processes in nature are interrelated', saw that the non-arbitrary, pictorial qualities of the Chinese language could not help but be 'poetic': 'Chinese notation is something much more than arbitrary symbols. It is based upon a vivid short-hand picture of the operations of nature', an economical picture which displayed its own process: 'First stands the man on his two legs. Second, his eye moves through space: a bold figure represented by running legs under an eye. . . . Third stands the horse on his four legs.' Fenollosa allied Emerson's argument to the Whitmanian 'poetry of things'; language's base in nature led him to celebrate its quiddity: 'The sentence form was forced upon primitive men by nature itself. . . . This brings language close to *things*, and in its strong reliance upon verbs it erects all speech into a kind of dramatic poetry.' And a 'poetry of things' concerned itself essentially with the 'lines of force', the 'transference of power' between those 'things',[84] with perceptions of relations that for Agassiz had been made possible by Cuvier's fourfold plan of internal morphology:

> With this new principle as the basis of investigation, it was no longer enough for the naturalist to know a certain amount of the features characteristic of a certain number of animals, – he must penetrate deep enough into their organization to find the secret of their internal structure. Till he can do this, he is like the traveller in a strange city, who looks on the exterior of edifices entirely new to him, but knows nothing of the plan of their internal architecture. To be able to read in the finished structure the plan on which the whole is built is now essential to every naturalist.

Agassiz's use of Cuvier was intellectual as well as empirical; in answering the problem that persistently worried the scientist during the nineteenth century – the problem of whether his accounts actually expressed the world or whether they were simply useful fictions – Agassiz argued for nature itself as 'the work of thought, the production of intelligence' and for the scientist's work as a deciphering of this 'thought'; it was exactly these intellectual lines of relation in the natural world that 'give such coherence and consistency to the whole, and make it intelligible to man'. In turn, these lines of thought ensured the economy and practical precision of scientific method:

> To study a vast number of Species without tracing the principles that combine them under more comprehensive groups is only to burden the mind with disconnected facts, and more may be learned by a faithful and careful comparison of a few Species than by a more cursory examination of a greater number.

The principle Agassiz learned from Cuvier, the principle whereby 'lines of force' were to be revealed, 'cette fécondation mutuelle des deux sciences',[85] provided the foundations for Agassiz's own revolutionary method of classification by comparison:

> It is deeply to be lamented that so many naturalists have entirely overlooked this significant advice of Cuvier's, with respect to combining zoological and anatomical studies in order to arrive at a clearer perception of the true affinities among animals. To sum it up in one word, he tells us that the secret of his method is 'comparison', – ever comparing and comparing throughout the enormous range of his knowledge of the organization of animals, and founding upon the differences as well as the similarities those broad generalizations under which he included all animal structures . . . the true method of obtaining independent knowledge is this very method of Cuvier's, – comparison.

The importance of Cuvier's comparative method was reflected in the deceptively simple statement in which Agassiz attempted to 'express all that I have done': 'I have shown that there is a correspondence between the succession of Fishes in geological times and the different stages of their growth in the egg. . . . It chanced to be a result that was found to apply to other groups and has led to other conclusions of a like nature.'[86] His popularization of Cuvier's method was the most widely received and applied lesson of all Agassiz's teaching. William James, who studied under Agassiz, wrote of Frederick Myers, one of the founders of the Society for Psychical Research: 'Myers's great principle of research was that in order to understand any one species of fact we ought to have all the species of the same general class of fact before us.'[87] The Society for Psychical Research was, of course, from the 1880s onwards, the major vehicle for the scientific exploration and translation of the ineffable, the immaterial. Within a prior system of terminology, Emerson wrote: 'A fact is the end or last issue of spirit. The visible creation is the terminus or the circumference of the invisible world.'[88]

Emerson was willing, as Pound was willing, to use the analogy of science to explain his more esoteric beliefs; he wrote of the 'charm' of the work of both philosopher and poet:

> It is, in both cases, that a spiritual life has been imparted to nature; that the solid seeming block of matter has been pervaded and dissolved by a thought: that this feeble human being has

penetrated the vast masses of nature with an informing soul, and recognized itself in their harmony, that is, seized their law. In physics, when this is attained, the memory disburdens itself of its cumbersome catalogues of particulars, and carries centuries of observation in a single formula.[89]

The dissolution of the world's materiality and the dissolution of cognition's weightier, abstractive procedures were intimate partners in Emerson's admiration for science's synthetic economy. The physics of the nineteenth century achieved literally the dissolution of 'the solid seeming block of matter'; the field theories of Faraday and Clerk Maxwell, in particular, reconstructed matter into lines of force. With the consequent fallacy of following traditional divisions between material and immaterial phenomena, the psychical researcher could claim a scientific basis for his investigations into the paranormal and the poet could offer to a sceptical public discussions of the 'gods' and of medieval sexual mysticism through the translations of physics. Emerson's 'informing soul' of a 'spiritual life' could be explained without resort to metaphysics but rather by the lines of force that were held to constitute matter, and Fenollosa could claim that 'Green is only a certain rapidity of vibration, hardness a degree of tenseness in cohering' and that 'Valid scientific thought consists in following as closely as may be the actual and entangled lines of force as they pulse through things'.[90]

As Pound was to employ science in a claim for the moral status of the writer in 'The Serious Artist', so Emerson asserted that 'every natural process is a version of a moral sentence', an assertion substantiated through examples from physics in elaborating the metaphoric qualities of language:

The word is emblematic. Parts of speech are metaphors, because the whole of nature is a metaphor of the human mind. The laws of moral nature answer to those of matter as face to face in a glass. 'The visible world and the relation of its parts, is the dial-plate of the invisible.' The axioms of physics translate the laws of ethics. Thus: 'The whole is greater than its parts'; 'Reaction is equal to action'; 'The smallest weight may be made to lift the greatest, the difference of weight being compensated by time': and many the like propositions, which have an ethical as well as physical sense.

Because of this intimate relationship revealed by science between the laws of nature and the laws of ethics, language itself within this metaphoric system of translation bore a large responsibility towards the culture that produced it; in times of social corruption, the malaise of the state became manifest in the perversion of its language. In an extraordinarily Poundian passage, Emerson anticipated Pound's lifelong concern with the health of language:

> The corruption of man is followed by the corruption of language. When simplicity of character and the sovereignty of ideas is broken up by the prevalence of secondary desires, the desire of riches, of pleasure, of power, and of praise, and duplicity and falsehood take place of simplicity and truth, the power over nature as an interpreter of the will is in a degree lost; new imagery ceases to be created, and old words are perverted to stand for things which are not; a paper currency is employed, when there is no bullion in the vaults. In due time, the fraud is manifest, and words lose all power to stimulate the understanding or the affections.[91]

Pound's most famous statement on the subject inverted Emerson's order; it was kidnapped from Chinese thought, that area in which Fenollosa found the most energetic illustrations of Emerson's views on language. In posing the question of literature's societal function, Pound offered a Confucian answer which had to do with 'maintaining the very cleanliness of the tools', of the 'solidity and validity' of words which were 'in the care of the damned and despised *literati*': 'When their work goes rotten . . . when their very medium the very essence of their work, the application of word to thing goes rotten, *i.e.* becomes slushy and inexact, or excessive and bloated, the whole machinery of social and of individual thought and order goes to pot.'[92]

And for a poetics of the 'real', we have Whitman's poetry of lists, of objects conceived in terms of a transcendentalism underwritten by science, which offered not only accuracy of perception but a confirmation of the primitivist unity, previously understood intuitively, that was the true meaning of phenomena, the lines of relation (geological, evolutionary, atomic or whatever) that constituted their reality. Whitman used the relations revealed by geology to make one of his most explicit statements on the subject:

I am the poet of reality
I say the earth is not an echo
Nor man an apparition;
But that all the things seen are real,
The witness and albic dawn of things equally real
I have split the earth and the hard coal and rocks and the solid
    bed of the sea
And went down to reconnoitre there a long time,
And bring back a report,
And I understand that those are positive and dense every one
And what they seem to the child they are.[93]

The transcendentalist poetics of Emerson and Whitman present a solid line of ancestry for the epistemological struggles of Pound's early poetry and prose,[94] the lexicographical catalogues whereby he perceived the world. They offer a reassurance for the problems of exile and, mediated by Ernest Fenollosa, a reassurance for the mode of debate that Pound wanted to construct for modernism, the materiality and availability of a language of the ineffable; the language that Whitman always praised:

> Kosmos words, Words of the *Free Expression of Thought, History, Chronology, Literature*, are showing themselves, with foreheads, muscular necks and breasts. – These gladden me. – I put my arms around them – touch my lips to theirs.[95]

It was within such a gristly acquisition of words that Pound discovered 'our American keynote', words whose closest equivalent was sought in the Anglo-Saxon period, when they incorporated the 'national chemical' of their time.[96]

Nature is always self-similar

Transcendentalist poetics suggest a special problematic of the 'real' in that the 'real' manifests itself only through metaphor, which is the major expression of a world-view conceived in terms of correspondence and interaction. For the Poundian modernist, this problematic is sited in the dialectic of Emerson *plus* Whitman, Fenollosa *plus* Ford and 'French scientific prose': the testimonies of integrated pattern *plus* arguments for commonplace words, the language of the ordinary.

Emerson's proposition that 'the whole of nature is a metaphor of the human mind' suggests the hermeneutics of total enclosure by the concealing of origin, of lines of production. Self and other, past and present are not formally separated but always considered together as an organic totality, a version of the later totality propounded by the Cambridge anthropologists and, in a sense, crude but containing elements of truth, the totality implicit in reactionary politics. Such totality immediately gives rise to the question of authority within a system where it is impossible to gain access to a product so conceived; rules of responsibility, reflecting the interrelational structure in which they flourish, become internalized: their procedure and their truth is only to themselves and to the enclosed world that constructs them, sealing them off from any wider ethical matrix. The notion that material experience explains the immaterial and vice versa allows no final discrimination between the two, save for the purposes of lexical convenience, but predicates an interlocking system that provides no access extraneous to its own terms. For Emerson, 'nature is always self-similar', constituted by its 'grand rhymes or returns', which focus the strategy of idealist discourse where nothing is recognized as having a beginning or, by extension, an end. For a certain kind of temperament, such a view would instigate the free play of 'open field' writing; for another, a prime means of disguising control. Emerson's 'grand rhymes' inscribed a particular ethical system whereby 'The laws of moral nature answer to those of matter as face to face in a glass' and the 'axioms of physics translate the laws of ethics'. The harmony expressed by this function of translation was that which ensured a consequent basis of morality for language itself; language's corruption was inevitably emblematic of societal corruption. Nowhere is the self-sealing inwardness of correspondence more clearly revealed than here where ethics, and all its attendant problems of authority and responsibility, becomes a matter of reflective translation, of repetition through the lexicographies of different discourses. Neither of these discourses displays any discernible priority of the one over the other; Emerson's equation of mimesis is one of equality, not of hierarchy, and so language itself functions as a further repetition of repetition.

The act of metaphor that deciphers a world conceived as correspondence follows this pattern of self-reflecting repetitions by proclaiming simultaneously that all natural facts are symbols of spiritual facts and that all spiritual facts are represented by natural symbols. By its very nature, metaphor is a defiance of the literal; it avowedly instigates further supplementation (paradoxically, the literal reading of metaphor may lead not only to absurdity but to myth which is, of course, the prime example of a mode of expression that disinherits its origin by evincing no authorship). It has to rely on a theory of correspondence to save it from sheer nonsense, but its special ambition for originality, for novelty, means that its own rules of procedure are peculiar only to itself; they can seek justification or truth from no other system external to the particular analogy being offered. As a one-off act, metaphor insists on its divorce from any larger scheme of things and thus implicitly displays the contradiction of correspondence theory; its rules can be sought only within and it can, in practice, draw attention to nothing but its own procedure which, by its disguising of its origins (and hence its mode of control), is mysterious: as Eliot remarked, the hallmark of a good metaphor is its concealment of divisions between categories.

An epistemology of correspondence demands above all an idea of centre, be it divine intelligence or the principle of unity (order, control) itself, and, as Derrida has argued, any ideology of the centre is invariably a surrogate for something else, just as metaphor is an act of displacement whose concern is to suggest a new centre in order to fill the void which (we are told) nature abhors. The argument for centre advertises itself as an argument for balance, for a system of potentially damaging or painful oppositions which the proposed centre holds in equilibrium, thereby anaesthetizing the damage or pain of their actual clash and presenting itself as a means for maintaining order. As the making of analogies within a system of correspondence proceeds from an assumption of unity, which is usually hidden in that we cannot trace the origins of its coherence, so metaphor insists on its coherence by minimizing the difference between the *explanans* and the *explanandum*, the signified and the signifier. The adjustments of metaphor are designed to predicate symmetry; the continuity that metaphor proposes relies on a something behind itself, as it were, some mysterious and invisible force of coherence. Now, the Whitmanian catalogue and the Fenollosan ideogram rely exactly on such force as a salvation from chaos, and Pound's 'sufficient phalanx of particulars' has meaning only through a presumed anterior matrix of ideas or community of interest by which its reductive, economical suggestions, its discrete items of 'luminous detail', may be restored to plenitude, fleshed out again. In this sense, the catalogue, the ideogram and the 'sufficient phalanx' (the major constituents of Pound's modernism) share the epistemology of metaphor; they stand in place of their full range of meaning, and their act of reduction, the economical cipher of their range, removes its fullness from us and makes its reconstruction possible only according to the rules of their reduction itself, their own terms of restriction.

For Emerson, Whitman, Fenollosa and Pound, proposed origins of the 'real' are always offered as accessible through the items of the ordinary world as we see them, accessible through the language of everyday things that Ford demanded, the lexicography of the naturalistic novel. But this access has its own contradictions: Flaubert taught Maupassant to describe the events of ordinary life in ordinary language, but the function of that language was to differentiate, to ensure that Flaubert would not mistake one concierge, or one horse, for a neighbouring concierge or horse. Just as Joycean epiphany sought revelation through the grittily itemized particular, so the language of ordinary things was meaningful only in its capacity to suggest both differences *and* a shared, available world, and also its further suggestion of a hidden metaphysic of choice for such language – that it incorporated a larger truth which was not evident to the immediate senses. This contradiction is that of Emerson's enterprise, of the titles of two famous essays, 'Self-Reliance' and 'The Over-Soul'. The way to the truth of universal unity, the 'over-soul', is by an insistence on the reliance of the self to the extent that it becomes alienated from the commonly shared concerns of society. While the 'over-soul' seeks the unity 'within which every man's particular being is contained and made one with all other', the universal beauty which is manifest in the fact that 'the act of seeing and the thing seen, the seer and the spectacle, the subject and the object are one', the practice of 'the transcendentalist' involves divorce from the world of action, since he who has the habit of 'self-reliance' denies history and 'cannot be happy and strong until he too lives with nature in the present, above time, puts off all external support and stands alone'. Metaphor's value in seeing things afresh each time, its organic vitality as opposed to the fixity imposed by the mediating functions of institutions, thus carries a burden of wholesale isolation, the isolation of the opaque sphere that Eliot took from F. H. Bradley, the 'circle closed on the outside', whose privacy matches the isolation of *The Waste Land* itself by its privileged access to past literatures (in that both resist real history and both aim to inhabit an idealist world as a resistance to the contingencies of the present), a gesture that, paradoxically, circumscribes correspondence's myth of an 'objective correlative' for the psyche which sought such access in the first place.

Two further points should be noted here. At the domestic level of biography, we may remember the atmosphere of the household in which Henry James grew up, an atmosphere of almost unlimited freedom instigated by the vehement anti-puritanism of Henry James Sr and his Swedenborgian refusal of the material world's imposition upon the individual. A belief in universal personality and in salvation through a release from materialism extended to the prohibition of remunerative employment for his family. Ideally, of course, this was all very well, but it had the effect of rendering his children curiously unfit for the world at large: Alice suffered a nervous breakdown at the age of nineteen and until her death was almost wholly bedridden through hypochondria, while it was not until the age of thirty that William managed to escape into the limited freedom of a job. The domestic crisis of unlimited freedom, the subject of so much of Henry's fiction, was emblematic of the wider crisis in which an absence of limit resulted in an absence of any framework in which that freedom could be meaningfully used. This particular mode of amorphousness, of dissolution, was reflected in transcendentalist notions of language: we are dealing not with any system of archetypes, of the natural merely offering a flawed copy of the supernatural, but with a system in which the two deeply interpenetrate. As transcendentalist science so clearly testifies, the spiritual is *in* the world, not inhabiting some mystical bubble above it.

In 'Spring', the penultimate chapter of *Walden*, where Thoreau evinces most explicitly his Emersonian leanings, there is a famous description of the movement of a sandbank literally melting into the life of a new year. Thoreau's description relies primarily on actions of flowing and merging, the sand 'exhibiting a sort of hybrid product, which obeys half way the laws of currents, and half way that of vegetation'. He insists on the 'hybrid' forms produced by the flow of this 'grotesque vegetation' (a sort of prior vegetation, 'architectural foliage more ancient and typical than acanthus, chicory, ivy, vine, or any vegetable leaves'), which suggests a variety of confusing shapes:

> As it flows it takes the forms of sappy leaves or vines, making heaps of pulpy sprays a foot or more in depth, and resembling, as you look down on them, the lacinated, lobed, and imbricated thalluses of some lichens; or you are reminded of coral, of leopards' paws or birds' feet, of brains or lungs or bowels, and excrements of all kinds.

The shapes that Thoreau sees move from the crystalline specificity of coral to the amorphousness of excrement, shapes that ultimately become lost altogether in the stream at the foot of the sandbank. This experience affects Thoreau 'as if in a peculiar sense I stood in the laboratory of the Artist who made the world and me', and this impression instigates a particular analogy: 'I feel as if I were nearer to the vitals of the globe, for this sandy over-flow is something such a foliaceous mass as the vitals of the animal body.' In his analogy Thoreau defines the vegetable leaf anticipated in the flow of sand as a shape for life itself ('No wonder that the earth expresses itself outwardly in leaves, it so labours with the idea inwardly. The atoms have already learned this law, and are pregnant by it') and as a determinant for language:

> The overhanging leaf sees here its prototype. *Internally*, whether in the globe or animal body, it is a moist thick *lobe*, a word especially applicable to the liver and lungs and the *leaves* of fat (λείβω, *labor*, *lapsus*, to flow or slip downward, a lapsing; λοβός, *globus*, lobe, globe; also lap, flap, and many other words); *externally* a dry thin *leaf*, even as the *f* and *v* are a pressed and dried *b*. The radicals of *lobe* are *lb*, the soft mass of the *b* (single-lobed, or B, double-lobed), with the liquid *l* behind it pressing it forward. In globe, *glb*, the guttural *g* adds to the meaning the capacity of the throat.

Words themselves thus partake of nature's characteristics and can share nature's liquidity, a flow towards absolute dissolution, as 'lobe' is constituted wholly by 'o' figures (the 'l' is only a pure vertical in print; in script it partakes of the organic roundness of its succeeding characters, 'o' 'b' and 'e'), figures that in another discourse suggest both nothingness and, when joined together in a 'double-lobe', infinity.[97] For Thoreau, this is how language appropriates the world; and it is a mysterious process, a 'hieroglyphic' whose mystery, compounded by its liquidity (which both suggests and then dissolves shape), circumscribes its urge for concealed control. The special quality of this 'hieroglyphic' – it is 'somewhat excrementitious in its character, and there is no end to the heaps of liver, lights, and bowels' – is non-social in the most obvious sense, and Thoreau, revealingly, attempts to anaesthetize that sense by suggesting it as evidence for a belief that 'Nature has some bowels, and there again is mother of humanity'. This is the final product of a philosophy of correspondence sustained by a view of science that dissolves 'the solid seeming block of matter' and of man as self-reliant: the dissolution of language in order to maintain mysterious orders of control, disguised by the 'hieroglyphic', the sacred and secret symbol, that nature thus becomes. It is not fortuitous that an Emersonian care for the health of language coincided with, in Thoreau's version, an excremental dissolution of language, its liquifying of the material, and that the modernism of Pound and Joyce, as I suggested earlier, while maintaining the antisepsis of the serious writer, incorporated exactly such excremental liquidity.

4 The vortex: shapes ancient and modern

> The worlds come into being thus. There were borne along by 'abscision from the infinite' many bodies of all sorts of figures 'into a mighty void', and they being gathered together produce a single vortex. (Leukippos)

> In an incompressible frictionless fluid rotatory movement can neither originate nor disappear; the vorticity . . . then is an unchangeable quantity . . . the vortex rings have perpetuity.
> (J. G. McKendrick, *H. L. F. von Helmholtz*)

Talk of the gods

Wyndham Lewis's 'Composition' (1913) was characterized by a fierce abstraction in its distribution of mathematical shapes, which had been closely anticipated by the designs in his *Timon* sequence of the previous year. By comparison, however, the designs in *Timon* were far more naturalistic and owed their impulse in part to the cave-paintings discovered at Lascaux in 1897, which in turn were used by contemporary anthropologists to sustain a view of the totality evinced by primitive anthropomorphism. Much later, Lewis described the composition of vorticist design as 'a mental-emotive impulse – and by this is meant subjective intellection, like magic or religion'. He was implying that the energy of vorticism belonged to that of these ancient paintings, the energy of a mystical correspondence between the gods, nature and man. This shared impulse was possible because for the modernist temperament that very energy was currently substantiated by science, which had revealed the world as a series of vibrations of varying kinds; energy had simply shifted its vocabulary. When Pound wrote of *Timon* that it perfectly reflected the contemporary age, he was not referring to the deceptively machine-like appearance of Lewis's designs, not the 'accelerated grimace' of the Mauberleyan age, but to the system of energy that science shared with primitive 'magic or religion', the gods and immaterial forces that were being redescribed by contemporary physics. As Hugh Kenner has insisted, it was no accident that Eliot, after visiting the cave-paintings himself, prior to writing 'Tradition and the Individual Talent', discerned in Lewis 'the thought of the modern and the energy of the cave-man'. It was also no accident that 1912–13 marked the first peak of Pound's efforts to assimilate the formulae of science to the mysticism of the pagan and medieval worlds. The excessive abstraction of Lewis's 'Composition', its advance from *Timon*, suggests above all this shift in vocabulary for describing the gods, the vibrations disclosed by science. At the same time, however, a mode of naturalism remained necessary for the camerawork of Alvin Langdon Coburn. This was a naturalism in which ideas of science played a more visible role; the *Octopus* of 1912, for example, was composed to reveal a 'beauty of design displayed by the microscope' and took as its subject the amoeba-like paths of Central Park. These paths, visualized as a cell under a microscopic lens, thus in a sense naturalized the formal landscape of the park, but the composition did not allow such unproblematical tensions to remain. As the perfected artifice of Yeats's golden bird was to be disturbed by the anarchy of felt life, so Coburn's photograph held a hint of human intrusion across its top; and it was dominated by the immense shadow of another artefact, a skyscraper, which filled virtually all of the left-hand side as (to continue the metaphor of microscopic vision) a scalpel poised to dissect. Such conjunctions resisted the possibility of an organized completeness; like Kandinsky's exercises, the photograph recognized the awkwardness of the conjunction between the organic and the hard edge, the awkwardness to which Pound testified at the end of his diagnosis of his London years, *Hugh Selwyn Mauberley*: 'Beneath half-watt rays, / The eyes turn topaz.' These perceptions, like the Virgin and the Dynamo of Henry Adams, existed within a tensile relationship as a means of exploration and struggle, not as a means of complete definition.

Pound adopted analogies from electromagnetism to explain the 'unofficial mysticism' of Provence in 'Psychology and Troubadours' (1912). The reader's attention is drawn to the linguistic shifts that organized his explanation; having posed the question of this mysticism, Pound immediately deconstructed it into another, more famous form: 'I believe in a sort of permanent basis in humanity, that is to say, I believe that Greek myth arose when someone having passed through delightful psychic experience tried to communicate it to others and found it necessary to screen himself from persecution.' Commentators have rightly attended to the notion of 'delightful psychic experience' but have usually ignored its coda, the possibility of 'persecution' as its consequence. This form of experience entered the world as 'myth', as a mode of fiction, but its primary reality was never in doubt:

> Certain it is that these myths are only intelligible in a vivid glittering sense to those people to whom they occur. I know, I mean, one man who understands Persephone and Demeter, and one who understands the Laurel, and another who has, I should say, met Artemis. These things are for them *real*.[1]

As Pound's 1915 essay on Arnold Dolmetsch testified,[2] he was concerned throughout his early years in London with a 'persecution' that took the form of mockery at all his talk of the 'gods' or consisted in simply calling him a liar. 'Masks', a poem from his first volume of 1908, shows this concern:

> These tales of old disguisings, are they not
> Strange myths of souls that found themselves among
> Unwonted folk that spake an hostile tongue . . .[3]

The problem, again, was that of the translation required by modernity: of finding an available lexicon for experience that was seemingly arcane and certainly private and communicatively unintelligible; of sustaining a public, and publishable, status for the myths of psychic or mystic phenomena. The truth of these myths was the truth of their 'permanent basis in humanity' which Pound celebrated lyrically in 'Und Drang', the sequence of poems that concluded the *Canzoni* of 1911; section VIII, 'The Flame', attested to the presence of 'gods':

> There *is* the subtler music, the clear light
> Where time burns back about th' eternal embers.
> We are not shut from all the thousand heavens:
> Lo, there are many gods whom we have seen,

Folks of unearthly fashion, places splendid,
Bulwarks of beryl and of chrysoprase.

But Pound was acutely aware of the impossibility of 'Bulwarks of beryl and of chrysoprase' for articulating such a belief; within the shifts of voice that characterized the sequence, Pound offered, in section XI, 'Au Salon', an alternative version:

I suppose, when poetry comes down to facts,
When our souls are returned to the gods and the spheres they
   belong in,
Here in the every-day where our acts
Rise up and judge us . . .[4]

Pound's shifts here from the tone of the 1890s to that of his own day mimed exactly the struggle for modernity of diction, the lesson of Ford Madox Ford. When Pound proposed in 1910 that 'Poetry is a sort of inspired mathematics', instigating certain equations for human emotions, he noted: 'If one have a mind which inclines to magic rather than to science, one will prefer to speak of these equations as spells or incantations; it sounds more arcane, mysterious, recondite.' These antitheses matched in an important sense the antitheses of tone in the 'Und Drang' sequence; Pound used them as a prelude to distinguishing between the 'floridity' of Apuleius' 'Golden Ass' and the prose clarity of Ovid's 'Metamorphoses': while both wrote of 'wonders, and transformations, and of things supernatural', Ovid, 'urbane, sceptical, a Roman of the city', produced not 'florid prose' but 'verse which has the clarity of French scientific prose'. Ovid's style resulted in a radically different way of talking about the 'gods' where we have not the 'oriental quality' of Apuleius, 'analogous to the superficial decorations of Byzantine architecture', but the plausible clarity of 'Convenit esse deos et ergo esse credemus', which Pound glossed:

'It is convenient to have Gods, and therefore we believe they exist,' says the sophisticated Naso; and with all pretence of scientific accuracy he ushers in his gods, demigods, monsters and transformations. His mind, trained to the system of empire, demands the definite. The sceptical age hungers after the definite, after something it can pretend to believe. The marvellous thing is made plausible, the gods are humanized, their annals are written as if copied from a parish register; the heroes might have been acquaintances of the author's father.

In other words, Ovid's tone was that of a naturalistic novelist with an eye for detail; Pound, with a similar Joycean eye, chose for his illustration Ovid's account of the mechanically minded Daedalus:

> Thus: in Crete, in the reign of Minos, to take a definite instance, Daedalus is constructing the first monoplane, and 'the boy Icarus laughing, snatches at the feathers which are fluttering in the stray breeze, pokes soft the yellow wax with his thumb, and with his play hinders the wonderful work of his father.'
> A few lines further on Ovid writes in witness of Daedalus's skill as a mechanic, that it was he who, observing the backbone of a fish, invented the first saw; it might be the incident of Newton and the apple. On the whole there is nothing that need excite our incredulity. The inventor of the saw invents an aeroplane.[5]

Pound, also the inhabitant of a 'sceptical age', found such practicality and such plain words essential to his own discourse, if he was to make the 'gods' and psychic experience plausible. His *Ripostes* of 1912 began with 'Silet', where the sturdy plainness of 'It is enough that we once came together' translated the mannered beauty of 'Ballatetta' from the *Canzoni* of the previous year, 'Lo, how the light doth melt us into song'.[6] The linguistic shifts of 'Psychology and Troubadours' inscribe these efforts to seek a public voice; Pound's explanation of the 'unofficial mysticism' of Provence translated the language of Aristotelianism, of 'cosmic consciousness' ('the universe of fluid force', the 'phantastikon' and the 'germinal') into the language of contemporary physics ('the common electric machine' and the 'wireless telegraph receiver').

It was not fortuitous that 'Psychology and Troubadours' was first published in G. R. S. Mead's *Quest*, a journal devoted to the explication of psychic and mystic phenomena. In his excellent discussion of this essay, Herbert Schneidau has noted:

> Pound was aware of a long occult tradition behind the idea of mind he employed there. This tradition was probably outlined for him by Mead, who was gathering material that was to appear in his *Doctrine of the Subtle Body in Western Tradition*. This work summarizes ancient conceptions of the *sensorium*, a per-

ceptive apparatus not limited to the gross physical body nor severed from it, but extending outward from it into the 'vital universe'. Mead tries to find a common ground for ancient and modern postulations of an 'intimate correspondence between man's psychical and sensible apparatus, or his inner embodiment, and the subtle nature of the universe.'

Schneidau is interested in the 'sexual mysticism' of 'Psychology and Troubadours' in order to elaborate 'Pound's own version of "Unity of Being"' and to argue for a temperament of 'exteriorized sensibilities' as a full response to the 'Upwardian conception of a universe full of vital forces'.[7] Schneidau's argument seems to me to be absolutely right, but it misses out the *struggle* to maintain for the modern world the value of mystical perception, the struggle that is everywhere revealed in Pound's urge towards analogies from science to clarify and make plausible that perception. Pound's programme was for a vocabulary, not for conveying ideas, but for making 'a language to think in',[8] and, as *Hugh Selwyn Mauberley* so clearly shows,[9] it was not as easy as Schneidau implicitly assumes. Schneidau rightly insists on the tone of Pound's voice, the solidity of his mysticism, which was rooted not only in science but in medieval precision:

> The important point to be made is that Pound does not think of mysticism, such as he finds in the Troubadours, as bodiless transmission of vague visions. He wrote of such cultists that for them 'ecstasy is not a whirl or a madness of the senses, but a glow arising from the exact nature of the perception'. Even of mystic visions Pound predicated exactness, precision, definition as the life-giving component. It was in this essay ['Psychology and Troubadours'] that Pound proclaimed that 'hyper-scientific precision' *alone* gives any matter 'immortality'. . . . The great example is clearly Dante: 'Dante's precision both in the *Vita Nuova* and the *Commedia* comes from the attempt to reproduce exactly the thing which has been clearly seen. The "Lord of terrible aspect" is no abstraction, no figure of speech.' Pound's comments on the Middle Ages ceaselessly reiterate that they teach a lesson of precision.[10]

While Schneidau is concerned predominantly with the ideas of Pound's mysticism, its substantiation and its 'reality' through its connections with the more familiar areas of Pound's thought, I am interested in the lexicon of that mysticism, its place in Pound's linguistic experiments and the contexts of the vocabulary he chose for giving modernity to mysticism. Certainly, Schneidau's suggestion of Mead takes us in the right direction.

The Doctrine of the Subtle Body (1919) was Mead's account of the doctrine as used by the later Platonists.[11] His opening sentence summarized the doctrine and noted its antiquity: 'The notion that the physical body of man is as it were the exteriorization of the invisible subtle embodiment of the life of the mind is a very ancient belief.' The purpose of the book was the defence and explication of this belief against 'the prevailing habit of the sceptical rationalism of the present day to dismiss summarily all such beliefs of antiquity as the baseless dreams of a pre-scientific age, and to dump them all indiscriminately into the midden of exploded superstitions.' Here, exactly, was Pound's problem: in what language was the value of supposedly 'pre-scientific' perception to be presented to the scepticism of modernity? As I shall demonstrate more fully in my discussion of 'tradition', part of the answer lay in what was a contemporary version of 'unity of being' which relied heavily on the increasingly interrelated nature of scientific research; Mead's programme for giving legitimacy to the 'exploded superstitions' of mysticism claimed:

It is beginning to be seen on all sides that the physical, the biological and the psychological activities of man as a unitary reality are so intimately interblended, that no arbitrary selection of any one of these stand-points can provide a satisfactory solution to the nature of the concrete whole which human personality presents.

The relational nature of the world exhibited by the different disciplines of science emphasized one crucial postulate: 'It is now a general persuasion in scientific circles that the static conception of matter, which once reigned supreme, explains nothing. Physical nature is found to be dynamic through and through.' A view of the world as a series of forces was what made possible the use of science to claim 'reality' for the mystical temperament by Mead and by the transcendentalist leanings of Pound. This view also removed Mead's argument from the familiar domain of the materialist/idealist, mind/body problem; with the aid of physics, he made an essential distinction:

> We are dealing with what invariably purports to be a corporeal entity, and not with the soul proper, much less with the mind. . . . Man's subtle body is of the material order, but of a more dynamic nature than his physically sensible frame. It pertains to the normally invisible. Nevertheless, the latest concepts of modern physics come in as a potent aid in elucidating the most enlightened ancient notions on the subject.

It was this special notion of materiality that physics elucidated, in order to displace the primitivist notion of the 'subtle body' as 'a thin replica of the gross body, as a diaphanous double of the dense frame' that was available to the physical senses; its 'fundamental constitution' was of 'a dynamic system of energy', conceived in the manner in which 'we are now being taught to regard the under-work of all natural objects by the ever more assured results of electronic analysis', and thus 'we have the advantage today of basing this ancient hypothesis on the demonstrated concrete facts of positive physical scientific research'.[12] Mead also defined the 'subtle body' in terms familiar to Pound from his reading in medieval philosophy and poetry, seeing it as 'the very soul' of astrology and alchemy in that it incorporated notions of 'an intimate correspondence between man's physical and sensible apparatus, or his inner embodiment, and the subtle nature of the universe' whereby man's nature was conceived as 'a germ or seed as it were of the universal tree of life'. This is very much the vocabulary of cosmic consciousness which Pound explicated in 'Psychology and Troubadours' and which instigated for Mead a model of alchemy as a ritual expression of psychic progress, 'a ladder of ascent from earth to the light-world' that led finally to 'man's perfection in spiritual reality', a 'bringing to birth of man's perfected subtle body'.[13]

Pound's essay, as I suggested earlier, combined the discourses of alchemy, cosmic consciousness and electromagnetism to sustain his view of the tensile and sexual mysticism of Provence. In Mead's discussion of Origen's treatise on the spiritual view of the Resurrection, we find an important gloss on Pound's view. Origen's belief in 'a real *continuum* of individuality, a substantial ground of personal identity', was distinct from the materialist view of the Resurrection (propounded by 'flesh-lovers') and that which asserted the resurrection-body to be 'of a purely phantasmal nature'. He explicated this *continuum* thus: 'Hidden in the seed of the tree is the principle (*ratio*, *logos*) of the tree. This is the formative power (*virtus*, *dynamis*) in the seed, the spermatic principle, which is called symbolically in Greek *Spinthērismos*.' These are familiar Poundian terms, although he never conflated *logos* (which he saw as 'germinal' consciousness) and *virtus* as fully as did Mead. Mead's conflation of the two as '*Spinthērismos*' was the 'spermatic principle' that Pound was to elaborate in his Postscript to Gourmont's *Natural Philosophy of Love* (published some two years after Mead's book), but here Mead's context was directly relevant for the translations of 'Psychology and Troubadours':

> What the precise meaning of the last term may be is difficult to say, for the lexicons are silent. It means, literally, 'emission of sparks', 'sparkling'.
> 'Light-spark', or 'light-emanation', as is well known, is used by a number of Gnostic schools as a symbolic expression for the 'germ' of the spiritual man.

The movement of Mead's explanation thus paralleled that of Pound, proceeding from the principle of '*logos*' ('the thought of the tree is in the seed', in Pound's formulation) to the 'Light-spark' (in Pound, the 'charged surface' between the two poles of electrical/sexual transmission). Origen's use of '*Spinthērismos*' ('the invisible principle of the visible seed') sustained Mead's notion of a special order of materiality for the 'subtle body', for:

> It seems to be conceived of as a 'substantial' something; for in it, in the case of human bodies developed from this germinal ground, is said to inhere the immemorial principles of resurrection.
> It is likened to the innermost part or 'pith' of plants; and is called by Origen, in the case of man, the 'nursery' or 'seed-plot' (*seminarium*) of the dead.[14]

Macrocosmic forms

The syntheses of discourse elaborated by Mead to discuss the doctrine of the 'subtle body' displayed concisely the areas of activity that informed the modernist lexicon. In the same year that Pound chose the analogy of the telegraph's 'charged surface' for the tensile 'chivalric' temperament in 'Psychology and Troubadours', he constructed what he coyly termed a 'cumbersome simile' to describe 'the masterly use of words':

> Let us imagine that words are like great hollow cones of steel of different dullness and acuteness. . . . Let us imagine them charged with a force like electricity, or, rather, radiating a force from their apex – some radiating, some sucking in. We must have a greater variety of activity than with electricity – not merely positive and negative; but let us say +, ÷, ×, −, +a, −a, ×a, ÷a etc. Some of these kinds of force neutralize each other, some augment; but the only way any two cones can be got to act without waste is for them to be so placed that their apexes and a line of surface meet exactly. When this conjunction occurs let us say their force is not added one's to the other's, but multiplied the one's by the other's; thus three or four words in exact juxtaposition are capable of radiating this energy at a very high potentiality; mind you, the juxtaposition of their vertices must be exact and the angles or 'signs' of discharge must augment and not neutralize each other.

Pound's analogy indicated a far more complex activity than that of the bipartite system of opposites (north and south, sun and moon) he used to explain the Provençal sensibility. The simile was designed to express not simply the general energy of words and their interactive suggestiveness but a particular mode of force: 'This peculiar energy which fills the cones is the power of tradition, of centuries of race-consciousness, of agreement, of association.'[15] It belonged to Pound's increasing use of the idea of a confluence of forces to describe both the activities of words and their historicity prior to his acquaintance with the work of Fenollosa; it belonged to the same order of language as those other famous similes from electromagnetism that Pound adopted during the next two years, the 'rose in the steel dust' and the 'vortex' itself. In all cases, they were a mode of translation and of revitalization; as he had renewed the sexual mysticism of Provence through his analogy from the telegraph, so in the notion of the 'vortex' did he find ancient cosmology, in the form of pre-Socratic atomism, elucidated and made new by nineteenth-century field-theory physics, that branch of science which sought to examine the areas wherein the exchange of forces took place.

Pound first used the word 'vortex' in 'Plotinus', a poem collected in his *A Lume Spento* of 1908, where he anticipated his later simile of the 'cone': 'As one that would draw through the node of things, / Back sweeping to the vortex of the cone, / . . . / I was an atom on creation's throne'.[16] This was a 'pre-scientific' use of the word, derived from Pound's reading in philosophy, while his later, more famous use was explicitly informed by electromagnetic theory; the persistence of the word in these two forms illustrates the entire enterprise of Pound's reliance on scientific vocabulary. Timothy Materer has briefly suggested a source for Pound's 'pre-scientific' usage: John Burnet, *Early Greek Philosophy* (1892). He centres his argument on Burnet's account of atomist theory:

> Burnet writes of the early Greek thinkers who believed that the elements of water, earth, fire and air were formed as they whirled in a 'vortex'. The later Atomists also considered the vortex an ordering force, as Burnet demonstrates when he translates a passage concerning Leukippos: 'The worlds come into being thus. There were borne along by "abscision from the infinite" many bodies of all sorts of figures "into a mighty void", and they being gathered together produce a single vortex.'[17]

Materer's discussion is limited to 'Plotinus'; since (as he notes) classical scholars do not generally use the word 'vortex', his argument is worth expanding.[18]

We should note that, in John Burnet, Pound was responding to a distinctive temperament. I have found only one reference to Burnet in Pound's published work; it occurs in his discussion of Book VI of the *Nichomachean Ethics* in *Guide to Kulchur*: 'There seems to be a good deal of commentative superstructure, all quite intelligent. "Definitions are the first principles of science." Rackham, Burnet here taking arms against a sea of stupidities.'[19] Pound was thinking primarily of Rackham; it was Rackham's commentary that he used throughout his discussion of Aristotle, but it is significant that he included Burnet as part of a quasi-scientific approach, since Burnet's temperament may best be seen in his account of the transition from the primitivist cosmology of Thales to the more 'scientific' approach of the Ionian school and, further, since this account was constructed in reaction to the methods offered by other commentators:

What, then, was the step that placed the Ionian cosmologists once for all above the level of the Maoris? Grote and Zeller make it consist in the substitution of impersonal causes acting according to law for personal causes acting arbitrarily. But the distinction between personal and impersonal was not really felt in antiquity. . . . It seems rather that the real advance made by the scientific men of Miletos was that they left off telling tales. They gave up the hopeless task of describing what was when as yet there was nothing, and asked instead what all things really are now.[20]

The importance of Burnet's substitution is clear; he was not only acknowledging an advance by the 'scientific' mind but also replacing the abstractions of scholars like Grote and Zeller with the concrete simplicity of the observation that the Miletians 'left off telling tales', a simplicity further enhanced by a sense of a more accurate scholarship that could actually touch, as it were, the period: 'the distinction between personal and impersonal was not really felt in antiquity.' Here was an order of the real matched by Ovid's superiority over Apuleius, Schliemann's excavation of Troy and indeed the whole burden of the naturalistic novel carried by the 'scientific prose' of Flaubert and Joyce. It was also that order of the real available to Pound in the Allen Upward who asked 'When is the good not good?' and answered 'When it is an abstract noun', who disrupted 'the old cloistered scholarship' which had 'toiled to understand the word "*glaukopis*" given to the goddess Athene' by pointing out that 'they had not only the word glaux staring them in the face, but they had the owl itself cut at the foot of every statue of Athene and stamped on every coin of Athens, to tell them that she was the owl-eyed goddess, the lightning that blinks like an owl', and sustaining his point with a novelist's detail: 'what is characteristic of the owl's eyes is not that they glare, but that they suddenly leave off glaring like lighthouses whose light is shut off. We may see the shutter of the lightning in the mask that overhangs Athene's brow and hear its click in the word glaukos.' Upward chose to describe *glaukopis* not only to make a point against conventional scholarship but to explicate the lexical problems ('Did it mean blue-eyed or grey-eyed, or – by the aid of Sanskrit – merely glare-eyed?') attached to anthropological accounts of myths:

The old talk about the Gods, which is called mythology, is confused in many ways, partly because all language is confused,
partly because it is a layer of many languages. When the talkers
no longer used the beast as an idol, they used it as a symbol, in
short a word; when they no longer slew the real Christ at Easter
they named the sun at Easter, Christ. Their language is tangled
and twisted beyond our power wholly to unravel because it was
beyond their power; because it began as a tangle when man's
mind was still a blur, and he saw men as trees walking, and trees
as men standing still.[21]

Upward's concern with the stories that myths told and with the
ways in which they were used is paralleled in Burnet's account of
the demise of stories and the consequent rise of empirical science in
the Greek world, a science that would do away with the confusions
of the 'tangled and twisted' language of myth. To substantiate his
thesis that this change in ways of looking at the world began when
the Greeks 'left off telling tales', Burnet put forward the lexicon of
the real as one of the possible causes of that change:

Foremost among these [causes] was undoubtedly the widening of
the Greek horizon occasioned by the great extension of maritime
enterprise which followed the decay of the Phoenician naval
supremacy. The scene of the old stories had, as a rule, been laid
just outside the boundaries of the world known to the men who
believed them. Odysseus does not meet with Kirke or the
Kyklops or the Sirens in the familiar Aegean, but in regions
which lay beyond the ken of the Greeks at the time the Odyssey
was composed. Now, however, the West was beginning to be
familiar too, and the fancy of the Greek explorers led them to
identify the lands which they discovered with the places which
the hero of the national fairytale had come to in his wanderings.
It was soon discovered that the monstrous beings in question
were no longer to be found there, and the belief grew up that they
never had been there at all.

Burnet was not simply describing a theoretical *Weltanschauung*; as
Upward was to substitute the sturdily empirical details of *glaukopis*
for the bloodless philology of the scholars, so Burnet, after the
excavations at Troy and five years prior to Butler's *The Authoress*

of the Odyssey, substituted for the abstractions of Grote and Zeller the 'luminous detail' of the Atlas story:

> According to the primitive view, the heavens were supported by a giant called Atlas. No one had even seen him, though he was supposed to live in Arkadia. The Phokaian explorers identified him with a cloud-capped mountain in Africa, and once they had done this, the old belief was doomed. It was impossible to go on believing in a god who was also a mountain, conveniently situated for a trader to steer by, as he sailed to Tarshish in quest of silver.[22]

One consequence of this mode of reading was Joyce's carefully (excessively so) detailed topography of Dublin; another was Pound's concern with the verity of myth as cognition, as a form of ritualizing perception during the linguistic crisis of 1911–15. That period culminated in the rhetoric of vorticism and matched the period when Rutherford and Bohr contributed to the new order of materiality by proposing an atomic model that combined theories of electromagnetism with those of matter; their model bore a significant visual relation to that of early Greek cosmology: 'Rutherford and Bohr conceived the atom, analogous to a planetary system, as a nucleus around which a number of electrons move in different orbits.'[23] Burnet's account showed how myth's claims on the real were disturbed by Ionian empiricism; for Pound, a different science, electromagnetism, was to provide myth with a recognizable public status. The use of myth was essentially a subjective means of establishing a relationship with the world; it marked, in a sense, a failure to objectify experience, to make experience communal. The problem was to render that subjectivity available, and Pound's answer was through the accessibility of contemporary physics. What helped in this immediate case was a specific continuity of ideas, the sharing of the concept of vortex motion by Burnet's version of pre-Socratic cosmology and by nineteenth-century field-theory physics.

Burnet's use of the word 'vortex' itself is confined to his discussion of Leukippos, 'the originator of atomic theory',[24] that Materer partially quotes, but his index lists under 'Vortex' two discussions of figures who preceded Leukippos; in both these discussions Burnet describes the activity of vortical motion without using the word itself. The first discussion concerns the cosmology of Empedokles:

The accumulation of fire in the upper hemisphere disturbs the equilibrium of the heavens and causes them to revolve; and this revolution not only produces the alternation of day and night, but by its rapidity keeps the heavens and the earth in their places. This was illustrated, Aristotle tells us [*De Caelo*, B13, 295 a16], by the simile of a cup of water whirled round at the end of a piece of string.

Burnet's second discussion describes Anaxagoras' theory of world formation:

The formation of a world starts with a rotary motion which Nous [Mind] imparts to a portion of the mixed mass in which 'all things are together' (fr 13), and this rotary motion gradually extends over a wider and wider space. Its rapidity (fr 9) produced a separation of the rare and the dense, the cold and the hot, the dark and the light, the moist and the dry (fr 15). This separation produces two great masses, the one consisting of the rare, hot, light and dry, called the 'Aether'; the other, in which the opposite qualities predominate, called 'Air' (fr 1). Of these the Aether or fire took the outside while the Air occupied the centre (fr 15).[25]

Both Empedokles and Anaxagoras offered essentially figurative, metaphysical cosmologies; Empedokles gave, avowedly, a simile to illustrate a principle of order, while Anaxagoras gave an abstraction, 'rotary motion', for a mind-orientated principle of separation. Admittedly Anaxagoras, demonstrating the empiricism of the Ionian school, marked an advance on the position of Empedokles, but, nevertheless, both accounts were ultimately teleological rather than scientific. By comparison, Leukippos' account of vortex motion was mechanical, a grittier version of Anaxagoras' argument that such motion was due to the action of 'Nous'. Leukippos was admired by Burnet for the physical, concrete nature of his thought, for giving, among other things 'a purely mechanical account of sensation'.[26] I would suggest that it was on the basis of this intellectual characteristic that Burnet used 'vortex' as a defining *word* rather than as a general activity to distinguish his account of Leukippos from his discussions of Empedokles and Anaxagoras; in Leukippos he discovered those qualities of exact empirical observation that displaced the metaphysics of previous thinkers, just as 'vortex' itself displaced the imprecise notions of revolving or rotary motion.

Here was more than a matter of language, for Leukippos demanded a further mode of solid specification. The question of space, the void, had traditionally provoked contention among pre-Socratic thinkers; for Leukippos, space had to be 'empty' for the movement of matter to be possible, but existent accounts of the nature of space were unsatisfactory for his theory of atomism, as Burnet explained:

> he had to assume the existence of empty space, which the Eleatics had denied in order to make his explanation of the nature of body possible. Here again he is developing a Pythagorean view. The Pythagoreans had spoken of the void, which kept the units apart; but they had not distinguished it from atmospheric air, which Empedokles had shown to be a corporeal substance. Parmenides, indeed, had formed a clearer conception of space, but only to deny its reality. Leukippos started from this.

The problem was this: how to assert the emptiness of something while simultaneously claiming its reality? Or, in terms of the Poundian problem, in what sense could mystical experience, 'empty' in the sense of potential 'nonsense', be also real in the function of its communal availability, lacking any observable sanction? Leukippos was unable to find a satisfactory answer (interestingly, as Burnet claimed, because he did not have access to the necessary vocabulary), but he did reconstruct the possibilities:

> He admitted, indeed, that space was not real, that is to say, corporeal; but he maintained that it existed all the same. He hardly, it is true, had words to express his discovery in; for the verb 'to be' had hitherto been used by philosophers only of body. But he did his best to make his meaning clear by saying that 'what is not' (in the old corporealist sense) 'is' (in another sense) just as much as 'what is'. The void is as real as the body.

This was partly the problem, particularly acute for Pound, of experience or knowledge that had yet to find its appropriate articulation; it was also the problem for the special mode of materiality that G. R. S. Mead sought to define for his notion of the 'subtle body'. For Burnet, this substanceless order of reality was particularly worthy of note in a thinker who was rigorously mechanistic and practical: 'It is a curious fact that the Atomists, who are commonly regarded as the great materialists of antiquity, were actually the first to say distinctly that a thing might be real without being a body.'[27] What Leukippos was in fact suggesting was an order of the material approaching that of the 'ether' so central to nineteenth-century field-theory physics, the branch of physics that, as we shall see, adopted as one of its principal tools another version of the vortex. It was also that branch of physics that provided the fuller account of Leukippos' non-corporeal reality in the form of electromagnetism; what else, for example, were Hertzian light-waves?

Burnet's use of the word 'vortex' itself in his account of Leukippos' theory of world formation warrants reprinting in full (rather than merely the introductory sentence Materer quotes), partly because of the extent of its reliance on vortex motion (and the rare extent of his use of the word itself) and partly because it suggests a further text in which Pound remembered Burnet:

The worlds came into being thus. There were borne along by 'abscision from the infinite' many bodies of all sorts of figures 'into a mighty void', and they being gathered together produce a single vortex. In it, as they came into collision with one another and were whirled round in all manner of ways, those which were alike were separated apart and came to their likes. But, as they were no longer able to revolve in equilibrium owing to their multitude, those of them that were fine went out to the external void as if passed through a sieve; the rest stayed together, and becoming entangled with one another, ran down together, and made a first spherical structure. This was in substance like a membrane or skin containing in itself all kinds of bodies. And, as these bodies were borne round in a vortex, in virtue of the resistance of the middle, the surrounding membrane became thin, as the contiguous bodies kept flowing together from contact with the vortex. And in this way the earth came into being, those things which had been towards the middle abiding there. Moreover, the containing membrane was increased by the further separating out of bodies from outside; and, being itself carried round in a vortex, it further got possession of all with which it had come in contact. Some of these becoming entangled, produce a structure, which was at first moist and muddy; but, when they had been dried and were revolving along with the vortex of the whole, they were then ignited and produced the substance of the heavenly bodies.

What is initially striking about this passage is the detail with which it observes a formation that is complexly interactive, resulting in a clear specificity to replace Anaxagoras' abstract principle of separation: 'it is only in the vortex that the atoms acquire weight and lightness. . . . Leukippos held that one effect of the vortex was that like atoms were brought together with their likes. . . . It is the finer atoms that are forced to the circumference, while the larger tend to the centre.' The detail of Leukippos' description was clearly puzzling to some commentators; Burnet felt it necessary to answer the charge that the 'vortex' was merely an impoverished substitute for 'centrifugal force' by which the heaviest substances would move furthest out from the centre, not the converse as Leukippos had claimed. Burnet's defence of the 'vortex' was a defence of the correct term, the accurate observation:

> We must remember that all the parts of the vortex are in contact, and that it is just this contact . . . by which the motion of the outermost parts is communicated to those within them. The larger bodies are more able to resist this communicated motion that the smaller, and in this way they make their way to the centre where the motion is least, and force the smaller bodies out. This resistance . . . is quite in accordance with this, that, on the atomist theory, the nearer a heavenly body is to the centre the slower is its revolution. There is no question of 'centrifugal force' at all, and the analogy of eddies in air and water is quite satisfactory.[28]

An insistence on the contact of all parts of the vortex to ensure communication of motion was in turn made by Pound's electromagnetic discussion of the 'masterly use of words'. It was such contact alone that precipitated the economical release of linguistic energy; 'the juxtaposition of their vertices must be exact, and the angles or "signs" of discharge must augment and not neutralize each other.'[29] The final sentence of Burnet's defence further proclaimed the accuracy of Leukippos' 'vortex' through the natural detail that first suggested the idea of vorticity, and he reiterated: 'we know from Aristotle that all those who accounted for the earth being in the centre of the world by means of a vortex appealed to the analogy of eddies in wind or water.'

The 'analogy of eddies in wind or water' defined the 'vortex' as an ordering device of a particular kind: the creation of order through an activity of separation. Leukippos had chosen a specific figure to illustrate this activity: 'those of them that were fine went out to the external void, as if passed through a sieve.' In 1914, the peak of the London Vortex, Burnet published *Greek Philosophy* where he reiterated Leukippos' 'vortex' and added another figure to that of the 'sieve', which further particularized the 'eddies in wind or water' and which had not appeared in his earlier treatise:

> The first effect of vortex motion . . . is to bring together those atoms which are alike in shape and size, and this is the origin of the four 'elements', fire, air, earth and water. The process was illustrated by the image of a sieve which brings the grains of millet, wheat, and barley together. . . . this image is found also in Plato's *Timaeus*. . . . Another image was that of the waves sorting the pebbles on a beach and heaping up long stones with long, and round with round.[30]

The conjunction of these two images, the sieve and the waves sorting the pebbles, suggests a further text in which Pound remembered Burnet: the poem that summarized the crises of Pound's early years in London, *Hugh Selwyn Mauberley*. In poem II of the 'Mauberley 1920' half of the sequence, Mauberley's 'sieve' is replaced by a 'seismograph';[31] his progression is from a valuable instrument of separation, selection and balance, sanctioned by Gourmont and Poincaré,[32] to a limited instrument of abstract measurement.[33] In the third poem of this half of the sequence, ' "The Age Demanded"', we have Mauberley 'delighted with the imaginary / Audition of the phantasmal sea-surge',[34] where 'phantasmal' operates not only as a complicated joke about modernist vocabulary[35] but also as a translation of the Homeric *poluphloisboio thalasses* which Pound later glossed as the 'scutter of receding pebbles'.[36] Not only does 'phantasmal' refer back to Burnet's citation of the vortical action of waves on pebbles as a device for organization, but as an act of Poundian translation it offers itself as a purely linguistic device for order; *poluphloisboio* is onomatopoeic, one of two qualities in Homer which for Pound remained 'untranslated',[37] and means literally 'any confused roaring noise': in Pound's Homeric source,

The Iliad at I.34, it is 'loud-resounding'. Pound's 'scutter of receding pebbles' is thus a lexical act of order, providing the particularity of the waves' action on pebbles for the amorphous, in any language, *poluphloisboio*.[38]

Burnet's *Greek Philosophy* made two further points, not included in *Early Greek Philosophy*, which seem to me to be relevant for Pound's position. Burnet upheld the empiricism of Leukippos' vortex theory by noting that it provoked a reaction against metaphysical cosmologies from those who believed in science as a practical discipline, based on 'experience and observation'; this reaction, claimed Burnet,

> came from specialists in the particular sciences, especially medicine, who disliked the sweeping generalizations of the cosmologists, and maintained the right of each science to deal with its own province. The Hippokratean treatise on *Ancient Medicine* (by which is meant the art of medicine based on experience and observation, as contrasted with the new-fangled medical theories of the school of Empedokles and others) is the best evidence of this.

And, while Burnet emphasized Leukippos' materialist bias, he did not impute any crude mechanicalism; he was eager to stress the influence of Pythagorean theory in which numbers were not to be considered as abstract but as having a capacity for creating form:

> the points of resemblance between Pythagoreanism and Atomism were already noted by Aristotle, and he had direct knowledge on the subject. 'Leukippos and Demokritos', he says, 'virtually make all things numbers too and produce them from numbers.' I do not see how this statement can have any meaning unless we regard the Pythagorean numbers as patterns or 'figurate numbers', and, in that case, it is still more striking that Demokritos called the atoms 'figures' or 'forms'.[39]

Pound, too, had an abiding interest in just this notion of numerology, the 'thrones and dominations' of analytical geometry that carried a potential for shaping experience. His most famous figure for the production of form was derived from observing an effect of electromagnetism, the 'rose in the steel-dust'; the patterning potential of electromagnetic energy was used as an analogy for the wider potential of energy in general, and its first occurrence was in 1913, in the very middle of the experimental period we have been discussing.[40] Its most immediate context was in contemporary physics, but we should remember that energy in all its forms always retained mystical properties for Pound; although quantifiable by science, it retained the signature of the 'gods', and the energy of electrical waves was to be seen not as a displacement of that mysticism but as a union of shared perceptions, as a testimony against the Bergsonian romanticism which divided the 'vital' and the 'mechanical'. Wyndham Lewis, in the 'Physiognomy of Our Time' section of *The Caliph's Design* (1919), gave a good summary of what this union meant for the modernist:

> Life, simply, however vivid and tangible, is too material to be anything but a mechanism, and the sea-gull is not far removed from the hydroplane. . . . I do not recommend any abstraction of our mental structure. No more definite unclothing than to strip till we come to the energetic lines is desirable . . . every living form is a miraculous mechanism, and every sanguinary, vicious or twisted need produces in Nature's workshop a series of mechanical gadgets extremely suggestive and interesting for the engineer, and almost invariably beautiful or interesting for the artist. . . . The rant around machinery is really, at bottom, adulation for the universe of creatures, and especially the world of insects. So the froth of a Futurist at the mere sight of a warplane or a tank is the same as a foaming ode to the dragonfly or the sea-gull; not for any super-mechanical attribute of the fly or the bird, but simply because one is a flying insect and the other a bird. And this all-inclusiveness of the direction of our thought is the result, primarily, of the all-inclusiveness of our knowledge.

Earlier, in 'A Review of Contemporary Art' (1914), Lewis made the simpler conjunction, pervasive in Pound and a determinant concept in vorticism, between the scientist and the seer of visions: 'The painters have cut away and cut away warily, till they have trapped some essential. European painting today is like the laboratory of an anatomist: things stand up stark and denuded everywhere as the result of endless visionary examinations.'[41]

Pound's 'rose in the steel-dust' received its fullest explication in the essay on 'Medievalism' which, although first published in 1928, was clearly an accumulative exercise, restating the argument of 'Psychology and Troubadours' and taking its impetus from the

complex of ideas that had formed his vorticist aesthetic. The essay
was a paean to what Pound called the 'medieval clean line', the
tensile clarity that he opposed to the Hellenic 'plastic moving towards coitus. . . . Plastic plus immediate satisfaction'; the Provençal
dogma that 'there is some proportion between the fine thing held in
the mind, and the inferior thing ready for instant consumption'.
There remained the problem of an appropriate vocabulary for this
aesthetic: 'The term metaphysic might be used if it were not so
appallingly associated in people's minds with unsupportable con-
jecture and devastated terms of abstraction.' To demonstrate that
'The Tuscan demands harmony in something more than the
plastic', he posited the 'interactive force' of the '*virtu*', the energy of
a sensory intelligence which moved beyond the plastic and which
invalidated 'the whole of monastic thought'. The vocabulary of
virtu was difficult; Pound was here somewhat fastidiously reluctant
to use a phrase such as 'the aesthetic or interactive vasomotor
magnetism is in relation to the consciousness' which, quite rightly,
he argued 'somewhat takes the bloom off the peach': it is, in any-
body's terms, a singularly ugly phrase whose awkwardness in no
way reflects his customary use of such analogies. He substituted a
traditional figure from sculpture, 'the god is inside the stone, *vacuos
exercet aera morsus*', again a component of the Mauberleyan
diagnosis, whereby 'shape occurs'. It was this energy that marked
the achievement of the medieval world prior to the 'carnal tissue' of
the sixteenth century, 'corpuscular', exhibiting 'a great deal of
meat' whose absorbency manifested no restraint and 'no longer the
body of air clothed in the body of fire'; an art form which 'no
longer radiates'. The loss of radiance was the loss of 'the Mediter-
ranean sanity' where 'one thought cuts through another with clean
edge', a world of 'moving energies' which displayed a special notion
of magnetism, 'magnetisms that take form, that are seen, or that
border the visible'. These were the energies and the magnetisms
constantly being revealed by contemporary science, but the discourse of science as it was customarily used, in Pound's eyes, failed
to account for their potential for creating 'forms', since it lacked the
innocence of the medieval perspective whereby such 'enchantments'
involved no disjunction with the real or the visible.[42] This was the
perspective celebrated by Pound in his Introduction to the 'Cavalcanti Poems' where *virtu* was seen to be analogous to radium, a
'spiritual chemistry' whose capacity for 'forms' was confirmed by

both modern mysticism and modern science. Here, the lady functioned as a 'magnet' for 'the invigorating forces of life and beauty'; she was conceived as a locus of the tensile energy that Pound was to define electromagnetically in 'Psychology and Troubadours' not as an 'object' but as 'the direction of a force'.[43]

The components of Pound's equation for *virtu*, the 'god inside the stone' and the forces of magnetism, were conjoined in exactly this way in a passage on Thales in Burnet's *Early Greek Philosophy*. Burnet transcribed Aristotle's précis of Thales' most famous argument: 'All things are full of gods. The magnet is alive; for it has the power of moving iron.'[44] This was in fact a compound of two separate propositions in Aristotle and a reversal of their order. In the Loeb translation we are given first: 'Thales, too, to judge from what is recorded of his views, seems to suppose that the soul is in a sense the cause of movement, since he says that a stone has a soul because it causes movement to iron' (*De anima*, A2, 405 a19); and second: 'Some think that the soul pervades the whole universe, whence perhaps came Thales' view that everything is full of gods' (*De anima*, A5, 411 a7). Aristotle argued for the absurdity of the doctrine, partly, one suspects, because of a too literal view of 'everything'. It was customary for Greek philosophers to substitute 'god' for the 'soul' and its energies; Plato, omitting Thales' detail of the magnetic stone, reiterated the notion that 'all things are full of gods':

> Concerning all the stars and the moon, and concerning the years and months and all seasons, what other account shall we give than this very same, – namely, that, inasmuch as it has been shown that they are all caused by one or more souls, which are good also with all goodness, we shall declare these souls to be gods, whether it be that they order the whole heaven by residing in bodies, as living creatures, or whatever the mode and method? Is there any man that agrees with this view who will stand hearing it denied that 'all things are full of gods'? (*Laws*, 10, 899B)

Burnet's conjunction and reversal of Aristotle's propositions gave them a connection they did not originally possess and brought them much closer to Pound's equation of magnetic energy and the 'god inside the stone'; the movement from Aristotle through Burnet to Pound is of an increasing proximity for initially separate statements. Most important of all, for Pound's discriminations between the 'medieval clean line', the Hellenic 'plastic moving towards coitus' and the 'carnal tissue' of the sixteenth century, Burnet insisted that the proposition 'all things are full of gods' did not entail the corollary, frequently assumed by commentators, that 'Thales attributed a "plastic life" to matter, or that he was a "hylozoist"'. It should not be construed as a dualistic understanding of things corporeal and incorporeal because such a distinction, in Burnet's thesis, simply did not exist for early Greek thought which saw the world as 'a single ultimate substance':

> Modern writers sometimes give the name of Hylozoism to this way of thinking, but the term is apt to be misleading. It suggests theories which deny the separate reality of life and spirit, whereas, in the days of Thales, and even far later, the distinction between matter and spirit had not been felt, still less formulated in such a way that it could be denied. The uncreated, indestructible reality of which these early thinkers tell us was a body, or even matter, if we choose to call it so; but it was not matter in the sense in which matter is opposed to spirit.[45]

A world-view which did not admit of these antinomies was an essential part of the transcendentalist syntheses constructed during Pound's experimental years to maintain the special reality of the ineffable; these syntheses were mimed, as it were, in the continuity of the word 'vortex' itself into the field theory of nineteenth-century physics.

Microcosmic forms

1914, the year of the London Vortex, was also the year of the pseudonym in Pound's critical prose. His most famous pseudonyms did not begin until 1917 in *The New Age* ('B. H. Dias', whose 'Art Notes' ran from November 1917 until April 1920, and 'William Atheling', whose 'Music' column ran from December 1917 until January 1921), but 1914 marked a more comical selection: 'Alf Arper', 'Henery Hawkins', 'Herrmann Karl Georg Jesus Maria', and those indistinguishable brothers 'Bastien' and 'Baptiste' 'von Helmholtz'. This last pair occasion interest because their surname was real; it belonged to Hermann Ludwig von Helmholtz (1821–94), one of the most famous German scientists of the nineteenth century whose work incorporated all the major disciplines of science, and for whom the divisions of professional categories of research were ultimately meaningless.

Helmholtz was renowned not only for the extensive range of his interests ('As each of seven cities contended for Homer, so seven sciences, mathematics, physics, chemistry, physiology, medicine, philosophy, and aesthetics, claimed Helmholtz') but for his far-sighted conclusions, which had to wait, sometimes for a considerable period, for acceptance and sanction by the scientific establishment. He was thus an ideal model for the interdisciplinary, polymathic approach (another version of the access to a unitary view of the world) that Pound admired in all branches of learning, and for the figure of a man isolated from his contemporaries by his distance from the mainstream of current thought. Helmholtz was another of those masters in practical 'looking', celebrated primarily for his invention of the opthalmoscope in 1851, for his textbook on *Physiological Optics* (1867), a work in which all the experiments he cited were performed by his own hand, and for a belief in the value of only the 'first rate', the work of real discovery; he wrote: 'Whoever comes into contact with men of the first rank has an altered scale of values in life. Such intellectual contact is the most interesting event life can offer.' As a student, Helmholtz was deeply impressed by Johannes Müller, one of the most influential biology teachers of the period, who 'powerfully stimulated thoughts leading in the direction of the correlation of all the physical forces of nature' and who emphasized 'the investigation of biological problems by the methods of physical and chemical science'; in other words, the ideal of the experimental comparative method as opposed to the metaphysical tradition of German *Naturphilosophie*: Louis Agassiz belonged to the same school of thought. It was Müller's stimulation that led Helmholtz and fellow students at the University of Berlin to found the Physical Society, whose purpose was to combat ideas that could not be demonstrated, in direct opposition to the metaphysicians' notion that the problem of vital action was quite beyond the domain of experimental science.[46]

The history that supplied this view of Helmholtz was Murray's *Science and Scientists in the Nineteenth Century* (1925). It had an Introduction by Sir Oliver Lodge who was not only a well-known conventional physicist but a leading member of the Society for Psychical Research; he had this to say about Murray's account of Helmholtz:

The chapter on Helmholtz, too little known in this country, is specially useful, though even so the Author has hardly succeeded in the almost impossible task of conveying to the general reader an adequate conception of the exceeding brilliance and wide scope of the 1847 thesis of Helmholtz on the Conservation of Energy; still less is it possible to deal with that epoch-making paper on Vortex theory, which may be said to have initiated modern hydrodynamics.[47]

These two works singled out by Lodge, the treatises on the conservation of energy and on vortex theory, inform Pound's choice of 'Helmholtz' as a pseudonym for six essays in 1914. Paradoxically, the essays themselves did little more than indirectly suggest models of science for the literary critic, being primarily a series of attacks on the various institutions that constituted and inhibited the world of letters,[48] but Pound's London period involved a whole range of rather complicated jokes about his literary situation and a complex manipulation of the distances, silences and diversions accompanying the use of mask and persona in which the pseudonym has an obvious part. Pound's stricture that a writer should always have the grace to exhibit his sources, his 'cribs', was a stricture he frequently ignored in his own practice, and, even when he obeyed it, his method of display was often far from direct. In any case, as John Berryman has said, 'for one thing, one forgets. . . . For another, there are trade secrets.'

It was chapter 3 of Hudson Maxim's *The Science of Poetry and the Philosophy of Language* (1910) that did much to focus Pound's attention on economy of force:

> Poetry obeys the law of conservation of energy. By poetry a thought is presented with the utmost economy of word symbols . . . selecting only those most pregnant with meaning; and this conserved energy is utilized by the hearer in perceiving the thought with unusual force and vividness.[49]

Helmholtz read his paper 'On the Conservation of Force' before the Physical Society at the University of Berlin on 23 July 1847. It established mathematically the principle of physical forces which later provided the basis for Kelvin's law of thermodynamics and a prime model for field-theory physics. Helmholtz's earliest biographer, J. G. McKendrick, called it 'one of the most epoch-making scientific papers of the century' which 'enunciated as a fundamental principle of physics the conservation of force, just as Lavoisier, seventy years before, had made that of the principle of matter the fundamental principle of chemistry.'[50] The original paper would not have been available to any but a narrow specialist audience; what did reach a wider public was a lecture of the same title delivered at Karlsruhe in 1862 and subsequently published in Helmholtz's *Popular Lectures on Scientific Subjects* of 1873. His opening remarks on the importance of 'law', and its permeation throughout the known universe, established his ideological framework, a belief in universal coherence:

> intellectual satisfaction we obtain only from a connection of the whole, just from its conformity with law . . . there is a kind, I might almost say, of artistic satisfaction, when we are able to survey the enormous wealth of Nature as a regularly-ordered whole – a kosmos, an image of the logical thought of our own mind.

Thus the purpose of the lecture was to demonstrate the applicability of the law of conservation to *all* natural processes; the law itself had a satisfyingly simple formulation: *'the quality of force which can be brought into action in the whole of Nature is unchangeable*, and can neither be increased nor diminished.' He felt it necessary to gloss the phrase 'quality of force': 'the same idea is more popularly expressed with reference to its technical application, what we call *amount of work* in the mechanical sense of the word', i.e. 'expenditure of force'. Helmholtz's gloss was designed to demystify the gnomic utterances of scientific formulae; as part of this design, he offered a more discursive account of his law:

> whenever the capacity for work of one natural force is destroyed, it is transformed into another kind of activity . . . working force may indeed disappear in one form, but then it reappears in exactly equivalent quantity in some other form; it is thus neither increased nor diminished, but always remains in exactly the same quantity.[51]

Helmholtz's theory of conservation was of obvious importance for his more extensive work on the interaction of forces in general; it was this work that led to his researches into the properties of matter, specifically into the ways in which the forces of matter connected with each other. Fundamental to these researches was his theory of vortex motion. Kelvin began his Preface to Koenigsberger's standard biography of Helmholtz in 1906 by claiming: 'His admirable theory of vortex rings is one of the most beautiful pieces of mathematical work hitherto done in the dynamics of incompressible fluids.'[52] Helmholtz's 'vortex rings' were a microcosmic version of the Greek atomists' cosmologies; the movement between them was from an explanation of the universe in terms of vortex motion to an explanation of the ultimate constituents of matter itself in terms of vortex motion. A letter from Kelvin to Helmholtz in January 1867, discussed by a modern commentator, made the point:

> [Kelvin] described the vortex rings of ether as being as permanent and indestructible as Lucretius' solid and hard atoms . . . he also pointed out that the variations and combinations of not only two but a long chain of vortex rings might contain all the possibilities needed for the explanation of all observable properties of matter.[53]

Helmholtz's paper 'On the Integrals of the Hydrodynamic Equations which Express Vortex-Motion' (translated into English in *The Philosophical Magazine*, 1867) was, as Koenigsberger remarked, 'intelligible in the first instance only to mathematical physicists';[54] it is certainly beyond the competence of the present writer to give a proper account of it, and so my description takes its material from the two major biographies.

Prior to Helmholtz's work, the assumptions of hydrodynamic theory were restricted to the motion of fluid resulting from the action of forces that had a potential of their own:

> Helmholtz abolished this limitation, and took into account the friction between the elements of the fluid, and against fixed bodies, the effect of which on fluids had not till then been determined mathematically, and endeavoured to determine the forms of the motion which friction produces in fluids.[55]

That Helmholtz's theory was concerned with fluids has its special significance; Burnet was to reiterate the pre-Socratic 'analogy of eddies in wind or water' in support of vortex theory, and Pound's 'world of moving energies' was clearly fluid in character, from his initial definition of the vortex in 1914, 'from which, and through which, and into which, ideas are constantly rushing',[56] to the 'radiant world' of 1928, 'the glass under water, the form that seems a form seen in a mirror'.[57] McKendrick gave the clearest account of the forms discerned by Helmholtz's mathematical investigation into the laws of vortex motion in a frictionless fluid:

> Wherever in a fluid vortex motion exists, there is a rotation of the smallest imaginable particle about some axis. Starting from this conception . . . Helmholtz proceeds to investigate the forms and behaviour of vortices. A vortex line he defines as a line drawn through the fluid in such a way that its direction at any point is the axis of rotation of the element at that point. A vortex filament is part of the fluid marked off from the surrounding fluid by drawing the corresponding vortex lines through all points of the circumference of an infinitely small plane area. Thus each vortex filament may be imagined to be shut off from the surrounding fluid by a thin layer or mantle of vortex lines. Vortex lines form closed curves in a finite fluid; and vortex filaments form closed filaments or rings, simple or knotted. The simplest type of a vortex ring is a circular anchor ring, every element rotating round the circular axis. Such a vortex ring advances through the fluid in the direction of motion of the elements on the inside of the ring. An ordinary smoke-ring shows the essential nature of the motion very well.

On the basis of the forms disclosed by vortex motion, McKendrick then considered the activity of these forms, the shapes created by their movement:

> If two vortex rings have the same axis and the same sense of rotation, and if they both advance through the fluid in the same direction, the first ring, *a*, will widen, and suffer retardation, and the second, *b*, will become narrower, and suffer acceleration, *b* ultimately overtaking *a*, and, under favourable conditions, passing through it. Then they will separate and again follow each other, but *b* will widen, and *a* contract, until *a* will pass through *b*. Thus the vortex rings will pass alternately through each other. On the other hand, if the coaxial rings have equal radii and equal rotational movements, but in opposite senses, they will approach each other and suffer distension, and this mutual approach and spreading out will go on indefinitely until the rings are infinitely close and infinitely wide.[58]

This beautiful sinuosity indeed provided figurability for the intuition of Emerson's Swedenborg, who saw nature 'wreathing through an everlasting spiral',[59] a figurability whose nature was characterized not only by the distinct shapes of its interactivity but also by the special permanence predicated by Helmholtz's earlier theory of energy's conservation:

> In an incompressible frictionless fluid rotatory movements can neither originate nor disappear; the vorticity . . . then is an unchangeable quantity. As they move in the surrounding fluid they are always composed of the same particles. Thus the vortex rings have perpetuity. They may jostle against each other and undergo changes of form, but they cannot be broken or dissolved. They have the indestructibility which is believed to belong to the ultimate constituents of matter.[60]

Vorticity was thus revealed as the indestructible, enduring constituent of matter; Helmholtz provided the most concrete image of the vortex, so necessary for Pound's aesthetic of the 'real', as a principle of shape and energy, the organization of all the forces Pound felt to be important and worthy of perpetuation. Helmholtz's mathematical explanation also alters our actual picture of the vortex; we can no longer be satisfied with the simple 'cone' suggested by Pound's essay 'On Technique', nor with any approximation to the Yeatsian 'gyre'. The picture of the whirlpool (Burnet's 'eddies in wind or water') retains its accuracy, but Helmholtz's work displayed the constitution of the whirlpool in more specific detail: a metaphor becomes vividly literal. We retain a picture of the action of the individual vortex rings in the motion of a whirlpool, but the action of those discrete rings is seen to take place within the complicated and integrated set of their relations to each other. To visualize this new picture of the vortex, we may pick up McKendrick's point that 'vortex filaments form closed filaments or rings, simple or knotted.' The 'knotted' variety belongs to a more complex mode of vortical action; McKendrick ended his account of Helmholtz's vortex by suggesting its pictorial aspect: 'Some idea may be formed of the possible variety of forms of vortex atoms by simply looking at the illustrations of Professor Tait's remarkable paper upon knots.'[61]

P. G. Tait (1831–1901), Professor of Physics in the Universities of Tokyo and Edinburgh, based his mathematical theory of 'knots', in a series of papers during the late 1870s and early 1880s, on Helmholtz's conception of the vortex atom. A 'knot' in mathematical physics was a complex version of Helmholtz's 'simple' vortex ring; Tait's biographer described it in 1911:

> If we take a cord or, better still, a long piece of rubber tubing, twist it round itself in and out in any arbitrary fashion, then join its ends so as to make a closed loop with a number of interlacings, on it, we get a vortex knot. . . . If we take a piece of rubber tubing plaited and then closed in the way suggested above, we shall be surprised at the many apparently different forms a given knot may take by simple deformations. Conversely, what appear to the eye to be different arrangements, become on closer inspection Proteus-like forms of the same.[62]

These 'knots', elaborations of the Helmholtzian 'vortex ring', clarify Hugh Kenner's metaphorical proposal of Buckminster Fuller's 'knots' as a means of explicating Pound's vortex.[63] Tait's 'knots' are a more accurate way, historically and visually, of locating Pound's usage, since they suggest a complexity and an interrelation necessary to a picture of the vortex as a model for tradition, linguistic energy and cultural forms. The 'knot' of Fuller is too simplistic to bear the weight of Kenner's metaphor; it cannot provide the picture essential to Kenner's perceptive comment that 'Leo Frobenius meant what Gaudier meant by a Vortex when he spoke of a Paideuma.'[64] What we need here is Tait's 'knot', the 'possible variety of forms of vortex atoms' in McKendrick's words, to offer a true visual counterpart for the complicated and integrated relations of the 'gristly roots of ideas that are in action'. It is exactly this essential notion of entanglement – available, too, in Leukippos' account of world formation – that, paradoxically, is missing in the picture of Fuller's 'knot'.

The Helmholtzian 'vortex' goes beyond the metaphor of Kenner's Fuller to provide a model for the permanent yet metamorphic nature of the relationship of language to the phenomenal world for which Pound used his own idea of the vortex. Furthermore, it held a special place in the theories of electromagnetism from which Pound chose his most significant analogies for creative behaviour. McKendrick pointed to the relationship between the vortex and electromagnetic theory:

In addition to the very remarkable theories in hydrodynamics, to which Helmholtz was led and on which Lord Kelvin and others have based whole theories of the ultimate constitution of matter, the investigation has another important side. The mathematical formulae are identical with certain formulae in electromagnetism, so that, as Helmholtz himself pointed out, there is a striking analogy between the two apparently distinct classes of phenomena, hydrokinetics and electrokinetics. Indeed all mechanical models that aim at explaining the reciprocal relations of electricity and magnetisms require rotating elements; and vorticity of some kind seems to be an essential feature of electromagnetic action. . . . Lord Kelvin made Helmholtz's investigation the basis of the splendid hypothesis, that the atoms of matter are composed of minute vortex rings in the ether, and he worked out in detail the analogy between such rotational movements and electromagnetic phenomena. . . . The element, according to this conception, is neither a solid atom, nor a mass of atoms, but a whirl in a fluid ether.

Here, again, we find a special notion of the material being advanced, not 'solid' nor a 'mass' but a 'whirl', that order of materiality necessary for an explication of the ineffable. Specifically, Helmholtz's work was an invaluable aid to the development of field-theory physics, those 'fields of force' on which Ernest Fenollosa based his entire theory of language. The final point of McKendrick's discussion was a gesture towards Faraday and Clerk Maxwell: 'Finally, the theory of vortex motions has made it possible to understand in some measure the transmission of magneto-electric effects through an intervening medium, and it has also helped to dispel the fiction of action at a distance.'[65]

Pound's 'vortex' with its attendant electrical analogies and Fenollosa's 'ideogram', the centres of their respective philosophies of language, share the same area of contemporary science: the notions of electromagnetic force established by field-theory physics to describe the ways in which bodies act upon one another. Max Nänny has posited the resemblance between vortex, ideogram and what he calls 'electric field',[66] but his account is circumscribed by his reading of Marshall McLuhan which, to my mind, suffers from the limitations of Kenner's metaphoric reliance on Buckminster Fuller. In addition, McLuhan's concept of 'electric field' as a 'unified field of *instant* relationship' (my emphasis)[67] is essentially Newtonian rather than Faradayan in character. McKendrick noted that Helmholtz's theory of vortex motion 'helped to dispel the fiction of action at a distance', which points exactly the difference between the views of Newton and Faraday: while Newton held that bodies consisted of corpuscles that acted upon each other from a distance, and instantaneously, Faraday established that all actions of one body on another took time to move between the bodies. By adopting Newton's postulate, via McLuhan, of 'instant relation-ships', Nänny suggests the converse of the true importance of the 'electric field' for the vortex and the ideogram, the time factor that governs the interaction of bodies in the field; it was precisely this fact of duration that was important for Fenollosa: 'The transfer-ences of force from agent to object, which constitute natural phenomena, occupy time.'[68]

There was a common element to field theories in the nineteenth century: 'all action of one body on a distant body, was held to be carried out by an *intervening medium*. In the case of Faraday, this medium was merely *force itself*, while for many others the medium was felt to be quasi-liquid or solid obeying Newton's laws, called the *ether*.' Field theories thus held that 'the field of forces – or ether – exists in space even where there is no matter',[69] and Fenollosa was able to maintain that 'Relations are more real and more important than the things which they relate';[70] his insistence on 'action' rather than 'things' again presumed the durational charac-ter that the notion of 'instant relationships' denies. The largest limitation of the theory of 'action at a distance' lay in its inability to account for electric, magnetic or chemical action, and it was most thoroughly undermined by Hertz, the pupil of Helmholtz who, in Helmholtz's laboratory, developed this theory of electromagnetic waves. Kelvin ended his Preface to Koenigsberger's biography of Helmholtz by stressing this point:

I cannot conclude this short preface without referring to the greatest debt which the world owes to Helmholtz, in having given to Hertz the inspiration to find experimental proof of Maxwell's electric waves; and giving him in the Physical Institute of the University of Berlin, the apparatus and appliances by means of which he carried out the investigation.

He noted its importance for one of Pound's favourite analogies, the telegraph:

> To this we owe the first practical demonstration of progressive electrical waves, and of stationary waves, in air, and therefore inferentially in ether undisturbed by ponderable matter. Thus in Helmholtz we find a prime factor in the grand series of theoretical and experimental researches through which wireless telegraphy has been achieved.[71]

Faraday's view of 'force' as the sole physical substance led him directly to the theory of electromagnetism. His experiments on electric and magnetic transmission demonstrated that lines of force were physical, not substanceless, even in fields where there was no matter; this was a final definition of the materiality that had led to Leukippos' argument that 'The void is as real as the body.'[72] So Faraday's final world-view was of 'an idea that matter and force were identical and that the world was one vast field of force',[73] and Fenollosa could argue that 'Valid scientific thought consists in following as closely as may be the actual and entangled lines of force as they pulse through things',[74] whereby the 'real' was conceived as the 'actual' and the 'entangled' qualities of the 'knots' formed by vortex rings.

What was crucial for field theory was the construction of 'models' to explain the 'physical' nature of the electromagnetic field. Clerk Maxwell sought to achieve a unified theory of electricity, magnetism and light; to this end, he had to find an ether model of the field which would incorporate all the known facts of these areas. The point of departure for a mechanical model was Faraday's theory that the distribution of magnetic lines of force could be determined by assuming a tension along those lines and a pressure between them, but there still remained the problem of what mechanical explanation could be given of the inequality of pressures in a fluid medium. The solution lay in the theory of vortex motion:

> Thomson had argued that it was necessary to suppose a vortex motion around the magnetic lines of force in diamagnetic media. He thought that there was no other way to explain the Faraday rotation of light. Maxwell took the idea of magnetic vortices and

applied it to all magnetic lines of force, in space as well as material media.[75]

Clerk Maxwell's explanation of lines of force by molecular vortices (1861–2) provided the major mechanical model of electromagnetic action that field theory needed in order to argue for its special materiality. In turn, it was only the mechanical model that made possible the practical results of field-theory physics, the telegraph, for example. Both were made 'real' by demonstrations of vortex motion, just as the sexual mysticism of Provence, for example, was offered as 'real' in the Poundian discourse by the principles of the telegraph. The vortex itself, prime model for the interaction of these syntheses, in terms both theoretical and practical, metaphorical and literal, inscribed itself for modernism as the major vehicle for carrying ideas into action.

5 Tradition and race-memory

We need the staff of tradition as well as the lamp of
reason. What is our faith in the future but
  'the rushing and expanding stream
Of thought, of feeling fed by all the past'?
What is our finest hope but finest memory?

(Edward Dowden)

The *historical sense* (or the capacity for divining
quickly the order of rank of the valuations according
to which a people, a community, or an individual has
lived, the 'divining instinct' for the relationships of
these valuations, for the relation of the authority of the
valuations to the authority of the operating forces) –
this historical sense, which we Europeans claim as our
speciality, has come to us in the train of the enchanting
and mad *semi-barbarity* into which Europe has been
plunged by the democratic mingling of classes and
races – it is only the 19th century that has recognized
this faculty as its sixth sense. Owing to this mingling,
the past of every form and mode of life, and of cultures
which were formerly contiguous and super-imposed
on one another, flows forth into us 'modern souls'.

(Nietzsche)

Puck is not dead

The years that we may call 'high modernism', during which the
self-consciousness of modernity strove to articulate itself, began
and ended with famous testaments to the function of 'tradition'. It
began in 1912 with Pound's analogy of words as 'great hollow
cones of steel . . . charged with a force like electricity', a 'force' he

defined as 'centuries of race-consciousness'.[1] It ended in 1919 when Eliot conceived of 'tradition' in terms of the 'relative spirit' that Pater had derived from the inductive sciences,[2] and when the relationship between 'tradition' and 'depersonalization' was figured as a chemical catalyst.[3] Thus one of the major hallmarks of modernity declared itself through specific images derived from contemporary science. There is no longer any quarrel with the place of Pater at the beginning of modernism in general, but what we need now is not so much a location of the 'line' of the modern but an explanation of the discourses through which it was announced, the particular and distinctive modes of debate that were used to convey ideas about 'tradition', which achieved their fullest expression in Pound and Eliot.[4]

These ideas took the form of 'race-memory' or 'race-consciousness'; they were part of the means whereby the seriousness of literary criticism could be maintained, as George Soule argued in 1914: 'Discerning critics must sift the true from the false. . . . They must fight eternally for the sincere. . . . They must bear sturdy witness to the fact that art is not an amusement for idle moments, but the consciousness of the race.'[5] By the middle of our period, claims for 'tradition' conceived in these terms had become so assimilated into the literary climate that they could survive as a modernist gesture without the scientific aid that Pound had explicitly invoked; thus John Gould Fletcher wrote of Richard Aldington:

> The task of a modern poet is not to shut his eyes to the past, but to see the work of the generations that preceded him as an uncompleted structure, the living intention of whose builders is again born in him, and seeks fruition in the additions he can make to it.[6]

Fletcher's proclamation did not display the specificity of analogy we find in Pound, but it clearly relied on an argument for a 'tradition' to be completed contemporaneously, just as the final human form completed the potential of the germ-cell; the 'uncompleted structure' of 'tradition' denied the easy satisfaction of fixity or self-sufficiency by its emphasis on process or growth which, in Pater's phrase, 'properly *is* not but is only always *becoming*'.[7] Contemporary participation within that unfinished (and, historically, unfinishable) morphology was, from the standpoint of the modernist biological metaphor, exactly what made it a *live* tradition.

A view of past events in literary history conceived in biological terms was partly dependent on a commonplace manipulation of theories of development (from Taine, Zola, *et al.*), but it received its major impetus from more precisely defined issues. The most urgent of these was the need to give legitimacy to certain kinds of experience and, in the case of the writer, certain kinds of material and practice seemingly at odds with the meta-contemporary world that modernist script was supposed to deal with. How, for example, was a dustbin at dawn or a London omnibus to share an imaginative world with the mythopoeic or the presence of the 'gods'; primitive cave-drawings or tales of metamorphosis with the aggressively mechanical edges of vorticist paintings or the scrupulous plan of Dublin? It was in the effort to provide legitimacy and justification for such conjunctions that modernist poetics sought a discourse from the sciences. A recent account of the theosophical movement, that it 'used the all-conquering concept of evolution as a springboard by means of which such ancient transcendental doctrines as Brahmanism and Neo-Platonism might be reasserted',[8] suggests how the movement reflected the modernist practice to offer respectability for seemingly mystical or metaphysical phenomena. This practice took its cue in part from the work of the Society for Psychical Research.[9]

G. R. S. Mead ended a discussion of the question of 'resurrection' by noting the new possibilities for science's relation to psychical matters:

> Indeed it is not too much to say that it is difficult for some of us to meet with anyone of culture now-a-days who believes in a crude physical resurrection. The purely rationalistic treatment of miracles, however, based on the prejudices of an exclusively materialistic view of science ... during the latter half of the xixth century, is no longer in fashion. ... A scientific psychology of religious experience is being inaugurated.[10]

Mead's testimony to a 'scientific psychology of religious experience' was a significant advance on earlier formulations of psychical method in that it sought to give the ineffable a new mode of materiality that could break down crudely held distinctions between the physical and the spiritual (in this instance, a materiality to account for the Neoplatonic doctrine of the 'subtle body'). The original psychical researchers had been obliged to assert a simple polemic to justify their work; Thomson Hudson introduced *The Law of Psychic Phenomena* in 1893 as an assistance in 'bringing Psychology within the domain of the exact sciences',[11] and Frederic Myers in 1886 was similarly eager to claim orthodoxy:

> we wish distinctly to say that so far from aiming at any paradoxical reversion of established scientific conclusions, we conceive ourselves to be working (however imperfectly) in the main track of discovery, and assailing a problem which, though strange and hard, does yet stand next in order among the new adventures on which Science must needs set forth.[12]

Once a kind of respectability was attained, however, the entrenched positions that any new idea requires for its protection became wider, more sophisticated, and significantly more interesting for the issues of modernism. Frank Podmore argued in 1908 that 'the most important of the investigations undertaken by the Society is that connected with Thought Transference or Telepathy', and he noted the 'distinguished pedigree' this theory exhibited:

> It is as old as the days when Chaldean shepherds, watching the stars by night, essayed to read therein the revelation of the Divine Will and to forecast the destiny of human kind. From these nightly vigils came the fruitful conception of an invisible influence radiating from the heavenly bodies – an influence potent for good and evil, yet transcending the limitations of mortal senses. At the hands of the later alchemists – Paracelsus and his successors – this conception received a remarkable extension. Not the stars only, but all substances in the universe, they taught, radiate influence and receive influence in turn.[13]

For Pound, of course, alchemy was the great revealer of what he called *virtu*, the potency that all things possess and exhibit in their intercourse with others; for the modern sensibility, it required no large imaginative leap for such *virtu* to be figured in the vocabulary of power supplied by electromagnetism, as Pound figured the tensile energy of Provençal mysticism through the principles of the telegraph, and Podmore himself chose the telegraph as an analogy, admittedly to a lesser degree of complication, for the telepathic process:

We have at either end of the chain a physical event – the changes in the cerebral tissues which are presumed to correspond to every act of thought or sensation. And it is not without interest to note in this connection that the arrangement of some of the nerve cells in the brain bears a superficial resemblance to the arrangement of the particles in the 'coherer' used for the reception of the message in wireless telegraphy.[14]

On a more formal level, the ambition of psychical research to provide a 'scientific' description of non-sensory experience may most easily be discerned in its attention to the ideology of such research. A Conference on the Extension of University Teaching held in Oxford during August 1905 produced a collection of essays designed to familiarize the non-specialist reader with the major areas of scientific methodology.[15] It included an essay on 'Psycho-Physical Method' by William McDougall, a member of the Society for Psychical Research and Wilde Reader in Mental Philosophy in the University. McDougall began by placing his own area in re-lation to the scope of conventional science with reference to an earlier lecture in the series delivered by Francis Gotch,[16] which described the nature of the universe as revealed by physics and mathematics, the 'objective world' apprehended by the senses, con-ceived solely in phenomenal terms and made intelligible 'by means of the principle of *physical causation*'.[17] What lay outside this schema were of course 'the facts of immediate experience, the states of our own consciousness'; McDougall argued that it was no longer possible to regard the material world as the exclusive object of scientific study, or the world of 'consciousness' merely as the pro-vince of metaphysics, and that there was observable 'a constant concurrence or concomitance of events of the two orders', which it was the business of psycho-physics to investigate.[18] McDougall's insistence on an interrelational method of approach to deconstruct the privacy of psychical cognition belonged to wider premises of contemporary thought; invoking the founder of psycho-physics, Gustav Theodor Fechner (Professor of Physics in the University of Leipzig, whose major work was the *Elemente der Psycho-Physik*, 1860), McDougall noted that the roots of the 'new' science were based on a version of Spinoza's monism which held that there was but one enduring substance in the world revealed to us under the two aspects of the physical and the psychical, the doctrine of 'universal animation': 'the view that every part of the whole universe not only exists as atoms swarming in scattered groups, but has also the feeling of its own existence and a joy in its own activity, and that this consciousness of each part is but an element in the universal world consciousness.'[19] Such a view explicitly dismissed the dualist perspective that traditionally had bedevilled all attempts to describe the relationship between the two aspects; it made possible the Poundian acceptance of an intelligence in nature where 'gods' were not only 'in the air' but also 'in the stone', awaiting release into shape by the artist's recognition.

William James, a founding member of the Society for Psychical Research, drew attention to the new order of materiality probed by its inquiries when, in discussing the 'positive content of primitive religions', he quoted W. C. Brownell: 'The influence of the Holy Spirit . . . is a matter of actual experience, as solid a reality as that of electro-magnetism.'[20] James was generally critical of mechanistic models of science, but he upheld their potential for describing events usually conceived as lying beyond the scientist's competence:

> the time-honoured phenomenon of diabolical possession is on the point of being admitted by the scientist as a fact, now that he has the name 'hysterodemonopathy' by which to apperceive it. No one can foresee just how far this legitimation of occultist phenomena under newly found scientist titles may proceed.

For James, this process of 'legitimation' had an important correspondence with a mythopoeic perception of the world: 'The divorce between scientist facts and religious facts may not necessarily be as eternal as it at first sight seems, nor the personalism and romanticism of the world, as they appeared to primitive thinking, be matters so irrevocably outgrown.'[21] Sidney Lanier offered this correspondence in its most familiar form in 1903 when he assessed the rise of physical science:

> Here are thousands upon thousands of acute and patient men today who are devoutly gazing into the great mysteries of Nature and fruitfully reporting what they see. These men have not destroyed the fairies: they have preserved them in more truthful and solid shapes. Puck is not dead: he has only changed his name to Electricity, and has increased his speed, and can now put a girdle round the earth in less than forty minutes.[22]

The synthesis that Lanier proposed relied on notions of force, which restated in a more picturesque way a prescription of 1890 for the 'scientific attitude' from Havelock Ellis:

> In its solvents all things are analyzed and atomized, the 'soul' of our religious world – the vast pulsating centre, at the bottom of which, according to the profound saying of the old mystic, lies that utterable sigh which we call God – is resolved into a momentary focus of ever-shifting rays of force; is but an incident in a huge evolution of shifting forces which we may, if we like, personify as Nature.[23]

In the same year, John Addington Symonds published a collection of essays which included 'The Philosophy of Evolution', an inquiry, like Ellis's, into the ways in which the methods of science were remoulding understandings of religion. For Symonds, as for the later modernists, the findings of science meant above all a substantiation of the 'seriousness' of literary enterprise for the public, delivering it from 'the caprice of connoisseurship and the whims of dilettantism', and, concomitantly, a substantiation of the 'seriousness' of mysticism in a sceptical world whereby evolution, preceded by the theories of conservation and correlation of energies, had displaced 'the old conception of miraculous occurrences'.[24]

Symonds and Ellis found it necessary to manipulate the legitimacy conferred by science in this way because of their larger roles, as part of a reaction against the dualism posited by much nineteenth-century science, in the current movement to restore 'unity' to the natural world. Evolutionary science, for Symonds, presented a view of the universe as 'one homogeneous whole, in which nothing can be lost and unaccounted for, through which there runs a continuity of energizing forces, and of which we are indisputably conscious members.' In its function of restoring man's unity with the universe, science was paralleled by mysticism and spiritual contemplation; Symonds affirmed that 'Science establishes the unity of the Kosmos, together with the exact correspondence and correlation of its parts', and hence 'we discover that we cannot think of it except as spiritual'.[25] In another essay from the same collection, Symonds offered this unity as fundamental for an understanding of myth. He talked of the impossibility for the contemporary mind of believing in the primitive myths of anthropomorphism, but, he argued, 'in its place the modern theory of the universe tends to establish the conviction that men and beasts and plants and inorganic substances are parts of one mind-penetrated unity.' The advent of such theory marked the demise of 'the leading principle of philosophy and religion during the last two thousand years', the 'abrupt separation of men from their environment', and testified to the validity of ancient myths conceived as 'forms found for uttering man's sensation of his affinity to woods and flowers and waters' in that their 'truth' was 'the perception of spirituality in the material world'. This was a familiar enough transcendentalism, but Symonds's point was that myths so conceived made sense only as a result of the lines of correlation revealed by science: 'science is leading us back by circuitous routes to the primitive belief in a life-penetrated universe.'[26] He concluded his essay with a useful comment on the state of contemporary ideas by speculating that his theory 'will probably find but scanty acceptance even now', but he finished forcefully: 'At the same time spirituality has been restored to the material universe by science, which forces us to regard the cosmos as a single whole, penetrated throughout with life-producing energy.'[27]

Symonds's view of science's potential for restoring universal unity was, of course, the converse of the more widely held understanding of science's relation to such matters, evident in T. E. Hulme, for example, as, in Kermode's phrase, 'the universe of death'. Symonds was right to have doubts about the reception of his theory; it needed to be reiterated time and again during the following three decades in order to establish itself fully as the fulcrum of modernist idealism. Confirmation of it, at a certain level of discourse, was provided by scientists themselves; even the hard-headed, anti-metaphysical J. Arthur Thomson declared in a popular textbook of 1911: 'The fundamental postulate of science is the Uniformity of Nature.'[28] But, substantially, it received its fullest explication from that body of scientifically minded men of letters during the period who were similarly concerned to maintain science's potential for translating mystical correspondences. Havelock Ellis returned to the issues raised by Symonds in an essay of 1913, where he argued that an opposition between science and mysticism was false. In primitive societies, he claimed, the two had been combined in the figure of the shaman: 'this harmony with the essence of the universe, this control of Nature through oneness with Nature, is not only at the heart of religion; it is also at the heart of science.'[29] Ellis offered his own case-history as symptomatic of the problems resulting from the disappearance of religious faith and from the alien nature of the world displayed by science, problems that were solved for Ellis by the revelation of James Hinton's *Life in Nature*. Hinton, claimed Ellis, showed that the world was still a mechanism, but 'As he viewed it, the mechanism was not the mechanism of a factory, it was vital, with all the glow and warmth and beauty of life.' What saved Ellis's position from the wearisomeness of a familiar debate was the electromagnetic vocabulary with which he described the effects of the revelation, the vocabulary that sustained a new order of materiality for modernism:

> Evidently by this time my mind had reached a stage of saturated solution which needed, by the shock of the right contact, to recrystallize in forms that were a revelation to me. . . . It acted with the swiftness of an electric contact; the dull aching tension was removed – the two opposing psychic tendencies were fused in delicious harmony.

Here was the 'harmony' that was implicit in Pound's electromagnetic explanation for the mysticism of Provence in his 'Psychology and Troubadours' of the previous year, and it was in this context that Ellis updated the position of Symonds's 1890 essay: 'matter', customarily used to create an 'artificial opposition between science and religion', was now conceived as 'electrical emanation', so that 'we now accept even that transmutation of the elements of which the alchemists once dreamed'. The mystic and the scientist affirmed identical worlds in which 'matter' was regarded as almost as 'ethereal' as 'spirit', and 'The spontaneous affirmation of the mystic that he lives in the spiritual world here and now, will then be, in other words, merely the same affirmation which the man of science has more laboriously revealed.'[30] As Pound's understanding of the medieval world so clearly showed, notably in his composite essay on 'Cavalcanti', the energies of medieval alchemy and modern physics consolidated each other.

Design and the permanence of type

If science consolidated mystical and transcendental intuitions of natural and cosmic harmony, so too did it consolidate the corollary of such harmony, the continuity of the organism itself. It was here that the function of memory became so important for the modernist ideology; the key text for our purposes was Samuel Butler's *Un-conscious Memory* (1880). Butler's thesis was a reaction against Darwinian natural selection and was concerned to emphasize in its place the doctrine of continued personality from generation to generation. For Butler, this continuity was ensured by the operations of memory: 'embryonic and youthful development . . . instinct and growth are due to a rapid unconscious memory of past experiences and developments in the persons of the ancestors of the living form in which they appear.'[31] As Butler was to argue at greater length in his subsequent work, 'whatever memory was, heredity was also':[32] 'it is this very possession of a common memory which has guided the offspring into the path taken by, and hence to a virtually same condition with, the parent, and which guided the parent in its turn to a state virtually identical with a corresponding state in the existence of its own parent.'[33] This con-junction of memory and heredity determined memory as the predi-cation of natural 'design':

> it is the binding power of memory which alone renders any consolidation or coherence of action possible, inasmuch as with-out this no action could have parts subordinate one to another, yet bearing upon a common end; no part of an action, great or small, could have reference to any other part, much less to a combination of all the parts; nothing, in fact, but ultimate atoms of actions could ever happen.[34]

The positing of the coherence of 'design' was one of Butler's major gestures against Darwinian notions of 'chance' and 'accident' in-herent in the principle of selection; an argument for 'design' as the cause of variation[35] established one of the points of Butler's departure from the main line of biological thought after the turn of the century. This departure was singled out for attention by a reviewer of the reprint of *Evolution Old and New* in 1914 who noted that the 'part of his book that will be of least importance at the present day' was Butler's version of Paley's 'deified architect idea of God' whereby 'evolution takes place in accordance with a design', a proposition that 'cannot be referred to the ordinary Darwinian explanations'. The main point of the book for the reviewer, however, lay in an important difference between Butler and Paley:

Butler differs from Paley, however, in placing the designer not outside the cosmic flux of his working materials, but within the organism. Not God, he says, but the ancestral memory of man is the designer. The individual perishes, but his memory endures in his offspring and alters them in accordance with the lessons of actual experience.

This was considered to be 'the least valuable part of the book' because 'recent work has added considerably to the data pertaining to these questions';[36] but it was exactly a notion of the materiality of hereditary memory – a force not external to, but *within* the organism – that underwrote the ideas on tradition of Pound and Eliot; for Pound, in particular, such principles of 'design' were indicative of the patterns suggested by an intelligence working in nature and hence available to sensory experience.

Butler sought the materiality of his idea of memory in a widely influential lecture by Ewald Hering, 'On Memory as a Universal Function of Organized Matter', delivered at the anniversary meeting of the Imperial Academy of Sciences in Vienna on 30 May 1870, and translated in its entirety by Butler as chapter 6 of *Unconscious Memory*. Hering's lecture was a physiological account of memory – 'I hope to show how far psychological investigations also afford not only permissible, but indispensable, aid to physiological inquiries' – and it is here that we find a large part of the lecture's innovatory influence. Hering claimed a 'mutual interdependence between the spiritual and the material' and argued:

> Thus regarded, the phenomena of consciousness become functions of the material changes of organized substance, and inversely . . . the material processes of brain substance become functions of the phenomena of consciousness. . . . By the help of this hypothesis of the functional interdependence of matter and spirit, modern physiology is enabled to bring the phenomena of consciousness within the domain of her investigations without leaving the *terra firma* of scientific methods.[37]

The methodological significance of the lecture, the claim for 'mutual interdependence', led, for Butler, to its main point, the notion of 'continuity of vibrations being the key to memory and heredity'.[38] The importance of memory conceived in terms of the 'vibrations' of the nervous system lay in its opposition to molecular

accounts of heredity. In 1876 Professor E. Ray Lankester reviewed
Haeckel's *Peregenesis der Plastidule* and noted that 'the theory of
emission from the constituent cells of an organism of material
gemmules which circulate through the system and affect every
living cell, and accumulate in sperm-cells and germ-cells', was being
substituted by 'the theory of transmission of force' and that the
relation of the two theories to each other was 'the same relation as
the emission and undulatory theories of light'.[39]

Lankester's 'transmission of force' was another formula for
'vibrations'; it was opposed to Darwinian pangenesis – the molecular description of heredity which proceeded according to a
standard morphological approach based on mechanistic 'units' –
and Lankester used Hering's lecture to illustrate the theory, offering
'memory' as a replacement for 'the continuity of Mr Herbert
Spencer's polar forces or polarities of physiological units'. As
memory conceived as 'transmission of vibrations or affectations
of material particles' marked an advance on the mechanism of
'units',[40] it is clear how the electromagnetism of a vorticist aesthetic, the 'mediaeval clean line' or Fenollosa's ideogram found its
counterpart in the new physiology in order to maintain its discourse. While retaining their local, concrete specificity, events or
organisms were integrated into wider, more fluid patterns of signifi-
cation: the epistemological shift from 'units' to 'vibrations'
replaced the synchronic with the diachronic. In 1913 the English
translation of Haeckel's *The Riddle of the Universe* (1899) drew
wide attention to the 'energetics' of memory. Haeckel used the term
'presentation' to mean 'an internal picture of the external object
which is given us in sensation' and argued that the four stages in the
development of its function (cellular, histionic, unconscious and
conscious) corresponded to the stages of the development of
memory. He then used this correspondence to stress the physio-
logical/psychological conjunction which comprised the function of
memory, of ideas going into action:

> The evolutionary scale of memory is closely connected with that
> of presentation; this extremely important function of the psy-
> choplasm – the condition of all further psychic development –
> consists essentially in the *reproduction of presentations*. The
> impressions in the bioplasm which the stimulus produced as
> sensations, and which became presentations in remaining, are

revived by memory; they pass from potentiality to actuality. The latent potential energy of the psychoplasm is transformed into kinetic energy.[41]

Haeckel's concern with the cellular basis of memory's activity is in itself instructive for our purposes, since it was a significant gesture towards the lengthy move away from metaphysical concerns with the 'essence' of vital phenomena to a concern with the constituents of those phenomena. The substance of this realignment was diagrammatized in the development of cell theory, initiated by Schleiden and Schwann in 1838–9, which was seen by J. Arthur Thomson in the only actual *history* of biology published in the nineteenth century as exerting a dominant influence from 1850 onwards. The value of the theory lay in the concreteness it offered for the hitherto abstract conception of the continuity of life; Thomson quoted a comment made by Schwann in 1839: 'The whole organism subsists only by means of the reciprocal action of the single elementary parts.'[42] The cell thus provided a major instrument at the microcosmic level for a material displacement of abstract speculation; a recent historian of biology has summarized its importance as a mode of description for both theory and practice:

> After mid-century the cell had become for the great majority of biologists the essential structural reference point for the interpretation of organic form . . . the cell, while always an architectural element of prime importance, is also the critical unit of organic function above the molecular level. The cell is thus the site of metabolism and energy exchange; it is the basis of nervous and secretory activity and therefore the foundation of harmonious, integrative, organic behaviour; the cell, as manifested in the reproductive products, ensures, finally, the very continuity of life across the generations.[43]

The concept of the cell not only dispelled metaphysics but rapidly became recognized as the crucial element in attempts to explain the problems of development, continuity and change, as a practical mechanism for deciding how perpetuation was possible. Above all, cytology (cell theory) provided a method whereby the mysterious power of historical transformation, a function of memory, could be revealed, and, by analogy, for the poetic imagination it offered a wholly apposite image for the nature of process.

Some thirty years after Hering's lecture, a professional biologist, G. Archdall Reid, found it necessary to reiterate the argument against the pangenetic theory. Reid claimed that most theories of development continued to base their explanations on morphological grounds: 'The "architecture" and composition of the germ-cell, the derivation and destination of its various "units", are the principal objects of study.' Reid's duplication of the earlier argument was for a specific and important reason; he wanted to urge an alternative doctrine of development:

> The theory of recapitulation, on the other hand, is essentially physiological. It supposes that the germ-cell is of such a 'nature', or has such a 'function', that under fit conditions it tends to develop by repeating the life-history of the race.

His concern to restore recapitulation to biological respectability led him to dismiss morphological theories of inheritance in which 'ancestors' were represented by 'discrete active or dormant "units" which are present during every stage of development'. By contrast, a recapitulationist perspective saw these 'ancestors' as represented 'not en-masse, but in orderly succession, beginning with the first and ending with the last'.[44] Evident here was the wider proposition that morphological theories were conceived a-historically, whereas recapitulation incorporated the signs of its own process or 'becoming'; in other words, a fundamental schema for the historicity of a notion of tradition seen as a form of 'race-memory' or 'race-consciousness'. The significance of Reid's book for a study of Poundian modernism was that it located the processes of development and heredity within the principles not of evolution but of recapitulation (a theory that had been discredited in scientific circles for some years); he stated the aim of his book in his Preface: 'In the fifth chapter I have sought to re-establish on a firm basis the doctrine that the development of the individual is a blurred recapitulation of the life-history of the race.' Reid noted that this theory had been 'controverted of late' but he argued strongly for its reinstatement: 'It follows logically and necessarily from the known fact that the child recapitulates the developmental footsteps of the parent. Unless it were true there could be no development of the individual and no evolution of the race.' The opening paragraph of the fifth chapter, 'the crux of the whole work', concisely proposed Reid's stance:

> Every individual who completes the span of days allotted to his kind follows in the footsteps of his parents . . . step by step, in orderly succession, he recapitulates the process by which his parents passed from ovum to embryo, to foetus, to infancy, to adult life. . . . No other method of development is known to us in Nature.[45]

The attractiveness of the recapitulationist doctrine for the modernist idea of tradition lay in its potential as a formula for understanding history from the standpoint of the present. In the proposal that the individual organism displayed its generic past within the compass of its own development, the doctrine offered a microcosmic version of the larger historical process, of the history of the race; Reid noted that 'We have a real history retold in every generation with the additions and omissions made by the preceding generation.'[46]

During the late nineteenth century, recapitulation was the rapidly diminishing alternative to Darwinian evolution. Its roots lay in German *Naturphilosophie* and it proclaimed physiological evidence for the manifestation of divine intelligence throughout the phenomenal world. The major spokesman for the doctrine was Louis Agassiz. For Agassiz, 'evolution' meant not 'change' as such but an unfolding of aspects of the original 'type', and was meaningfully understood only within strictly embryological terms; he stated his entire position in *Methods of Study in Natural History* (1863), the most widely read of his works:

> There are periods in the development of the germ in the higher members of all the types, when they transiently resemble in their general outline the lower representatives of the same type, just as we have seen that the higher orders of one class pass through stages of development in which they transiently resemble lower orders of the same class. The gradation of growth corresponds to the gradation of rank in adult animals, as established upon comparative complication of structure . . . the history of the individual is, in some sort, the history of its type.[47]

Agassiz insisted on the historicity of his enterprise; building on the argument of his earlier *An Essay on Classification* (1859), he argued for a correspondence between the embryological phases of recent fish and the geological succession of the class, a correspondence between past and present which he saw as the summation of his life's work.[48]

The unity of past and present proposed by Agassiz's recapitulationist embryology was also manifested in his major field of research, palaeontology; J. Arthur Thomson's description of palaeontology in 1899 clearly indicated its historicity: 'It is the task of palaeontology to spell out the history of the past, so far as that can be deciphered from the fossil-bearing rocks, to trace the rise and decline of races'.[49] Palaeontology displayed the relevance of extinct forms to those of the contemporary period on the 'principle of correlation', which was first coherently announced by one of Agassiz's earliest masters, Cuvier, 'the only man who exerted a scientific and personal influence over Agassiz'.[50] Cuvier met Agassiz in Paris and was so impressed by the young student that he presented him with his own notes on extinct species of fish, which Agassiz incorporated into his monumental *Poissons fossiles* (1833–44). Cuvier's 'principle of correlation' was, for Thomson, his greatest contribution to morphology: 'This fruitful idea is the morphological aspect of the unity of the organism. It suggests that the organism is not a hap-hazard aggregate of characters but a unified integration. Part is bound to part, so that if the one varies, the other varies with it.' The practical consequences of the principle came close to the Poundian 'luminous detail'; Thomson quoted from Cuvier's *Discourse on the Revolutions of the Surface of the Globe*:

> a claw, a shoulder-blade, a condyle, a leg or arm bone, or any other bone separately considered, enables us to discover the description of teeth to which they belonged; so also, reciprocally, we may determine the form of the other bones from the teeth. Thus, commencing our investigation by a careful survey of any one bone by itself, a person who is sufficiently master of the laws of organic structure may, as it were, reconstruct the whole animal to which that bone had belonged.[51]

On this basis, the palaeontologist 'makes the present intelligible in the light of the past', and Cuvier was the man who made it 'absolutely clear for the first time that fossils were in most cases remains of extinct organisms, different from and yet related to modern forms'; it was the 'reconstructive genius' of Cuvier's 'correlation' that 'brought the dead to life again, and insisted on their being ranked along with the modern types in a unified zoological system.'[52]

Palaeontological historicity confirmed Agassiz's conception of the world as the product of a unified and rational schema manifest in the morphology of both plant and animal kingdoms. It was a conception that held wide currency; T. H. Huxley, for example, remarked as a matter of fact in one of his American lectures in 1876: 'Biologists have arrived at the conclusion that a fundamental uniformity of structure pervades the animal and vegetable worlds, and that plants and animals differ from one another simply as diverse modifications of the same great general plan.'[53] Agassiz was the most important propounder of this 'same great general plan', predominantly through his argument for 'types' as the primary morphological components of nature. The main reaction of opponents to this argument was to see it as an unproblematic version of a Neoplatonic system of archetypes, but this was to do a great injustice to the tenor of Agassiz's mind. What constituted Agassiz's view of the natural world was not a theory of abstract forms but a theory that ultimately had its origins in the Aristotelian notion of immanence: it was not the case that individual members of each 'type' were seen as imperfect reflections of some ideal plan, but that the developmental pattern of each 'type' was immanent embryologically within each of its members, waiting to be unfurled as development progressed.[54] We are here at the fulcrum of the idealist science that was so attractive for Romanticism in general, for American transcendentalism in particular and, via not only Agassiz but the Emersonian leanings of Ernest Fenollosa, for Pound himself. Emerson, in 1849, pondered Schelling's notion that 'the form or type became transparent in the actual forms of successive ages as presented in geology' and wrote in his Journal:

> Schelling's *aperçu* and its statement was a forlorn hope, and all but fell into the pit. Yet just on the eve of ruin, Oken seized and made the most of it; of course, he was ridiculous, and nowhere but in Germany could have survived. Yet Hegel, a still more robust dreamer, clung to this identical piece of nonsense. Then it came rebounding to them in melody from songs of Goethe, and, strange to say, from Geoffroy Saint-Hilaire's *Mémoires* to the Institute in France. Agassiz brought it to America and tried it in

popular lectures on the towns. It succeeded to admiration, the lecturer having, of course, the prudence to disown these bad names of his authors.[55]

Emerson's whimsy did not conceal the sturdiness of Agassiz's notion of 'type' as a form of historical transmission, and it is here that we see most clearly why Pound chose to figure the power of words as 'centuries of race-consciousness' and Eliot chose to define the operations of tradition in biological terms to suggest both a mode of permanence and a means of contemporary participation. One of the firmest conclusions suggested to Agassiz by the comparative method and that further entrenched his opposition to Darwin was the theory that all the type-characteristics of a given group were present from the very beginning; adaptation, transmutation and transition between types, all of which assumed that the various different types were linked together as in a chain, were, for Agassiz, merely fictions: 'It is my belief that naturalists are chasing a phantom, in their search after some material gradation among created beings, by which the whole Animal kingdom may have been derived from a single germ, or from a few germs.'[56] Agassiz's belief in the permanent primacy of 'type' was a means to recapitulative order: 'When the first fish was called into existence, the Vertebrate type existed as a whole in the creative thought, and the first expression of it embraced potentially all the organic elements of that type, up to man himself.' Although he was prepared to admit 'transient resemblances of the young among the higher animals in one type to the adult condition of the lower animals in the same type', he always maintained that each of the four primary divisions of the animal kingdom established by Cuvier was bound by its own course of development, outside of which its members did not move: comparative evidence proved to Agassiz's satisfaction that there was no substantial divergence from the typical structural character. Laws of development were clearly defined for each type, and there was no evidence to suggest that they had ever been joined together to justify a theory of genuine transition between types: 'We shall seek as vainly to transform the lower animal types into the higher ones by way of our theories, as did the alchemists of old to change the baser metals into gold.'[57]

Agassiz's recapitulationist claim that 'the history of the individual is, in some sort, the history of its type' suggests a prime cipher for the traditionalism evinced by Pound and Eliot. His grittiest discussion, and one that is most illuminating for the modernist temperament, was given in his posthumously published essay of 1874, 'Evolution and the Permanence of Type', which began by arguing that what was actually known about the process of evolution was furnished by embryology, by men like Von Baer:

> The pioneers in the science of Embryology . . . have proved that all living beings produce eggs, and that these eggs contain a yolk-substance out of which new beings, identical with their parents, are evolved by a succession of gradual changes. The successive stages of growth constitute evolution, as understood by embryologists.

Evolution, in embryological terms, was thus a law of perpetuation rather than of transition, a law 'controlling development and keeping types within appointed cycles of growth, which revolve forever upon themselves, returning at appointed intervals to the same starting-point and repeating through a succession of phases the same course.'[58] Agassiz insisted on an embryological approach to counter what he saw as the speculative cast of Darwinian theory, its paucity of empirical grip; in Darwin, he wrote, 'the reader seeks in vain for any evidence of a transition between man and his fellow-creatures', claiming that 'Darwin and his followers thus throw off the responsibility of proof with respect both to embryonic growth and geological succession'.[59] The data of 'embryonic growth and geological succession' provided the firmest ground for Agassiz's notions of scientific method in general and for the theory of recapitulation in particular; the one complemented and illustrated the other to emphasize the historicity of his distinctive mode of investigation.

As part of his campaign for the 'type' revealed by embryology and illustrated for the contemporary world by successive geological eras, Agassiz had to reconstruct the definition of 'metamorphosis', which he saw as having been abused by the Darwinian emphasis on transmutation:

> Metamorphosis plays a large part in it, and is treated as evidence of transition from one animal into another. The truth is that metamorphosis, like all embryonic growth, is a normal process of development, moving in regular cycles, returning always to the

same starting-point, and leading always to the same end. . . . In some of these types the development lasts for a long time and the stages of embryonic growth are often so distinct that, until the connection between them is traced, each phase may seem like a separate existence, whereas they are only chapters in one and the same life.

It was on the basis of this conception of metamorphosis, with its origins in Goethe's view of the process as the operation whereby the same organ assumed various forms (all the organs of a plant being not separate but modifications of the leaf), that Agassiz maintained the permanence of the original 'types' as science's enduring truth: 'One thing only we know absolutely. . . . Whatever be the means of preserving and transmitting properties, the primitive types have remained permanent and unchanged.' And it was only such a system that could lay claim to a proper explanation for a specific kind of individualism, the individualism that the principle of trans-mutation could not account for:

> The most trifling and fantastic tricks of inheritance are quoted in support of the transmutation theory; but little is said of the sudden apparition of powerful original qualities which almost always rise like pure creations and are gone with their day and generation.[60]

It was, of course, precisely the ambition of modernist traditionalism to preserve such 'powerful original qualities' that were retained in the 'race-memory'; Eliot's 'ideal order' of 'existing monuments', for example, which were subject to modification by contemporary participation within that order.

A relative spirit

Cuvier's principle of 'correlation' and its function within the re-capitulationist theories of Agassiz was, of course, undeniably seductive for students of letters and of culture and particularly for modernism's concern with its own historicity: from Edward Taylor in 1865, 'the past is continually needed to explain the present, and the whole to explain the part',[61] to Pound in 1912, 'Sismondi said that one studied the past so as to learn how to deal with the present',[62] and to Eliot in 1919 for whom the 'historical sense' involved a perception 'not only of the pastness of the past, but of its presence'.[63] Specifically, the argument for 'tradition', understood as a function of 'race-memory' and modelled on biological procedure to determine, in Pound's later phrase, one's 'own ADDRESS (in time)', was primarily announced for modernism by Pater and Wilde.

In his essay on Coleridge, Pater defined the whole enterprise: 'Modern thought is distinguished from ancient by its cultivation of the "relative" spirit in place of the "absolute". . . . To the modern spirit, nothing is, or can be rightly known, except relatively.' This 'relative spirit' was grounded in the inductive sciences which were essentially 'the sciences of observation': 'The growth of those sciences consists in a continual analysis of facts of rough and general observation into groups of facts more precise and minute.'[64] Pater's practice was true to his theory; in the essay on Giorgione, for example, he examined his conception of the 'moment' from the point of view of its capacity for historical accumulation, claiming that it was part of the highest kind of art that it presents us with 'some brief and wholly concrete moment' in which 'all the motives, all the interests and effects of a long history, have condensed themselves, and which seem to absorb past and future in an intense conscious-ness of the present.'[65] Thus a major part of Giorgione's importance for Pater was his *influence*, and throughout *The Renaissance* Pater was concerned to place his subjects within a solid historical perspec-tive of figures and events that preceded and followed those subjects. Similarly, his later account of Plato in *Plato and Platonism* relied to a large extent on the versions of Platonism that succeeded Plato, and Pater's acute awareness of his own historical position, his own 'place in time'.

Wilde, too, stressed the importance of placing particular works within the compass of literature as a whole, rather than seeing them in isolation, echoing Pater's dictum that modernity involved above all a sense of its relative historical location. And from Wilde's Arnoldian advocation that the critic must proceed comparatively from the framework of 'the best that is known and thought in the world', it was but a short step to Pound's claim in 1913 that 'When we know to what extent each sort of expression has been driven in, say, half a dozen great literatures, we begin to be able to tell whether a given work has the excess of great art.'[66] Pater's sense of the 'relative' was partly a means towards establishing a distinctive version of the 'permanent'; in his essay on Winckelmann, he maintained that 'individual genius works ever under the conditions of time and place. . . . There is thus an element of change in art', but 'there is also an element of permanence, a standard of taste . . . maintained in a purely intellectual tradition.'[67] This 'standard' acted upon the artist through the art-products of previous cultures, providing a guide not only to his own contemporaneity but also to the practice he required for the perfection of his own art. The 'element of permanence' arose directly out of the 'relative spirit'; Pound was to note the problem of critical method in 1910 in the need for one 'balance' to weigh both Theocritus and Yeats simultaneously,[68] and in 1913 to plead for 'a Weltliteratur standard' derived from the comparative attitude instigated in the metropolis.[69]

It was Wilde who, to a larger extent than Pater, explicitly employed the models of heredity and memory to describe that sense of history which was to illuminate the idea of tradition in Pound and Eliot. His most famous definition of this historical sense was, appropriately, given in the course of a review of Pater's *Appreciations* in 1890 to gloss the term 'modernity' itself: 'For he to whom the present is the only thing that is present, knows nothing of the age in which he lives. To realize the nineteenth century, one must realize every century that has preceded it, and that has contributed to its making.' It was a definition completed by the historicity of heredity:

> The legacies of heredity may make us alter our views of moral responsibility, but they cannot but intensify our sense of the value of Criticism; for the true critic is he who bears within himself the dreams and ideas and feelings of myriad generations, and to whom no form of thought is alien, no emotional impulse obscure.[70]

In the same year, Wilde published that most 'modern' of his own works, 'The Critic as Artist', where he reiterated his definition but amplified his use of 'heredity' to sanction his notion of the 'contemplative' life: 'By revealing to us the absolute mechanism of all action, and so freeing us from the self-imposed and trammelling burden of moral responsibility, the scientific principle of Heredity has become, as it were, the warrant for the contemplative life.' Wilde's ideal of the 'contemplative' had as its instrument the 'critical spirit', synonymous with the imagination, which enabled the contemplator to live in his own time the 'countless lives' of the past and so maintain the contemporaneity of all the ages through the heredity which 'can help us to leave the age in which we were born, and to pass into other ages, and find ourselves not exiled from their air.' His description of this process of acquisition deliberately mimed the rhythm of Pater's famous testament to the accumulative potency of the *Mona Lisa*, which had been perceived in specifically biological terms (her beauty wrought out 'cell by cell'), and Wilde's model for the process was similarly biological: 'Do you think that it is the imagination that enables us to live these countless lives? Yes; it is the imagination; and the imagination is the result of heredity. It is simply concentrated race-experience.' The accumulative history witnessed by the 'contemplative' imagination, the 'critical spirit', was thus finally resolved into a view of heredity as 'concentrated race-experience': 'The culture that this transmission of racial experiences makes possible can be made perfect by the critical spirit alone, and indeed may be said to be one with it.' Wilde's 'critical spirit', the hallmark of his 'modernity', was enabled, with the aid of a notion of heredity, to realize 'the collective life of the race'.[71]

It was as a result of this biological view of history that Wilde claimed 'It is Criticism that makes us cosmopolitan', a view that became central for Pound's advocation of the standards of 'metropolis', and, as Pound was to mark the 'luminous detail' as a product of 'metropolis', so too had Wilde justified his claim on the basis of Cuvier's principle of 'correlation':

> where there is no record, and history is either lost, or was never written, Criticism can re-create the past for us from the very smallest fragment of language or art, just as surely as the man of science can from some tiny bone, or the mere impress of a foot upon a rock, re-create for us the winged dragon or Titan lizard that once made the earth shake beneath its tread, can call Behemoth out of his cave, and make Leviathan swim once more across the startled sea. . . . It can give us the exact science of the mind in the process of becoming.[72]

Furthermore, Wilde's significant phrase, 'the mind in the process of becoming', had a particular application for the notion of the 'permanent' within the complex of ideas that we have been discussing, since for Pater the evolutionary 'type' itself 'properly *is* not but is always only *becoming*'. The context of Pater's definition was his essay on 'Plato and the Doctrine of Motion', which was concerned to establish one of the most pervasive modernist dogmas, the confirmation by contemporary science of ancient philosophies; he asked of the 'entire modern theory of development': 'what is it but old Heracliteanism awake once more in a new world, and grown to full proportions?' In the process of elaborating this point, Pater adumbrated what was to be perhaps Pound's most famous technique of composition, the 'palimpsest'. Pater argued that 'The thoughts of Plato, like the language he has to use . . . are covered with the traces of previous labour and have had their earlier proprietors', and that 'as in many other very original products of human genius, the seemingly new is old also, a palimpsest, a tapestry of which the actual threads have served before, or like the animal frame itself, every particle of which has already lived and died many times over.'[73]

Pater's 'palimpsest' thus becomes an excellent cipher for a mode of writing informed by the complex of recapitulationist ideas we have been discussing.[74] These ideas found wider expression in letters than in science by the turn of the century; Agassiz's personal charisma had prolonged the intellectual life of recapitulation, but certainly G. Archdall Reid was right, in 1905, to recognize the doctrine as having suffered at the hands of professional scientists. His proposal for reinstatement did, however, achieve a measure of success; three years later, in another widely read textbook, J. Arthur Thomson admitted that although 'popular travesties have reduced a luminous idea to an absurdity, it remains in a general way true that the individual development, especially in the stages of organ-forming, is in some measure a recapitulation of the racial history.' This was a revealing, albeit grudging, admission of the fresh currency sought by the doctrine. Thomson continued:

> Although it is more picturesque than accurate to speak of 'every animal climbing up its own genealogical tree', there is a suggestive general resemblance between the stages in the individual development of organs . . . and the stages in the supposed racial evolution of the same.

Thomson's admission was especially significant, since it came from a theorist who was solidly opposed to the imaginative and metaphysical speculations of science (he had dismissed both Agassiz and recapitulation absolutely in his earlier *The Science of Life*), and he did pay tribute to Reid's book as 'An important study, *especially as to the practical aspects*' (my emphasis).[75]

A recapitulationist theory of memory provided not only a clear model for the operations of 'tradition' but also clear figurability for those operations. The 'branch' suggested by evolutionary theory was too flat a figure, and the 'circle' suggested by recapitulationist repetition was apt to be misleading. Samuel Butler proposed a 'spiral' as the most accurate figure, an illuminating choice in that it bore an obvious pictorial resemblance to the 'vortex' that Pound was to choose as his major figure for the accumulation and transmission of energy. Butler argued that memory did not instigate exact repetition (a circular reading of history) but that it was selective according to necessary modifications:

> memory of the most striking events of varied lifetimes I maintain . . . to be the differentiating cause, which, accumulated in countless generations, has led up from the amoeba to man. If there had been no such memory, the amoeba of one generation would have exactly resembled the amoeba of the preceding, and a perfect cycle would have been established – the modifying effects of an additional memory in each generation have made the cycle into a spiral.[76]

Pictorially, the 'spiral' evinced its superiority to the 'cycle' through its larger capacity for complication and integration and, by comparison, avoided the crude mechanism, manifestly false, of a deterministic repeat. Its layering effect, in addition, more closely represented the analogy of the 'palimpsest' as a mode of writing; for Pound, the 'repeat in history' was neither innocent nor neutral, but heavily overwritten by the appropriate signs of past and present in a relationship of entanglement. In his turn, Reid found it important to insist that recapitulation did not posit completeness or exact repetition; its integrated layers of connection operated through variation and gradual omission and addition: every variation could be seen as 'a structure capable of independent variation in an almost infinite number of directions' and as a consequence of which 'every species of plant and animal is in a condition of continual flux and change' so that 'As a whole the likeness to the parent is well-preserved', but 'in minutiae there is an immense amount of variation'. Reid distinguished two terms to describe the modes of variation, 'progressive' and 'regressive': by the former he intended 'a divergence from the ancestral type, a complete recapitulation plus an addition', and by the latter 'a reversion towards the ancestral type, an incomplete recapitulation'.[77] This distinction, when applied to literature, would suggest the difference between the effort to Make It New through events or works of the past and the debilitating enclosure of 'works gone dead', works of 'incomplete recapitulation', which offered merely shadows of the past: tradition, on the model of recapitulation, posited a form in which a work participated contemporaneously through an acknowledgement of its own historicity; neither implied any notion of completion and each anticipated further 'addition', further participation.

It was not accidental that the increasing attention to questions of heredity corresponded with the early modernist period itself. Mendel began publishing on the subject in German from 1865, but it remained a relatively minor area of study for several years (Mendel was not translated into English until 1901). As a major discipline, Galton's *Hereditary Genius* (1869) brought it to the notice of a wider audience, and from the 1880s onwards it found its most influential spokesmen in Weismann and de Vries.[78] Modernism's use of heredity, and, indeed, of science in general, was always at the level of analogy or metaphor; it thus declared its status *as* modern by rhetorical means, with a definite and attention-seeking verbal battle-cry. Despite Eliot's display of scientific analogy in earlier essays, particularly those published in *The Egoist* during 1918, the main point about the chemical catalyst that framed the argument from development in 'Tradition and the Individual Talent' is its place in the text. It was introduced at the end of the first instalment of the essay and then expanded and explained at the beginning of the second instalment. Deliberately, it operated as the fulcrum of the whole piece; its location emphasized above all its function as a public gesture of vocabulary. That function was further underscored by the fact that two months previously in the same magazine Eliot's 'Reflections on Contemporary Poetry' had also been concerned with the idea of 'tradition' but had eschewed any support from science; it was, as it were, a lexically neutral preparation for the modernist vocabulary of 'Tradition and the Individual Talent' which began in the following issue of *The Egoist*.

The art of creation

A diverse range of texts propagated an assumption of 'tradition' underwritten by biological theories of development, heredity and memory. Their diversity suggests the extent of a shared understanding, but it was in the nature of the mode of articulation chosen by this particular form of ideology that it should achieve expression through a single source, even a single text. That source was Edward Carpenter, whose audience during the Edwardian period was considerable. Emile Delavenay summarizes the focus of Carpenter's enterprise when he notes: 'being a man of the late nineteenth century, he needs, and in this he is not unlike the alchemists, to base his mysticism on some degree of scientific observation. This is why . . . he wants to find in neurology a justification for his beliefs.'[79] Carpenter's campaign to dislodge the primacy of the brain as the centre of response to the world by postulating 'the great sympathetic nerve' coincided with the work of those other anti-cerebralists so important to modernism, Bergson and, in particular, Gourmont, with his notion of the brain as a function of spermatic activity. Carpenter's starting-point was a familiar criticism of science in general: its 'failure' was seen as a result of 'the tendency to separate the logical and intellectual part of man from the emotional and instinctive, and to give it a *locus standi* of its own'.[80] As a counter to this 'failure' he emphasized the transitional function of the brain: 'behind the brain and determining its actions stands the great sympathetic nerve – the organ of the emotions. In fact here the brain appears as distinctly transitional. It stands between the nerves of sense on the one hand and the great sympathetic on the other.'[81] In his most important book for present purposes, *The Art of Creation* (1904), he reconstructed his earlier antinomies of the mechanist/vitalist question within the more immediate problematic of mind and matter as a version of Spinozan monism: 'There is a *distinction* between Mind and Matter (as of two aspects of the same thing), but no real separation.'[82]

The Art of Creation was the most comprehensive single exposition of the complex of ideas I have been discussing. Its premiss was an intelligence working throughout nature (another way of positing organization by design rather than by chance or accident), and Carpenter dramatized the seeds of the natural world as 'little dream-images in the brain of the great globe, waiting for their awakening' (p. 30). Nature, thus considered as 'an innumerable network and channel of intelligence and emotion', became expressive through its 'vibrations':

> the messages of light and sound and electricity and attraction penetrate everywhere; and as modern science shows us that the air, the sea, and the solid frame of the earth itself may be the vehicle of waves which without wire or definite channel may yet convey our thoughts safely to one another through intervening leagues of distance, so surely must we believe that the countless vibrations ever going on around, and ever radiating from and impinging on every known object, are messages too of endless meaning and feeling. (pp. 33–4)

Carpenter's 'vibrations' lacked the specificity of those advanced by Hering and Butler, but their function was rather different: Carpenter used 'vibrations' to suggest a union of discourse to articulate that unity of perception which ensured sympathy with the natural world, a sympathy whose 'Cosmic, or universal, Consciousness' refused the dichotomy of mind and matter. The universal knowledge so acquired further denied the distinctions of an earlier stage of epistemology (that between the knower and the thing known), which, argued Carpenter, was marked, in physiological terms, by the growth of the brain in conflict with 'the great sympathetic system' (pp. 58–9). By contrast, Carpenter's universal knowledge reconciled the self with the world; its echoes invoked not only the New England transcendentalists (Emerson and Whitman were among Carpenter's favourite sources of quotation) but the 'dissociation of sensibility' of Santayana, Gourmont and Eliot, and the metamorphic preoccupations of Pound. Carpenter had earlier admired Goethe's notion that all the 'separate' parts of a plant should be regarded as modifications of the leaves, 'the idea of leaf metamorphosis' ('In this view the distinctions between the parts are effaced and we have only the one part instead of the many')[83] which, in the present text, was elaborated as a metaphor of universal knowledge by a figure from physics:

> The external knowledge is transformed by being brought into relation with the original source of knowledge, i.e. the unity of all beings. It is, in fact, that hidden knowledge realized and made external. To borrow a simile from electricity, the luminous arc

springs into being when the circuit is complete, and is the evidence and manifestation of that completeness. (p. 63)

The unity that Carpenter proclaimed was thus heavily dependent on that 'assumed by all physical science', a relational unity conceived as 'a state where every object (or portion of the whole) is united to every other object (or portion) by infinite threads of relation – such infinitude of relations constituting the universal consciousness as embodied in that object' (p. 68).

What was distinctive about Carpenter's debate was his supplementation of the discourse from physics by the discourse of physiology; he proffered the Whitmanian question, 'How can the great Self also be millions of selves?', and answered at the cytological level, 'Well, we may ask, How can the self of the human body also be millions of selves in the component cells of the body?' on the grounds of the 'intimate relation' between them: 'The intelligence of each cell is an aspect or a differentiation of the intelligence of the body' (pp. 80–1). Arguing that 'modern science more and more attributes selfness and intelligence to cells', Carpenter consistently used the function of cell formation and action to describe 'mental' events as an ideal mechanism for the physiological unity between intellect and sensation and, further, to suggest the 'germinal consciousness' that was to become so important for Pound's 'Psychology and Troubadours': 'since the brain-cells are only differentiations of the primitive body-cells,' claimed Carpenter, 'we are compelled to think of the general cells as having a germinal consciousness', which, 'though they may convey their coenaesthesia or common sentiment to the brain', reveals, nevertheless that the brain 'originates, and has its first birth in them' (p. 97n.).

Crucially, Carpenter used cell function as the basis of his account of race-consciousness: a society or race, he claimed, 'has its individual members, its groups, and larger groups, culminating in the whole tribe or race as an entity, just the same as the cells with regard to the human body' (p. 99). This view of social organization was differentiated from the Spencerian 'social organism' by the effect of race-consciousness:

we see that at all times, in some mysterious way, the capacity of entering into the Race-consciousness is in us, and that daily and hourly this fact is moulding and modifying our lives: just the same as in every limb of my body there lurks the capacity of being thrilled by the great emotions of my total ego, and this fact in its turn guides and moulds the destinies and activities of my tiniest cells. (p. 100)

Carpenter's race-consciousness so conceived was a form of the immanent teleology popularized by Bergson. For Carpenter, a man's ego was at birth 'already affiliated to that of the race', a condensation of 'a ramifying thread of race-life' which stored 'the immense heritage of race-memory' (p. 104). In addition to the self-conscious brain, which, for the purposes of demarcating individuality, asserted the self dissociated from the race, Carpenter proposed this race-memory as communal hereditary experience, the 'subconscious hereditary Mind' as 'in the main represented by the Great Sympathetic nerve-system' (p. 107).

It was here that Carpenter exhibited one of the major hallmarks of modernism; he speculated on the forms in which race-memory expressed itself: 'the gods, the devils, and the great emotions represent our past in Race-consciousness' (p. 100). Like Pater before him and Pound after him, Carpenter found in modern science a confirmation of much older mythologies for describing the world; his notion of the immanence of the 'seeds' of material forms as 'little dream-images in the brain of the great globe, awaiting their awakening', was a version of a figure for 'Ideas' in, appropriately, the *Timaeus*:

> Thus Plato feigns in the 'Timaeus' that the universal spirit of God handed over the seeds of the immortal, imperishable Ideas to the lesser gods, who, each according to the race of men or animals over which he presided, was to embody these seeds in external forms. Thus the various races of living creatures arose – all vivified from within by the external Ideas, yet all having their various structures according to their races, and the genius of the particular god residing over the race.

The *Timaeus*, the most mathematically and physiologically orientated of all the dialogues, offered, to the temperament of Carpenter, a clear prediction of contemporary biology:

> In the language of modern Science, using the term 'Heredity' to cover much of the same ground as 'the genius of the race-god', we should say that while the ideas (say of melody and of flight in the case of birds) are the vivifying impulses of any class of

creatures, the particular forms (as of songs and of wings) are a matter of slowly growing heredity and the tradition of the race. (p. 129)[84]

As Butler insisted, memory was the key to heredity, and in his turn Carpenter's conjunction of heredity and Platonic idealism, of genetics and the notion of tradition, rested on memory: 'Thus we come near to Plato's *avauvnols*, and see how a kind of memory of celestial visions and powers may be roused by the sight of mortal things';[85] the essential ideas of a race were 'riveted and emphasized by Heredity' (p. 133).

The argument that such ideas were usually fictionalized as 'gods', that science reworded mythopoeic descriptions of psychic events, was one of the characteristic assumptions of Pound's perpetual reliance on ancient stories, much along the lines of Carpenter's testimony to the potency of beliefs in the 'gods': 'these figures derive their profound influence from the fact that they represent the *life of the race itself . . .* they are the manifestation and expression of that life' (p. 138). Furthermore, the continued presence of the 'gods' was a vestige of the Paterian 'relative spirit': 'In studying any phenomenon of the past it is always advisable to try and detect it in the life of today. And the moment we do so in this case we see that the gods are still living and real all around us' (pp. 138–9). The figure of, for example, the warrior hero, was 'an inherited composite image' with a physiological location, 'dwelling in or associated with a nerve-plexus' (p. 147n.). This 'image' had a twofold structure: 'in one sense this God-form is the result of the chiselling of thousands of minds, in another it is the Form which the Heroic Idea working through the centuries has fashioned for itself and has inspired the multitudinous minds to adore.' The 'image' was thus of 'the god himself, as one aspect of the race-life, whom we here see in his double activity', and its 'double activity' was both transcendental, 'as producing certain types of manhood, and as inspiring others to reverence and store in memory these types, so that at last through the mortal types the god himself may be beheld, and the race-life and race-consciousness entered into', and physiological, 'There in its appropriate centre or nerve-structure of the human body the heroic Idea dwells' (p. 147–8).

By means of this physiology, the 'gods', located within a 'nerve-plexus', entered into race-consciousness and were retained by race-memory. Myths and legends, in Carpenter's schema, arose out of 'the immense subconscious emotion of the race' as expressions of 'the selection and affectionate preservation from the memorial life of the race of events and stories which illustrate and symbolize some deep instinct and enthusiasm of the race' (pp. 154–5). This was a commonplace enough psychology; what differentiated Carpenter, however, from the more familiar expositions of anthropology or Jungian archetype or *anima mundi*, etc., was his insistence that the 'gods' and the myths that celebrated them were not '*mental* ideas', not 'handy little allegories and generalizations', but that 'the Ideas and enthusiasms which produce myths and legends lie deep down in the very structure and physical organization of humanity, and in its very *physiology*' (p. 156). Carpenter's preoccupation with neurological explanation was his major contribution to modernism's attempts to preserve traditionally metaphysical events from a sceptical and positivist world by elaborating new modes of materiality:

> there is among the nerves of the human body, of the brain and of the great sympathetic system, some kind of centre or plexus, or group of plexuses, which co-ordinates and dominates the love-instinct . . . connected and associated with this centre and its ramifications is a whole world of emotions, desires, mental images, thought activities . . . this centre, in both its physical and mental aspects, is the result and growth and embodiment of centuries and ages of race-experience. (p. 157)

The aim of *The Art of Creation* was to remove discussions of the 'gods' from fantasy and superstition, to reconstruct the merely anthropomorphic view of psychic experience by seeing them as representing not only 'very distinct centres and co-ordinations of feelings and activities in the race' but also 'very distinct centres of organic life in each human body' (each body which 'is indeed an epitome of the race'). As the physiological figures of the emotions, the 'gods' were seen not only to be 'aspects of the life of the race' but also to 'dwell in some sense in the organic nuclei and plexuses of the body, and to be the centres of command and service there' (p. 160).[86]

Carpenter took Hardy's 'The Well-Beloved' to demonstrate the contiguity between conceptions of memory envisaged by Platonism and by heredity: both derived the 'sentiment of Beauty' from 'our continuity with an order of existence beyond what we usually call our own' and, while in the Platonic view, 'the dream-figure which walked by the man's side was a reminiscence of some celestial form seen long ago, but still dwelling there, far in the heavens', heredity regarded the same figure as 'the revivescence within the mind, of a luminous form, the complex product or manifested presence of ages of race-consciousness and memory'. In either case, claimed Carpenter, 'it was the working of another order of consciousness within the man' (pp. 195–6). This particular form of Romantic transcendentalism was most pertinent to the new poetics of the 'real' that Pound based on exactly such reconstructed materiality defined in terms both mythopoeic and psycho-physiological. Carpenter contended that we cannot dismiss the vision in Hardy's poem 'as merely subjective':

> Taking the Heredity view, we cannot refuse to see that the race-life which builds up and projects these Visions, dreams, and glamours is intensely real, and that the visions, &c., are quite real and necessary manifestations of it. This race-life is, as a matter of fact, within each of us, and forms the chief, though a subconscious, part of our individual selves; we, as conscious individuals, are simply the limbs and prolongations of it. When, therefore, Hardy's pilgrim sees the 'god-created norm of womankind' walking beside him he sees something which, in a sense, is *more* real than the figures in the street, for he sees something that has lived and moved for thousands of years in the heart of the race . . . and which has done as much to create those very figures in the street as qualities in the circulation of the blood may do to form a finger or other limb. (pp. 196–7)

Carpenter's 'gods' were thus not considered as static, eternal embodiments but as integrated functions of the world of process. In conjunction with theories of biological development, they were 'no changeless, inviolate beings, but . . . may be thought of as continually growing, evolving' (p. 198), changing as the race-life continually varied and modified its aspirations. The individual conceived as 'our own race-mind made visible' (p. 212), as the 'consolidated racial mind' (p. 218), substantiated the unity of material and psychic phenomena and the concomitant unity of discourse which the whole purpose of *The Art of Creation* was designed to illustrate: 'New ideals, new qualities, new feelings and envisagements of the outer world, are perpetually descending from within . . . new centres and plexuses are forming among the nerves; new gods are presiding in the region of our dreams' (p. 223).

The unity advanced by Carpenter's discourse, of 'gods' and 'nerve-plexuses', marked his distinctive version of Pater's 'relative spirit'; Carpenter's larger synthesis of Platonic transcendentalism and contemporary physiology gave lexical affirmation to the historicity proclaimed by Pater's principle, a historicity conceived within the perspective of recapitulation. Towards the end of the book, Carpenter concerned himself with a case-study of the mayfly organized exactly according to this perspective: 'the successive changes in the embryo and the young form a kind of epitome of the history of the race to which the individual belongs . . . the growth of the individual thus resumes and rehearses in brief the agelong previous life and growth of the race' (p. 243). Race-history understood in recapitulationist terms could best be defined as a record of change and novelty consequent upon the necessity for the organism's continual variation and adaptation. A literary tradition conceived on analogous lines would consist in, to adopt Pound's vocabulary, the innovative or the 'donative' moments of 'luminous detail', moments charged with the force of 'centuries of race-consciousness' and capable of providing access to concrete historical situations. For Carpenter, memory was thus the articulator not only of heredity but of recapitulation: 'it is difficult not to see in this recapitulation by the individual of the general outlines of the history of his race, something very like the working of a racial memory transmitted to the individual' (p. 246). The various modes of unity discerned by Carpenter in his disquisitions on memory, heredity, neurology, mysticism and recapitulation – modes expressive at the lexical, material and intellectual levels – gave rise, eight years later, to one of modernism's most sustained testaments to contemporary science's potential for maintaining, primarily through a view of the world as a series of 'vibrations', the universal synthesis that manifested the ancient doctrine of nature's intelligence:

> The obvious signs of intelligence in the minutest cells, almost invisible to the naked eye, the very mysterious arcana of growth in such cells . . . the myriad action of similarly intelligent microbes, the strange psychology of plants, and the equally

strange psychic sensitiveness (apparently) of *metals*, the sudden transformations and variations both of plants and animals, the existence of the X and N rays of light, and of countless other vibrations of which our ordinary senses render no account, the phenomena of radium and radiant matter, the marvels of wireless telegraphy, the mysterious facts connected with hypnotism and the subliminal consciousness, and the certainty now that tele-pathic communication can take place between human beings thousands of miles apart – all these things have convinced us that the subtlest forces and energies, totally unmeasurable by our instruments, and saturated or at least suffused with intelligence, are at work all around us.[87]

Since Pound's understanding of 'tradition', and of the 'gods' that figured that 'tradition', belonged to this world of 'transformations', 'variations' and 'vibrations', his conception of memory was distinct from the more familiar conceptions held by his contemporaries, such as Yeats.[88] In Pound's thought the 'gods' were always associ-ated with metamorphosis; in the San Trovaso Notebook, he wrote of 'Shalott': 'Of such perceptions rise the ancient myths of the origin of demi-gods. Even as the ancient myths of metamorphosis rise out of flashes of cosmic consciousness.'[89] His most famous definition of metamorphosis was given in 1915: 'The undeniable tradition of metamorphoses teaches us that things do not remain always the same. They become other things by swift and unanalys-able process.'[90] This definition was taken from Pater's essay on 'Coleridge', at the point where Pater was dealing with the relation-ship between contemporary science and older philosophies. In the general context of his belief in heredity ('Man's physical organism is played upon not only by the physical conditions about it, but by remote laws of inheritance, the vibration of long-past acts, reaching him in the midst of the new order of things in which he lives'), Pater claimed that the fruits of the 'sciences of observation', the inductive sciences, 'reveal types of life evanescing into each other by in-expressible refinements of change. Things pass into their opposites by accumulation of undefinable qualities.'[91] Two years prior to his definition, Pound received the Fenollosa notes that were to become *The Chinese Written Character as a Medium for Poetry*, and there again he found a poetics integrated with science's concern with principles of change and development. It was metaphor, the linguistic counterpart to metamorphosis, that marked the essential difference between Chinese and phonetic languages, bringing words 'closer to the concreteness of natural process'. In this sense, the phonetic word was neutral – 'There is little or nothing in a phonetic word to exhibit the embryonic stages of its growth. It does not bear its metaphor on its face' – while the ideogram displayed a calligraphic recapitulation of its history:

> Its etymology is constantly visible. . . . Its uses . . . throw about it a nimbus of meanings. . . . The memory can hold them and use them. . . . With us the poet is the only one for whom the accumulated treasures of the race-words are real and active. Poetic language is always vibrant with fold on fold of overtones and with natural affinities, but in Chinese the visibility of the metaphor tends to raise this quality to its intensest power.[92]

Fenollosa's 'race-words', displaying the processes of their heredity by their calligraphic memory, thus ensured the ideographic method as the residual cipher of modernist traditionalism articulated through the analogies of biological development: the final exfoliation of a transcendentalist poetics which, in Pound's terms, offered control over 'race-long recurrent moods'.[93] Their self-consciousness exhibited the wider issues of modernism's programme for its own historical location; as Allen Upward, thinking in these terms, wrote in 1911: 'It is a sign of the times that so many of us should be busy in studying the signs of the times.'[94]

6 Towards a conclusion: the endless sentence

> There is no *is*. There is no present tense in the meta-strophe of time. The Present is the point at which the Future turns into the Past. (Upward)

Chemistry of the soul

'We turn back, we artists,' wrote Pound in 1914, 'to the powers of the air, to the djinns who were our allies aforetime, to the spirits of our ancestors.'[1] Myth and art ritualized the potency of valuable experience and knowledge and made it new through repetition in their own time, a repetition sealed, as it were, in organic continuity by the researches of contemporary science. This was not a condition of comfort; Yeats, in seeking to explain the 'transition' in the arts of the period (which was ultimately sited in the problematic of the material and the immaterial), sought its meaning in the line 'The very sunlight's weary, and it's time to quit the plough' which he glossed:

> Its importance is the greater because it comes to us at the moment when we are beginning to be interested in many things which positive science, the interpreter of exterior law, has always denied: communion of mind with mind in thought and without words, foreknowledge in dreams and in visions, and the coming among us of the dead, and of much else.

Yeats's anti-materialist stance of 1898 consequently proposed a priesthood of the arts to resist the limitations of a positivist world:

> The arts are, I believe, about to take upon their shoulders the burdens that have fallen from the shoulders of the priests, and to lead us back upon our journey by filling our thoughts with the

essences of things, and not with things. We are about to substitute once more the distillation of alchemy for the analyses of chemistry and for some other sciences; and certain of us are looking everywhere for the perfect alembic that no silver or golden drop may escape.[2]

The opposition between 'essences' and 'things', the search for 'the perfect alembic', was the basis for the reaction against Victorian materialism that Arthur Symons coded as symbolism, 'a literature in which the visible world is no longer a reality, and the unseen world no longer a dream'; literature's function was conceived as 'ritual' and 'religion':

Here, then, in this revolt against exteriority, against rhetoric, against a materialist tradition; in this endeavour to disengage the ultimate essence, the soul, of whatever exists and can be realized by the consciousness; in this dutiful waiting upon every symbol by which the soul of things can be made visible; literature, bowed down by so many burdens, may at last attain liberty, and its authentic speech. In attaining this liberty, it accepts a heavier burden; for in speaking to us so intimately, so solemnly, as only religion had hitherto spoken to us, it becomes itself a kind of religion, with all the duties and responsibilities of the sacred ritual.[3]

Symons's distrust of the 'materialist tradition' was to be only partially true for the later phase of modernism, which required a more complex notion of the 'real': in the Poundian system, the 'religion' and 'ritual' of 'good art'[4] was never understood as divorced from the conditions of science; the myths that constituted such a large part of ritual were conceived not as decorative stories but as a residue of truth presented in the form of 'an interpretation of nature'.[5] The substantial difference between the modernism of Symons and that of Pound was a difference of vocabulary; the ambition of both was to elaborate, in Symons's phrase, 'a new, an older sense in the so worn out forms of things'. This ideal of totality has been perceptively explained by John Goode: 'It is because Symbolism came to England not as the making of new forms, but as a new light on an organic, if occult, tradition that modernism could site itself within that ideology.'[6] While Pound shared Symons's distrust of mechanism, he also considered that, within this ideology, science had the function of confirming the mysticism of earlier myth and ritual; while Symons chose the model of religion to express the artist's responsibilities, Pound chose the model of the scientist's laboratory work. In fact, Symons's account of the symbolists' mysticism strongly resembled the propositions for cosmic unity that were available to Pound in pre-Socratic atomism and in New England transcendentalism; Symons wrote of Gérard de Nerval, for example:

> All things live, all things are in motion, all things correspond; the magnetic rays emanating from myself or others traverse without obstacle the infinite chain of created things: a transparent network covers the world, whose loose threads communicate more and more closely with the planets and the stars.

In claiming that here was the 'central secret of the mystics, from Pythagoras onwards', Symons pointed directly to two of the major sources for transcendentalist epistemology, Boehme's 'signatures' and Swedenborg's 'correspondences'.[7]

For Pound, the true mystic was he who abhorred the 'cloudy'; in 1912, he glossed his favourite quotation from Spinoza, 'The intellectual love of a thing consists in the understanding of its perfections', as a tribute to precision:

> Some mystic or other speaks of the intellect as standing in the same relation to the soul as do the senses to the mind; and beyond a certain border, surely we come to this place where the ecstasy is not a whirl or a madness of the senses, but a glow arising from the exact nature of the perception.[8]

This precision certainly marked a removal from the sensory world, a necessary displacement, but it did not involve the denial of that world's expression through science that we find in Symons, who had also insisted on the clarity of mysticism.[9] Consequently, the analogous precision of science became for Pound a wholly appropriate vehicle for the explication of mysticism and for the announcement of the artist's responsibilities to society at large. The precision of science and mysticism belonged to the same order of perception, a perception that sought meaning and value through the objects, the 'things' of the phenomenal world. As Max Nänny has suggested, on the basis of Whitehead's *Science and the Modern World*, empiricist modern science was 'through and through an anti-intellectualist movement, an anti-rationalist trend', and this 'anti-rationalist bias in favour of direct perception' was 'natural to the mystic or scientist'.[10] This recognition, in itself, seems to me to be correct, but it is severely limited; by 'direct perception' here, Nänny means a 'naïve faith in facts or things'. The vocabularies of biology and electromagnetism whereby Pound articulated his perceptions expressly denied the uncomplicated nature of 'facts' and 'things' that Nänny implies, and his struggle for those vocabularies with their complex range of reference certainly precluded any sense of the naïve. Furthermore, as I shall show, Nänny's proposal refuses utterly to approach the problematic of a poetics of the 'real' which incorporated such 'things'.

After spending over a decade of work on the *Cantos*, Pound returned to the issues of his London years to argue for a model of dissociation available in biological procedure, a model restricted from more general usage because 'we are slower to take over the ways of thinking and thought instruments from science than one wd. think were possible' and, remembering Fenollosa's lesson, because 'We continue with thought forms and with language structures used by monolinear medieval logic, when the aptitudes of human mind developed in course of bio-chemical studies have long since outrun such simple devices.' By this he meant that 'the biologist can often know and think clearly a number of things he can not put in a simple sentence; he can dissociate things for which there is as yet no dissociated language structure.'[11] In a context that reiterated not only Fenollosa but also Whistler's strictures on the particular materiality of painting ('lines', 'arrangements', 'harmonies') that resisted spurious questions of 'meaning' (seen to be extraneous to the truth of a painting as an object), Pound prescribed the function of dissociation as a means of distinguishing 'the great artist and the poor artist': it was the former who 'has so vigorously or so persistently, or so clearly or in such sudden and violent light dissociated some concept in some particular tone, shade, and set of implications that his expression becomes a new noun'.[12] By seeing the artist's 'dissociated concept' as a *noun*, Pound was arguing for its status as a special order of object; this 'noun', as the primary solid of a language structure, required, as an expression of dissociation, particular terms of reference: the terms of biology.

'We are as capable or almost as capable as the biologist', argued Pound, 'of thinking thoughts that join like spokes in a wheelhub

and that fuse in hyper-geometric amalgams.' As figures for the 'new
noun', these 'spokes in a wheelhub' and these 'hyper-geometric
amalgams' belonged to a habit of practicality that Pound had
always maintained could instigate access to the sensory actuality of
the world: 'In a general sense the quarrel is as old as Hippocrates,
but in a particular sense it has a new application not to science but
to verbal manifestation.' He was referring to a habit of engaged
experience: 'Berman goes as far as to deny real understanding even
to men who have had laboratory experience if they have not also
had experience as medical practitioners.'[13] Pound's choice of
Berman and Hippocrates as exemplars of this habit and of the
linguistic conflation of 'hyper-geometric amalgams' (where linguistic novelty matched phenomenal novelty) was indicative of the
new mode of the 'real' he sought for the 'noun' introduced by
dissociation.

Louis Berman was the author of *The Glands Regulating Personality* (1922), a study of physiology that Pound reviewed for *The
New Age* in 1922.[14] Berman's book postulated that the activity of
the glands was the source of both conscious and subconscious behaviour; its purpose was to illustrate the thesis that 'The human
animal has achieved no advance beyond the necessities of his
ancestors, nor freed himself from his bondage to their instincts and
automatic reflexes.'[15] As an exercise in material investigation,
Berman clearly marked a signal advance not only on the earlier
physiology of Butler, Ellis and Carpenter, which had sustained a
neurological basis for 'race-consciousness' and notions of tradition,
but also on the recapitulationist biology of Agassiz. Pound had
Berman's thesis in mind when he wrote 'On Criticism in General'
during the following year and noted what he saw as the weakness in
Ford Madox Ford's critical procedure: 'I think Hueffer goes wrong
because he bases his criticism on the eye, and almost solely on the
eye. Nearly everything he says applies to things *seen*.' It was as a
counter to this weakness that Pound remembered Berman: 'Man is
an animal . . . he is affected by interstitial pressures, from seven sets
of glands, and from the sensations of taste, sight, hearing, touch,
etc., etc.' Pound's point was not only to suggest the limitations of
Ford's criticism but also to comment on the fact that Ford's
'impressionist' criteria simply 'let in too many people' and consequently allowed for imprecision; the 'seven sets of glands', argued
Pound, 'leave a residuum, dangerous to Mr Hueffer's theories, and

doubly dangerous to everyone else, because this residuum can be talked about in vague terms.'[16]

Pound's use of Berman here suggests the distinct urge to power he saw being dissipated, as modes of knowledge such as those expressed by Berman's physiology became more widely diffused. The gesture towards determinism implicit in Berman's thesis would, of course, promise an obvious means of control, but not in the crude reading offered by a recent commentator who argues that it 'proclaims the doctrine that a person's emotions, his physique, his actions and what we call his personality are all rigidly determined by his particular glandular structure.'[17] Such a reading confuses the difference between a merely mechanical account of the relationship between physiology and certain psychic states, and the more flexible postulation of a physiological explanation for those states, the explanation that assumes a physio-chemical rather than a psychological description. The confusion in turn disguises the real function of control attendant upon physiological explanation, its concealment within an argument for freedom. Berman wrote that 'the history of mankind is, too, a long research into the nature of the machinery of freedom', and he insisted that the aim of his own work was to participate in that record of freedom:

> All recorded history, indeed, is but the demonstration of that research. Viewed thus, customs, laws, institutions, sciences, arts, codes of morality and honour, systems of life, become inventions, come upon, tried out, standardized, established until scrapped in ever-lasting search for more and more perfect means of freeing body and soul from their congenital thralldom to a host of in-numerable masters.[18]

Pound shared this view; Berman diagnosed 'types' on the basis of glandular activity (which, for Pound, was the foundation for the book's 'revolution'), and Pound remarked:

> A whole new field of research is opened . . . the general tendency is to recognize that human beings can differ widely from each other without being abnormal; and a strong scientific support for this 'humanity' can only make for civilization, tolerance, and an end of Fabian and Puritan endeavours to cram all human beings into one button-mould.[19]

Here was how the 'new noun' produced by the dissociative temperament added, in Allen Upward's phrase, 'a new thing to the contents of the universe' and not merely 'a new word to the dictionary'; the dissociative 'noun' resisted the abstract vocabulary that occurred 'when, instead of thinking of men one by one, you think of them all at once, and call your thought humanity'.[20] Pound had remembered Upward's lesson in 1914, and we can begin to see clearly how this argument incorporated a non-social aesthetic: Upward's view reiterated what he called 'the heresy of the Nominalists' – the proposition that 'names are not things' – whereby abstract terms inevitably fudged dissociation as, for Pound, Ford's impressionism led to 'vague terms' when it 'let in too many people'.[21] Pound claimed in a later essay which recalled Berman: 'The artist, if he is any good, expresses his own dissociated concept. . . . He puts forward this concept as distinct from the blurred, messy, less defined or by-the-public-demanded formulation of the to-the-public-familiar.'[22]

The précis of Berman's position in his review was one of Pound's major acknowledgements of a physiological basis for experiences traditionally understood to be beyond the range of physiology:

> The present belief is that the body has slowly developed about the endocrine glands; the pineal, pituitary, thyroid, parathyroid, thymus, adrenals, pancreas, and the gonads; that these are older than the brain (cerebrum), and that they control the unconscious, or that they are the subconscious; that when the secretions of these glands interact in certain ways, they produce definite chemical pressure, and that when this pressure reaches a certain intensity it forces itself on the consciousness.

The book's value lay not only in its glandular physiology but in its practical, experimental method, which offered a sure guide to the 'real'. Pound began his review by noting that the book 'offers us a comforting relief from Freudian excess'. By comparison with Berman's 'experiment', the Freudians 'try continually to relieve complexes by psychological means before considering whether chemical means would not be simpler', and Pound accused Freud's work of being limited by his 'working in a vacuum': 'You have all this talk of suppressed wishes, but no analysis of the charged wish itself.'[23] It was thus on the basis of Berman's method as well as his thesis that Pound claimed: 'the book marks presumably one of the great revolutions in medicine.' Berman's theoretical and practical achievement was consequently the most complete demolition of the division between the material and the non-material:

> Berman uses the term 'chemistry of the soul', and one may accept it or qualify it; certainly he has demonstrated the impossibility of an independent or separate soul-entity manifesting itself through a body in which the thyroid supply falls below a certain minimum.[24]

Berman's research into glandular activity confirmed the epistemology that underwrote Pound's use of scientific analogy during his London years; here was the final evidence for the shared physiology of body and soul that had been implicit in his poetics since 'Psychology and Troubadours', as well as for the materiality of the new 'real', which marked the resolution of a transcendentalist aesthetic. Its immediate application was to his reading of Gourmont's *The Natural Philosophy of Love*, which had appeared the previous year in Pound's own translation, and which had speculatively suggested to him similar conclusions to those of Berman.[25] Specifically, Pound wanted to elaborate on the notion of the brain as 'maker or presenter of images' by virtue of its nature as 'a sort of great clot of genital fluid held in suspense or reserve'.[26] In one sense, this was an updating of the tensile sexual energy Pound had discerned in Provence, but it also reminds us that the notion of the brain as a gland had its origins in Hippocrates (whom Pound was to pair with Berman to support his advocation of the biologist as an exemplar of the dissociative sensibility in his essay on 'Epstein, Belgion and Meaning' of 1928), a fact that Pound would have read in, among other places, Emerson's essay on 'Swedenborg',[27] which provided the fullest account of the doctrine of correspondence. As the 'vortex' of field-theory physics had confirmed that of pre-Socratic cosmology, as theories of heredity sanctioned the notions of race-consciousness in modernist traditionalism, so contemporary endocrinology sustained one of the most potent conjectures of Greek medicine in its early experimental stage and implied a final, most intimate and concrete proof for the patterns of correspondence that Pound's poetics, through the discourses of science, always assumed.

Prior to his reading of Berman, Pound had found evidence for patterns of correspondence between material and non-material

experience in Gourmont's less disciplined physiology, in a 'complicated sensuous wisdom' which, as Pound wrote in 1919, 'if not of
the senses, is at any rate via the senses' and which instigated an
epistemology of 'osmosis' for the interstitiality of the 'real': 'He
does not grant the duality of body and soul . . . there is an interpenetration, an osmosis of body and soul, at least for hypothesis.'[28]
Pound returned to the vocabulary of electromagnetism to express
this 'osmosis' in his Postscript to *The Natural Philosophy of Love*:
'Take it that usual thought is a sort of shaking or shifting of a fluid
in the viscous cells of the brain; one has seen electricity stripping the
particles of silver from a plated knife in a chemical bath, with order
and celerity, and gathering them on the other pole of a magnet.' His
vocabulary stamped his reading as a reworking of the Provençal
tensile energy of 1912; he wrote of the brain lobes as 'two great
seas of fecundative matter, mutually magnetized', and proposed
that the glands themselves 'may serve rather as fuses in an electric
system, to prevent short circuits, or in some variant or allotropic
form.'[29] Pound's vocabulary again asserted a further mode of
expression, that of the truths of experience ritualized by myth and
by talk of the gods. For Pound, such truths were a necessary
counter to what he saw as the increasingly mechanistic nature of
contemporary life, which denied the 'sensuous wisdom', the response of the full body, he found valuable in Gourmont:

> In his growing subservience to, and adoration of, and entangle-
> ment in machines, in utility, man rounds the circle almost into
> insect life, the absence of flesh; and may have need even of
> horned gods to save him, or at least a form of thought which
> permits them.[30]

A request for a 'form of thought' that would permit talk of such
'gods' was a further request for 'a language to think in', the ambition of all Pound's critical prose during his London years. The
vocabulary of electromagnetism expressing glandular activity indicated the provenance of this ambition at the lexical level, and
reflected the famous summary at the end of Pound's Postscript to
Gourmont, which described the composition of the ambition by
explicating a 'clue' from Propertius, '*Ingenium nobis ipsa puella
fecit*':

> There is the whole of the twelfth century love cult, and Dante's
> metaphysics a little to one side, and Gourmont's Latin Mystique;

and for image-making both Fenollosa on *The Chinese Written Character*, and the paragraphs in *Le Problème du Style*. At any rate the quarrel between cerebralist and viveur and ignorantist ends, if the brain is thus conceived not as a separate and desiccated organ, but as the very fluid of life itself.[31]

Pound's 'clue' was given its full material status in Gourmont's *Le Chemin de velours* (1902):

> Unless our organism is such that the abstract notion redescends towards the senses the moment it has been understood; unless the word beauty gives you a visual sensation; unless handling ideas gives you a physical pleasure, almost like caressing a shoulder or a fabric, let ideas alone.[32]

Physics of thought

It was his reading of Gourmont that instigated Pound's acceptance of a totally physiological view of creative behaviour:

> Thought is a 'chemical process' in relation to the organ, the brain; creative thought is an act like fecundation, like the male cast of the human seed. . . . Gourmont has the phrase 'fecundating a generation of bodies as genius fecundates a generation of minds'.[33]

Pound's attention to Gourmont's physiology had been shared by James Huneker who similarly approached Gourmont from the standpoint of science's potential for dislocating orthodoxies and displaying new modes of reality: 'Old frontiers have disappeared in science and art and literature. We have Maeterlinck, a poet writing of bees, Poincaré, a mathematician opening our eyes to the mystic gulfs of space; solid matter resolved into mist, and the law of gravitation questioned.'[34] Huneker was almost singlehandedly responsible for introducing Gourmont to an American audience, featuring him in *Mlle New York* in 1895, reviewing the *Livres des masques* in 1897 and providing the first substantial account of Gourmont for America in the *New York Sun* in 1900.[35] Huneker's admiration was reciprocated; Gourmont wrote of Huneker's collection of stories, *Visionaries* (1905), in 1906: 'I am convinced that you have written a very curious, very beautiful book, and one of that sort comes to us rarely.'[36]

In part, the relationship between Huneker and Gourmont was a response of like to like; both were versatile in their knowledge not only of the arts but also of the sciences, and both delighted particularly in the dislocations of received ideas that resulted from contemporary scientific research. Huneker's essay of 1917 on Gourmont proclaimed that 'The image of the concrete is De Gourmont's touchstone'. That 'image' was applicable not only to Gourmont's prose but to the materiality of his thought: Huneker saw *Un Cœur virginal* (1907), for example, as a sequel to the *Physique de l'amour* (1903), noting that in the former, 'we touch earth, fleshly, and spiritually. . . . It shows mankind as a gigantic insect indulging in the same apparently blind pursuit of sex sensation as a beetle.'[37] In Pound's version, this was Gourmont's 'sexual intelligence', manifest in a line he quoted from the earlier *Songe d'une femme* (1899): 'La virginité n'est pas une vertu, c'est un état; c'est une sousdivision des couleurs.'[38] Gourmont's physiology rescued the misguided abstraction of a condition like virginity from a perverse and prohibitive puritan theology; Huneker's essay underlined the materialist context of that physiology, a context whose testimony to universal correspondence played so large a part in Pound's own aesthetics:

> The universe had no beginning, it will have no end. There is no first link or last in the chain of causality. Everything must submit to the law of causality; to explain a blade of grass we must dismount the stars. . . . There are no isolated phenomena in time or space. The mass of matter is eternal. Man is an animal submitting to the same laws that govern crystals or brutes. He is the expression of matter in physique or chemistry. Repetition is the law of life. Thought is a physiological product; intelligence the secretion of matter and is amenable to the law of causality.

Huneker was careful to distinguish Gourmont's materialism from the mechanistic version, claiming that it was 'not the rigid old-fashioned materialism, but a return to the more plastic theories of Lamarck and the transformism of the Dutch botanist, Hugo de Vries'. It was a means of dislodging the primacy of man himself – 'the Darwinian notion that man is at the topmost notch of creation is as antique and absurd as most cosmogonies'[39] – and Pound, too, sought to dislodge such primacy by means of Gourmont's account of sexual energy: 'From the studies of insects to Christine evoked from the thoughts of Diomède, sex is not a monstrosity or an

exclusively German study.' While admiring Gourmont's proposal
of a shared basis of sexuality among all species, however, Pound
felt it important to urge that beyond 'a purely physiological reproductive mechanism' there also existed a sexual energy such as he
had discerned in Provence, which lay 'in the domain of aesthetics,
the junction of tactile and magnetic senses'.[40] Two years later, in his
Postcript to *The Natural Philosophy of Love*, Pound clearly felt
that such distinctions were small beer in maintaining the 'sper-
matozoic act of the brain'.[41]

Huneker's insistence on Gourmont's materialism drew attention
to that cast of Gourmont's mind which only Huneker and Pound
appeared to recognize fully. Significantly for our present argument,
Gourmont used his materialism to redefine idealism; he advocated
a 'physics of thought':

> We know that it is a product, since we can curtail it by injuring the
> producing organ. Thought is not only a product, but a material
> product, measurable, ponderable. Unformulated externally, it
> nevertheless manifests its physical existence by the weight which
> it imposes upon the nervous system.

On the basis of this 'physics of thought', Gourmont then sought to
dispel idealism (the 'reigning doctrine in philosophy') as an abstract
notion: 'Idealism is definitely founded on the very materiality of
thought, considered as a physiological product. . . . The reasons for
idealism plunge deeply into matter. Idealism means materialism,
and conversely, materialism means idealism.'[42] This redefinition
was fully within the transcendentalist tradition of Emerson and
Whitman which signally informed the responses of Pound and
Huneker to Gourmont (Huneker had recognized in Whitman a
'concrete imagination' which 'automatically rejected metaphysics'[43]), and it was Huneker's own relationship to that tradition
and its current formulations that gave his materialism a provenance
remarkably akin to Pound's.

Being of a 'practical temperament', Huneker read Browning
every morning 'to prepare myself for the struggle with the world'[44]
and acknowledged the materiality of Bergson's 'vital idea' of time
whereby the historicity of the past was not 'abstract' but 'concrete,
real'; this idea merited Bergson a phrase Huneker was later to use
for Gourmont, 'a mighty maker of images'.[45] While Pound was
lightly to touch on Laforgue's scientific interests ('He has dipped his

wings in the dye of scientific terminology'[46]), Huneker attended to
those interests with the full force of transcendentalist epistemology:
'He would have welcomed Maeterlinck's test question: "Are you
one of those who name or those who only repeat names?" Laforgue
was essentially a namer – with Gallic glee he would have enjoyed
renaming the animals as they left the Noachian ark.'[47] Maeterlinck
was the most available literary figure of scientific persuasion (his
most famous scientific work, *La Vie des abeilles* (1901), was listed
in the bibliography for *The Natural Philosophy of Love*), but Noah
himself provided an even more suitable example of science's lexicography: two years later, in 'Four Dimensional Vistas', Huneker
wrote of him as 'the supreme symbol of science, he the first namer
of the animals in the ark'. The subject of Huneker's essay was the
'mysticism' of Claude Bragdon's *Four Dimensional Vistas*, and,
after a lifetime of elaborating a concrete base for a diverse range of
esoteric thought, Huneker was concerned to do away with much of
the vagueness that customarily characterized discussion of subjects
such as the 'fourth dimension': 'After studying Saint Teresa, John
of the Cross, Saint Ignatius, or the selections in Vaughan's Hours
with the Mystics, even the doubting Thomas is forced to admit that
there is no trace of rambling discourse, fugitive ideation, half-
stammered enigmas.' Contrary to such vagueness was the 'true
mystic' who 'abhors the cloudy' and whose vision 'pierces with
crystalline clearness the veil of the visible world'.[48] Here was the
materialist clarity that Aldington noted on behalf of Gourmont –
'one sees that there is a mystical sort of beauty even in science and
under his pen mysticism itself appears almost as exact as a
science'[49] – and that Pound, using Gourmont to focus the accumulative provenance of his London aesthetics, discovered to be the
'exact expression' of 'mysticism' that characterized the 'profound
psychological knowledge' of Provence.[50] Huneker's 'practical
temperament', too, connected mystical perception with precision of
style:

> As literary style we find sharp contours and affirmations. Mysti-
> cism is not all cobweb lace and opal fire. Remember that we are
> not stressing the validity of either the vision or its consequent
> judgements; we only wish to emphasize the absence of muddy
> thinking in these writings. This quality of precision . . . we en-
> counter in Claude Bragdon's Four Dimensional Vistas.[51]

Bragdon, an architect and author of theosophical tracts, provided an excellent combination as an exemplar of concrete clarity: 'He is a mystic. He is also eminently practical . . . both a mathematician and a poet.' This combination enabled entry to an order of perception not available to 'the grosser senses'; mystical mathematics (Pound's Cartesian geometry) returned us, argued Huneker, to transcendentalist world:

> Nature geometrizes, said Emerson, and it is interesting to note the imagery of transcendentalism through the ages. It is invariably geometrical. Spheres, planes, cones, circles, spirals, tetragrams, pentagrams, ellipses, and what-not. A cubistic universe. Xenophanes said that God is a sphere. And then there are the geometrical patterns made by birds on the wing. Heaven in any religion is another sphere. Swedenborg offers a series of planes, many mansions for the soul at its various stages of existence.

Huneker's major contribution to this world was to claim that its geometrical patterns were a product of a discernible physiology:

> The precise patterns in our brain, like those of the ant, bee, and beaver, which enable us to perceive and build the universe (otherwise called innate ideas) are geometrical. . . . That 'astral trunk' once so fervently believed in may prove a reality; it is situated behind the ear and is a long tube that ascends to the planet Saturn, and by its aid we should be enabled to converse with spirits! The pineal gland is the seat of the soul, and miracles fence us in at every step.[52]

There was, of course, an element of whimsy in Huneker's tone here, a deliberate strategy in a collection of essays that began in praise of the 'reality' of unicorns and chose its epigraph from Emerson: 'I would write on the lintels of the door-post, "Whim".' But the principle of Huneker's argument, that mystical beliefs had a mathematical and physiological base, was seriously held. For Huneker, Bragdon's treatise, Howard Hinton's *The Fourth Dimension* and Cora Lenore Williams's *Creative Involution*, texts of a renewed transcendentalism, served to reaffirm 'the arcana of the ancient wisdom':

> Their thought is not new; it was hoary with age when the Greeks went to Old Egypt for fresh learning; Noah conversed with his

wives in the same terminology. But its application is novel. . . .
The idea of a fourth spatial dimension may be likened to a fresh
lens in the telescope or microscope of speculation.[53]

In his discussion of Cora Williams's book, Huneker again felt it
necessary to rescue his subject from quackery: 'she is not a New
Thoughter, a Christian Scientist, or a member of any of the other
queer rag-tag and bobtail beliefs and superstitions.' As 'an authority in mathematics', her thesis had scientific respectability; not
'verbal wind-pudding' but having 'a basis of mathematics and the
investigations of the laboratory' where 'chemists and physicists are
finding that the conduct of certain molecules and crystals is best
explained as a fourth-dimensional activity.' And again Huneker
saw contemporary mathematics as a continuation of 'ancient
wisdom': 'Perpetual motion, squaring the circle, are only variants
of the alchemical pursuit of the philosopher's stone, the transmutation of the baser metals, the cabalistic Abracadabra, the quest of
the absolute.' The 'spiritual' notion of a fourth dimension freed
thought from the 'cast-iron determinism of the seventies and
eighties' precisely because of science's new account of matter,
which permitted more concrete explanations for older mystical
typologies: 'Matter, in the light of recent experiment, is become
spirit, energy, anything but gross matter'. These conceptions were
apparent not only at the level of force but at the level of physiology:
'From a macrocosmic monster our gods are become microcosmic;
god may be a molecule, a cell. A god to put in a phial.'[54]

This shift from the macrocosmic to the microcosmic, to 'gods' in
a molecule or a cell, was the hallmark of the new transcendentalism
and both literally and metaphorically coded the apotheosis of transcendentalism's organicist epistemology. Huneker's physiological
account of the geometrical imagery that traditionally expressed
'transcendentalism through the ages' ended with the Cartesian proposal of the pineal gland as 'the seat of the soul', but Pound, with
the aid of Louis Berman's more detailed endocrinology, was able to
offer a clearer picture. Pound isolated the pineal gland as the site of
original image-making; the '*new* juxtaposition of images', potential
for 'original thought, as distinct from imitative thought', was made
possible only by a conception of the pineal considered as

gland of 'lucidity', of the sense of light analogous to the eye,
perhaps as the fibres of Corti in the ear show analogy to stringed

instrument. gland of metamorphosis, of original thought, the secretion being very probably just the lime salt crystals well known to lie in it, but they may be secreted not as a slow effusion, but ejected suddenly into sensitized area, analogy to the tests.

The word 'tests' was presumably a misprint for 'testes', given his prior Gourmontian proposal of creative activity as a function of spermatic activity. The pineal so conceived marked Pound's most complete acceptance of physiological aesthetics; the gland's function was of a special order of sight, 'sense of vision, sense of light flowing along the nerves and making one aware where one's hands are in the dark', a particular mode of vision, 'luminosity in vision, "gates of beryl and chrysoprase" effect, power of visualization as distinct from hallucination', and the prime exercise of the *Cantos*, 'Intelligence developed from seeing, telescopic as opposed to telepathic intelligence'. Pound stressed that he wanted to dissociate this 'orderly visualization', which 'neither confuses nor annoys the visionary', from the 'D.T.s., or any other sort of hallucination'.[55]

This use of physiology to formulate aesthetics represented the most intimate means whereby the organicist epistemology incorporated in transcendentalism sought a materiality for the correspondences that structured its being. By arguing for the interpenetration of the 'material' and the 'spiritual', transcendentalism dismissed the distinctions traditionally held between them in order to suggest a new materiality, which found its final location not only in the world of forces revealed by physics but also in the sensory microcosmic world of glandular and cellular physiology. Science, in any of its forms, always signalled for Pound a mode of transformational unity; 'the thing that matters in art', he wrote in 1913, 'is a sort of energy, something more or less like electricity or radio-activity, a force transfusing, welding, unifying.'[56] The function of this 'transfusing' process was to dissolve the seeming solidity of the world by postulating either fields of force or cellular activity in order to suggest a new materiality. The point is, that it was only by its own privileged systems that any semblance of the positive could be restored, by its own concealed means of control that the sensory world could be regained. Here is science's largest contradiction: its removal of the old order of the material in favour of the new required almost a neurosis with regard to 'things', apparently solid objects, and con-

sequently a loss of the full plenitude of life. As Norman O. Brown
has argued, 'The commitment to mathematize the world, intrinsic
to modern science, is a commitment to sublimation.' Plato, in
Brown's system, was right to claim that 'God geometrizes' because
mathematics is 'the crucial discipline in converting human love to a
suprasensual life'. The notion of sublimation here suggests hidden
sources of control and above all *denial* whereby mathematical
thinking 'specifies what part of the life of the body is affirmed by
negation' in order to construct the 'non-bodily life'. Science's contradiction lies in the fact that sublimations are 'negations of the
body which simultaneously affirm it' by their mechanism of 'projecting the repressed body into things'. Thus, 'The more the life of
the body passes into things, the less life there is in the body, and at
the same time the increasing accumulation of things represents an
ever fuller articulation of the lost life of the body.'[57]

Brown refers to this process of sublimation and denial as 'the
anal character of mathematical thinking'; it clearly holds important
implications for modernist writing, which sought its place in the
world not only by a geometrized aesthetic, but in two crucial
places, in Pound's 'Hell' cantos and in the monologue that ended
Ulysses, as we have seen, by the problematical vocabulary of excrement and emission. Faced with the loss of the sensual body, conceivable only in terms of a cellular paradigm, and the concomitant
loss of the body's necessary vocabulary, modernism strove after the
physical items of the world, via a poetics of the 'real', as a means of
compensation. The effort to rematerialize the world by its physical
items and, paradoxically, by cellular physiology was the final contradiction of the transcendentalist temperament: in straining after
harmony and correspondences, it moved its interests from the
macrocosmic to the microcosmic and succeeded in appropriating
the world through its ultimate constituents, the cells and molecules
of matter, but in the process lost the service of matter itself, of
'things' themselves. This contradiction of what we might call the
mathematical imagination was most clearly sited in James's famous
proposition in the Preface to *Roderick Hudson*: 'Really, univer-
sally, relations stop nowhere, and the exquisite problem of the
artist is eternally but to draw, by a geometry of his own, the circle
within which they shall happily *appear* to do so.'[58] Here was a
geometry whose cipher signified everything and nothing simultaneously, appropriate for the Jamesian sentence that sublimated

the material world in the interests of the transcendent consciousness which was its true subject and which was so manifestly ill equipped to confront the hazards of that world.

James's geometry shared the provenance of a philosophy known as unanimism, most famously expressed by Jules Romains in 'Reflexions', a short essay appended to his *Puissances de Paris* (1911). Pound translated this essay in 1918 for *The Little Review*; it testified to the 'organic consciousness' that saw the world in terms of a total interdependence:

> One ceases to believe that a definite limit is the indispensable means of existence. Where does La Place de la Trinité begin? The streets mingle their bodies. The squares isolate themselves with great difficulty. . . . A being (*être*) has a centre, or centres in harmony, but a being is not compelled to have limits. He exists a great deal in one place, rather less in others, and further on a second being commences before the first has left off. . . . Space is no one's possession. No being has succeeded in appropriating one scrap of space and saturating it with his own unique existence. Everything over-crosses, coincides, and cohabits. Every point is a perch for a thousand birds. Paris, the rue Montmartre, a crowd, a man, a protoplasm are on the same spot of pavement. A thousand existences are concentric.

Here was Pound's 'fluid universe' figured in the contemporary city:

> groups are not truly born. Their life makes and unmakes itself like an unstable state of matter, a condensation which does not endure. They show us that life, at its origin, is a provisory attitude, a moment of exception, an intensity between two relaxations, not continuity, nothing decisive.[59]

A view of life as 'a provisory attitude' in this sense indicated the extent to which the organic consciousness both willed and feared the simultaneous materialization of the spiritual and the spiritualization of the material that science offered; an 'intensity between two relaxations' is an excellent phrase for the interstices that located the new world of physics and biology. Appropriately, Romains's 'Mort de quelqu'un' – a story whose subject was death, the final negation – had been singled out as expressive of a unanimist position six months previously in *The Egoist* by Muriel

Ciolkowska. Ciolkowska found it 'reminiscent of Mr Joyce', and its subject (ideologically coded as: 'M. Jules Romains proves how all in this world diverges to converge. And he is always alive to its incessant metamorphosis from concrete to abstract, abstract to concrete')[60] certainly belonged to the 'paralysis' of *Dubliners*. In the case of both James and Joyce, death or an emotional freezing was the ultimate consequence of, respectively, a misappropriation of the material world through rarefied consciousness and through a detailed topography which, sustained by its mythopoeia, created a flattened street-map of reality for the purposes of control.

As we have seen, the organic consciousness relied on science to elaborate the two major areas of its enterprise: the seriousness of aesthetic behaviour, its practical and responsible role in society, and the gritty concreteness of the material it derived from the various arguments for correspondence that it sustained. Both were responses to the historical nexus of the rise of industrial capitalism and its threat to the harmony the artist had previously enjoyed in his social role. It was in an attempt to heal this disruption that the organic discourse of transcendentalism emphasized the new reality of its material and the consequent seriousness of its programme, and here, exactly, lay the contradiction of that programme, for the result was a further mode of commodity (to the artist, another kind of negation, or death) which would compete in the market with the commodities produced by the commercial system it resisted. The case of Allen Upward will serve to remind us of the organicist issues we have been discussing and to bring into focus the contradiction of their role in history. His case is particularly convenient for the present argument since, as Donald Davie has instructed us, Upward held many views that were parallel to the London aesthetics of Pound.

Although Upward was sceptical about science's potential for determining the shapes necessary for a true picture of the world,[61] he was willing to use the scientific analogies to which we have become accustomed in Pound as expressions of the new materiality and of the seriousness it attested. The proposition that 'all knowledge is of relations', for example, was figured by geology:

Just as the geologist can discern in the same cliff-face layers of rock that are separated in time by myriads of ages, so the anthropologist has to distinguish in the same religion, in the same rite,

and even in the same word, meanings and ideas that have orig-
inated at intervals of millenniums.[62]

Upward's insistence on the reciprocal relation between consciousness and the outer world, the self and the universe, mind and
matter, was of the 'double understanding' of the brain as 'a fold of
skin stuff' and matter itself as 'skin'.[63] This reciprocity led him to
conceive his main subject, 'genius', in terms of electricity,[64] to
anticipate in the patterns of magnetism Pound's figure of the 'rose
in the steel dust',[65] and to see the function of ideas in his own mind
as a form of chemical catalyst.[66] For Upward, writing, avowedly,
'in the spirit of a naturalist marking for different orders of plants
and animals',[67] the primal shapes of matter itself were a waterspout
and a whirlpool, shapes that, when pressed for figurability, were
visualized as a 'spring',[68] a clear anticipation of the Poundian
'vortex', particularly since Upward conceived of the 'spring' in
terms of knots and entanglement. 'Matter is electric charge,' he
wrote, 'or electric charge is Matter, whichever way we like to put
it', and so, invoking the support of Lord Kelvin: 'And what else is it
but a network – a thousand knots tied up in one knot?'[69] And as
Pound was to use the 'vortex' as a vehicle for synthesis, so Upward
noted with regard to this view of 'matter' that 'The pick of the
physicist has chimed against the pick of the psychologist, as in the
middle of a tunnel, and wrought a thorough-fare for light.' Here,
fully within the transcendentalism inherited by Pound was, to
Upward, 'what I call a Rhyme'.

Upward's sense of 'rhyme' lay at the core of the etymologies that
structured virtually all his major arguments; he wrote later that
'The bestowal of the name Puritan upon the English revival of the
Zarathustrian morality is one of those significant coincidences, or
Universal Rhymes, which teach us how small our universe is.'[70] The
rhyme whereby Upward was able to conceive of matter in the elec-
trically charged knotted entanglement of the 'spring' had its
corollary in his materialization of words themselves, in the
distinctly concrete etymologies that more than anything ensured his
attractiveness for Pound. Upward's persistent reluctance to use
words of Greek or Latin origin stressed, rather like Whitman, the
physicality of the Anglo-Saxon language: 'most words have taken
shape by coming into touch with outside sounds, and with the
sights and scents, the tastes and touches, that go together with the

sounds. Whether the word *thing* or *think* comes first in history, a thought is a feeling outlined by means of things.'[71] So, in the sense made familiar by Pound, the abstractions of ideas were 'embodied in wood or stone', they were 'the names of actions':[72] a non-concrete word like 'atom' (a word 'in a state of celibacy') was thus glossed as 'crumb', where 'crumb' itself in this context was 'made up of electricity'.[73] On the Fenollosan principle that the Chinese written characters 'carry in them a verbal idea of action', Upward replaced 'metabolism' with 'metastrophe' and, with a marvellous literalness for the present argument, traced the etymology of 'God' to 'go'.[74]

The active materiality of Upward's etymologies incorporated an affirmation of the seriousness of the artist as practical workman: 'he who hews away marble, and lays bare a statue, is not less a creator than he who builds a wall.'[75] It was this model of practical workmanship, everywhere evident in his etymologies, that led Pound to discern in Upward the 'modern value of the creative, constructive individual'.[76] The value of construction in this primary sense had a double interest for Pound because of Upward's major assertion of the individual of 'genius' against the dilutions of the mass. Upward chose to define 'genius' by means of an electrical analogy that Pound was to use throughout his defence of the seriousness of the modern writer, which culminated in the famous claim of the *ABC of Reading* that artists were 'the antennae of the race'. 'Genius', claimed Upward,

> is the power of being sensitive to what is divine. The man of genius, the last delicate bud that sprouts from the tree of man, may be compared to the slender wire that rises from the receiving station to catch the unseen message that comes across the sea from an unseen continent. His duty, like the duty of the wire, is to record that message as he receives it.[77]

The analogy had the double function of offering 'genius' as a form of highly sensitized instrument (as Pound pervasively figured Henry James) and of arguing for the seriousness of its activity by invoking the dispassionate attitude of the scientist who would simply 'record that message as he receives it'. Furthermore, the analogy in this particular context displayed the additional double function of all organicist uses of science within modernist transcendentalism by dematerializing the world in order to rematerialize it on behalf of a different order of materiality.

This double process of dematerialization and rematerialization marked a special means of appropriating the world; words themselves, within the organic metaphor, shared the materiality of the larger metaphor of relation between traditional antinomies, between the individual consciousness and the outer life. The larger relation was one of reciprocity or, crucially, exchange: the artist's words, in the Romantic tradition we have been discussing, adopted their materiality as a means of simultaneously resisting *and* playing a responsible part in a world conceived as a series of markets for the disposal of commodities. Paradoxically, they thus became a mode of commodity themselves, and the process was finally manifest in the modernist urge to revitalize and cleanse language. A transcendentalist view of language established a materialist base for words (Pound, Fenollosa and Upward following in the line of Emerson, Whitman and Thoreau) in a programme for the universal harmony that its organic metaphors explicitly maintained. Within this view, words became a medium for exchange not only in its wider sense of reciprocity but also in its commercial sense: 'Words', for Upward, 'are, like money, a medium of exchange, and the sureness with which they can be used varies not only with the character of the coins themselves, but also with the character of the things they are offered for, and that of the men who tender and receive them.' Words as 'signs for sounds', which in turn are signs for 'feeling', thus constitute a manipulation of language as 'a cheque drawn on your mind'.[78]

As a means of 'exchange', words incorporated an etymological version of the new conception of matter as a conversion of energy in scientific discourse where we 'watch heat converted into pressure, and pressure into heat' and we 'transfer the strength of a waterfall to an electric dynamo'. The 'Catholic word' for this conversion, noted Upward, was 'transubstantiation', and he chose a particularly revealing metaphor for its expression: 'we meet it in the form most easily understood by the savage, and perhaps the scientific, mind in cannibalism. Every meal is a scientific communion by which the strength of the bread and wine is received into the communicant.'[79] To see transubstantiation, the primal rite of energy's transformation, as a cannibalistic act, an act of transformation through the organs of digestion, was to imply an intensively intimate means of material acquisition, a means of power whereby the immaterial was appropriated by the material and hence controlled. Eating, the essential means of physical sustenance, involves the most fundamental act of exchange as a mode of acquisition. Upward's view of such exchange in monetary terms revealed exactly the relationship between organicist language, a mode of power and the world as market-place, that transcendentalism usually assumed in a more covert manner. Cannibalism was thus further seen as 'good business' and Christ, the object of transubstantiation, as 'speaking in favour of the Budget'.[80]

For the writer, the disintegration of the world into a series of markets with the rise of industrial capitalism was reflected in the more immediate problem of the disruption of his relationship with his audience: 'alienation' may have become a truism for the later manifestation of this problem in the modernist period, but it retains its accuracy. As I suggested in a previous chapter, modernist writing shared an ideology of work with the earlier phase of American transcendentalism, elaborating metaphors of practicality and construction to present an image of the artist as a builder, a participant in the everyday business of living, in order to seal his relationship with society. As this ideology became increasingly fragile for obvious historical reasons, so this image became increasingly untenable, but the writer, particularly the modernist writer, continued to rely on such metaphors of shared activity as a means of healing his alienation by elaborating them in support of his seriousness and his social responsibility. The problem of the market became exacerbated at the turn of the century and in the years leading to the First World War, as the larger nations sought to shore up the outlets for their commodities, the years of what is known in history textbooks as the 'scramble for Africa'. Consequently, the artist had to renew his efforts to proclaim his fiction as work (technique) which was productive (diagnostic) and which was, with the aid of the new science and the new psychology, a truly accurate account of men's affairs, a truly 'real' account of the world of matter. Simultaneously, his organic ideal sought its means of order through the very cells and molecules of people and of things, projecting a barrier of unity and correspondence against the unruly awkwardness of contemporary life. As Terry Eagleton has suggested, such totalization necessarily involved a remoteness from felt history, a sealing off of empirical difficulties in the interests of 'an authoritarian cultural ideology'.[81] Its materialization of language, in particular, marked its urge for control and, paradoxically, constituted words and the artefacts built upon them as in themselves further modes of commodity, as objects to be acquired and sold.

Fields of action

Pound's resources for a language of dissociation in the glandular models of Gourmont and Berman obviously provided for 'things', human and non-human, a more complex and more solid context of the 'real'. Physiological dissociation re-emphasized the quiddity of those 'things' by stressing what Fenollosa called the 'lines of force', or what Emerson and Upward called 'rhymes', which brought them together within a harmonious unity. Here was the function of the light that suffuses the *Cantos*, the light (received through the pineal gland, as Pound understood it from Berman) of intelligent seeing, of metamorphosis, transformation and the receiving of visions; the *claritas* that was ultimately the result of observation liberated from 'monolinear medieval logic' and enlivened by science. The operation of these protean patterns constituted, in William Carlos Williams's instructive term, a poem's 'field of action',[82] and provided an implicit model for Fenollosa's 'essay on verbs'. Structured by Pound's composite discourse from geometry, electromagnetism and biology, the notion of a 'field of action' offered a morphological flexibility, an openness of function and operation, even of meaning, that replaced the linguistic confinement of 'monolinear medieval logic'. Paradoxically, this notion resulted in the opposite of this promise of flexibility and openness; we confront in fact a poetics of enclosure, the consequence of the linguistic crises that trapped Hugh Selwyn Mauberley and left his art confined by the very processes of metamorphosis which that art and its scientific provenance were designed to control.[83] A rarely cited essay of Hugh Kenner's, 'Art in a Closed World', has attended to this promise of openness. The essay is doubly useful for present purposes not only because of its characteristically fascinating explication of field theory but also because that explication itself clearly demonstrates how Poundian commentary so often perpetuates the ideology of its subject and becomes itself a self-sealing paradigm: metaphors repeat themselves to create an enclosed harmony of their own.

Kenner begins, with Joyce and Beckett in mind, by arguing that the major form of twentieth-century literature is that of the 'closed field', which he sees as 'the dominant intellectual analogy of our time'. This 'closed field' contains 'a finite number of elements to be combined according to fixed rules', rules that govern the arrangement of 'discrete counters'. Kenner finds the sources of this procedure in the European traditions of lexicography, the concern with 'fixing the language',[84] and in the parallel work of mathematics; he provides the mathematician's use of the term 'field':

> A field, he says, contains a set of elements, and a set of laws for dealing with these elements. He does not specify what the elements are. . . . The laws, in the same way, are any laws we like to prescribe, so long as they are consistent with one another. The purpose of this manoeuvre is to set mathematics free from our inescapable structure of intuitions about the familiar world, in which space has three dimensions and every calculation can be verified by counting. Once we have a theory of fields we can invent as many mathematical systems as we like, and so long as they are internally consistent their degree of correspondence with the familiar world is irrelevant.[85]

Although Kenner does not acknowledge it as such, his definition belongs to the reductionist philosophy of scientific language that I discussed earlier; in this context, as formulated by Sir Arthur Eddington, here was the 'shadowgraph performance of the drama of familiar life' that we witness in the measurements offered by physics: 'Science has at last revolted against attaching the exact knowledge contained in these measurements to a traditional picture-gallery of conceptions which convey no authentic information of the background and obtrude irrelevancies into the scheme of knowledge.' It was important to recognize this account of scientific language within the terms of its own limits in order to prevent the deceit of shadows:

> It is difficult to school ourselves to treat the world as purely symbolic. We are always relapsing and mixing with the symbols incongruous conceptions taken from the world of consciousness. Untaught by long experience we stretch a hand to grasp the shadow, instead of accepting its shadowy nature. Indeed, unless we confine ourselves altogether to mathematical symbolism it is hard to avoid dressing our symbols in deceitful clothing.[86]

Kenner's error is exactly that against which Eddington offered his warning, taking the 'shadows' of scientific discourse for solid things. Indeed, freedom from 'our inescapable structure of intuitions about the familiar world' was precisely the covert ambition of modernism's geometry: the creation of equations as 'lords' over 'fact', which categorically exhibited its removal from the tangle of history.

Kenner argues that creative procedure within a 'closed field' is a predominantly European activity, and that it is inappropriate for a discussion of American literature because of the latter's relationship to a special notion of 'speech', which is conceived as spontaneous 'naked utterance' and not as part of the codes (a 'closed set of patterns') that organize conversation. He takes Williams as his best example:

> A poem by William Carlos Williams is speech, all the time, but either it is not speech we are to think of as spoken *to* anyone, but merely *uttered*, or else it is spoken to his wife, or an intimate friend, someone who might answer out of hidden depths of intimacy with the poet, but never according to a social stereotype.[87]

To claim that 'naked utterance' freed words from stereotyped fields of language is to revive the idealism that demands the superiority of oral to written language on the grounds that it is more flexible and more immediately 'real', that it is not confined by the artificial, arbitrary materiality of the printed sign and hence has access to the natural and the spontaneous; or, within the Adamic tradition distinctive of American writing, that to utter the name of an object is somehow to incorporate the special essence of that object. As a means of avoiding the stereotypical threat of a social and communal structure of language, 'naked utterance' includes that further code of privacy which establishes its hermetic character: it is not 'spoken *to* anyone', and it draws its power from sources of 'hidden depths of intimacy'.

The primacy of the oral was intrinsic to the organicism of a transcendentalist view of language. Whitman famously acclaimed the physicality of language and its relationship to felt experience:

> Language, be it remembered, is not an abstract construction of the learned, or of dictionary-makers, but is something arising out of the work, needs, ties, joys, affections, tastes, of long generations of humanity, and has its bases broad and low, close to the ground. Its final decisions are made by the masses, people nearest the concrete, having most to do with actual land and sea.

Thus the vernacular, and particularly slang, provided 'the lawless, germinal element' of language, instigating its capacity for concrete novelty, for overcoming the *typos* of social code; its 'indirection' was 'an attempt of common humanity to escape from bold literalism, and express itself illimitably'; it was the 'wholesome fermentation or eructation of those processes eternally active in language'.[88] The antinomianistic function of language's physicality relied in turn on its use in speech 'living' in the 'real world', not in print, and so demonstrated the oral sanction that was the corollary of its physicality. In the nature of the paradox we have noted with regard to transcendentalism, words were thus conceived as 'eluding, fluid, beautiful, fleshless, realities'. Whitman claimed that 'nothing is more spiritual than words'[89] and, on the principle that 'nothing is better than a superb vocalism', he defined 'Pronounciation' as 'the stamina of language, – it is language'.[90]

A materialist epistemology of language is seen here clearly to carry a hidden source of communal elusiveness, finding its most powerful resource in 'Pronounciation', which is the exercise of that most elusive of phenomena, breath itself, the traditionally Romantic figure for 'spirit'. In Whitman's case, the strategy of opposing oral to written language was a means of salvaging words from their institutional uses and meanings; its occasion was an ambition for a diction and a terminology that would be commensurate to the need of a historical object, the nebulous state of America itself, to declare its own distinctive place in the world as a resistance to the hegemony of European culture and tradition. Within the organicist metaphor, words became breath – like eating, a particularly individualistic means of appropriation – the breath of the body, which was Whitman's final source for the sinewy function of their activity. The paradox here was that, while bodies are the ultimate things we all share, they are simultaneously our most intimate and private possessions. A mode of acquisition in this context shares exactly such privacy. Allen Upward's constructivist insistence on people as 'makers' demonstrated a similar reliance on breath as the fundamental constituent of language: 'When we look deep enough we find only two sounds beneath all spoken words, one made by in-breathing, and the other by breathing out. That is the whirl-swirl in language.'[91] And as Upward was to figure the appropriation of energy as cannibalism, so Whitman chose a metaphor from eating to figure the appropriation of words; maintaining that 'a true composition in words, returns the human body, male or female', he argued for the 'fitness' and 'charm' of 'aboriginal names': 'Monongahela – it rolls with venison richness upon the palate.'[92] Again we see here how the reciprocity between the material and the immaterial was to give physicality to the immaterial, to make it an object, to appropriate it for consumption, and, further, to recode that object by the interstices of rematerialization so that it belonged to none of the communally held categories of knowledge but to a new, inevitably mysterious category of its own.

Such mystery was another aspect of privacy, analogous to the secret that required no words for its expression among the initiates, or, rather, words that were understandable only to the initiates. Testifying to his debt to Ford, Pound stressed the importance of the oral: 'One might summarize it by saying that he believes one should write in a contemporary spoken or at least speakable language; in some sort of idiom that one can imagine oneself using in actual speech, i.e. in private life.'[93] And, for Pound, the only form of 'actual speech' that really mattered was solely in the custody of an élite: 'THE CULTURE OF AN AGE is what you can pick up and/or get in touch with, by talk with the most intelligent men of the period.'[94] This 'talk' is clearly different from Kenner's notion of Williams's 'naked utterance', but equally clearly its potential for actual conversation is severely restricted by its paradigm of 'the most intelligent'. Hence it shares the non-social privacy of spontaneous speech in the sense that it relies on a model of *agreement* (the shared code of 'the most intelligent') which refuses the proper function of *difference* implicit in any true conversation. Since difference holds the possibility for instigating change, its muted function within flawed conversation presents access to that order of manipulation and control which belongs to the privacy of utterance considered autonomously.[95]

Arguments for the seriousness of the artist were part of an attempt to heal fractured relationships with an audience and thus sought the support of the phenomenal world. So, too, arguments for the primacy of oral language, belonging to the same transcendentalist urge, resulted, through their reliance on 'utterance', in the paradoxical effect of establishing faith in the discreteness of objects. Any page of Whitman's, in both poetry and prose, would provide an obvious example, but we may also remember the seriousness of the joke about Ouan Jin in Canto LXXIV which Pound used to demonstrate *sinceritas*, the *verbum perfectum*:

> Ouan Jin spoke and thereby created the named thereby making
>   clutter
> the bane of men moving
> and so his mouth was removed[96]

Kenner recognizes, of course, that Williams's attempt to 'turn the poem into an autonomous utterance' resulted in a new set of laws which, as proper to 'utterance', were simply different from the more familiar laws of conversation but were laws nevertheless, and hence another version of the 'closed field' that, in Kenner's argument, it was the impetus of 'utterance' to avoid.[97] But quite what is this 'autonomous utterance'? Kenner's formalism, with its paradoxical fear of the stereotype, finds it impossible to acknowledge that words, whether written or spoken, cannot help but partake in a nexus of relations; that there can be no such thing as an *autonomous* utterance, and, if there were, then it would be communally unintelligible.

In the case of Pound himself, Kenner argues for an assumption of the 'closed field' in the form of the 'curriculum' offered by the *Cantos*. This 'curriculum' belongs to the acts of selection which for Kenner have characterized American cultural history; he makes his point vividly by distinguishing between the structures of American and European libraries:

> The first American universities were founded with gifts of books; and every American library since then has reflected a long series of deliberate acts of choice. A library like the Bodleian contains hundreds of thousands of books; nobody knows how most of them got there. If many of those same books are in collection at Yale or Harvard, it is because they were chosen and ordered for people who had some immediate use for them. For the same reason, American education is focussed, as European education is not, on the curriculum. The curriculum is an act of selection.

An illuminating parallel would be Agassiz's handwriting visible on the labels of specimens in the Jardin des Plantes, which Emerson visited. This sturdily pictorial idea of the 'curriculum' enables Kenner to invert the function of the 'closed field' in its American context: 'I want to suggest, in concluding, its highly American quality, which suffices to turn the closed field inside out, and make it an instrument of possibilities, not foreclosures.' Kenner is imitating here his own view of the expatriate character in Pound and Eliot, 'speaking as an American who has assumed European categories'.

Kenner's point is his most influential contribution to the ways in which the *Cantos* are read: that order is achieved through the principles of selection and concentration whereby the energies of the reader are renewed and whereby 'possibilities' are maintained against 'foreclosures':

> What happens in the 'Cantos', in short, is the deliberate imposition of the closed field on material virtually infinite . . . this closed field, since it implies that what is left out the author has examined and determined not to put in, offers to sharpen our attention rather than mock at our poverty of resource. . . . One way or another, when it is focussed by art, the closed field becomes that point of concentration which in proportion as it grows smaller concentrates more intensely the radiant energies of all that we feel and know.[98]

We have to be suspicious about this assumption of authorial purposiveness, and, even if we subscribe to it, we need to recognize again the mysteriousness of the authorial choice and its privacy on the page. Furthermore, as a version of Pound's maxim in the *Guide to Kulchur*, 'Dichten = Condensare', Kenner's reading of 'curriculum' as selection and concentration provides one of the clearest statements we have on the nature of authoritarian rhetoric: curricular concentration is inevitably a seeking after power, the power derived from a selective process designed to refine language for the purposes of manipulation and which always imposes 'foreclosures' exactly in the disguise of 'possibilities'. The assumption of patterns of correspondence, right down to the level of physiology, becomes, for the modernist writer, a justification for omitting or denying the full range of discourse in favour of the stark solidity of objects which in effect stand on their own and merely signal silently towards the discourse of their hidden unity. This justification announces itself exactly as an ambition for the increased activity of the reader, for the energizing of his perceptions, as a recent commentator, implicitly following Kenner's criterion, has demonstrated: 'Pound presents the reader with a "palimpsest" – a parchment from which the writing has been partially removed to make room for another text. Such a document requires completion by someone other than its author; alone it is fragmentary, elliptical and obscure.'[99] As we have seen, this was explicitly the demand made by the modernist conception of 'tradition', heavily coded by transcendentalist physiology, which required with the authority of organic truth a contemporary participation within an existing and incomplete cultural structure.

Terry Eagleton has rightly argued, with regard to Eliot, that 'tradition' in the context I have described 'is a labile, self-transformative organism extended in space and time, constantly reorganized by the present'. This 'radical historical relativism' then becomes endowed with 'the status of absolute classical authority': 'What Eliot does, in fact, is to adopt the aesthetics of a late phase of Romanticism (symbolism), with its view of the individual artefact as organic, impersonal and autonomous, and then project this doctrine into an authoritarian cultural ideology.' By historicizing organicism, 'tradition' thus 'extends rather than escapes from a sealed, intersubjective circuit, replacing real history with a self-evolving idealist whole in which all time is eternally present, and so unredeemable.'[100] The implicit practice of the transcendentalist sensibility was exactly such a sealed intersubjectivity: Eliot's formulation of 'tradition' offered no 'objects' as such because it included no sense of historical or social production, and presented merely a series of 'subjects', which were conceived as autonomous and available to be debated only within the terms they themselves constituted. James Huneker read Gourmont to claim the axiom 'Repetition is the law of life', and his argument for the geometrical patterns revealed by transcendentalist mathematics as products of a discernible physiology returned his axiom to an Emersonian world: repeats have a tendency to repeat repeats.

Emerson's account of Swedenborg's 'identity-philosophy' placed it in the tradition of the 'old aphorism' that 'nature is always self-similar', illustrated through the Goethean principle that 'the whole art of the plant is still to repeat leaf on leaf without end' ('the eye or germinative point opens to a leaf, then to another leaf, with a power of transforming the leaf into radicle, stamen, pistil, petal, bract, sepal, or seed'). The law of repetition applied equally to the animal form where 'nature makes a vertebra, or a spine of vertebrae

. . . spine on spine, to the end of the world'. Within this law, the 'mind' itself was viewed as a further modification of the spine where 'all that was done in the trunk repeats itself. Nature recites her lesson once more in a higher mood.' The consequence of this repetition was a thorough materialization of the brain:

> The mind is a finer body, and resumes its functions of feeding, digesting, absorbing, excluding, and generating, in a new and ethereal element. Here, in the brain, is all the process of alimentation repeated, in the acquiring, comparing, digesting, and assimilating of experience.

It was a materialism that came close to anticipating the physiological account of creativity we find in Gourmont: 'Here again is the mystery of generation repeated. In the brain are male and female faculties: here is marriage, here is fruit.' What was absent was Gourmont's *tensile* sense of this interaction; 'marriage' is altogether too comfortable a term for the way in which Gourmont – and Pound with his understanding of Provençal sexuality – saw creativity seeking its place by the oppositions against which it structured its forms. Nevertheless, we see here the extent to which transcendentalist materialism sealed its circuit of reference: 'there is no limit to this ascending scale, but series on series. Everything, at the end of one use, is taken up into the next, each series punctually repeating every organ and process of the last.'[101] This sealed circuit was the covert strategy of an organicist overt refusal of difference: from the law of perpetuation inscribed by Agassiz's theory of 'types' which, by its denial of transmission between 'types' through their repetition, paradoxically attested to the distinctness of those 'types' (in other words, the ground of an élitist epistemology), to Eliot's admiration for that form of metaphor in which it was impossible to distinguish between its components. Refusal of difference within the contradiction of the organic metaphor thus endorses a concealed and hence controllable assumption of distinction: metaphors, as indices of repeats and harmonies, while proclaiming similarity among dissimilarity, implicitly manipulate that similarity to suggest hidden dissimilarity. The interstitial space that metaphor inhabits between its simultaneous proposals for '*a* is viewed as if it is *b*' and '*a* is not *b*' promises both the tension through which imaginative language operates *and* language's means to control.

A language of objects

Laws of repetition offered clear ciphers for the patterns of corre-spondence that sealed the harmony of the transcendentalist world at the level of theory. At the level of practice, this results in an absence of full discourse on the grounds that such fullness is implicitly ever-present and can therefore be suggested in terms of allusion. Fullness is replaced by a poetics of 'things', of a non-discursive reality whereby phenomenal objects are simply given and achieve their resonance through their allusion to the full system of completeness that inhabits a ghostly meta-world of coherence, of 'rhymes', behind the text itself. A poetics of 'things' thus becomes a poetics of selection, which disguises its full procedure in favour, paradoxically, of the solidity and discreteness of the objects it offers, objects whose nature is then inevitably one of condensation and a means towards a manipulative refinement.[102] The energizing of the reader is a device for concealing a rhetoric of power. We may begin to detect the manipulation consequent upon a poetics of the 'real' expressed through 'things' by a brief consideration of another famous style of another American expatriate, Ernest Hemingway.

Hemingway's best-known statement about composition relied on 'selection' as a principle of omission:

> If a writer of prose knows enough about what he is writing about he may omit things that he knows and the reader, if the writer is writing truly enough, will have a feeling of those things as strongly as though the writer had stated them. The dignity of movement of an iceberg is due to only one-eighth of it being above water.[103]

Again we are presented with the mysteriousness of this process, a mysteriousness and a concealment reflected in Hemingway's con-ditional clauses and in his metaphor of the 'iceberg'. Its practice was to instigate a language of objects whose very solidity would cleanse all the 'dirty, easy labels'. Fredric Jameson has perceptively described the experience of such a language: 'Hemingway's great discovery was that there was possible a kind of return to the very sources of verbal productivity if you forgot about words entirely and merely concentrated on prearranging the objects that the words were supposed to describe.'[104] What the reader is offered, then, is not a complex social reality (traditionally impossible for modernist writing) but, as Jameson observes, a 'reality thinned out', a reality of 'foreign cultures and of foreign languages' in which 'the individual beings come before us not in the density of a concrete social situation in which we also are involved, but rather with the cleanness of objects which can be verbally circumscribed.' A literature constituted by such objects inevitably denies the full range of discourse: 'Something is left out: both the actual movement itself and that full style or *parole pleine* which would have somehow "rendered" it.'[105]

Paul Goodman, approaching Hemingway's prose from a similar angle, arrives at a more strident conclusion. He addresses our attention to the largest contradiction of a poetics that objectifies the world and seeks by its selectivity to energize the reader. Goodman stresses the *passivity* of Hemingway's fiction, which is partly a consequence of the action or, rather, the non-action, of the narrative itself:

> The characters, including the narrator, are held off in such a way
> . . . that they influence nothing; events happen to them. The
> actions that they initiate . . . do not add up to actualizing them; it
> is one thing after another . . . the events turn out to be happen-
> ings.[106]

The problem is one of accessibility: 'The persons are held at arm's length, there is no way to get inside them or identify with them, it is happening to them.' This is particularly true of Hemingway's early fiction. In *The Sun Also Rises* (1926), to take the clearest instance, the specialized vocabulary shared by the main protagonists has the double function of constructing a self-sealed élitism as a means of protection, and of discriminating against all those who cannot share that vocabulary and the hidden experience that prompts it. The process of inclusion within this sealed world is wholly mysterious: the path whereby a character may become 'one of us' is as concealed as the hidden understandings of 'afición' itself; you either have it, or you haven't, and the 'how' of appropriation is never given to the uninitiate (a category that extends to Hemingway's readers themselves). Significantly, the novel took its title and one of its epigraphs from the beginning of *Ecclesiastes* ('The sun also ariseth, and the sun goeth down, and hasteth to the place where he arose', and 'One generation passeth away, and another generation cometh: but the earth abideth for ever'); these lines testify to the circularity and repetition of natural cycles as a refuge, a sealing off, against the haphazard contingencies of the world.[107]

The inaccessibility of the text and the passivity of the narrative are curious results for a theory of composition noted for its reliance on active verbs. The reason has to do with the reader's inability to participate in its 'objective' world: 'The verbs are active and the sentences indicative, but since the *persons* do not do it, we feel that they do not *do* it.' As Goodman notes, the point is that 'the events do not happen to the prose; rather the prose influences the events.' And the prose not only influences the passive 'happenings' of the narrative, it also imposes passivity on the reader himself; it is exactly the 'succession of short, active indicative sentences' which instigates passivity in the reader by the intolerance of its syntax, its 'objective' selectivity: 'There is not enough syntactical leeway for the author or reader to become engaged actively or contemplatively or as one who desires or one who interprets.'[108]

The 'objective' worlds of both Hemingway and Pound, largely different though they obviously are, share this problem: a reliance on the solid cleanliness of concrete objects results in a narrative of inaccessibility because of its refusal to incorporate the reader within an open discourse, and this refusal is sanctioned by the implicit proposition of a fuller, hidden, discourse of harmony. The immediacy of the relationship between language and objects, particularly emphasized by a materialist linguistics, requires for the reader a syntax that will allow him room to manoeuvre; the absence of such room makes it impossible to construct the necessary field of linguistic reference that will overcome the discreteness of immediacy and locate the objects within an accessible field of action: the reader's problems are not dissimilar to those of Lambert Strether.

Goodman's argument for passivity cannot be applied in quite the same sense to a reader of Pound. With Hemingway, we deal with a fiction that keeps itself to itself, whereas with Pound our task has to do with the intertextuality of the poetry; in any case, passivity would tend to be misleading if only because of all the leg-work necessary for Pound's readers. Nevertheless, the problem of accessibility remains, because of the difficulty of finding our way through the phenomena produced by a poetics of objectivity. In this sense, the *Cantos* becomes a very curious object itself in that we can never be sure of quite where the text *is* that we are reading. The 'palimpsest' offered by the work requires a more complicated version of what we are asked to do in reading a less diverse poem such as the *Homage to Sextus Propertius* where we have, at a minimum, Pound's poem on one side of the desk, an edition of Propertius on the other side, and in the middle our own attempt to reinscribe the interaction between the volumes to either side. This activity of reinscription is the programme of the 'palimpsest', directing us to the events of experience which have left 'traces in the air' in the hope that our connection with these 'traces' will make 'the fragmentary coherent, even if momentarily'.[109] Such hopes are illusory, as illusory as the habit, increasingly common among commentators following Kenner's guide, of miming Pound's organicist idealism by making the elements of the *Cantos* 'rhyme' together. These 'rhymes' confine us further within the items of Pound's own poetics, demonstrating more clearly than anything the extent to which the repetitions of his idealism spiral out to ensnare the reader by the mysteriousness of its process: we find ourselves repeating repeats which in themselves seal the world by their own repetitions.

One of the few attempts in print to describe the situation of Pound's reader is a recent essay by Stephen Fender which charts his own experience in editing the Jefferson Cantos for a new anthology, *The American Long Poem* (1977). Fender confronts the primary problem of considering the allusions to American history by Whitman, Crane, Pound and Williams; the first two seem to be 'much more public' than the last two, and, while 'historical emphasis in Crane and Whitman is that of the ordinary American public school', the American history of Pound and Williams 'is precisely not that found in the contemporary educational system.'[110] Obviously, Whitman's allusions, say, to Columbus in 'Passage to India' are more 'open', more accessible than those to the complicated correspondence of Jefferson and Adams in the *Nuevo Mundo* Cantos, but that is inevitable, given Pound's ambition exactly to replace the 'contemporary educational system' with a new curriculum of his own. The difficulties of access to arcane allusions is not what I mean by a 'closed' field of action in a poem: considered as items of material, there is, at root, no difference in kind between the availability of Columbus and that of the correspondence between Jefferson and Adams; the latter requires, initially, only a larger effort of research. A 'closed' field involves something more than merely an appeal to areas of knowledge that are presumably beyond an audience's customary range of reading; it involves formal principles of composition resulting from a poetics of 'things', a language system that denies 'syntactical leeway' and, in terms of structure, has little to do with the status of the information being conveyed.

A curriculum is a *guide* to knowledge and as such it offers a particular gesture towards completeness: contained herein, it proclaims, is all the knowledge worth knowing, all the works of literature worth reading. To suggest this completeness, its strategy is one of fragmentation, a series of signposts that point towards the wider area condensed by its selection and that are 'open' by virtue of their status as indicators. Here is the contradiction within the practical function of a curriculum: by offering a series of objects in this supposedly provisional manner, it in fact traps us within the field of those objects. If the curriculum happens to express itself in the form of a poem, then we are forced back to the original of the objects constituting the poem's material, and the reading of the poem becomes confined by the instructions of the curriculum as a sealed epistemology. At the level of reading practice, we are thus not talking about the relationship of 'sources' or 'allusions' in the poem to the poem itself but about the radically changed status of the way in which the poem functions in the world as an object; as Fender notes, 'the documents are indispensable, not only to an understanding but also to a *reading* of the *Jefferson* Cantos'. The poems cannot be construed without these documents: 'they are not just sources but parts of the poem. I mean this literally.'[111] Fender's literalness can be extended beyond the immediate problems of the *Nuevo Mundo* Cantos to the problems of the sequence as a whole in its habit of incorporating whole chunks of quotations from primary sources as part of its insistence on its own objectivity, its capacity for the 'real', through a materialist poetics. Words themselves are offered in the form of tangible objects as, following Richard Sieburth, 'quotation involves shifting the emphasis from language as a means of representation to language as the very object of representation', a shift that involves 'a mode not merely of copying or reflecting but of including the real'.[112] Needless to say, the diversity of Pound's linguistics and his typography cannot help but focus our attention on the status of words *as* words, as a species of print, which is their own special materiality.

The poem on the page in this sense is compositionally incomplete in a different way from a poetry of allusion, which more simply requires a recognition of the extent and resonance of the allusions that constitute its substance. Unless we attend to this difference, to the *Cantos* as a different sort of object with different demands on the reader, demands that themselves exhibit this difference, then we cannot begin to give an account of a poetics where the selection of objects compositionally establishes a problematic of practice for the reader. Fender's literalness provides an excellent index to how the promise of 'open' activity in fact mystifies and conceals enclosure, but he seems unwilling to recognize the implications of his own experience: he views the activity of reading the Jefferson Cantos as 'not different in kind' from the activity of reading any other allusory text, merely more difficult. His concern is to defend this difficulty, to reassure the reader that he is being asked to engage in a more complicated activity than is required by customary reading habits but which, in the end, is no different: 'Like a huge metaphor, the thing and the thing compared, the prospectus and the course, seem at first unrelated, then more congruent and harmonious than what was imagined before.'[113] By seeking the consolation and security of metaphor, Fender offers ease for the strain of the *Cantos* by falling back on the advertised programme of modernism: the running of order through chaos, the making things cohere, the wish that a language system of diverse objects will, through its very diversity and concentration, provide for heterogeneity a solid power of nomination. He thus conceals the significance of his experience in editing these four cantos by displacing it within a familiar model of harmony, which in turn exhibits the formalist fear of stereotype that we noted in Kenner:

> [Pound and Williams] make no *immediate* appeal to shared knowledge, much less to shared prejudice. In fact, their citations of documents are not allusions at all. The reader is not expected to have anticipated their cultural set; he is 'ignorant' only in that he has yet to follow their course.[114]

To claim that 'citations' are not 'allusions' is rightly to imply their new objectification, but Fender refuses to extend this implication to the reader's practice, which is to produce a further text on his own behalf. The promise of 'open' structure and a corresponding flexibility of behaviour by the reader turns out to be a false promise because the objects of his material turn out to be restricted by the list from which he began. This is not the same as saying, with

Fender, that the reader constructs his own closure;[115] this closure is the inevitable consequence of a poetics of objectivity in which a reliance on 'things' refuses anything other than a skeletal construction that encourages and dominates a natural willingness to put those 'things' together. A poetics that advertises possibilities for correspondence through a language structure of dissociation[116] in fact obliges the reader to reiterate the shadow language of its own programme, confined as he is by the shadow of its original promise.

Pound's main vehicle of selection and concentration, the ideogram coded by the materialism of the new transcendentalism, thus incorporates its authoritarian patterns in much the same way that the modernist notion of 'tradition' incorporates the determinant ideology of heredity. A poetics that denies the security of a text 'on the page' by a structure of intertextuality incorporates the double authoritarianism of a false promise. As a means of 'including the real', of objectifying words themselves, the intertextuality of Pound's work offers its programme as fragmented, unmediated, provisory: its displacement matches the displacement of our reading experience, the empty space in the middle of the desk where the reader is instructed to transcribe his own centre. Authorship is diffused, as the 'seemingly solid block of matter' was diffused by field-theory physics, so that the reader participates in the concealment of origins as in his turn he further decentres the text before him in an effort to reconstruct the hidden harmony that its curriculum promises. The curriculum asks the reader to participate in the larger unity of a special version of ideas going into action: action becomes here another mode of writing, not of writing freely, but of writing only within the terms prescribed by the prior text. The supplementation of reading practice becomes itself a means to order, a striving after the ideal centre signalled by the objects of the poem, rather than a radical interactivity of free minds.

The proposition of this concealed, ideal centre is true of the major exercises in modernist writing: as Terry Eagleton has written of *The Waste Land*, 'behind the back of this ruptured, radically decentred poem runs an alternative text which is nothing less than the closed, coherent, authoritative discourse of the mythologies which frame it',[117] and as Fredric Jameson has written of *Ulysses*, it points 'toward a unity that transcends the reality of the individual, of the individual character or individual life, and this is to be found in some vaster impersonal system of relationship . . . there rises up, behind the finite, realized work itself, the mirage of some more perfect totality, to which the former makes allusion at every moment as to its own ultimate meaning, but to which we as readers can never accede.'[118] Our practice in reading such texts thus becomes an exercise in trying to tie their signals together, paradoxically, in the process, removing ourselves further from any substantial reality by the insistent objectification of their material which relies on a physiological view of the correspondence it signifies as its primary resource against the alternative dominance of abstract values.

Hence the potential figurability of the *Cantos* incorporates only a system of harmonious correspondence signalled by the items of its curriculum. But because of the special nature of the work as an object itself, the product of a poetics underwritten by the idealist science I have been describing and of our special function as readers in that we are offered the promise of free participation in its fragmented, provisory structure, the historical reality it alludes to is not domesticated in the usual way; it is not collapsed and made safe by a reassuring narrative. The point is that the reader himself performs the office of reassurance by his own practice of transcription. As all the commentaries assume, it is we who do the work, we who affirm the items of the curriculum and we who create the final consolation that is the function of the modernist art-object against actual contingency by repeating its repetitions. The satisfaction that we inevitably feel at the end of such an exercise thus becomes worrying not only because we have been manoeuvred into it by the compositional strictures of the *Cantos*, but also because we have been particularly active in participating in its ideology, actively involved, literally, in writing history in a form that will protect us from its vagaries. This is worrying because instead of simply reading a domesticated history, a version of the past flattened out into the comforting fiction that conventionally representational art promises, we are ourselves completing the sentences of the 'palimpsest', and the satisfaction we thereby derive is that much more immediate to us.

The 'endless sentence' weaved by Henry James in Canto VII[119] is the object we have to deal with, the 'endless sentence' proposed against 'a shell of speech', against 'Words like the locust-shells, moved by no inner being'.[120] It is a sentence that conceals its origins and, like the 'palimpsest', it incorporates only incompleteness: 'Nor began nor ends anything',[121] we learn from Canto CXIV, and the

Cantos as a whole, of course, 'begin' not only *in media res* but in mid-sentence with the conjunctive 'And'. A sentence, 'endless' or not, always implies the possibility of a syntactical form artificially enclosed, but, as Fenollosa observed, there could be no complete sentence but one that 'it would take all time to pronounce'.[122] Here is the central problematic of the poem's structure: the proposition of an 'endless sentence' contradicts itself by its own practice; it suggests the limitless extent of a linguistic unit we are forced to close ourselves, for the purposes of convenience and intelligibility, by our act of transcription.

The objects in the poem, the texts displaced by Pound's concentrated selection, are offered to us as meaningful only through the nexus of relationship, of 'rhyme', they share with each other and with the idealist unity they signal by their special objectivity. The poem begins with a reflection of a reflection, with Andreas Divus's translation of Homer, a displacement of an earlier displacement.[123] Thus the act of displacement, a promise of renewed energy, of openness and flexibility through the function of intertextuality, exhibits a contradiction parallel to that of the 'endless sentence': our act of transcription, our own act of supplementation, can only replace a series of other replacements or, on the model of correspondence, repeat what has already been repeated.

Notes

Unless otherwise indicated, the place of publication is London.

Abbreviations

ABC	Ezra Pound, *ABC of Reading* (1934)
Analects	Ezra Pound, *Confucian Analects* (1956)
CEP	*Collected Early Poems of Ezra Pound*, ed. Michael King (1977)
CSP	Ezra Pound, *Collected Shorter Poems* (1952; 1968)
CWC	Ernest Fenollosa, *The Chinese Written Character as a Medium for Poetry*, ed. Ezra Pound (1920; San Francisco, n.d.)
G-B	Ezra Pound, *Gaudier-Brzeska: A Memoir* (1916; New York, 1970)
GK	Ezra Pound, *Guide to Kulchur* (1938; 1966)
H to R	Ezra Pound, *How to Read* (1931)
LE	*The Literary Essays of Ezra Pound*, ed. T. S. Eliot (1954; 1960)
Letters	*The Letters of Ezra Pound*, ed. D. D. Paige (1951)
MN	Ezra Pound, *Make It New* (1934)
Nat. Phil.	Remy de Gourmont, *The Natural Philosophy of Love*, trans. Ezra Pound (1922; 1926)
Pav. Div.	Ezra Pound, *Pavannes and Divisions* (New York, 1918)
P/J	*Pound/Joyce: The Letters of Ezra Pound to James Joyce, with Pound's Essays on Joyce*, ed. Forrest Read (1968)
SP	*Ezra Pound: Selected Prose 1909–1965*, ed. William Cookson (1973)

Sp. Rom.   Ezra Pound, *The Spirit of Romance* (1910)
Translations   *The Translations of Ezra Pound*, ed. Hugh Kenner (1953)

Introduction

1 *ABC*, p. 1.

2 *Sp. Rom.*, p. vi.

3 Ibid., p. 3. In 1913 the problem of terminology was provided with a model from the exact sciences: 'it is nearly impossible to write with scientific preciseness about "prose and verse" unless one writes a complete treatise on the "art of writing", defining each work as one would define the terms in a treatise on chemistry' ('The Serious Artist, III', *The New Freewoman*, I, 10 (1 November 1913), p. 194). It had been a problem insisted upon by T. E. Hulme: 'The great difficulty in any talk about art lies in the extreme indefiniteness of the vocabulary you are obliged to employ' (*Speculations*, ed. Herbert Read (1924; 1960), p. 143).

4 I agree with Samuel Hynes's proposal: 'Pound's poetic theory was fixed by the time he was thirty. . . . His most important statements date from the years 1913–16 – the years immediately preceding the first *Cantos*' ('Whitman, Pound and the Prose Tradition', *The Presence of Walt Whitman: Selected Papers from the English Institute*, ed. R. W. B. Lewis (New York and London, 1962), p. 113). Pound acknowledged this proposal in 1923: 'I consider criticism merely a preliminary excitement, a statement of things a writer has to clear up in his own head sometime or other, probably antecedent to writing' ('On Criticism in General', *The Criterion*, I, 3 (January 1923), p. 146). Hynes's suggestion of 1913–16 as the crucial period for Pound is, as I shall show, rather too restrictive in that it ignores the crises of vocabulary in 1910–12; equally restrictive is Herbert Schneidau's proposal: 'In a sense, everything that is part of Pound's mature poetics was latent in the earlier conceptions of Imagism' (*Ezra Pound: The Image and the Real* (Baton Rouge, 1969), pp. 159–60). But the general point of both commentators is surely right – that the major years of Pound's achievements as a theoretician were those he spent in London.

5 'Guido's Relations', *The Dial* (July 1929); reprinted as part of 'Cavalcanti', *LE*, p. 194.

6 Arthur Symons, *The Symbolist Movement in Literature* (1899; 1911), p. 4.

7 Noel Stock's gesture in the 'Confucius and Nineteenth Century Science' chapter of his *Poet in Exile* (Manchester, 1964) promises a great deal more than it actually delivers: he glances only briefly at Louis Agassiz, and the only texts that he cites in support of Pound's science are works of anthropology.

8 Max Nänny's *Ezra Pound: Poetics for an Electric Age* (Berne, 1973)
   offers a whole series of stimulating ideas, but his commitment to the
   theories of Marshall McLuhan, although never unquestioning, results
   in several distortions. Nevertheless, his treatise is based on the essential
   recognition that 'no other poet or critic of our time . . . has made such a
   profuse and illuminating use of electric analogies' (p. 20), and one of his
   most valuable conclusions suggests the necessary connection between
   Pound's mystical temperament and its reliance on science: 'As paradoxical as it may sound, it was exactly Pound's "mystical" desire for
   immediate experience and perception that was instrumental in his replacing the purely verbal "approach of logic" by the intuitional and
   factual approach of science' (p. 63).
9 Kenner's acknowledgements of Pound's science in *The Pound Era*
   (1972) are characteristically diffuse and invigorating, but they are also
   deeply ingrained with the idealism of Pound himself:

   And the chemists, the physicists, the biologists, were everywhere
   discovering a pattern-making faculty inherent in nature. Salt was
   crystalline, bubbles were vectorial equilibria, Marconi's pulses
   patterned the very ether, D'Arcy Thompson in 1917 explained how
   the bird's skeleton and the cantilever bridge utilize identical
   principles. (pp. 269–70).

   This is Kenner's most explicit statement on the subject, and, brilliant
   and economical though it is, vestigially it is stamped by that miming
   of the master into which so many of the commentaries, following
   Kenner's lessons, fall. As I hope my subsequent arguments will show,
   the reiteration of Pound's transcendentalist idealism is, in the nature of
   this epistemology, a further sealing-off of a world conceived originally
   in correspondential terms from the awkwardnesses of actuality.
10 'I Gather the Limbs of Osiris, II', *The New Age*, X, 6 (7 December
   1911), p. 130.
11 G. Thomas Tanselle, 'Two Early Letters of Ezra Pound', *American
   Literature*, XXXIV, 1 (March 1962), pp. 117, 115. Cf. 'Psychology and
   Troubadours', *Quest* (October 1912); in *The Spirit of Romance*, rev.
   ed. (1970), p. 88.

1 Poet as geometer

1 References to *A Portrait of the Artist as a Young Man* are from the
   Viking Press edition, ed. Chester G. Anderson and Richard Ellmann
   (New York, 1964), pp. 191–3, 213, 217–19.
2 *The Education of Henry Adams* (1907; Boston, 1918), pp. ix–x. Within the complicated lines of relationship through which the culture of

New England expressed itself, we may remember that, during his visit to Japan in 1886 with John La Farge, Adams met another proclaimer of scientific method, Ernest Fenollosa, and Basil Bunting has suggested that Pound's idea of physics 'seemed to me to be taken from the later chapters of Henry Adams's *Education*'. (Letter to I.F.A.B., 12 September 1972.)

3 An untitled essay, *Ezra Pound: A Collection of Essays to be Presented on his Sixty-Fifth Birthday*, ed. Peter Russell (1950), p. 262. There are pertinent comments on Pound's American 'tradition' in Noel Stock, *Poet in Exile* (Manchester, 1964), chapters 1 and 14; Charles Norman, *Ezra Pound: A Biography* (1960; 1966), pp. 70–1; Donald Davie, *Pound*, Fontana Modern Masters (1975), p. 32.

4 'Patria Mia', *The New Age* (1912); in *Patria Mia and the Treatise on Harmony* (1962), pp. 45, 34, 18, 13–14. 'The Condolence' is in *CSP*, pp. 91–2.

5 'Letters to Viola Baxter Jordan', ed. Donald Gallup, *Paideuma*, I, 1 (Spring and Summer 1972), p. 110. 'Malrin' is in *CEP*, pp. 33–4.

6 'Patria Mia', p. 19; *CSP*, p. 74. The volume to which 'NY' belongs, *Ripostes* (1912), charts with remarkable clarity the dilemma of imaginative worlds that confronted Pound during this period of his life.

7 'Patria Mia', pp. 45, 34.

8 Marshall McLuhan, 'Ezra Pound's Critical Prose', *Ezra Pound: A Collection of Essays to be Presented on his Sixty-Fifth Birthday*, ed. Peter Russell (1950), pp. 165–6.

9 Ibid., p. 167.

10 *G-B*, pp. 116, 134, 117.

11 'Criterionism', *Hound and Horn*, IV, 1 (October–December 1930), p. 114.

12 *G-B*, pp. 119–20.

13 J. M. Whistler, *The Gentle Art of Making Enemies* (1890), pp. 26–7, 32, 33.

14 Whistler, op. cit., pp. 33–4; Pound, 'An Anachronism at Chinon', *The Little Review* (June 1917); in *Pavannes and Divigations* (1960), p. 91.

15 See 'Letters to Viola Baxter Jordan', p. 109.

16 E. R. and J. Pennell, *The Life of James McNeill Whistler*, 2 vols (1908; 5th rev. ed. 1911), p. 242.

17 *CSP*, p. 251. Pound reiterated the poem's tribute in 'Patria Mia', pp. 34–5.

18 *Sp. Rom.*, p. 162.

19 'Affirmations, II: Vorticism', *The New Age*, XVI, 11 (14 January 1915), p. 278.

20 'Edward Wadsworth, Vorticist', *The Egoist*, I, 16 (15 August 1914), p. 306. Here Pound viewed the painter in the composite phrase

'Whistler and the Japanese' to define the anti-representational meaning of 'arrangements' in place, line or colour. Another American of scientific temperament, Ernest Fenollosa, his perceptions alive with the shapes of Japanese paintings, wrote:

> That a picture represents a man does not interest us. . . . It is a question of spacing, of how the pattern is worked out, that interests us . . . not the representational element but the structural element . . . not the realistic motive but the desire to find finer and finer space relations and line relations. (Quoted, Van Wyck Brooks, *Fenollosa and His Circle. With Other Essays in Biography* (New York, 1962), p. 49.)

21 'Affirmations, II: Vorticism', p. 277–8.

22 'Psychology and Troubadours', *Quest* (October 1912); in *Sp. Rom.*, rev. ed. (1970), pp. 92–4.

23 'Affirmations, II: Vorticism', p. 278.

24 'Vorticism', *The Fortnightly Review* (September 1914); in *G-B*, pp. 90–2.

25 Oliver Lodge, *Pioneers of Science* (1893; 1913), p. 150.

26 'Vorticism', p. 91.

27 Lodge, op. cit., p. 151.

28 Pound, in 'Vorticism', p. 85, was misquoting from Whistler's 'Red Rag' of 1878 (*The Gentle Art of Making Enemies*, pp. 126–7).

29 Lodge, op. cit., pp. 152–4.

30 *G-B*, pp. 122, 126.

31 Ibid., pp. 137–8.

32 Whistler, op. cit., pp. 50, 130, 15.

33 'Patria Mia,' pp. 24–5, 33. The vocabulary of technology had the benefit of emphasizing the practical achievements of scientific research. Shortly after the composition of 'Patria Mia', in another essay of confessed exile, Pound wrote of a visit to the House of Commons: 'I heard two things that sounded like sense – one from a man who knew something about the inside of a coal mine, and later, another argument from a man who knew something about marine engines' ('Through Alien Eyes, III', *The New Age*, XII, 13 (30 January 1913), p. 301).

34 *G-B*, pp. 119, 88, 78, 49, 120–1.

35 *GK*, pp. 180–1.

36 Charles B. Willard, 'Ezra Pound's Debt to Walt Whitman', *Studies in Philology*, LIV (October 1957), p. 574.

37 'The Renaissance, I: The Palette', *Poetry* (1915); in *LE*, p. 218.

38 'What I Feel About Walt Whitman', *SP*, p. 115.

39 Walt Whitman, *The Complete Poems*, ed. Francis Murphy (Harmondsworth, 1975), pp. 485, 517, 726.

40 See especially the essay that Whitman wrote during the 1850s but never published: *An American Primer*, ed. Horace Traubel (1904; San Francisco, 1970).

41 Walt Whitman, *A Critical Anthology*, ed. Francis Murphy (Harmondsworth, 1969), p. 41.

42 'Patria Mia', pp. 24, 47.

43 'What I Feel About Walt Whitman', p. 115.

44 Walt Whitman, *Selected Poems and Prose*, ed. A. Norman Jeffares (Oxford, 1966), p. 220.

45 Newton Arvin, *Walt Whitman* (1938), pp. 212–13.

46 E. C. Stedman, *Poets of America* (New York, 1885), pp. 382–3.

47 Joseph Beaver, *Walt Whitman – Poet of Science* (New York, 1951), p. 140.

48 Walt Whitman, *Selected Poems and Prose*, pp. 221–2.

49 'The Wisdom of Poetry', *Forum* (1912); in *SP*, pp. 332, 330.

50 The classic account is A. N. Whitehead, *Principles of Natural Knowledge* (1919).

51 Bertrand Russell, Preface to Henri Poincaré, *Science and Method*, trans. Francis Maitland (1914), pp. 6–7.

52 Adams, op. cit., p. 456.

53 Ibid., ch. 31; A. R. Jones, *The Life and Opinions of T. E. Hulme* (1960), p. 19.

54 William Bayliss, *Principles of General Physiology* (1913); quoted, William Coleman, *Biology in the Nineteenth Century: Problems of Form, Function and Transformation* (New York, 1971), p. 143.

55 Karl Pearson, *The Grammar of Science* (1892; 1900), pp. vii, 181.

56 A. D. Ritchie, *Scientific Method: An Inquiry into the Character and Validity of Natural Laws* (1923), p. 183.

57 Pearson, op. cit., p. 513.

58 A. S. Eddington, *The Nature of the Physical World* (Cambridge, 1928), pp. 294, 301.

59 Hudson Maxim, *The Science of Poetry and the Philosophy of Language* (New York, 1910), p. ix. All further references will be inserted in the main text.

60 *Sp. Rom.*, p. vi.

61 'A Visiting Card' (1942), *SP*, pp. 297, 304.

62 Herbert Spencer, 'The Philosophy of Style', *Westminster Review* (October 1852); in *Essays: Moral, Political and Aesthetic* (1864; New York, 1884), pp. 21, 10–11.

63 'The Wisdom of Poetry', pp. 329, 330.

64 'Patria Mia', p. 53.

65 'The Science of Poetry', *Book News Monthly*, XXIX, 4 (December 1910), pp. 282–3.

66 Ibid., p. 283.

67 'The Science of Poetry', p. 283; Maxim, op. cit., p. 95.

68 'The Science of Poetry', p. 283; Maxim, op. cit., p. 43.

69 'The Science of Poetry', p. 283.

70 'The Wisdom of Poetry', p. 329. Pound also amplified here the first clause of the definition by reallocating the reference to physics in order to sharpen the concerns of a practising poet:

> The Art of Poetry consists in combining these 'essentials to thought', these dynamic particles, *si licet*, this radium, with that melody of words which shall most draw the emotions of the hearer toward accord with their import, and with that 'form' which shall most delight the intellect. (p. 330)

Pound's 'form' here referred back to his preceding discussion of art's 'liberation', and was to be understood as the freedom instigated by the design of a work.

71 Pound began the essay by describing the unnamed book as having been 'mercifully forgotten' and as displaying 'considerable vigorous, inaccurate thought, fathomless ignorance, and no taste whatever' (p. 329). The only other reference that Pound made to Maxim occurred in the satirical 'L'Homme Moyen Sensuel' of 1915 where Maxim was included in the general diatribe of the opening section:

> Dulness herself, that abject spirit, chortles
> To see your forty self-baptised immortals,
> And holds her sides where swelling laughter cracks 'em
> Before the 'Ars Poetica' of Hiram Maxim. (*CSP*, p. 256)

72 'The Wisdom of Poetry', p. 331.

73 Ibid., pp. 331–2.

74 *G-B*, pp. 81–94.

75 'Reviews' (Signed 'Z'), *The New Freewoman*, I, 8 (1 October 1913), p. 149.

76 *Sp. Rom.*, p. 5.

77 'Vorticism', *G-B*, p. 92. These equations were to be seen as having a 'variable' significance, unlike those of arithmetic which had a 'fixed value' (p. 84). The latter merely predicated, for Pound, the 'association' whereby symbolism operated, resulting only in a language of substitution.

78 *Sp. Rom.*, pp. 115–16.

79 Ibid., p. 117.

80 'Psychology and Troubadours', pp. 92–3.

81 Ibid., pp. 95, 93.

82 Ibid., p. 94.

83 *Nat. Phil.*, p. 170.

84 'Psychology and Troubadours', p. 97. Pound's celebration of the Provençal aesthetic has ramifications far beyond its immediate context; this enormous topic has been thoroughly and brilliantly explicated by Peter Makin in 'Pound's Provence and the Medieval Paideuma', *Ezra Pound: The London Years 1908–1921*, ed. Philip Grover (New York, 1978), pp. 31–60, 139–54, and in *Provence and Pound* (Berkeley and Los Angeles, 1978).

2 The seriousness of the artist

1 Walter Pater, *The Renaissance* (1873; 1910), pp. viii–x.

2 Introduction to the 'Cavalcanti Poems', *Translations*, p. 18. Cf. Hugh Witemeyer, *The Poetry of Ezra Pound: Forms and Renewal 1908–1920* (Berkeley and Los Angeles, 1969), p. 9.

3 'I Gather the Limbs of Osiris, II', *The New Age*, X, 6 (7 December 1911), p. 130.

4 *GK*, pp. 60–1. Cf. a similar anecdote about Pound's scientific mentor, Louis Agassiz, in Elizabeth Cary Agassiz, *Louis Agassiz: His Life and Correspondence*, 2 vols (Boston, 1885), vol. I, p. 337.

5 Karl Pearson, *The Grammar of Science* (1892; 1900), pp. 34–7.

6 'I Gather the Limbs of Osiris, XI', *The New Age*, X, 16 (15 February 1912), p. 370.

7 'I Gather the Limbs of Osiris, IV', *The New Age*, X, 8 (21 December 1911), p. 178.

8 E. C. Stedman, *The Nature and Elements of Poetry* (1892), p. 14. Stedman had begun his campaign for 'the harmony of Poetry and Science' in the opening chapter of an earlier book, *Victorian Poets* (1875; 1877), pp. 7–21. A recent biographer of Stedman has noted of *Victorian Poets*: 'As the first extended demonstration of Tainean critical principles by an American, it marked the beginning of a new approach to criticism in America' (Robert J. Scholnick, *Edmund Clarence Stedman* (Boston, 1977), p. 38).

9 'The Serious Artist, I', *The New Freewoman*, I, 9 (15 October 1913), p. 161. Pound's irritability did not blunt his wit; he offered a very neat parody of his own willingness for scientific analogy: 'From medicine we learn that man thrives best when duly washed, aired and sunned. From the arts we learn that man is whimsical, that one man differs from another.'

10 Ibid., p. 162.

11 'Joyce', *The Future* (May 1918); in *LE*, pp. 416–17.

12 'Cooperation', *The Little Review*, V, 3 (July 1918), pp. 56–7. Pound

had begun to canonize the Goncourts two years earlier: 'If a man has not in the year of grace 1915 or 1916 arrived at the point of enlightenment carefully marked by the brothers De Goncourt in A.D. 1863, one is not admitted to the acquaintance of anyone worth knowing' ('Meditatio', *The Egoist* (March 1916); in *Pav. Div.*, p. 163).

13 'Paris Letter', *The Dial* (June 1922); in *LE*, p. 408.

14 'Patria Mia', *The New Age* (1912); in *Patria Mia and the Treatise on Harmony* (1962), pp. 24–5.

15 'The Renaissance, III', *Poetry*, VI, 2 (May 1915), p. 90.

16 'Meditatio', *The Egoist* (March 1916); in *Pav. Div.*, pp. 163–4.

17 Grant Allen, *Physiological Aesthetics* (1877), p. viii.

18 'Meditatio', p. 165.

19 'A Shake Down', *The Little Review* (August 1918); in *MN*, p. 258.

20 'In Explanation', *The Little Review* (August 1918); in *MN*, p. 254.

21 'James Joyce: At Last the Novel Appears', *The Egoist* (February 1917); in *P/J*, p. 90.

22 'Patria Mia', p. 32; 'A Shake Down', pp. 282, 257.

23 *GK*, p. 96.

24 J. P. Pritchard, *Criticism in America* (Norman, Oklahoma, 1956), p. 201. The best biography of Huneker is Arnold T. Schwab, *James Gibbons Huneker: Critic of the Seven Arts* (Stanford, 1963).

25 Van Wyck Brooks, *The Confident Years 1885–1915* (1952), pp. 2, 95–6.

26 T. S. Eliot, review of James Huneker, *Egoists* (New York, 1909), *Harvard Advocate*, LXXXVIII, 1 (5 October 1909), p. 16. Ludwig Lewisohn, in an influential book published in the same year as Pound's *How to Read*, insisted on the same point: 'The entire modern period of American culture is scarcely thinkable without the long energetic and fruitful activity of James Huneker ... if by 1909 there had come to exist an American minority that was aware of the direction of human culture, that group was largely the creation of James Huneker.' (*Expression in America* (New York and London, 1931), pp. 350–1.)

27 Eliot, op. cit., p. 16.

28 Donald Hall, 'The Art of Poetry, V: Ezra Pound: An Interview', *Paris Review*, No. 28 (Summer/Fall 1962), p. 26.

29 *P/J*, pp. 290, 105. Quinn, patron of the modernist avant-garde, was Huneker's legal adviser and remained a close friend throughout the later part of his life; Huneker dedicated *Ivory Apes and Peacocks* (1915) to Quinn.

30 James Huneker, *Unicorns* (New York, 1917), pp. 187–8.

31 Ibid., pp. 190–1.

32 Ibid., pp. 192–3.

33 'Joyce', p. 411. When Pound included this essay in *Instigations* (1920), he added a note on *Ulysses* which consisted mainly in another of his reprintings of the Preface to *Germinie Lacerteux*.

34 '"Dubliners" and Mr James Joyce', *The Egoist* (July 1914); in *LE*, p. 399.

35 Quoted, Pound, 'Remy de Gourmont: A Distinction', *The Little Review* (February–March 1919); in *LE*, p. 353.

36 James Huneker, *Egoists* (New York, 1909), pp. 111, 114.

37 Ibid., p. 113.

38 Ibid., pp. 129, 121–2.

39 'The Serious Artist, I', p. 162.

40 'Remy de Gourmont', *The Fortnightly Review* (N.S.), XCVIII, 588 (December 1915), p. 1161.

41 Ibid., pp. 1163, 1164. Pound also explained the 'scientific dryness' of Gourmont's *Sonnets in Prose*: 'He has worn off the trivialities of the day, he has conquered the fret of contemporaneousness by exhausting it in his pages of dry discussion, and we come on the feeling, the poignancy' (p. 1166).

42 'A Retrospect', *Pav. Div.*, p. 4.

43 'The Renaissance, I: The Palette', *Poetry*, V, 5 (February 1915), p. 227.

44 Matthew Arnold, 'The Study of Poetry', *Essays in Criticism* (First and Second Series), Everyman edition (n.d.), p. 239.

45 'Arnold Dolmetsch', *The Egoist* (August 1917); in *Pav. Div.*, p. 261.

46 *Letters*, p. 168.

47 'Dreiser Protest', *The Egoist*, III, 10 (October 1916), p. 159.

48 Anon., 'Correspondence', *The Egoist*, III, 12 (December 1916), p. 191.

49 *CSP*, p. 43.

50 'Correspondence', *The Egoist*, IV, 2 (February 1917), p. 30.

51 *Selected Letters of James Joyce*, ed. Richard Ellmann (1975), pp. 83, 81.

52 Canto XIV: 63/67. When referring to the *Cantos*, I follow Hugh Kenner's model of giving first the canto number, then the page reference to the New Directions edition (1972), followed by the page reference to the Faber edition (1964).

53 Pound's use of *Ulysses* in his revisions of the early *Cantos* is well described in Ronald Bush, *The Genesis of Ezra Pound's Cantos* (Princeton, 1976), pp. 194 ff.

54 Richard Godden, 'James Joyce: He do the Police in no Voices at all', *Essays in Poetics*, V, 1 (April 1980), p. 82.

55 Canto XII: 59/63.

56 *Confucius: The Great Digest and the Unwobbling Pivot*, trans. Ezra Pound (New York, 1951), p. 31.

57 Richard Sieburth, *Instigations: Ezra Pound and Remy de Gourmont* (Cambridge, Mass., and London, 1978), pp. 18, 78 ff., 129–30.

58 'Remy de Gourmont: A Distinction', p. 342.

59 Pater, op. cit., p. 24.

60 Sieburth, op. cit., pp. 134–5.

61 Norman O. Brown, *Life Against Death* (1959; 1968), pp. 163–207.

62 'Medievalism', *The Dial* (March 1928); included in 'Cavalcanti', *LE*, pp. 150–1. Cf. Peter Makin, *Provence and Pound* (Berkeley and Los Angeles, 1978), pp. 32–3.

63 Canto XV: 64/68.

64 'Salutation the Second', *CSP*, p. 95.

65 See Godden, op. cit., *passim*.

66 Anon., 'The Art of the Future', *The New Freewoman*, I, 10 (1 November 1913), p. 181.

67 Ibid., p. 182.

68 'The Serious Artist, I', p. 163.

69 *Letters*, p. 37.

70 Pearson, op. cit., pp. 6–7. Pearson's mode of investigation was available in the demands of Zola, the Goncourts and Flaubert for the novel, but its reiteration was deemed necessary for the confusions of the twentieth century, particularly by men of science. As late as 1929, J. H. Woodger's textbook on biology gave it, in a distinctly Poundian moment, the status of an ethical axiom: 'That the whole pursuit of science rest upon moral judgements is clear from the fact that a man of science who falsifies his results does not break a logical law but an ethical one' (*Biological Principles* (1929), pp. 65–6).

71 Ibid., p. 515.

72 A. N. Whitehead, *An Introduction to Mathematics* (1911), p. 91. J. H. Woodger again marked the continuing need to reiterate the principle of proper definition throughout Pound's early years by picking up Whitehead's 'blot of ink':

> A great number of the words used in biological books are nothing more than ink marks without a clear meaning, and it is because no one considers it necessary, either to assign a clear meaning to such terms, or to abandon them altogether, that much biological controversy is apt to be so fruitless. But so long as this is the state of affairs there is no hope for clear thinking or for the application of any sort of symbolic technique. (op. cit., pp. 482–3)

73 Anon., 'Views and Comments', *The New Freewoman*, I, 9 (15 October 1913), pp. 165–6.

74 Walter Pater, *Plato and Platonism* (1893; 1928), pp. 253–4.

75 'The Serious Artist, IV', *The New Freewoman*, I, 11 (15 November 1913), p. 214.

76 See especially *Letters*, pp. 42, 43, 46, 51, 124, 140.

77 *GK*, pp. 327–8.

78 'Patria Mia', p. 53. Pound wrote of the importance of learning from practising craftsmen: 'What we know about the arts we know from practitioners, usually from their work, occasionally from their comments. Our knowledge is sometimes second hand and becomes more wafty with each remove.' (*GK*, p. 59.)

79 Pearson, op. cit., p. 517.

80 T. H. Huxley, 'Lecture on the Study of Biology' (1876), *American Addresses* (1877), p. 141.

81 Pearson, op. cit., pp. 18–19. In essence, as J. H. Woodger put it on behalf of biological investigation, 'we require to think primarily about biological facts, not about hypothetical billiard balls' (op. cit., p. 486).

82 'It is perhaps hardly sufficiently realized how important a part the mechanical arts play in the development of science and how absolutely essential they are for the purpose of physical measurement. The screw-cutting lathe is as important an instrument of knowledge as the differential calculus.' (A. D. Ritchie, *Scientific Method: An Inquiry into the Character and Validity of Natural Laws* (1923), pp. 3–4.) For Ritchie 'the relation of formal laws to facts can only be found by experience. . . . Deductive reasoning by itself can never tell us about facts' (pp. 12–13). And for Ernest Fenollosa the deductive process was a function of the 'medieval tyranny of logic', obstructing access to phenomenal objects.

83 T. H. Huxley, 'Lecture on the Study of Biology', pp. 151–3.

84 Ibid., pp. 159–60, 154–6.

85 'Things to be Done', *Poetry*, IX, 6 (March 1917), p. 313.

86 F. O. Matthiessen, *American Renaissance* (1941; 1968), p. 173.

87 Richard Poirier, *A World Elsewhere* (1966; Oxford, 1968), pp. 17–21.

88 Hugh Kenner, *The Pound Era* (1972), pp. 42, 47. Kenner's version of an archaeological Homer has been explored in detail by Michael Seidel, *Epic Geography* (Princeton, 1976). Ronald Bush has suggested the partiality of Kenner's position in that it ignores the mythological Homer of the Cambridge anthropologists (op. cit., pp. 125 ff.), but that partiality hardly detracts from the significance of Kenner's position in that (as the whole burden of my present enterprise is designed to illustrate) Pound's aesthetics rely exactly on the problematic of the concrete and the mythopoeic, and for too long critical attention has been devoted, misleadingly, to the mythopoeic at the expense of the concrete.

89 'I Gather the Limbs of Osiris, VI: On Virtue', *The New Age*, X, 10 (4 January 1912), p. 224.

90 'Early Translators of Homer', *The Egoist* (January–February 1919); in *LE*, p. 267.

91 Ibid., pp. 254, 250.

92 'Jewel stairs, therefore a palace. Grievance, therefore there is something to complain of. Gauze stockings, therefore a court lady, not a servant who complains. Clear autumn, therefore he has no excuse on account of the weather. Also she has come early, for the dew has not merely whitened the stairs, but has soaked her stockings.' (*CSP*, p. 142.)

93 'Affirmations, I: Arnold Dolmetsch', *The New Age* (January 1915); in *LE*, pp. 431–6.

94 Samuel Butler, *The Authoress of the Odyssey* (1897; 1922), pp. 15–18. Butler's plan of the house faces p. 17.

95 Ibid., p. 75.

96 Ibid., pp. 40, 43.

97 Ibid., pp. 88, 98.

98 Poirier, op. cit., pp. 18, 21.

99 Harriet Monroe, 'Rhythms of English Verse, II', *Poetry*, III, 3 (December 1913), pp. 110–11. Monroe's was a familiar reliance on the supposed immutability of scientific law: 'Rhythm is rhythm, and its laws are unchangeable, in poetry, in music, in the motion of tides and stars, in the vibration of sound-waves, light-waves, or the still more minute waves of molecular motion' ('Rhythms of English Verse, I', *Poetry*, III, 2 (November 1913), p. 61).
    The distance between such loose usage and that of Pound can be gauged most accurately by the quality of argument in the small debate concerning the relationship between science and poetry set up by Harriet Monroe at the end of the decade ('A Scientist's Challenge', *Poetry*, XV, 3 (December 1919), pp. 149–52, and 'Science and Art Again', *Poetry*, XV, 4 (January 1920), pp. 204–11). The debate returned to the old theme of whether the arts were possible in an age of science, a theme that in itself is sufficient indication of anachronism. After a decade of instruction by Pound in the possibilities of science for modernist literature, it would be difficult to find a more trivial, unsophisticated response, which, intellectually, was naïve and, stylistically, was obfuscatory and mystifying. It was characterized by axioms such as the proposal that it was not 'inventions' themselves that were important but 'the creative human spirit beneath the invention that counts' (p. 204), and 'The inquiry is essentially this: Is not the truth one and indivisible, whether of science, art, philosophy, or anything else?' (p. 208).

100 George Soule, 'The Vision of Wells', *The Little Review*, I, 3 (May 1914), p. 29.

101 Anon., 'A Brilliant Enemy', *The Little Review*, II, 7 (November 1915), p. 25.

102 To say that *The Egoist*, of all the literary magazines of the period, was most willing to incorporate the discourse of science, is really to say that the articles constituting the editorial column by Dora Marsden from July 1916 to December 1919 were willing to incorporate that discourse. They employed an intensive combination of philosophy, psychology and the physical sciences, to define a material base for the major terms usually associated with abstract speculation: imagination, memory, will and, indeed, knowledge itself. An account of this series is beyond the scope of the present work, and its manipulation of science is really too late significantly to have informed Pound's usage which, by the time they were begun in 1916, was virtually fully developed.

103 Huntley Carter, 'Art and Drama: The Theatre and Armageddon', *The Egoist*, I, 22 (16 November 1914), p. 430. Despite his disapproval of scientific terminology (see his pejorative use of vocabulary from electricity in 'The New Driving Force', *The Egoist*, I, 13 (1 July 1914), pp. 257–8, published two months after a bitter attack on quasi-scientific approaches to literature in Edgar A. Mowrer, 'Georges Polti: A Sign of the Times', *The Egoist*, I, 10 (15 May 1914), pp. 190–3), Carter's present essay did recognize the need for a more vigorous discussion of his subject, based on scientific precepts:

> If we are to have a wonderful form of creative dramatic effect, and more than one person is to produce it, then clearly we must have not only a definite statement of the basic laws or principles governing its production, but a careful consideration of the best methods of applying such laws or principles, for the guidance of all who are to take part in producing it. Besides the 'art' of the theatre there is the science of the theatre. Besides the electric current there is the wireless apparatus for its absorption and transmission. (p. 430)

104 The best discussion of the topic is Tom Gibbons, *Rooms in the Darwin Hotel: Studies in English Literary Criticism and Ideas 1880–1920* (Nedlands, W. Australia, 1973). Gibbons's study examines the effect of evolutionary principles on the critical thinking of Havelock Ellis, Arthur Symons and A. R. Orage, providing an excellent account of the ways in which scientific thought explains many of the problems and contradictions of modernism.

105 Sidney Lanier, *The Science of English Verse* (New York, 1880), p. vii. Lanier championed scientific method generally in America as a means of approach: 'It was as a scientist, of course, analyzing and detecting, discovering adherence to or deviation from natural laws that Lanier

undertook his work as a critic' (Aubrey Harrison Starke, *Sidney Lanier: A Biographical and Critical Study* (N. Carolina, 1933), p. 440). But Lanier was certainly capable of a more sustained organicist theorizing: 'As the embryo is wont in its growth to reproduce successively all the stages of the race, so we may say there is a Hebrew stage of culture, a Greek stage, an English stage' (*Shakespeare and His Forerunners*, 2 vols (1903), vol. I, p. 53). Significantly for Poundian purposes, Lanier was one of those men of letters who persistently denied the doctrine of evolution; his view of embryonic growth suggested here was rather that of a recapitulationist. During his education at Oglethorpe College in the late 1850s, the chair of science was held by James Woodrow – like Lanier firmly imbued by Presbyterian thought – who had spent the summer of 1853 at the Lawrence Scientific School in Harvard (Philip Graham, 'Lanier and Science', *American Literature*, IV (November 1932), pp. 288–92). This was the school established and headed by Pound's scientific mentor from the 1930s onwards, Louis Agassiz, the major spokesman in America for the principles of recapitulation against the influence of Darwin (see Ian F. A. Bell, 'Divine Patterns: Louis Agassiz and American Men of Letters', *Journal of American Studies*, X, 3 (December 1976), pp. 349–81).

It is important to distinguish thinkers like Lanier from the issues popularized by French naturalist theory. Lanier attacked Zola's pretensions to 'scientific experiment' as wholly specious. (*The English Novel* (1883; 1903), p. 69. Cf. Gay Wilson Allen, 'Sidney Lanier as a Literary Critic', *Philological Quarterly*, XVII, 2 (April 1938), p. 134.) His prose was occasionally illuminated by the more precise form of analogy so characteristic of Pound himself:

> just as the chemist in causing chlorine and hydrogen to form hydrochloric acid, finds that he must not only put the chlorine and hydrogen together, but must put them together in the presence of light in order to make them combine: so the poet of our time will find that his best combinations, his greatest syntheses of wisdom, own His law, and they too must be effected in the presence of the awful light of science. (*The English Novel*, p. 50)

106 Havelock Ellis, 'The Present Position of English Criticism', *Time* (December 1885); in *Views and Reviews, First Series: 1884–1919* (1932), p. 37. In practice, Ellis's criticism often involved merely the tracing of genealogy; see, for example, his celebration of racial crossbreeding in 'The Ancestry of Genius', *The Atlantic Monthly* (March 1893); in *Views and Reviews*, pp. 68–85.

107 John Addington Symonds, 'On the Application of Evolutionary Prin-

ciples to Art and Literature', *Essays Speculative and Suggestive* (1890; 1907), p. 37. Symonds's title meant simply an attention to the three-fold process of development:

> the development of a complex artistic structure out of elements existing in a national character, which structure is only completed by the action of successive generations and individual men of genius, all of whom in their turn are compelled to contribute either to the formation of the rudimentary type, or to its perfection, or to its decline and final dissolution . . . the inevitable progression from the embryo, through ascending stages of growth to maturity, and from maturity by declining stages to decrepitude and dissolution, has not been sufficiently insisted on. (p. 30)

108 Quoted in Valerie Eliot's Introduction, *The Waste Land: A Facsimile and Transcript of the Original Drafts* (1971), pp. xii, xiii.

109 T. S. Eliot, 'Tradition and the Individual Talent, I', *The Egoist*, VI, 4 (September 1919), p. 55.

110 T. S. Eliot, 'Humanist, Artist, and Scientist', *The Athenaeum*, 4667 (10 October 1919), pp. 1014–15.

111 T. S. Eliot, 'In Memory of Henry James', *The Egoist*, V, 1 (January 1918), p. 2.

112 'The Middle Years', *The Egoist*, V, 1 (January 1918), p. 2.

113 T. S. Eliot, 'Contemporanea', *The Egoist*, V, 6 (June–July 1918), p. 84.

114 Eliot, 'Tradition and the Individual Talent, I', p. 55.

115 See 'Patria Mia', p. 53. This series of essays also presented one of Pound's earlier statements on the notion of tradition for which Eliot was to provide his famous definition in 1919: 'Sismondi said that one studied the past so as to learn how to deal with the present. . . . One wants to find out what sort of things endure, and what sort of things are transient; what sort of things recur' (pp. 48–9).

116 'A Few Don'ts by an Imagiste', *Poetry* (March 1913); in *LE*, p. 6.

117 T. S. Eliot, 'Studies in Contemporary Criticism, I', *The Egoist*, V, 9 (October 1918), p. 113. Eliot's concern with the tools of vocabulary indicated the interest he shared with Pound in practical craftsmanship. Two years later he used mathematics to sanction such craftsmanship: 'The critic is interested in technique – technique in the widest sense. You cannot understand a book on mathematics unless you are actively, not merely passively, a mathematician, unless you can perform operations, not merely follow them.' ('A Brief Treatise on the Criticism of Poetry', *Chapbook* (London), II, 9 (March 1920), p. 3.)

118 'The Renaissance, III', *Poetry*, VI, 2 (May 1915), p. 90.

119 Eliot, 'Studies in Contemporary Criticism, I', p. 114. The second in-

stalment of this essay contained the following proposal for critical aids for the reading public: 'I propose at some future date a convenient encheiridion, *A Guide to Useless Books*, prepared in such an order that it will be possible at once to refer any new book to its category.' This proposal was for 'a classification which would enable the reader to determine immediately whether a critic fulfils any of the legitimate critical functions or fulfils more than one without confusion' ('Studies in Contemporary Criticism, II', *The Egoist*, V, 10 (November– December 1918), p. 131). Eliot's proposal, significantly following one of the rare instances where he employed the discourse of science, echoed the joke of the 'scientific norm' that Pound had suggested in 1913.

120 Paul Ricœur, *The Rule of Metaphor*, trans. Robert Czerny (1978), p. 7.

121 'Affirmations, I: Arnold Dolmetsch', p. 431.

122 *International Journal of Ethics*, XXVII, 1 (October 1916), p. 116.

123 T. S. Eliot, Introduction to *Collected Works of Paul Valéry*, vol. VII, ed. Jackson Mathews (1958), pp. xviii–xx. Valéry's essay lay unpublished until 1946 (note, p. 345).

124 Paul Valéry, 'On Literary Technique', *Collected Works*, vol. VII, pp. 315–16.

125 Judith Robinson has written of Valéry's disposal of his scientific knowledge:

> The recent publication of Valéry's personal notebooks calls for a major change of emphasis in many of the generally accepted critical attitudes towards this most complex of all modern French thinkers. In particular, the Cahiers make it abundantly clear that nothing was more central or fundamental in Valéry's thought than his preoccupation with the methods and achievements of science, and especially of physics and mathematics. Throughout the whole of his adult life, the Cahiers show him reading widely and intensively in the field of classical physics . . . and studying with the greatest interest the development of mathematics. . . . They show him as well following in detail, and with tremendous intellectual excitement, the remarkable advances which were taking place in scientific thought during his own lifetime. ('Language, Physics, and Mathematics in Valéry's Cahiers', *Modern Language Review* (October 1960), p. 519)

To judge from the information given in Ms Robinson's excellent article, it is a great pity that Valéry's thoughts on science and their connections with poetic modernity were not expressed in print as fully as in the notebooks since, time and again, they coincided with Pound's

uses of science. Ms Robinson writes, for example, of Valéry's fascination with the syntheses of diverse materials and ideas achieved by
late nineteenth- and early twentieth-century mathematical physics,
such as Maxwell's fusion of the three previously separate branches of
physics (electricity, magnetism and light) into the single subject of
electromagnetism, the syntheses that were to be central for Pound's
thinking about tradition and the vortex:

> In the broadest sense, the whole development of scientific inquiry
> can be regarded as a systematic search for affinities and analogies
> of this type. Physics, as Valéry realized, is basically concerned not
> with phenomena 'in themselves' ... but with the relationships
> between phenomena. The same is true of mathematics, whose
> primary purpose is the working out of abstract relationships be-
> tween general classes of phenomena and the operations linking
> them. In Valéry's words, mathematics deals with 'les propriétés des
> actes indépendantes de l'objet et de la matière particulière de ces
> actes' – or, more simply, with 'les propriétés d'une forme'. This idea
> of the essentially formal character of the physical and mathematical
> sciences was undoubtedly confirmed in Valéry's mind by his reading
> of Poincaré, whose profound influence on his thought cannot be too
> strongly emphasized. In one of many typical passages, Poincaré
> writes: 'Les mathématiciens n'etudient pas des objets, mais des
> relations entre les objets; il leur est donc indifférent de remplacer ces
> objets par d'autres, pourvu que les relations ne changent pas. La
> matière ne leur importe pas, la forme seule les intéresse.' (p. 524)

Ernest Fenollosa, somewhat earlier, had admired exactly such syntheses and interested himself precisely in Poincaré's opposition between relations and *relata*.

126   Edith Wyatt, 'True to Life', *The Little Review*, III, 3 (May 1914),
p. 14.

127   *Letters*, p. 143. The anecdote was to become one of Pound's perennial
lessons in looking; it shared the *ABC of Reading* with the scientific
lesson of Louis Agassiz's postgraduate student (*ABC*, pp. 1–2, 48–9).

128   The relationship between Pound and Ford is familiar and needs little
reiteration here. There are good discussions in Hugh Kenner, *The
Poetry of Ezra Pound* (1951), and particularly in Herbert N.
Schneidau, *Ezra Pound: The Image and the Real* (Baton Rouge,
1969), where, in chapter 1, Schneidau revealingly uses Ford in his
account of imagism. The widest account of the relationship is in Eric
Homberger, 'Pound, Ford and "Prose": The Making of a Modern
Poet', *Journal of American Studies*, V, 3 (Decmber 1971), pp.
281–92. My purpose differs from these accounts in that it attends not

to a series of shared ideas but to the development of a distinctive vocabulary for their articulation.

129 Ford Madox Hueffer, *Ancient Lights* (1911), pp. 243, 110.

130 Donald Davie, *Pound* (1975), p. 32. Davie also quotes Pound's important letter to Thomas Hardy in 1921 to illustrate a further problem of his exile: 'I come from an American suburb – where I was not born – where both parents were really foreigners, i.e., one from New York and one from Wisconsin. The suburb has no roots, no centre of life' (p. 49). This was why Whistler and Whitman (rather than Eliot or James) were so important for Pound. Charles Norman has commented: 'in moments of doubt and despair, the achievement of Whitman sustained him; and along with Whitman, the other re-nowned American, Whistler' (*Ezra Pound: A Biography* (1960; 1969), p. 33). Cf. Walter Baumann, *The Rose in the Steel Dust* (Miami, 1970), p. 145.

One of the elements that deeply distinguishes Pound from Eliot lies precisely in their attitude towards this particular heritage; as Davie notes of Eliot, 'Not a hint of Whistler is *his* demeanour!' (p. 33). Eliot did not have much time for Whitman either, to the extent of per-versely denying him for Pound: 'Whitman is certainly not an in-fluence; there is not a trace of him anywhere; Whitman and Mr Pound are antipodean to each other' ('Ezra Pound: His Metric and Poetry' (1917), in *To Criticise the Critic* (1965), p. 177). Cf. Eliot's patronizing comments on Whitman in his Introduction to *Ezra Pound: Selected Poems* (1928; 1948), p. 10.

131 Hueffer, *Ancient Lights*, p. 293.

132 Ibid., pp. 58–62. Ford's mourning for the loss of 'the sense of a whole' was to be answered for Pound two years later by the transcendentalist bias of Fenollosa's science.

133 Ibid., p. 185.

134 Ford Madox Hueffer, *The Critical Attitude* (1911), p. 134. All further references will be included in the text.

135 Ibid., p. 97. Ford was assuming here the familiar distinction from the post-Jamesian novel between 'showing' and 'telling' a story, a re-formulation of Flaubertian *impassibilité*. Herbert Schneidau makes a good case for this 'objective predication' as the 'key to Pound's idea of a "poetry of reality"' (op. cit., pp. 65–8).

136 Ford Madox Hueffer, 'The Poet's Eye, I', *The New Freewoman*, I, 6 (1 September 1913), pp. 108–9. Pound had earlier maintained the modernity of diction by incorporating the word 'uxorious' in 'Portrait d'Une Femme' (*CSP*, p. 73); see 'Patria Mia', p. 30.

137 Ford Madox Hueffer, *Henry James: A Critical Study* (1913), pp. 22–4. All further references will be included in the text.

138 'A Shake Down', *The Little Review* (August 1918); in *MN*, p. 257.

139 Ibid., pp. 260–1.

140 Ford was also capable of using more practical scientific analogies; see, for example, his use of the 'nine-cylinder, 160 horse-power, non-rotary Bréguet engine' as part of his discussion of the 'Pre-Jamesian writer' (pp. 123–4).

141 Eric Homberger, 'Pound, Ford, and "Prose": The Making of a Modern Poet', *Journal of American Studies*, V, 3 (December 1971), p. 285.

142 Ibid., pp. 287, 291–2.

143 Hueffer, *Ancient Lights*, p. 110.

3 Correspondences

1 A. R. Jones, *The Life and Opinions of T. E. Hulme* (1960), p. 19.

2 Herbert N. Schneidau, *Ezra Pound: The Image and the Real* (Baton Rouge, 1969), p. 56. Schneidau's masterly critique of Hulme (pp. 46–56) demonstrated once and for all the paucity of Hulme's mind and the fundamental ideological incompatibility between Hulme and Pound.

3 T. E. Hulme, 'Romanticism and Classicism', *Speculations* (1924; 1960), pp. 134–5.

4 'Real work, history and scientific researches, the accidental, the excrescences, like digging, and necessary just as digging is. Poetry the permanent humanity, the expression of man freed from his digging, digging for poetry when it is over' (T. E. Hulme, 'Notes on Language and Style', incl. as appendix III in Michael Roberts, *T. E. Hulme* (1938), p. 271). For Pound, such 'digging' was a necessary display of the artist's seriousness, his struggle; Hulme's is an argument for, paradoxically, an alternative mode of abstraction, the flattening out of this struggle.

5 A. S. Eddington, *The Nature of the Physical World* (Cambridge, 1928), pp. xv–xvi.

6 Ibid., pp. 252–4.

7 Eddington wrote that symbols in physics were 'definable only in terms of the other symbols belonging to the cyclic scheme of physics' (op. cit., p. 269).

8 T. E. Hulme, 'Notes on Language and Style', incl. as appendix III in Roberts, op. cit., p. 272.

9 T. E. Hulme, 'Lecture on Modern Poetry', incl. as appendix II in Roberts, op. cit., pp. 268–9.

10 T. E. Hulme, 'A Personal Impression of Bergson', incl. in A. R. Jones, op. cit., p. 206.

11 'Remy de Gourmont', *The Fortnightly Review* (N.S.), XCVIII, 588 (December 1915), p. 1161.

12 T. E. Hulme, 'Cinders', *Speculations*, pp. 223–4.

13 T. E. Hulme, 'The Philosophy of Intensive Manifolds', *Speculations*, pp. 177–8. Earlier, in 'Humanism and the Religious Attitude', Hulme offered a familiar and simplistic account of nineteenth-century 'materialism': 'Vital phenomena were only extremely complicated forms of mechanical change (cf. Spencer's Biology and the entirely mechanical view involved in the definition of life as adaptation to environment)' (*Speculations*, p. 7).

14 Frank Kermode, *Romantic Image* (1957; 1966), pp. 129–30.

15 T. E. Hulme, 'Humanism and the Religious Attitude', *Speculations*, pp. 13–15; 'Notes on Language and Style', p. 282. A similar demand for a philosophy that was both intuitive and scientific was made in Henri Bergson, *An Introduction to Metaphysics*, trans. T. E. Hulme (1913), p. 63.

16 Karl Pearson, *The Grammar of Science* (1892; 1900), pp. 18–19.

17 Bergson, op. cit., pp. 6–7.

18 T. E. Hulme, 'Bergson's Theory of Art', *Speculations*, p. 147.

19 Bergson, op. cit., p. 35.

20 Hulme, 'Bergson's Theory of Art', pp. 154–5.

21 Hulme, 'Humanism and the Religious Attitude', p. 53.

22 Schneidau (op. cit., pp. 55–6) records his agreement with Hynes's Introduction to T. E. Hulme, *Further Speculations* (Lincoln, Neb., 1962), p. xxxi.

23 *Translations*, p. 379.

24 T. E. Hulme, 'A Tory Philosophy', incl. in Jones, op. cit., p. 194.

25 *CWC*, pp. 25–8. Bergson recounted a similar idea of science's struggle against logic:

> Modern science dates from the day when mobility was set up as an independent reality. It dates from the day when Galileo, setting a ball rolling down an inclined plane, firmly resolved to study this movement from top to bottom for itself, in itself, instead of seeking its principle in the concepts of *high* and *low*, two immobilities by which Aristotle believed he could adequately explain the mobility. (op. cit., pp. 64–5)

26 Bergson, op. cit., pp. 37–8, 56, 40.

27 T. E. Hulme, 'The Philosophy of Intensive Manifolds', p. 196.

28 *ABC*, p. 7.

29 Maud Ellmann, 'Floating the Pound: The Circulation of the Subject of *The Cantos*', *The Oxford Literary Review*, III, 3 (Spring 1979), p. 18.

30 Walter Pater, *The Renaissance* (1873; 1910), pp. vii–viii.

31 *ABC*, pp. 40, 2.

32 Interest in *japonisme* was widespread in centres of culture on both sides of the Atlantic, notably in Boston and London. Present space refuses a detailed bibliography, but the best start may be made with D. J. Gordon and Ian Fletcher, 'The Poet and the Theatre', in D. J. Gordon, *Images of a Poet* (1961; Manchester, 1970); Van Wyck Brooks, *New England: Indian Summer* (1940); and Lawrence W. Chisholm, *Fenollosa: The Far East and American Culture* (New Haven, 1963).

33 Alice Corbin Henderson, 'Japanese Poetry', *Poetry*, VII, 2 (November 1915), pp. 89–90, 91.

34 Aristotle, *Poetics*, ch. 22. Pound first used the quotation in *Sp. Rom.*, p. 166.

35 *Sp. Rom.*, p. 167.

36 Henderson, op. cit., pp. 93, 90, 92.

37 *Analects*, p. 5.

38 *CWC*, p. 21. All further references will be included in the main text.

39 Pearson, op. cit., pp. 87, 179.

40 Herbert Spencer, *The Principles of Biology*, 2 vols (1864 and 1867), vol. I, pp. 80, 95.

41 Ernest Mach, 'The Economical Nature of Physical Inquiry' (1882), *Popular Scientific Lectures*, trans. T. J. McCormack (1943) (from the third edition of 1898), pp. 205, 211, 206.

42 Ernest Mach, 'On the Principle of Comparison in Physics' (1894), *Popular Scientific Lectures*, pp. 238–9.

43 Ernest Mach, *The Analysis of Sensations* (1897), trans. C. M. Williams (New York, 1959), p. 89.

44 J. Arthur Thomson, *The Science of Life* (London and New York, 1899), pp. 8, 14, 15.

45 Van Wyck Brooks, *Fenollosa and His Circle. With Other Essays in Biography* (New York, 1962), pp. 9, 4. Hearn's recognition of a world shared by Spencerian biology and Eastern mysticism was the result of a strong distrust of Western materialist science (see p. 60), a distrust shared by another friend of Fenollosa's in Tokyo, Sturgis Bigelow (see p. 55).

46 Quoted, ibid., p. 45. Brooks demonstrates the synthesizing activity of Fenollosa's mind by quoting a letter of 1897 in which he outlined his current programme of study:

> Monday evenings our subject is Philosophy, and at present we are studying Hegel's logic. On Tuesday it is Poetry, and we have begun with the Elizabethan dramatists. Wednesday, History, at present English, Thursday, the History of Art, Bosanquet's Aesthetics. Friday, Science, just now mechanics. Saturday, Japanese language. (p. 63)

47 Quoted, Lawrence W. Chisholm, *Fenollosa: The Far East and American Culture* (New Haven and London, 1963), pp. 133–4, 216. Chisholm's excellent treatise (inexplicably neglected by commentators on Pound), which provides the bulk of the material for my following account of Fenollosa, pays little attention to Fenóllosa's science, but he begins his book by noting the general relations between Fenollosa's thought and the scientific revolution at the beginning of the twentieth century:

> To many artists and philosophers the publication in 1905 of Einstein's *Special Theory of Relativity* revealed the inadequacy of basic conventions underlying man's knowledge of physical reality, namely long-held assumptions of absolute time and absolute space, anchors of certainty in modern conceptions of the universe. At a more general level, William James, lecturing on 'Pragmatism' in 1906, was attacking the pretensions of a variety of 'block universes' which seemed to close the future. James pictured reality as multiple and moving, a various stream of possibilities ordered by the purposive force of thought into solutions which were tentative, not certain. Fenollosa's attacks on cultural parochialism and on formalisms of every sort . . . anticipated a looser, relational pattern of thinking. (pp. 8–9)

48 Quoted, ibid., p. 185.

49 In the 'Brief Concordance' he appended to the English edition of *Confucian Analects* (1956), Pound instructed the reader to compare Agassiz with the proposition of Bk VI, xi: 'Observe the phenomena of nature as one in whom the ancestral voices speak, don't just watch in a mean way.' Fenollosa's ideal of an art museum (see Chisholm, op. cit., pp. 175–6) exhibited principles of structure very similar to Agassiz's Museum of Comparative Zoology at Cambridge. Pound's pairing of Agassiz and Confucius was his own configuration of transcendentalist ideology.

50 Quoted, Chisholm, op. cit., p. 177 (source unattributed).

51 Fenollosa's theories of education are discussed fully in Chisholm, op. cit., pp. 177–95. He championed Whistler's cause in 'The Place in History of Mr Whistler's Art', *Lotus* (Boston), I, 1 (1903), and 'The Collection of Mr Charles L. Freer', *Pacific Era*, 1 (November 1907); see Chisholm, op. cit., pp. 173–4.

52 Chisholm, op. cit., p. 183. Fenollosa's effect as a theorist of art education was achieved not so much via his own works as via those of his friend Arthur Wesley Dow whom he first met in 1891. Dow's major book was *Composition* (1899), a widely influential work that went through nineteen editions; its emphasis followed the revolutionary

principles of Fenollosa, stressing manual training and the non-representational elements of line, *notan* and colour. (See Chisholm, op. cit., p. 187.)

53 Quoted, Chisholm, op. cit., p. 191.

54 Quoted, ibid., pp. 216–17.

55 E. C. Stedman, 'Victorian Poets', *Scribner's Monthly*, V (January 1873), p. 364.

56 Quoted, Van Wyck Brooks, op. cit., p. 28. Morse's reminiscences of Agassiz were: 'Jean Louis Rudolphe Agassiz', *The Popular Science Monthly*, 71 (December 1907), and 'Agassiz and the School at Penikese', *Science* (N.S.), 58 (12 October 1923). Extensive documentation concerning his relationship with both Agassiz and Fenollosa, 'my most intimate friend', is to be found in Dorothy G. Wayman, *Edward Sylvester Morse: A Biography* (Cambridge, Mass., 1942), which, despite its uncritical anecdotal tone, is useful for the large amount of material it draws from Morse's own journal.

57 Quoted, Brooks, op. cit., p. 251.

58 Elizabeth Cary Agassiz, *Louis Agassiz: His Life and Correspondence*, 2 vols (Boston, 1885), vol. II, pp. 556–7, 669; vol. I, p. 336.

59 Theodore Lyman, 'Recollections of Agassiz', *Atlantic Monthly*, 33 (February 1874), p. 223. Lyman's use of Agassiz's handwriting also served to illustrate his lifestyle in Paris, an impoverishment with which Pound would sympathize:

> we can understand why Agassiz said in America, 'I have no time to make money.' In that very laboratory, and in others like it, he worked for years, never knowing the value of silver. . . . His small handwriting, which seemed unnatural in so broad and impulsive a character, was a result of early necessity. On the backs of old letters, and on odd scraps of paper, he copied, as closely as possibly, many volumes which he needed but which he could not buy. (p. 222)

60 Ralph Waldo Emerson, 'Nature' (1836), *Complete Prose Works of Ralph Waldo Emerson* (Ward Lock, n.d.), pp. 310, 312, 315.

61 Hugh Kenner, in one of his hugely tantalizing hints, has suggested: 'From Emerson's lectures on "The Poet" (1844) and on "The Method of Nature" (1841) we can collect without trouble a body of propositions indistinguishable in import from the statements about reality out of which Fenollosa's great Ars Poetica is educed' (*The Pound Era* (1972), p. 158). I agree, and with Kenner's wonderfully dense paragraph summarizing Fenollosa's debt to Emerson (p. 230; cf. pp. 105–6), but Kenner's voice is so intent on miming that of his subject ('the universe is alive, and the live mind part of the universe, and each one of these brilliant pictures [Fenollosa's ideograms] made by some

live mind is a living cell, specializing the life of the totality') that we are presented with a latter-day idealism facing a mirror-image of its earlier self, a tautology of discourse to which Poundian commentators are particularly prone. Such feeding off one's material inevitably involves a mode of mystification, not to say incest. Kenner's choice of texts follows the customary pattern of promoting the metaphysical Emerson; the Emerson to whom Pound would have responded was the sturdier, more practical Emerson of the treatise on *Nature* (1836) and the essay on Swedenborg (1845). In any case, it is rarely ideas, 'propositions', that are new; they require specific frameworks of vocabulary to revitalize them for the responsive mind.

62 Quoted, Harry Hayden Clark, 'Emerson and Science', *Philological Quarterly*, X, 3 (July 1931), p. 244.

63 Louis Agassiz, *Methods of Study in Natural History* (Boston, 1863), pp. 199, 231–2, 42–3, 129.

64 Lyman, op. cit., p. 229.

65 Jules Marcou, *Life, Letters and Works of Louis Agassiz*, 2 vols (New York, 1896), vol. II, pp. 123, 125.

66 Lyman, op. cit., pp. 223–4.

67 Louise Hall Tharp, *Adventurous Alliance: The Story of the Agassiz Family in Boston* (Boston, 1959), p. 213. Modern commentary has sustained the lesson; E. C. Herber writes: 'Agassiz inspired by example; once he examined the developing stages of a turtle for 60 days and nights consecutively at regular intervals until all stages of its development were established' (*Correspondence between Spencer Fullerton Baird and Louis Agassiz*, ed. E. C. Herber (Washington, 1963), p. 18).

68 Samuel Hubbard Scudder, 'In the Laboratory with Agassiz', *Every Saturday*, 16 (4 April 1874), pp. 369–70. Scudder's essay was reprinted in the two standard contemporary biographies of Agassiz by Jules Marcou (op. cit., vol. II, pp. 94–7) and Elizabeth Cary Agassiz (op. cit., vol. II, p. 567). It was published separately as a leaflet for the Agassiz Fund on behalf of the Museum of Comparative Zoology at Cambridge by James Barnard, again a former student of Agassiz (see Marcou, op. cit., vol. II, p. 97).

69 See, for example, Agassiz's description of the different kinds of movement attributable to different animals in *Methods of Study in Natural History*, pp. 124–5.

70 Elizabeth Cary Agassiz, op. cit., vol. II, p. 405.

71 The best of these examples are to be found in Marcou, op. cit., vol. II, p. 150.

72 Ralph Waldo Emerson, 'Swedenborg; or, The Mystic' (1845), *Complete Prose Works*, pp. 187, 184, 185, 186–7.

73 *Letters*, p. 285.

74 Emerson, 'Swedenborg', pp. 187–8.
75 'Letters to Viola Baxter Jordan', ed. Donald Gallup, *Paideuma*, I, 1 (Spring and Summer 1972), pp. 109, 110.
76 Emerson, 'Nature', pp. 327, 326.
77 Clark, op. cit., p. 229.
78 Emerson, 'Nature', p. 315.
79 Alice Corbin Henderson, 'Japanese Poetry', p. 91.
80 *CWC*, pp. 22–3.
81 Emerson, 'Nature', p. 315.
82 *CWC*, p. 35.
83 Emerson, 'Nature', pp. 315, 316.
84 *CWC*, pp. 11, 8, 13, 12.
85 Louis Agassiz, op. cit., pp. 9–10, 13–14, 192, 134, 19–21.
86 Ibid., pp. 20–1, 23–4. Cf. Agassiz's Prospectus for his *Contributions to the Natural History of the United States* in 1855; *Correspondence between Spencer Fullerton Baird and Louis Agassiz*, ed. E. C. Herber (Washington, 1963), p. 83.
87 William James, *Memories and Studies* (1911), p. 152. The standard account of Agassiz is Edward Lurie, *Louis Agassiz: A Life in Science* (Chicago, 1960). Lurie has continued the groundwork of this account with a series of fascinating speculations on the place of Agassiz and the implications of scientific thought in the wider cultural issues of American intellectual history, in 'Science in American Thought', *Journal of World History*, VIII (April 1965), pp. 638–65; 'American Scholarship: A Subjective Interpretation of Nineteenth Century Cultural History', *Essays on History and Literature*, ed. Robert M. Bremner (Columbus, Ohio, 1966), pp. 31–80; *Nature and the American Mind* (New York, 1974). Agassiz's importance for Pound in particular is explored in Guy Davenport, *The Intelligence of Louis Agassiz* (Boston, 1963), and I. F. A. Bell, 'Divine Patterns: Louis Agassiz and American Men of Letters', *Journal of American Studies*, X, 3 (December 1976), pp. 349–81.
88 Emerson, 'Nature', p. 318.
89 Ibid., p. 323.
90 *CWC*, pp. 19, 12.
91 Emerson, 'Nature', pp. 319, 317, 316.
92 *H to R*, pp. 17–18.
93 *Uncollected Poetry and Prose of Walt Whitman*, ed. Emory Holloway (Garden City, 1921), vol. II, pp. 69–70.
94 Benjamin T. Spencer has noted: 'though Pound's concentration on and exaltation of the factual, objective world were secular and affective rather than cosmic in intent and implication, his massing of discrete particulars often resembles passages of the Transcendentalists and their

followers for whom a sense of wonder suffused all objects and held them together in mystic unity' ('Pound: The American Strain', *PMLA*, LXXXI, 7 (December 1966), p. 464).

95 Walt Whitman, *An American Primer*, ed. Horace Traubel (1904; San Francisco, 1970), p. 12.

96 'Patria Mia', *The New Age* (1912); in *Patria Mia and the Treatise on Harmony* (1962), p. 45.

97 References to *Walden* are from the Signet edition (1960), pp. 203–5. I am grateful to the conversation of Richard Godden for help in eluci- dating this passage. We may note further how Thoreau adapts his principle of the 'lobe' to the human face itself:

> The ear may be regarded, fancifully, as a lichen, *Umbilicaria*, on the side of the head, with its lobe or drop. The lip – *labium*, for *labor* (?) – laps or lapses from the sides of the cavernous mouth. The nose is a manifest congealed drop or stalactite. The chin is a still larger drop, the confluent dripping of the face. The cheeks are a slide from the brows into the valley of the face, opposed and diffused by the cheek bones. Each rounded lobe of the vegetable leaf, too, is a thick and now loitering drop, larger or smaller; the lobes are the fingers of the leaf; and as many lobes as it has, in so many directions it tends to flow, and more heat or other genial influences would have caused it to flow yet farther.

The extent to which Thoreau is thinking in Emersonian terms, and terms particularly interesting for Fenollosa and Pound, may be seen in a passage from his next paragraph:

> The earth is not a mere fragment of dead history, stratum upon stratum like the leaves of a book, to be studied by geologists and antiquaries chiefly, but living poetry like the leaves of a tree, which precede flower and fruit, – not a fossil earth, but a living earth; compared with whose great central life all animal and vegetable life is merely parasitic.

Thoreau's final clause suggests again the extent to which a theory of correspondence is in many ways a subterfuge for a non-social indi- vidualism.

4 The vortex

1 'Psychology and Troubadours', *Quest* (October 1912); in *Sp. Rom.*, rev. ed. (1970), pp. 91–2.

2 'Affirmations, I: Arnold Dolmetsch', *The New Age* (January 1915); in *LE*, p. 431. Pound began the essay with a discussion of myth in order to

elaborate the important access that Dolmetsch provided to earlier forms of music, and he wrote: 'the early music starts with the mystery of pattern; if you like, with the vortex of pattern' (p. 434). Pound's move from 'mystery' to 'vortex', from the arcane to the contemporary, circumscribes exactly the area of our present concerns.

3 *CEP*, p. 34.

4 *CEP*, pp. 172, 173.

5 *Sp. Rom.*, pp. 5–7.

6 *CSP*, pp. 71, 52. Within another mode of translation, Pound made the 'scurrilous, bejewelled prose' of Apuleius (*Sp. Rom.*, p. 10) into the fragile beauty of 'Speech for Psyche' (*CEP*, p. 149).

7 Herbert N. Schneidau, *Ezra Pound: The Image and the Real* (Baton Rouge, 1969), pp. 126, 119–21. Schneidau's account of this area of Pound's thought is the most intelligent and stimulating of such discussions; I have found chapter 4, 'Tradition, Myth and Imagist Poetics' (pp. 110–46), particularly useful and exciting in the present context.

Schneidau indicates the parity between the theses of Mead and Upward: 'Mead's "subtle universe" is similar to Upward's universe of "fluid force"; it implies many existences not immaterial but of an order of corporeality too fine for the gross sense to perceive' (p. 126). It has been one of the achievements of more recent commentaries to establish with commendable precision the relationship between Pound's thought and that of Upward: see in particular Bryant Knox, 'Allen Upward and Ezra Pound', *Paideuma*, III, 1 (Spring 1974), pp. 71–83; A. D. Moody, 'Pound's Allen Upward', *Paideuma*, IV, 1 (Spring 1975), pp. 55–70; Donald Davie, *Pound* (1975), pp. 62–74; Ronald Bush, *The Genesis of Ezra Pound's Cantos* (Princeton, 1976), pp. 91–102.

8 'Guido's Relations', *The Dial* (July 1929); in 'Cavalcanti', *LE*, p. 194.

9 I have argued for the poem's expressions of modernist crisis in 'The Phantasmagoria of Hugh Selwyn Mauberley', *Paideuma*, V, 3 (Winter 1976), pp. 361–85, and 'Mauberley's Barrier of Style', in *Ezra Pound: The London Years 1908–1920*, ed. Philip Grover (New York, 1978), pp. 89–115, 155–64.

10 Schneidau, op. cit., p. 124.

11 The general point should be made that Pound's efforts to confirm mystical speculation by the public rhetoric of scientific analogy can very fruitfully be seen as a contemporary version of Neoplatonist thought, but that, as a result of his metamorphic view of the world, there is little indication of any radical discontinuity between the real and the ideal; as the *Cantos* instruct us, 'le paradis n'est pas artificiel'. Mead, in his own attempt to confirm the doctrine of the 'subtle body' by modern science, noted the contemporary 'powerful renascence of Platonic

studies in their wider sense' (*The Doctrine of the Subtle Body in Western Tradition* (1919), p. 9).

12 G. R. S. Mead, op. cit., pp. 1–5.

13 Ibid., pp. 11–13, 17, 41.

14 Ibid., pp. 112–14. Cf. 'Psychology and Troubadours', pp. 92–4. Pound's notion of *virtu* was, of course, habitually figured by images of light – 'Apparuit' (*CSP*, pp. 80–1) is the most obvious example among many – and, since Hertz's discovery of electromagnetic waves in the middle of the nineteenth century, it would have seemed natural to envisage light and potency in electrical terms.

15 'I Gather the Limbs of Osiris, IX: On Technique', *The New Age*, X, 13 (25 January 1912), pp. 298–9.

16 *CEP*, p. 36.

17 Timothy Materer, 'Pound's Vortex', *Paideuma*, VI, 2 (Fall 1977), p. 175.

18 The function of vortex motion in the formation of worlds helps to explain Pound's rather puzzling biological comparison several years after the initial clamour over the vorticist movement had died down: 'Vorticism is, in the realm of biology, the hypothesis of the dominant cell' ('A Study in French Poets', *The Little Review*, IV, 10 (February 1918), p. 55). Pound's most immediate source for this comparison must have been Allen Upward's notion of the 'vorticell' which he put into print in a series of articles, 'The Nebular Origin of Life', for *The New Age* in 1921–2. (These articles were reprinted as an appendix to the recent edition of Upward's *The Divine Mystery* (1913; Santa Barbara, 1976), pp. 364–84.) Upward, in an eccentric synthesis of contemporary science and what looks suspiciously like early Greek atomic theory, used the notion of the 'vorticell' to explain the origins of organic life, to provide a 'physical basis' for those origins (pp. 380–3). Donald Davie has recommended: 'One has only to read chapters 13 and 14 of his [Upward's] *The New Word* (1908) to recognize a powerful and original mind clearly and trenchantly concerned with matters that bear directly on what Pound meant by "vortex" ' (*Pound* (1975), p. 45).

   Poe, in his prose-poem 'On the Material and Spiritual Universe', similarly testified to the primacy of vortical movement in the formation of stellar bodies ('Eureka', *The Science Fiction of Edgar Allan Poe*, ed. Harold Beaver (Harmondsworth, 1976), p. 300).

19 *GK*, p. 327. The only citation of Pound's awareness of Burnet that Materer provides is from an unpublished letter to Wyndham Lewis in 1954: 'Ever hear of John Burnet: "Early greek philosophy" 1892/some items on numbers by diagram, as dice and dominoes. . . . Also a few quotes from Empedokles' (Materer, op. cit., pp. 175–6).

   It is interesting that Burnet, as I shall show, proves to be a rich source for much that Pound sympathized with yet, like Hudson Maxim and James Huneker, only enters the Poundian pantheon by name to such a limited extent.

20 John Burnet, *Early Greek Philosophy* (1892; 1908), p. 10 (cited here-after as Burnet, *EGP*).

21 'Allen Upward Serious', *The New Age* (April 1914); in *SP*, pp. 377–9. It was Upward's capacity for the 'real' that for Pound 'distinguishes him from all the encyclopaedists who have written endlessly upon the corn gods, etc.' ('The Divine Mystery', *The New Freewoman* (November 1913); in *SP*, p. 374).

22 Burnet, *EGP*, pp. 16–17.

23 Andrew G. Van Melsen, *From Atomos to Atom* (1952), trans. Henry J. Koren (New York, 1960), p. 167.

24 Burnet, *EGP*, p. 380. Leukippos' notion that 'the atom may be known by its mass' was included by Emerson in his list of Swedenborg's 'favourite dogmas' (*Complete Prose Works* (Ward Lock, n.d.), p. 187). Usefully for Pound's later interest in Gourmont's *Natural Philosophy of Love*, Emerson's list also included 'The ancient doctrine of Hippocrates that the brain is a gland', and he quoted Swedenborg's hierarchy of forms which was differentiated by geometrical figures; here, vortical shape itself was used to describe the two penultimate forms, prior to the 'perpetual-celestial, or spiritual' (p. 188).

25 Burnet, *EGP*, pp. 274, 311–12.

26 John Burnet, *Greek Philosophy* (1914; 1964), p. 159 (cited hereafter as Burnet, *GP*).

27 Burnet, *EGP*, p. 389.

28 Ibid., pp. 390–1, 397, 400–1.

29 Burnet, in his reiteration of vortex theory in 1914, added the question of neutralization: 'The larger bodies offer more resistance . . . to this communicated motion than the smaller, simply because they are larger and therefore more exposed to impacts in different directions which neutralize the vortex motion' (*GP*, p. 80).

30 Burnet, *GP*, p. 80. The only difference between Burnet's accounts of Leukippos in his two volumes is a firmer assurance of argument, characterized by the absence of any debate with other commentators over the correctness of Leukippos' theory. The later volume did, how-ever, insist more strongly on Leukippos' anti-metaphysical tempera-ment in a way that was particularly relevant to Pound's current preoccupations; Burnet isolated for attention his mechanical expla-nation of weight consequent upon vortex theory in which weight 'is not an occult quality', but arises from purely mechanical causes' (p. 80).

31 *CSP*, p. 217.

32 See *Nat. Phil.*, pp. 178, 179, 180, and Henri Poincaré, *Science and*

Method (1909), trans. Francis Maitland (1914), pp. 57–66. Pound's assimilation of Gourmont and Poincaré was a good index to his efforts to synthesize the subject matter of idealist biology with the imaginative strictures of mathematics.

33 See Bell, 'Mauberley's Barrier of Style', pp. 103–4. Burnet's suggestion of Plato's use of the 'sieve' for the version of world formation we find in the *Timaeus* is worth following up as a further context for Mauberley's 'sieve', since it provides an indication of quite what is lost through Mauberley's preference for the 'seismograph', as Plato, too, used it as a simile for the principle of separation that instigated the bringing of order and pattern to chaos; I quote from the Loeb translation:

> The Nurse of Becoming, being liquefied and ignified and receiving also the forms of earth and of air, and submitting to all the other affections which accompany these, exhibits every variety of appearance; but owing to being filled with potencies that are neither similar nor balanced, in no part of herself is she equally balanced, but sways unevenly in every part, and is herself shaken by these forms and shakes them in turn as she is moved. And the forms, as they are moved, fly continually in various directions and are dissipated; just as the particles that are shaken and winnowed by the sieves and other instruments used for the cleansing of corn fall in one place if they are solid and heavy, but fly off and settle elsewhere if they are spongy and light. So it was also with the Four kinds when shaken by the Recipient: her motion, like an instrument which causes shaking, was separating farthest from one another the dissimilar, and pushing most closely together the similar; wherefore also these Kinds occupied different places even before that the Universe was organized and generated out of them. Before that time, in truth, all these things were in a state devoid of reason or measure, but when the work of setting in order this Universe was being undertaken, fire and water and earth and air, although possessing some traces of their own nature, were yet so disposed as everything is likely to be in the absence of God; and inasmuch as this was then their natural condition, God began by first marking them out into shapes by means of forms and numbers. (*Timaeus*, 52d–53b)

Analogously, at the level of language, Leukippos' 'sieve' and his 'vortex' particularized and ordered the rather vague conception of rotary movement through which Empedokles and Anaxagoras had articulated their notions of cosmological nascence.

34 *CSP*, p. 220.

35 See Bell, 'The Phantasmagoria of Hugh Selwyn Mauberley', pp. 378–81.

36 *Letters*, p. 364.

37 'Early Translators of Homer . . . I: Hugues Salel', *The Egoist* (August 1918); in *LE*, p. 250.

38 That such lexical order, such particularity of observation, is reversed in the 'inferior' (*Letters*, p. 364) version of 'phantasmal' is, of course, entirely suitable for the crisis of Mauberley's temperament.

39 Burnet, *GP*, pp. 81, 79.

40 'Through Alien Eyes, I', *The New Age*, XII, 11 (16 January 1913), p. 252.

41 *Wyndham Lewis on Art*, ed. Walter Michel and C. J. Fox (1969), pp. 155–8, 59. Hugh Kenner has made the point succinctly: 'Salt was crystalline, bubbles were vectorial equilibria, Marconi's pulses patterned the very ether, D'Arcy Thompson in 1917 explained how the bird's skeleton and the cantilever bridge utilize identical principles' (*The Pound Era* (1972), pp. 269–70).

42 'Medievalism', *The Dial* (March 1928); in *LE*, pp. 150–5.

43 *Translations*, pp. 18, 19–20.

44 Burnet, *EGP*, p. 48.

45 Ibid., pp. 51, 15–16.

46 Robert H. Murray, *Science and Scientists in the Nineteenth Century* (1925), pp. 70–2, 84.

47 Oliver Lodge, Introduction to ibid., p. xvii.

48 These essays, in order of their appearance in *The Egoist*, were:

1 'The Bourgeois', I, 3 (2 February 1914), p. 53. A didactic, programmatic attack on contemporary journalism: 'The bourgeois . . . is, in brief, digestive. He is the stomach and gross intestines of the body politic and social, as distinct from the artist, who is the nostrils and the invisible antennae.'

2 'John Synge and the Habits of Criticism', I, 3 (2 February 1914), pp. 53–4. An attack on the indiscriminating attitude of literary journalism, its inability and unwillingness to applaud the new rather than the mediocre: 'There is no truce between art and the vulgo. There is a constant and irrefutable alliance between art and the oppressed. . . . There is a bond between the artist and the inventor and the able man in a system. Each is feared by the inefficient man who holds the administrative grade just above him. I have seen an inventor treated by capitalists exactly as a good writer before he is "recognized" is treated by inefficient editors. . . . The "Times" reporter . . . is therefore against the discoverer.'

3 'Reviews: Poetry, A Magazine of Verse', I, 11 (1 June 1914), p. 215. Praise for 'an American paper that seems every now and again, for the fraction of a number to be trying to introduce an international standard.'

4 'Reviews: First Novels', I, 11 (1 June 1914), p. 215. An attack on the publishing system that indiscriminately and for pecuniary purposes advertises on the basis of the 'first emanation' of a first novel: 'There is no peace between art and any commercial system.'

5 'On the Imbecility of the Rich', I, 20 (15 October 1914), pp. 389–90. A mourning for the economic situation of the artist and for the decline of aristocratic patronage: 'There remains an aristocracy of the creative arts and an aristocracy of inventive science.'

6 'Those American Publications', I, 20 (15 October 1914), p. 390. A complaint about the prudish and antiquated editorial policy of American magazines: 'The little old ladies, male and female, of those aged editorial offices, dare not face the fact of individual personality; of writers who will not be *made*.'

49 Hudson Maxim, *The Science of Poetry and the Philosophy of Language* (New York, 1910), pp. 36–7.

50 J. G. McKendrick, *H. L. F. von Helmholtz* (1899), pp. 40–1.

51 Hermann von Helmholtz, 'On the Conservation of Force', *Popular Lectures on Scientific Subjects*, First Series (1873; 1892), trans. E. Atkinson, pp. 279, 280, 281, 315.

52 Leo Koenigsberger, *Hermann von Helmholtz* (1902), trans. F. A. Welby (Oxford, 1906), p. iii.

53 Stanley L. Jaki, *The Relevance of Physics* (Chicago and London, 1966), p. 168. The urge to confirm older philosophies by contemporary science was a familiar ambition for the temperament of transcendentalist cast. In that essay on 'Swedenborg' which contained so many modernist roots, Emerson described the 'atmosphere of great ideas' into which Swedenborg was born and he drew attention to vortex theory: 'Gilbert had shown that the earth was a magnet; Descartes, taught by Gilbert's magnet, with its vortex, spiral, and polarity, had filled Europe with the leading thought of vortical motion, as the secret of nature' (*Complete Prose Works* (Ward Lock, n.d.), p. 185). Swedenborg's particular aptness for cosmology was a result of his 'native perception of identity which made mere size of no account to him', seeing in 'the atom of magnetic iron' the 'quality which would generate the spiral motion of sun and planet' (p. 185). Later in the same essay, Emerson used vortex motion as a figure for the 'rhymes' of nature, the 'strange sympathies' he had perceived in the Jardin des Plantes where Agassiz had studied, that united all aspects of the known universe: 'vortical motion, which is seen in eggs as in planets' (p. 187). This was a figure used by Swedenborg himself, who saw nature 'wreathing through an everlasting spiral', and whose theory of ascending degrees of forms placed the form of the 'perpetual-vortical' second only to the highest form, that of the 'spiritual' (pp. 187, 188).

54 Koenigsberger, op. cit., p. 171.
55 Ibid., p. 167.
56 'Vorticism', *The Fortnightly Review* (September 1914); in *G-B*, p. 92.
57 'Medievalism', p. 154. In Canto XXV we have 'the waves taking form as crystal' (XXV: 119/124).
58 McKendrick, op. cit., pp. 197–8.
59 Ralph Waldo Emerson, 'Swedenborg; or, the Mystic', *Complete Prose Works* (Ward Lock, n.d.), p. 187.
60 McKendrick, op. cit., p. 198. Koenigsberger made the same point about Kelvin's derivation of the 'indestructibility' of matter from Helmholtz's vortex theory:

> Lord Kelvin has associated his Theory of the Constitution of Matter with Helmholtz's law that a vortex in a frictionless fluid persists as an invariable quantity. Kelvin sees a fundamental analogy between the indestructibility of the vortex and the indestructibility of matter. He conceives an atom as a whirl or vortex in the ether, and accounts for the chemical disparity of the atoms on the supposition that we have in them different combinations of vortex rings. (Koenigsberger, op. cit., p. 171)

61 Ibid., p. 200. Tait read three papers on 'knots' before the Royal Society of Edinburgh in 1877, 1884 and 1885, which were collected in his *Scientific Papers*, 2 vols (Cambridge, 1898), vol. I, pp. 273–317, 318–34, 335–47, respectively. The illustrations to these papers were plates IV–V (following p. 316), plate VI (following p. 334) and plates VII–IX (following p. 346).
62 C. G. Knott, *Life and Scientific Work of P. G. Tait* (Cambridge, 1911), pp. 106–7.
63 Hugh Kenner, *The Pound Era* (1972), pp. 145–7. Kenner takes Fuller's 'knots' as examples of 'patterned energies'. Fuller, claims Kenner,

> grasps and tenses an invisible rope, on which we are to understand a common overhand knot, two 360° rotations in intersecting planes, each passed through the other. . . . Pull, and whatever your effort each lobe of the knot makes it impossible that the other shall disappear. It is a *self-interfering pattern . . . a patterned integrity.* (p. 145)

64 Ibid., p. 239. Ronald Bush has offered an excellent, although brief, account of the relationship between the 'vortex' as 'knot' and systems of etymological and hereditary energy via Allen Upward's *The New Word* (1908); see *The Genesis of Ezra Pound's Cantos* (Princeton, 1976), pp. 92–3.
65 McKendrick, op. cit., pp. 196–9, 199—200.

66 Max Nänny, *Ezra Pound: Poetics for an Electric Age* (Berne, 1973), pp. 86–7.
67 Quoted, Nänny, op. cit., p. 86n.
68 *CWC*, p. 7.
69 William Berkson, *Fields of Force: The Development of a World View from Faraday to Einstein* (1974), p. 3. The main texts on which Berkson bases his fascinating study are Faraday, *Experimental Researches in Electricity*, 3 vols (1839, 1844, 1855), and *The Scientific Papers of James Clerk Maxwell*, ed. W. D. Niven (Cambridge, 1890).
70 *CWC*, p. 22.
71 Koenigsberger, op. cit., p. v.
72 Burnet, *EGP*, p. 389.
73 Berkson, op. cit., p. 125.
74 *CWC*, p. 12.
75 Berkson, op. cit., p. 149.

5 Tradition and race-memory

1 'I Gather the Limbs of Osiris, IX: On Technique', *The New Age*, X, 13 (25 January 1912), p. 299.
2 Walter Pater, 'Coleridge', *Appreciations* (1889; 1910), p. 66.
3 T. S. Eliot, 'Tradition and the Individual Talent, I', *The Egoist*, VI, 4 (September 1919), p. 55.
4 P. G. Ellis has noted the 'common vocabulary concerning history, development, memory, and tradition' which united the modern line from Pater to Eliot ('The Development of T. S. Eliot's Historical Sense', *Review of English Studies* (N.S.), XXIII, 91 (1972), pp. 291–301).
5 George Soule, 'New York Letter', *The Little Review*, I, 5 (July 1914), p. 43. Soule's demands for the seriousness of literature were, of course, a restatement of Pound's arguments throughout his London period for that seriousness.
6 John Gould Fletcher, 'Three Imagist Poets', *The Little Review*, III, 3 (May 1916), p. 32.
7 Walter Pater, *Plato and Platonism* (1893; 1928), p. 14.
8 Tom Gibbons, *Rooms in the Darwin Hotel: Studies in English Literary Criticism and Ideas 1880–1920* (Nedlands, W. Australia, 1973), pp. 128–9.
9 Indispensable work on the relationship between the Society for Psychical Research (and the wider issues of contemporary formal science) and the question of modernism has been done by Martin Kayman in his PhD thesis, 'Ezra Pound and the Phantasy of Science' (University of York, 1978), a monograph which, inexplicably, has yet to find a publisher.

10 G. R. S. Mead, *The Doctrine of the Subtle Body in Western Tradition* (1919), p. 117.

11 Thomson Jay Hudson, *The Law of Psychic Phenomena* (1893; London and Chicago, 1905), p. v.

12 Edmund Gurney, Frederic Myers and Frank Podmore, *Phantasms of the Living* (1886), abridged edition, ed. Mrs Henry Sidgwick (London and New York, 1918), p. xxxiv.

13 Frank Podmore, *The Naturalisation of the Supernatural* (London and New York, 1908), p. 7.

14 Ibid., pp. 10–11. This use of electromagnetism had, of course, a lengthy history in the literature of the nineteenth century, most recently explicated by Maria M. Tatar who asks:

> What is one to make of the electrical energy vibrating through Kleist's dramas, the 'streams of magnetic fluid' coursing through Balzac's novels, the 'electrical heat' radiating from figures in E. T. A. Hoffman's tales, and the 'magnetic chain of humanity' joining together the characters in Hawthorne's novels? And why is it that Rodolphe woos Emma Bovary by entertaining her with 'dreams, forebodings, magnetism'? Why does Charles Bovary, distraught by his wife's death, recall stories about the 'miracles of animal magnetism' and imagine that, by 'straining his will', he can resuscitate his wife? (*Spellbound: Studies in Mesmerism and Literature* (Princeton, 1978), p. xi.)

The answer to these questions lay in applications of the work of Anton Mesmer:

> In the decades following the French Revolution, mesmerism escaped the control of its founder to become enmeshed with a wide range of mystical, spiritual, and metaphysical doctrines. The magnetic fluid that had once streamed so abundantly through Mesmer's clinic was transformed by mystics into a divine afflatus, by spiritualists into ethereal specters, and by metaphysicians into an impalpable force designated as the will . . . mesmerism now promised to endow man with a sixth sense that would expand his cognitive consciousness. (ibid., p. xiii)

15 *Lectures on the Method of Science*, ed. T. B. Strong (Oxford, 1906).

16 Francis Gotch, 'On Some Aspects of the Scientific Method', in Strong, op. cit., pp. 25–58.

17 William McDougall, 'Psycho-Physical Method', in Strong, op. cit., pp. 111–12.

18 Ibid., pp. 112–14.

19 Ibid., pp. 115–16.

20 William James, *The Varieties of Religious Experience* (1902; 1977), p. 490n.

21 Ibid., p. 478n.

22 Sidney Lanier, *Shakespeare and His Forerunners*, 2 vols (1903), vol. I, p. 72.

23 Havelock Ellis, *The New Spirit* (1890; 1926), p. 246.

24 John Addington Symonds, 'The Philosophy of Evolution', *Essays Speculative and Suggestive* (1890; 1907), pp. 7, 4.

25 Ibid., pp. 10–11.

26 John Addington Symonds, 'Nature Myths and Allegories', *Essays Speculative and Suggestive*, pp. 303, 305, 311.

27 Ibid., p. 314.

28 J. Arthur Thomson, *Introduction to Science* (1911), p. 81.

29 Havelock Ellis, 'Science and Mysticism', *Atlantic Monthly*, III, 6 (June 1913), p. 771.

30 Ibid., pp. 779, 782–3. Cf. the section on 'Mind and Matter' in *The Notebooks of Samuel Butler*, ed. Henry Festing Jones (1912), pp. 74–92. Ellis's synthesis of science and mysticism involved attention to the literary trope most appropriate, within the transcendentalist discourse shared by Emerson and Pound, to that synthesis: metaphor. He quoted that proposition from Aristotle to which Pound himself returned so often: 'It was a fine and deep saying of Aristotle's that "the greatest thing by far is to be a master of metaphor." That is the mark of genius, for, said he, it implies an intuitive perception of the similarity in dissimilars', and he expanded the proposition in a distinctly Poundian manner: 'All the great thinkers have been masters of metaphor, because all vivid thinking must be in images, and the philosopher whose metaphors are blurred or diluted is one whose thinking is blurred and diluted.' To think in metaphorical terms was to see the world as 'an infinite series of analogies', and those who employed metaphor 'were alive; they had realized what they meant; they embodied their thoughts in definite images which are a perpetual challenge to thought for all who come after' (*Impressions and Comments* (1914), pp. 80–2).

31 Samuel Butler, *Unconscious Memory* (1880; 1910), p. 161. Butler extended his argument to claim memory as the base for any definition of the individuality of a given organism:

> a chrysalis . . . is as much one and the same person with the chrysalis of its preceding generation, as this last is one and the same person with the egg or caterpillar from which it sprang. You cannot deny personal identity between two successive generations without sooner or later denying it during the successive stages in the single life of what we call one individual. (pp. 161–2)

32 Ibid., p. 54. This had been the thesis of *Life and Habit* (1877) and was to be the core of a lecture delivered in December 1882: 'the connection between memory and heredity is so close that there is no reason for regarding the two as generically different' (*The Notebooks of Samuel Butler*, p. 57).

33 Ibid., pp. 163–4. Cf. the section on 'Memory and Design' in *The Notebooks of Samuel Butler*, pp. 56–65.

34 Ibid., p. 175.

35 Samuel Butler, 'The Deadlock in Darwinism', *Universal Review* (1890); in *Essays on Life and Art and Science* (1904; 1908), pp. 234–40.

36 Illiam Drone, 'The Growth of Evolutionary Theory', *The Little Review*, I, 7 (October 1914), p. 45.

37 Butler, *Unconscious Memory*, pp. 64, 66–7.

38 Ibid., p. 58. Cf. the concluding chapter of Butler's *Luck or Cunning?* (1887) and the section on 'Vibrations' in *The Notebooks of Samuel Butler*, pp. 66–73.

39 E. Ray Lankester, 'A Theory of Heredity', *Nature* (1876); in *The Advancement of Science* (1890), pp. 279–80.

40 Ibid., p. 283.

41 Ernst Haeckel, *The Riddle of the Universe*, trans. Joseph McCabe (1913), pp. 95–7.

42 J. Arthur Thomson, *The Science of Life* (London and New York, 1899), p. 103.

43 William Coleman, *Biology in the Nineteenth Century: Problems of Form, Function and Transformation* (New York, 1971), p. 17.

44 G. Archdall Reid, *The Principles of Heredity* (1905), pp. 57, 63.

45 Ibid., pp. vii, 52.

46 Ibid., p. 56. Reid's divergence from the scientific establishment was formally announced on the next page: 'It is a remarkable fact . . . that the doctrine of recapitulation is almost completely ignored in every formal theory of heredity that is at all well known' (p. 57).

47 Louis Agassiz, *Methods of Study in Natural History* (Boston, 1863), pp. 90–1.

48 Ibid., pp. 23–4. Cf. J. Arthur Thomson, *The Science of Life*, pp. 133–4.

49 Thomson, *The Science of Life*, p. 162.

50 Jules Marcou, *Life, Letters and Works of Louis Agassiz*, 2 vols (New York, 1896), vol. I, p. 43.

51 Thomson, *The Science of Life*, p. 29. While applauding the innovatory importance of Cuvier's principle of 'correlation', Thomson pointed to its distance from current practice; this is again suggestive of how the ideas we are dealing with diverged from the mainstream of scientific thought: 'There is no living morphologist who would accept so exaggerated a statement.'

52 Ibid., p. 164. The principle of 'correlation' was developed by Cuvier into the method of comparison, and this method, from Thomson's stance at the very end of the nineteenth century, marked the peak of that century's achievement in biological research. Success in that research was to be measured primarily by its willingness to incorporate comparative procedure – a procedure that, as a mechanism, matched the unity revealed by its results, as we can see from Thomson's account of Johannes Müller and the beginnings of comparative physiology:

> he was especially distinguished by the ease with which he turned from one method to another in seeking to solve a problem. Now he would appeal to physics and again to psychology, here he sought the chemist's aid and there the embryologist's; he tried all methods to gain his end. In showing how animals of high and low degree shed light upon one another, he founded comparative physiology, and gave a new dignity to zoology. (ibid., p. 56)

Cf. Thomson's account of Von Baer and the instigation of comparative embryology, p. 123.

53 T. H. Huxley, 'Lecture on the Study of Biology' (1876), in *American Addresses* (1877), p. 146.

54 The notion of 'immanence' provided an important means whereby post-Darwinian thinkers attempted to reconcile the competing views of science and religion. According to this argument, the deity's presence in the material world was manifest in the workings of evolutionary process; the design of that process was the divine mode of function in nature; that design itself was taken as evidence for the intelligent operation of the deity. One of the best-known proponents of this argument and an excellent index to its conduct was John Fiske, who engaged the support of Agassiz's work in 'Agassiz and Darwinism', *Popular Science Monthly*, III (1873), pp. 692–705.

55 Quoted, F. W. Conner, *Cosmic Optimism: A Study of the Interpretation of Evolution by American Poets from Emerson to Robinson* (1949; New York, 1973), p. 18.

56 Agassiz, *Methods of Study in Natural History*, p. iii.

57 Ibid., pp. 317–19. Despite the force of his opposition to particular aspects of Darwinism, to the notion of adaptation, for example, we should note the shared area of concern that in fact united Agassiz with a substantial part of evolutionary thought. In an early lecture of 1837, 'Discours prononcé à l'ouverture des séances de la Société Helvétique des Sciences Naturelles, à Neuchâtel' (reprinted, Marcou, op. cit., vol. I, pp. 89–108), Agassiz proposed his controversial theory of glacial 'catastrophe' and, towards the beginning of the lecture, he talked of the bond he saw as uniting all scientific thought, the point of view organ-

izing the ways in which research was conducted: 'C'est l'idée d'un développement progressif dans tout ce qui existe, d'une métamorphose à travers différents états dépendants les uns des autres, l'idée d'une création intelligible, dont notre tâche est de saisir la liaison dans tous ses phénomènes' (p. 90). As Marcou pointed out (p. 90n.), such a position came close to prefiguring Darwin himself.

58 Louis Agassiz, 'Evolution and the Permanence of Type', *Atlantic Monthly* (1874); in *The Intelligence of Louis Agassiz*, ed. Guy Davenport (Boston, 1963), p. 215.

59 Ibid., pp. 222–3. Cf. p. 232.

60 Ibid., pp. 226–8.

61 Quoted, Coleman, op. cit., p. 108.

62 'Patria Mia', *The New Age* (1912); in *Patria Mia and the Treatise on Harmony* (1962), p. 49.

63 T. S. Eliot, 'Tradition and the Individual Talent, I', *The Egoist*, VI, 4 (September 1919), p. 54.

64 Walter Pater, 'Coleridge', p. 66. For a good account of Pater's indebtedness to science, see Anthony Ward, *Walter Pater: The Idea in Nature* (1966), pp. 25–52.

65 Walter Pater, *The Renaissance* (1873; 1910), p. 150.

66 'The Serious Artist, IV', *The New Freewoman*, I, 11 (15 November 1913), p. 214.

67 Pater, *The Renaissance*, p. 199.

68 *Sp. Rom.*, p. vi.

69 *Letters*, p. 62. This most familiar of Pound's modernist claims was most forcefully articulated in 'The Renaissance', *Poetry* (1915); in *LE*, pp. 214, 220, 225.

70 Oscar Wilde, 'Mr Pater's Last Volume', *The Artist as Critic*, ed. Richard Ellmann (1970), p. 230.

71 Oscar Wilde, 'The Critic as Artist', *Complete Works*, ed. Vyvyan Holland (1966; 1969), pp. 1040–1. Wilde's 'critical spirit' owed as much to Arnold as it did to Pater, particularly to Arnold's inaugural lecture as Professor of Poetry at Oxford in 1857, 'On the Modern Element in Literature' (*Complete Prose Works* (Ann Arbor, 1960), vol. I, pp. 18–37), a lecture which announced a programme for modernity very similar to that of Pound himself. Arnold began with a demand for an 'intellectual deliverance' which was 'the peculiar demand of those ages which are called modern', those ages whose 'modern spirit' had made the demand 'with most zeal, and satisfied with most completeness' (p. 19). This deliverance consisted in a particular historical perspective, 'in man's comprehension of this present past . . . when our mind begins to enter into possession of the general ideas which are the law of this vast multitude of facts', and the 'harmony' of such 'posses-

sion' was a distinguishing feature of modernity: 'This, then, is what distinguishes certain epochs in the history of the human race, and our own amongst the number; – on the one hand, the presence of a significant spectacle to contemplate; on the other hand, the desire to find the true point of view from which to contemplate this spectacle' (p. 20). Arnold's 'spectacle' was 'the collective life of humanity', and the 'true point of view' for its contemplation was the result of historical self-consciousness: 'everywhere there is connexion, everywhere there is illustration: no single event, no single literature, is adequately comprehended except in its relation to other events, to other literatures.' For Arnold, 'it is adequate comprehension which is the demand of the present age. . . . To know how others stand, that we may know how we ourselves stand; and to know how we ourselves stand, that we may correct our mistakes and achieve our deliverance – that is our problem' (pp. 20–1). The 'supreme characteristic' of such a 'modern age' was the 'manifestation of a critical spirit' (p. 25), manifested by its willingness to compare, and, in a wonderfully Poundian passage, Arnold demonstrated his point by comparing the language of Thucydides (found to be concrete and realistic) with that of Ralegh (found to be abstract and inflated) to offer a cultural discrimination on the basis of the modes of terminology employed by each (pp. 25–7). In other words, modernity was discerned in their prose itself to answer modernity's major question of any writer: '*Is he adequate? Does he represent the epoch in which he lived?*' (p. 34).

72 Ibid., p. 1056.
73 Walter Pater, *Plato and Platonism* (1893; 1928), pp. 14, 13, 3.
74 As Ian Fletcher has noted, 'In Pater's view, an organic development involved the notion that though the organism was in constant change, at each moment in its development it vestigially contained legible upon it a sort of synoptic history of development' (*Walter Pater* (1959; rev. ed. 1971), p. 26).
75 J. Arthur Thomson, *Heredity* (1908), pp. 125, 572.
76 Butler, *Unconscious Memory*, p. 174.
77 Reid, op. cit., pp. 60–1.
78 August Weismann, *Essays upon Heredity and Kindred Subjects*, 2 vols (Oxford, 1891 and 1892), and *The Germ-Plasm: A Theory of Heredity*, trans. Parker and Rönnfeldt (1893); Hugo de Vries, *Intracellular Pangenesis* (1889) and *Species and Varieties, Their Origin by Mutation*, ed. D. T. MacDougal (1905). There is a very good bibliography of works on heredity from 1857 to 1907 in Thomson, *Heredity*, pp. 539–86.
79 Emile Delavenay, *D. H. Lawrence and Edward Carpenter: A Study in Edwardian Transition* (1971), p. 129.

80 Edward Carpenter, 'Modern Science – A Criticism', *Civilisation: Its Cause and Cure, and Other Essays* (1889), pp. 51–2.

81 Edward Carpenter, 'The Science of the Future – A Forecast', *Civilisation: Its Cause and Cure, and Other Essays* (1889), p. 85.

82 Edward Carpenter, *The Art of Creation* (1904; rev. ed. 1907), p. 4. All further references will be inserted in the main text.

83 Carpenter, 'The Science of the Future – A Forecast', p. 94. Arguments for the unity of psychical and material phenomena, implicit in a poetics underwritten by analogies from psycho-physiology, suggest 'metamorphosis' as the prime emblem of a sensibility that is not 'dissociated'. William James's axiom, 'All consciousness is motor', was refurbished by Carpenter into the instruction 'Do not *think* – or at any rate delay the process of thinking as much as you can – but retain the mind in its state of feeling' (*The Art of Creation*, pp. 231–2), and by Eliot, in an essay three years prior to 'The Metaphysical Poets', accepting Gourmont's proposition from *Le Problème du style* that 'all thought and all language is based ultimately upon a few simple physical moments' ('Studies in Contemporary Criticism, I', *The Egoist*, V, 9 (October 1918), p. 114).

84 Emerson, in observing the function of 'intellectual science' to beget doubts as to the existence of matter, noted:

> It fastens the attention upon immortal necessary uncreated natures, that is, upon Ideas; and in their presence, we feel that the outward circumstance is a dream and a shade. Whilst we wait in this Olympus of gods, we think of nature as an appendix to the soul. We ascend into their region, and know that these are the thoughts of the Supreme Being. ('Nature' (1836), *Complete Prose Works* (Ward Lock, n. d.), p. 323)

85 Pater, similarly aware of science's confirmation of Greek thought, whereby modern theories of 'development' were but a reawakening of 'old Heracliteanism' (*Plato and Platonism*, p. 13), emphasized in 'Coleridge', the most 'scientific' of his essays, the relationship between science and Platonic memory: 'Science, the real knowledge of that natural world, is to be attained, not by observation, experiment, analysis, patient generalization, but by the evolution or recovery of those ideas directly from within, by a sort of Platonic "recollection"' (*Appreciations*, p. 77). Carpenter used Platonic 'recollection' to claim that, when ordinary people or objects suddenly became invested with divine attributes, auras or qualities of great beauty, what happened was that they awoke in the perceiver a memory of a divine idea: 'The countless memories of the race, all associated for generations with the particular object – or the sum and result of these memories – wake the

Idea in the mind of the present individual with a seemingly supernatural force' (*The Art of Creation*, p. 143). Thus the beloved lady, for example, was an awakening of divine love or beauty, a visionary figure who, as Carpenter quoted Lafcadio Hearn, was 'a composite of numberless race-memories . . . a beautiful luminous ghost made of centillions of memories' (p. 150). It was from this perception exactly that Pound admired the description of Dante's first sight of Beatrice in *La Vita Nuova*.

86 Carpenter further asked: 'Whether the microbial organisms which our scientific instruments reveal to us are not indeed the eternal forms of beings which seen from within would appear to us as simple or rudimentary states of mind. . . . Shall we actually discover, ere long, the bacillus of Fear, or of Money-greed, or of Vanity, or of Ambition' (pp. 215–16).

87 Edward Carpenter, *The Drama of Love and Death* (1912), p. 113.

88 Yeats's understanding of memory was wholly mystical; in his essay on 'Magic' (1901) he gave as the second of the three magical doctrines he held: 'That the borders of our memories are as shifting, and that our memories are part of one great memory, the memory of Nature herself' (*Essays and Introductions* (1961), p. 28). This was the uncomplicated belief that 'there is a memory of Nature that reveals events and symbols of distant centuries' (p. 46). It never sought consolidation in the physiology determined by contemporary science.

89 *CEP*, p. 322. 'Shalott' is at p. 252.

90 'Affirmations, I: Arnold Dolmetsch', *The New Age*, XVI, 10 (7 January 1915), p. 246.

91 Pater, 'Coleridge', pp. 66–7.

92 *CWC*, pp. 24–5.

93 'Vorticism', *Fortnightly Review* (September 1914); in *G-B*, p. 92.

94 Allen Upward, 'The New Age', *The New Age*, VIII, 13 (26 January 1911), p. 297. Upward's major figure for modernist energy transformations was an anticipation of the Poundian 'vortex', the 'whirl-swirl' which had the function, primarily, to focus historical self-consciousness:

> It is a magic crystal, and by looking long into it, you will see wonderful meanings come and go. It will change colour like an opal while you gaze, reflecting the thoughts in your own mind. It is a most chameleon-like ball. It has this deeper magic that it will show you, not only the thoughts you knew about before, but other thoughts you did not know of, old, drowned thoughts, hereditary thoughts; it will awaken the slumbering ancestral ghosts that haunt the brain; you will remember things you used to know and feel long, long ago. (*The New Word* (1908), p. 197)

6 Towards a conclusion

1 'The New Sculpture', *The Egoist*, I, 4 (19 February 1914), p. 67. Ronald Bush has observed of Pound in this respect: 'He conceived of all ritual as a cyclical return to the clues of divine presence until revelation transformed an initiate's understanding of those clues' (*The Genesis of Ezra Pound's Cantos* (Princeton, 1976), p. 105).

2 W. B. Yeats, 'The Autumn of the Body' (1898), *Essays and Introductions* (1961), pp. 191–3.

3 Arthur Symons, *The Symbolist Movement in Literature* (1899; 1911), pp. 4, 8–9. Symons's most programmatic attack on mechanistic science occurs at p. 162.

4 Pound wrote of Dante's canzone: 'They are good art as the high mass is good art . . . [they] must be conceived and approached as ritual' ('Psychology and Troubadours', *Quest* (October 1912); in *The Spirit of Romance*, rev. ed. (1970), p. 89).

5 *Sp. Rom.*, p. 235. Pound's conjunction of science and religion was matched by Allen Upward for whom 'religion is rudimentary science' ('Anthropolatry', *The New Age*, VI, 11 (13 January 1910), p. 249; cf. '"Christ." An Interpretation', *The New Age*, VI, 5 (2 December 1909), p. 106, and *The Divine Mystery* (1913; Santa Barbara, 1976), p. 29).

6 John Goode, 'The Decadent Writer as Producer', in *Decadence and the 1890's*, ed. Ian Fletcher (1979), p. 126.

7 Symons, op. cit., pp. 29–30. Symons stressed the allusiveness of the new poetry on the principle of 'eternal correspondences':

> it is on the lines of that spiritualizing of the word, that perfecting of form in its capacity for allusion and suggestion, that confidence in the eternal correspondences between the visible and the invisible universe, which Mallarmé taught . . . that literature must now move, if it is in any sense to move forward. (pp. 134–5)

His definition of symbolism itself relied on the relational view of the world that was the corollary of such correspondences: 'What is Symbolism if not an establishing of the links which hold the world together, the affirmation of an eternal, minute, intricate, almost invisible life, which runs through the whole universe?' (p. 145). These 'links' were variously figured as Emerson's 'rhymes or returns in nature', or Fenollosa's 'lines of force', or Pound's 'gods', the functions of 'race-consciousness'.

8 'Psychology and Troubadours', p. 91.

9 'All art hates the vague; not the mysterious, but the vague. . . . And the artist who is also a mystic hates the vague with a more profound hatred than any other artist' (Symons, op. cit., p. 153).

10 Max Nänny, *Ezra Pound: Poetics for an Electric Age* (Berne, 1973), p. 63.

11 'Simplicities', *The Exile*, I, 4 (Autumn 1928), pp. 3–4.

12 'Epstein, Belgion and Meaning', *The Criterion*, IX, 36 (April 1930), p. 472. Pound's essay was a reply to Montgomery Belgion, 'Meaning in Art' (*The Criterion*, IX, 35 (January 1930), pp. 201–16), an essay that reawakened the argument for 'meaning' that Pound had fought during the vorticist battles. He noted the tautologous nature of the judgements about 'meaning' that Belgion had offered:

> The error of making a statue *of* 'Night' or *of* 'Charity' lies in taut-ology. The idea has already found its way into language. The func-tion of the artist is precisely the formulation of what has not found its way into language, i.e., any language verbal, plastic or musical. (p. 471)

It was exactly such a tautology of discourse that Pound's 'dissociated language structure' was designed to prevent; the 'new noun' proposed by dissociation was thus not a purely linguistic affair, but incorporated a new object.

13 Ibid., p. 475.

14 Pound was so impressed by Berman's book that he persuaded Joyce to consult Berman in Paris about the deterioration of his eyesight. See Richard Ellmann, *James Joyce* (1959; 1966), p. 550; *P/J*, p. 212; Noel Stock, *The Life of Ezra Pound* (1970), p. 251.

15 Louis Berman, *The Glands Regulating Personality* (New York, 1922), p. 2.

16 'On Criticism in General', *The Criterion*, I, 2 (January 1923), p. 146.

17 Mick Gidley, 'Another Psychologist, a Physiologist and William Faulkner', *Ariel*, II, 4 (October 1971), p. 82.

18 Berman, op. cit., p. 2.

19 'The New Therapy', *The New Age*, XXX, 20 (16 March 1922), p. 260.

20 Allen Upward, *The New Word* (1908), p. 73.

21 'Allen Upward Serious', *The New Age* (April 1914); in *SP*, p. 379.

22 'Epstein, Belgion and Meaning', p. 472. Agassiz's account of 'type' had emphasized its impermeability, its function as a medium for the con-tinuity and transmission of permanence and hence its sanction for a particular means of stabilizing change. (At the very least, such a view argues for a familiar racism; see Stephen Jay Gould, 'Flaws in a Vic-torian Veil', *New Scientist*, LXXIX, 1118 (31 August 1978), pp. 632–3.) Pound's use of Berman suggested the further function of 'type' as a medium for dissociation, the dissociation that, earlier, Pound had admired in Henry James within a looser scientific analogy:

As Armageddon has only too clearly shown, national qualities are the great gods of the present and Henry James spent himself from the beginning in an analysis of these potent chemicals; trying to determine from the given microscopic slide the nature of the French-ness, Englishness, Germanness, Americanness. . . . They are the permanent and fundamental hostilities and incompatibles. ('A Shake Down', *The Little Review* (August 1918); in *LE*, pp. 300–1)

23 'The New Therapy', p. 259.

24 Ibid., p. 260.

25 Pound introduced Berman's book as 'one of the most interesting works on physiology that has been given to a lay public since Gourmont's "Physique de l'Amour"' ('The New Therapy', p. 259).

26 *Nat. Phil.*, p. 169.

27 Ralph Waldo Emerson, 'Swedenborg; or, the Mystic', *Complete Prose Works* (Ward Lock, n.d.), p. 187. Nietzsche had made the same point in *The Will to Power* (see Joseph N. Riddel, 'Pound and the Decentred Image', *The Georgia Review*, XXIX, 3 (Fall 1975), p. 567).

28 'Remy de Gourmont: A Distinction', *The Little Review* (February–March 1919); in *LE*, pp. 341, 345. 'Style', wrote Gourmont, 'is a physiological product' ('All abstract words are the figuration of a material act'), and as Richard Sieburth, the best commentator on the subject, has noted: 'At its most basic, Gourmont's problem of style can be reduced to the relation of the world of sensations to the world of words or ideas' (*Instigations: Ezra Pound and Remy de Gourmont* (Cambridge, Mass., and London, 1978), p. 62).

29 *Nat. Phil.*, pp. 172, 179, 178.

30 Ibid., p. 172.

31 Ibid., p. 180.

32 Quoted, Guy Davenport, 'The Perpendicular Honeycombe: Pound, de Gourmont, Frobenius', *Meanjin*, XIV (December 1955), p. 493.

33 *Nat. Phil.*, p. 173.

34 James Huneker, *Unicorns* (New York, 1917), p. 20.

35 See Glenn S. Burne, *Remy de Gourmont: His Ideas and Influence in England and America* (Carbondale, 1963), p. 111.

36 Quoted in the publisher's 'blurb' for Huneker's *Unicorns*.

37 James Huneker, 'Remy de Gourmont: His Ideas. The Colour of His Mind', *Unicorns*, pp. 30, 25.

38 'Remy de Gourmont: A Distinction', p. 342.

39 Huneker, 'Remy de Gourmont: His Ideas. The Colour of His Mind', pp. 27–8.

40 'Remy de Gourmont: A Distinction', p. 341.

41 *Nat. Phil.*, p. 179.

42 Remy de Gourmont, *Selected Writings*, ed. Glenn S. Burne (Ann Arbor, 1966), pp. 166–7, 167–8.

43 *Essays by James Huneker*, ed. H. L. Mencken (1930), p. 421.

44 James Huneker, *The Pathos of Distance* (New York, 1913), p. 4.

45 Ibid., pp. 381, 374, 369. Huneker applies this phrase to Gourmont in *Unicorns*, p. 31.

46 'Irony, Laforgue and Some Satire', *Poetry* (November 1917); in *LE*, p. 283.

47 James Huneker, *Ivory Apes and Peacocks* (New York, 1915), p. 35.

48 Huneker, *Unicorns*, pp. 203–4.

49 Richard Aldington, 'Remy de Gourmont', *The Little Review*, III, 3 (May 1915), p. 11.

50 'Remy de Gourmont: A Distinction', p. 344.

51 Huneker, *Unicorns*, p. 204.

52 Ibid., pp. 204–5, 206, 208–9.

53 Ibid., p. 210.

54 Ibid., pp. 195–6, 197–8.

55 'The New Therapy', p. 260.

56 'The Serious Artist, III: Emotion and Poesy', *The New Freewoman*, I, 10 (1 November 1913), p. 194.

57 Norman O. Brown, *Life Against Death* (1959; 1968), pp. 259–60.

58 Henry James, *The Art of the Novel*, ed. R. P. Blackmur (1962), p. 5.

59 'Unanimism', *The Little Review*, IV, 12 (April 1918), pp. 29–30.

60 Muriel Ciolkowska, 'The French Word in Modern Prose, VIII', *The Egoist*, IV, 8 (September 1917), p. 120.

61 See, for example, *The New Word* (1908), pp. 138–9 (hereafter cited as NW), and his articles on 'The Nebular Origin of Life', first published in *The New Age* (1921–2) and conveniently reprinted in the new edition of *The Divine Mystery* (1913; Santa Barbara, 1976), pp. 364–84 (hereafter cited as *DM*).

62 Upward, *NW*, p. 203; *DM*, p. 96.

63 Upward, *NW*, pp. 229, 195.

64 Upward, *DM*, p. 4. Upward first used this analogy in 'The Order of the Seraphim, II', *The New Age*, VI, 19 (10 March 1910), p. 447.

65 Upward, *NW*, p. 218.

66 Ibid., p. 31.

67 Allen Upward, 'The Order of the Seraphim, I', *The New Age*, VI, 15 (10 February 1910), p. 349.

68 Upward, *NW*, pp. 174, 193–4.

69 Ibid., p. 122; cf. pp. 111, 191–2. Upward cited Kelvin's support at p. 112.

70 Upward, *DM*, p. 198. Here, Upward demonstrated the 'Universal Rhymes' displayed in etymology by maintaining that 'the English word

fire is but another spelling of the same ancient European word that meets us in the Greek *pur* (fire), and the Latin *purus* (bright, clean), from which our word *pure* is directly copied.'

71 Upward, *NW*, p. 53.

72 Ibid., pp. 55, 66.

73 Ibid., pp. 118, 121.

74 Upward, *NW*, p. 200; *DM*, p. 194.

75 Upward, 'The Order of the Seraphim, I', p. 349.

76 *G-B*, p. 116.

77 Allen Upward, 'The Order of the Seraphim, II', *The New Age*, VI, 19 (10 March 1910), p. 447.

78 Upward, *NW*, p. 189. Pound used the vocabulary of commercial exchange when he wrote of the poet's function to 'new-mint the speech' ('The Wisdom of Poetry', *Forum* (April 1912); in *SP*, p. 331), and Eliot distinguished 'paper currency' from 'actual coinage' on behalf of language ('Eeldrop and Appleplex', *The Little Review*, IV, 1 (May 1917), p. 10). Glenn S. Burne (*Remy de Gourmont: His Ideas and Influence in England and America* (Carbondale, 1963), p. 117) and Richard Sieburth (*Instigations: Ezra Pound and Remy de Gourmont* (Cambridge, Mass., and London, 1978), p. 67) have suggested Gourmont's metaphor of 'médailles usées' as a probable source (*Le Problème du style* (Paris, 1902), p. 36).

79 Upward, *DM*, pp. 54, 57. The complications of relationship between the writer's defence of his seriousness to an alienated audience and the contradiction of that defence were attested in the vocabulary with which Pound attacked contemporary journalism in an essay published under the pseudonym of 'Helmholtz' during the following year: 'The bourgeois . . . is, in brief, digestive. He is the stomach and gross intestines of the body politic and social, as distinct from the artist, who is the nostrils and the invisible antennae.' ('The Bourgeois', *The Egoist*, I, 3 (2 February 1914), p. 53.)

80 Allen Upward, 'The Son of Man', *The New Age*, VI, 13 (27 January 1910), p. 298.

81 Terry Eagleton, *Criticism and Ideology* (1976), pp. 102–61. The ideology was most insidiously expressed by Eliot, and Eagleton has given an excellent summary of his programme:

> By framing his classicist doctrine in the organicist terms of the Romantic tradition, Eliot is able to combine an idealist totality with the sensuous empiricism which is its other aspect. . . . Eliot's ideal of the organic society is one in which a finely conscious élite transmits its values through rhythm, habit and resonance to the largely unconscious masses, infiltrating the nervous system rather than engaging the mind. (p. 147)

82 See William Carlos Williams's essay of 1948, 'The Poem as a Field of Action', *Selected Essays* (New York, 1969), pp. 280–91. There is a good discussion of the scientific basis for Williams's theory in L. S. Dembo, *Conceptions of Reality in Modern American Poetry* (Berkeley and Los Angeles, 1966), pp. 48–80.

83 See I. F. A. Bell, 'Mauberley's Barrier of Style', *Ezra Pound: The London Years, 1908–1920,* ed, Philip Grover (New York, 1978), pp. 89–115, 155–64.

84 Hugh Kenner, 'Art in a Closed World', *Virginia Quarterly Review,* 38 (Autumn 1966), pp. 605, 600–1.

85 Ibid., p. 606.

86 A. S. Eddington, *The Nature of the Physical World* (Cambridge, 1928), pp. xiii, xvii.

87 Kenner, 'Art in a Closed World', p. 609.

88 Walt Whitman, 'Slang' (1885), *Walt Whitman: A Critical Anthology,* ed. Francis Murphy (Harmondsworth, 1969), pp. 103–4.

89 Walt Whitman, *An American Primer,* ed. Horace Traubel (1904; San Francisco, 1970), p. 1.

90 Ibid., pp. 29, 12. Cf. pp. 9–10, 20.

91 Upward, *NW,* p. 267.

92 Whitman, *An American Primer,* pp. 27, 30.

93 'On Criticism in General', pp. 144–5.

94 *GK,* p. 217.

95 Again, I am indebted to conversations with Richard Godden.

96 Canto LXXIV: 427/453.

97 Kenner, 'Art in a Closed World', p. 610.

98 Ibid., pp. 610–13.

99 Fred Moramarco, 'Concluding an Epic: The Drafts and Fragments of the *Cantos*', *American Literature,* XLIX, 3 (November 1977), p. 323.

100 Eagleton, op. cit., pp. 147, 150–1.

101 Emerson, 'Swedenborg; or, the Mystic', p. 186.

102 For an excellent discussion of this condensation, see Herbert N. Schneidau, *Ezra Pound: The Image and the Real* (Baton Rouge, 1969), pp. 173–87.

103 Ernest Hemingway, *Death in the Afternoon* (1932; Harmondsworth, 1966), p. 182.

104 Fredric Jameson, *Marxism and Form: Twentieth Century Dialectical Theories of Literature* (1971; Princeton, 1974), p. 410. I should register my agreement with Jameson's proposition that 'it is a mistake to think, for instance, that the books of Hemingway deal essentially with such things as courage, love, and death; in reality, their deepest subject is simply the writing of a certain type of sentence, the practice

of a determinant style. This is indeed the most "concrete" experience in Hemingway' (p. 409).

105 Ibid., pp. 412, 410.
106 Paul Goodman, *Speaking and Language* (1971; 1973), p. 181.
107 It was Lionel Kelly who first drew my attention to the importance of *Ecclesiastes* for this text.
108 Goodman, op. cit., pp. 184, 186.
109 Moramarco, 'Concluding an Epic', p. 323.
110 Stephen Fender, 'Ezra Pound and the Words off the Page: Historical Allusions in Some American Long Poems', *The Yearbook of English Studies*, vol. VIII (1978), pp. 96–7.
111 Ibid., p. 105.
112 Richard Sieburth, *Instigations: Ezra Pound and Remy de Gourmont* (Cambridge, Mass., and London, 1978), p. 121.
113 Fender, 'Ezra Pound and the Words off the Page', pp. 106, 107.
114 Ibid., pp. 107–8.
115 Stephen Fender, *The American Long Poem* (1977), p. 10.
116 We need to remember, of course, that 'correspondence' for Pound never predicated the hegemony of a crudely mechanistic 'unity'; he wrote in 1921: 'The greatest tyrannies have arisen from the dogma that the *theos* is one, or that there is a unity above various strata of theos which imposes its will upon the substrata, and thence upon human individuals' ('Axiomata', *The New Age* (January 1921); in *SP*, p. 51).
117 Eagleton, op. cit., pp. 149–50.
118 Fredric Jameson, 'Seriality in Modern Literature', *Bucknell Review*, XVIII, 1 (Spring 1970), p. 69.
119 Canto VII: 24/28.
120 Canto VII: 26/30.
121 Canto CXIV: 793.
122 *CWC*, p. 11.
123 For a perceptive application of the notion of 'displacement', see Joseph N. Riddel, 'Pound and the Decentred Image', *Georgia Review*, XXIX, 3 (Fall 1975), pp. 565–91. Riddel's conclusion is, however, different from mine: he is not worried by his recognition that 'The poem's structure can only be described by a number of metaphors it already bears within itself' (p. 590), a recognition of the incestuousness that is one of the most disturbing characteristics of the 'Pound Industry', and he sees the *Cantos* as in fact defeating the threat of enclosure, as an 'attack upon the dream of the Book, of totalization or closure' (p. 588). The *Cantos* certainly promise such an attack, but the act of reading them constantly contradicts that promise by its confinement within a further 'dream', that of their hidden unity and intelligibility.

Name index